GENDER IN THE POLITICAL SCIENCE CLASSROOM

SCHOLARSHIP OF TEACHING AND
LEARNING

Jennifer Meta Robinson, Whitney M. Schlegel, and
Mary Taylor Huber, *Editors*

GENDER IN THE POLITICAL SCIENCE CLASSROOM

Edited by Ekaterina M. Levintova and
Alison Kathryn Staudinger

Indiana University Press

This book is a publication of

Indiana University Press
Office of Scholarly Publishing
Herman B Wells Library 350
1320 East 10th Street
Bloomington, Indiana 47405 USA

iupress.indiana.edu

© 2018 by Indiana University Press
All rights reserved

No part of this book may be reproduced or utilized in any form or by any means, electronic or mechanical, including photocopying and recording, or by any information storage and retrieval system, without permission in writing from the publisher.

The paper used in this publication meets the minimum requirements of the American National Standard for Information Sciences—Permanence of Paper for Printed Library Materials, ANSI Z39.48-1992.

Manufactured in the United States of America

Cataloging information is available from the Library of Congress.

ISBN 978-0-253-03320-8 (cloth)
ISBN 978-0-253-03321-5 (paperback)
ISBN 978-0-253-03322-2 (ebook)

1 2 3 4 5   23 22 21 20 19 18

Contents

Acknowledgments   vii

Teach It Forward: Gender in the Political Science Classroom and Beyond / *Ekaterina M. Levintova and Alison Kathryn Staudinger*   1

Part One: National and Institutional Trends

1. Gendering the Political Science Classroom While Mainstreaming Gender in the Discipline: Understanding the Barriers and Exploring Solutions / *Ingrid Bego*   31

2. Divergent? Gender and Methodological Diversity in Recent Political Science Dissertations / *Rina Verma Williams and Laura Dudley Jenkins*   60

3. Gendered Representation in Political Science Textbooks / *Daniel Mueller*   89

4. Gender Mainstreaming and Political Science Teaching in New Zealand: Still a Work in Progress / *Jennifer Curtin*   116

5. Student Perceptions of Gender in Political Science Teaching and Advising / *Ekaterina M. Levintova*   137

Part Two: Classroom Evidence and Solutions

6. Getting to No: The Need for Gender-Conscious Pedagogy in Service-Learning Courses / *Daisy Rooks*   167

7. Class Format, Gender, and Student Attitudes toward Political Participation / *Sara Rinfret and Michelle Pautz*   196

8. Beyond Gender Neutrality in the Scholarship of Teaching and Learning and the Classroom / *Alison Kathryn Staudinger*   214

9 Thinking through Movement: Embodied Learning as
Feminist Pedagogy for the Social Sciences / *Valerie Barske*   237

Gender Forward: Momentum for the Future /
Ekaterina M. Levintova and Alison Kathryn Staudinger   263

Index   277

Acknowledgments

We would like to thank the many people and groups who supported this book and made it better. University of Wisconsin Office of Professional Development (OPID), Wisconsin Teaching Fellows and Scholars Program (WTFS), University of Wisconsin–Green Bay Center for Advancement of Teaching and Learning (CATL) and its Teaching Scholars Program provided us with funding and logistical support and often enabled us to make connections with scholars interested in our topic. Jennifer Robinson (Indiana University) encouraged us at various stages of the manuscript preparation to move along and push ourselves to make this book happen. Two anonymous reviewers, Aaron Haynie (University of New Mexico), Indiana University Press (IUP) Series on Scholarship of Teaching and Learning editors, and the IUP Editorial Board gave us invaluable feedback that improved this book dramatically.

A Note on the Cover: As discussed in chapter three, political science textbooks currently depict the world of politics in a gendered way, reinforcing the continued overrepresentation of certain groups in the ranks of the powerful. Although our discipline has the same inequalities, we choose not represent them pictorially, but rather center an image of the political science students of the twenty-first century.

GENDER IN THE POLITICAL SCIENCE CLASSROOM

Teach It Forward: Gender in the Political Science Classroom and Beyond

Ekaterina M. Levintova and
Alison Kathryn Staudinger

In 1991, John Wahlke published his groundbreaking "Liberal Learning and the Political Science Major: A Report to the Profession," one of the first in-depth studies of curriculum in political science since the 1960s. The 1991 Wahlke report, as it came to be known, called for more structured curricula overall and for attention to gender specifically. Among other recommendations, the Wahlke report prescribed "that the character of... gender... diversity... of particular problems and policies *be addressed in all relevant courses*—'mainstreamed,' in the pedagogical vernacular—not treated as a separate and unique problem to be dealt with in a particular course or two by a particular faculty member." This call went largely unanswered, following historical patterns in political science of waxing and waning attention to teaching and learning (Ishiyama 2006).

Others have made the same call, arguing that mainstreaming gender in the social sciences would extend their analytical reach (Kramer and Martin 1988), given that gender "underpins the modern political system" (Elison 1997, 204). The absence of gender analysis parallels an absence of attention to other facets of inequality and oppression. As a 2011 American Political Science Association (APSA) report noted, the discipline is less diverse because "it tends to treat identity as given and outside of analysis" (2). The APSA report recommended treating "diversity, inclusivity and inequality" as a category of analysis "that inform[s] each unit of study rather than be[ing] seen as a separate or supplementary unit" (2011, 3). Yet, this also has not yet occurred (Cassese, Bos, and Duncan 2012). One reason may be that "gender mainstreaming," although it aims to suffuse the curriculum, is insufficient for producing shifts in how knowledge is produced and shared in political science or for gender justice, because it offers gender as an analytical tool while shying away from the normative implications of such analysis.

Gender mainstreaming is sometimes criticized as a potential justification for the elimination of social-justice or identity-focused programs, such as Women's and Gender Studies (WGS), and as a depoliticizing force (Hawthorne 2004).

Certainly WGS programs, along with ethnic studies and other politically targeted fields, are often attacked under the banner of austerity and budget cuts. The need to support these programs in intellectual solidarity does not relieve political science, or any discipline, of the responsibility to consider and integrate the insights of WGS and LGBTQ+ studies in the classroom and the world, or to develop gender-forward scholarship and teaching in their own disciplines. Whether this should be called "mainstreaming" is debatable. *PS: Political Science and Politics*, published by APSA, recently printed "The Teacher Symposium: Mainstreaming Gender in the Teaching and Learning of Politics," featuring six compelling arguments for why and how to mainstream gender, especially in introductory and methods courses (Ackerly and Mügge 2016). However, this symposium also demonstrates that, thus far, calls for gender mainstreaming have yet to succeed. Most contributors to the symposium argue that "it is possible to teach the need for feminist analysis without teaching theories of gender and feminism" (Ibid., 543). Although we agree, we worry that without these theories, we will struggle to make clear the stakes in terms of democratic and just outcomes. We want to respond and extend the work of that symposium by pursuing the questions it raises through close study of evidence of student learning as well as practical approaches in the classroom. As Cassese, Bos, and Duncan (2012) argued, departments still need to assess and promote equality; the same researchers also demonstrated the continued need for studies of the results of gender mainstreaming and asked what comes after mainstreaming, or what would make it possible. Our book responds to this challenge, arguing that, if gender-mainstreaming is to work, some scholarship and teaching in political science needs to be explicitly gender-forward, making connections to WGS and to gender-forward instructors in cognate disciplines.

While we speak to political scientists directly, we also include voices from kindred disciplines, and these classroom approaches are applicable in many fields. In particular, we are interested in how political science can serve as a "trading zone," just as the Scholarship of Teaching and Learning (SoTL) does, for linking the hard sciences with the social sciences and the humanities, as aspects of all of these disciplinary cultures thrive in political science.[1] SoTL, which we discuss in relation to political science below, serves as a reflective and yet systematic approach to understanding and improving our work as teachers. While SoTL builds on classic works of pedagogy and traditional education research, for us it is unique in its focus on public dissemination of work with our colleagues and its thoughtful reconsideration of our practice in light of our shared inquiry. Because SoTL brings instructors from many disciplines together with each other, as well as with students, librarians, and instructional designers, it fruitfully allows for the sharing of new methods, ideas, and strategies—what is traded in the "trading zone." We model this in our volume, and in our suggestions that social sciences be more inclusive of concepts of gender. Students who never choose to take a WGS class or who are not required to take any coursework in ethnic studies will, in all but the rare university without any general studies requirements, still take courses in the humanities and the social sciences. These courses are an opportunity to put gender front-and-center and to frame the political and ethical development of students. One of our goals is to show how this is possible through classroom-focused Scholarship of Teaching and Learning (SoTL). Another goal is to examine the barriers that have perhaps kept this sort of centralization from happening thus far by seeing what work gender does at the level of doctoral education, textbook and curriculum development, and professional advancement. These same dynamics are applicable to other fields and so is the gender-forward approach.

To meet these goals, we begin by tracing the ways in which gender—both conceptually and in terms of the lived experiences of those in the discipline—is a continuing problem. We discuss the effects gender inequality seems to have on students, practitioners, and faculty, especially in the context of the barriers women face in the political world that the 2016 election so powerfully exposed. Gender is not a simple concept, so the call to put it "forward" is itself a call to import plural methods and political stakes into the classroom. For example, 2016 has seen a rise of so-called bathroom bills, which target those whose gender identity or expression does not match the gender they were assigned at birth. To unpack and discuss this salient political issue in class requires much groundwork, starting from the distinctions between gender, sex, and sexual orientation—not to mention identity and expression—linked up with ideas seen as the core of political science, such as majority rule, rights, religious freedom, and, in the case of many state legislatures who make these laws, the power of redistricting. It also might be useful to include a sense of the electoral politics of social issues, the history of the LGBTQ+ movement and the role of trans people as (often erased) leaders within it, and the rise of the New Right since the late 1970s. Given the background work required and the stress of supporting a conversation about such weighty and controversial issues of identity and politics, we might be tempted to avoid the topic of bathroom bills. This is why to "do" gender in a classroom and curriculum is not as simple as "add women and stir." The debates about sameness and difference, liberalism and radicalism, and essentialism and intersectionality that characterize broader political conversations also emerge when thinking about gender, teaching, and learning. And, putting gender forward is costly, both in terms of the space it takes in a course syllabus or curriculum, and the exhausting intellectual and emotional labor of discussing issues such as bathroom bills. But the contested and complex concept of gender can also enrich and deepen discussions, helping explain, for example, *why* bathrooms matter. Unless there is a political benefit for marking the boundaries of gender at the door of the bathroom or insisting on particular forms of families, the move to create such laws is confusing.

In this volume, we remain conscious of the multiple ways that gender is deployed in political science research and the classroom and make the work it does visible. In particular, we are interested in the way that political science as a discipline is a place where gender is (re)produced, both for teachers and students. The classroom is a place of learning, but it is also a workplace, a site where gendered meanings and identities are learned and reaffirmed. Thus it matters how student attitudes about faculty might relate to implicit bias about gender and other factors, and it also matters how faculty interact with different students as they learn how to perform their particular genders. Recent national research, for example, demonstrates that women dominate the ranks of contingent faculty (62 percent in 2012), while men take up a majority of tenure-track positions (59 percent), a problem especially exacerbated in traditionally male-dominated fields, including political science (Baker 2015). We have even less data on faculty outside the gender binary. While much attention is rightly focused on the "leaky pipeline" that continues to thin the ranks of women and other historically marginalized groups at the top of the field, graduate and undergraduate classrooms are among the first inputs to this pipeline. And, even beyond the leaky pipeline, there may be gendered divisions of labor and expected performances that limit both individuals and our collective inquiry into the social and political world.

This volume is not an attempt to put an end to debates about gender as a contested concept but to illustrate and problematize them through an exploration of the political science classroom, in a broad sense and within a context of the social sciences proper, and in dialogue with the latest work in other fields, such as the essays in Dewar and Bennett (2015) and Blessinger and Carfora (2015) or the arguments laid out in Schwartz and Gurung (2012). What we hope to show is that the discipline of political science is not only a source of continued gender inequality, but a potential site for transformative and creative pedagogy and partnerships that are mindful of gender and that may extend to other social science disciplines. This two-pronged approach to both the problem and its possibilities also has implications for the broader political sphere, where undergraduates practice what they learn in general education courses and as political science majors. We begin with treatments of gender differences in political science education at a structural level for both faculty and students, from national and international perspectives. This structural examination considers gender disparity both in the political science classroom and as part of the profession. We then focus our discussion on the particular importance of perception and gender roles and how they affect diversity in research and teaching. Finally, we drill down on evidence of identity-specific student learning in the classroom to offer research-based suggestions for creating a more gender-equitable classroom, discipline, and university. We include authors from the cognate disciplines of history and sociology and incorporate an international perspective from New Zealand to attempt to show some of the linkages and rifts within and beyond political science. Each author argues for classrooms that are attentive to gender rather than gender neutral, although there is productive tension over what that means in practice. Built around a new vision of gender-forward disciplines and classrooms, the proposed pedagogies offer an alternative to feminism of the "lean-in" variety represented by gender mainstreaming.

Gender as a Threshold Concept in Political Science

Political science bridges the social sciences and humanities, making it a prime site for contesting gender. However, there are also challenges. Highly segregated by subfield in graduate education and research agendas, political scientists often identify with one of the four dominant subfields: American politics, international relations, comparative politics, and political theory.[2] Many curricula are still arranged around these subfields at the undergraduate level. There are also vibrant and growing specializations in research methods, public administration, public law, and public policy. Political scientists range from the practice-oriented—who work in think tanks, field research, and for campaigns—to theory-building and research-intensive academics. Political scientists also use a wide-range of methods: quantitative, qualitative, and even, especially in political theory, humanistic approaches to inquiry. The combined breadth and segmentation of political science makes it a fertile ground for studying broader currents in academia, particularly related to political socialization and gender. Despite a somewhat unique disciplinary culture, political science ultimately shares many challenges with and engages in methodological, theoretical, and pedagogical debates that also animate other social sciences and humanities, including sociology, anthropology, economics, history, and philosophy. In fact, some political science subfields are cross-pollinated by these very disciplines, borrowing their insights to explain political phenomena on individual, institutional, and societal levels. Our discipline is, in a sense, an "eclectic messy center" of social sciences, to borrow Peter Evans's phrase (Kohli et al. 1995, 2), operating with the premise that people, institutions, and culture all matter. It is in this disciplinary context that gender uneasily sits.

Gender is treated differently in these subfields, highlighting (or perhaps reinforcing) the boundaries between them. For example, Sharon Krause (2011) identifies the powerful role that feminist theory has played in shaping political theory through a commitment to intersectionality, the theorization of nonsovereign agency, and the linkage of political theory with empirical work; this needs to be extended throughout the entire subfield, which still teaches a canon that is overwhelmingly male (Moore 2011). Yet, in the subfield of American politics, which tends to be quantitatively focused, identity is often studied narrowly or not at all. For example, voting behavior studies often use sex as an independent variable and "women in politics" is a research agenda in American government that tends to take the shared interests and identity of biological women as a starting point. In international relations and comparative politics, where methods are a bit more mixed, gender, or even sexuality, might be included as units of analysis, but not always, and especially not in work on security theory or other masculine coded areas (Blanchard 2003). As Weldon (2006) argues, there is ample room for the development of a comparative analysis of gender relations that denaturalizes gender and other axes of disadvantage by comparing them across countries, exposing their construction. There are of course bright spots. Authors like Ange-Marie Hancock (2011) infuse their intellectual work with insights from many subfields and an intersectional and critical feminist awareness.

In this volume, we include authors who write from various subfields and perspectives, including those who see gender as a binary or ask questions primarily about the different experiences of men and women. Put another way, political science often seems focused on a first or second wave conceptualization of gender and equality. Even the insights of feminist political theory may not make their way into other subfields, reflecting the "separate tables" of the discipline. Essentialism may be passé in many fields, but it is still current in political science. Valerie Barske, one of our contributors, resists this move by advancing a bodily pedagogy, reflecting a broader "mobilities turn" in feminist studies. This shows some of the implicit tension in political science on the question of gender and the possibilities of better integrating subfields through explicit conversations about the concept and through changes in graduate education and curricular development.

The rich diversity within political science means that SoTL work in the discipline can speak to many audiences, but also struggles to capture all of political science at once. Some of the key insights in SoTL have uncovered disciplinary ways of knowing and learning, including common pitfalls for new learners. What, for example, are political science's "threshold concepts"—those that serve as a doorway where students often get stuck? The threshold or liminal space has been analogized to a rite of passage through which students must pass to enter the discipline; once threshold concepts are learned, they transform the way students see the world and their own learning (Meyer and Land 2005, 2006). These concepts can also be a form of "troublesome knowledge" because they can be counter-intuitive to students or novice practitioners (Meyer and Land 2005; Perkins 1999). Yet mastering threshold concepts is essential in student learning, due to the transformative (leading to a significant shift in student perceptions) and the integrative (exposing previously hidden interrelatedness) nature of any such concept (Meyer and Land 2006).

Like every mainstream discipline, political science relies on teaching disciplinary habits of mind to preserve and extend its knowledge base and having bottlenecks and misunderstood threshold concepts should be treated as an important pedagogical and methodological problem. Yet surprisingly, for a discipline that teaches and accumulates knowledge about such subjective and contested concepts as power or conflict, political science seems to be a late comer to the conversation about threshold concepts. *Threshold Concepts within the Disciplines* (Land, Meyer, and Smith 2008), for example, does not feature political science, although the section on economics may be useful for some political scientists who use economic concepts or methods, such as rational choice theory.

Our disciplinary difficulties are confounded even further by the existence of not one but multiple threshold concepts and bottlenecks. Williams (2014) argues that power is a threshold concept in political science, but certainly power is also a contested concept with variations ranging from the Schumpeterian to the Gramscian and Foucaultian.[3] Furthermore, power is also central for sociology and important for many other disciplines, so whether it is a particularly disciplinary threshold is unclear. Bernstein (2012, 76) focuses on several "bottlenecks" that prevent students from learning "how to approach a disciplinary question as an expert would, in other words, how to think like a political scientist." Importantly, Bernstein (2012, 78–79) identifies two interrelated bottlenecks—conflict as a part of a healthy political system and tension between majority rules and minority rights—as two of the most troublesome potential bottlenecks or uncrossed thresholds for students.

Yet another complication involves the remarkable cross-cultural and chronological range of political science research questions. For example, while Bernstein's (2012) article persuasively identifies strategies for addressing bottlenecks in students' understanding of conflict and tension between majorities and minorities, it is less clear whether these strategies are broadly applicable; for instance, Bernstein explores these conflicts and tensions as part of contemporary democratic systems, when, of course, many political scientists study nondemocratic or historical political spaces. Kustrar and Kärner, in Meyer, Baille, and Land (2010), even use the idea of threshold concepts and liminal space to describe and understand the experiences of societies in political transition; in this work, the threshold concepts are society-wide, rather than in the classroom.

This diversity of threshold concepts and bottlenecks and their spillage into actual societal and political realms reflects the eclectic nature of the discipline itself. It is, of course, also a function of being a discipline on the forefront of debates about equity, fairness, and justice, both currently and historically, domestically and internationally, and on macro- (national), meso- (institutional), and micro- (individual) levels. Yet, the fact that threshold concepts are plural in political science and have broader societal implications offers more opportunities to foreground gender—one of the most pressing threshold concepts—than mainstreaming can.

It is possible that, at least in our discipline, there are portals to different areas of inquiry rather than one threshold that all political scientists cross (Farganis and Kirk 2012). Indeed, what we advocate is the addition of threshold concepts from WGS to increase the number of portals into a gender-forward approach to studying and doing politics. Here we follow Launius and Hassel (2014, vii), who offer four critical threshold concepts in WGS: "the social construction of gender; privilege and oppression; intersectionality; and feminist praxis." Each of these four concepts could open a portal to a political science discipline that is at the forefront of gender studies, which would behoove a discipline dedicated to exploring, explaining, and improving the political world. We offer work that speaks to all of Launius and Hassel's four concepts in this text. Most important, we offer it in the spirit of "feminist praxis," which we find lacking in political science as a whole, if not in many political scientists. Launius and Hassel (2014) define this praxis as integrating teaching, learning, and the classroom with social justice, which in the classroom takes the form of empowering students through critical evaluation of current events.

Feminist praxis is urgently needed because gender is a complex concept that is still undertheorized in political science and often folded into "sex" or treated as an afterthought. There is insufficient borrowing from WGS. For example, political science is often blind to differences between gender and sex, although this is a nearly axiomatic distinction in WGS. This distinction is also elided in educational research more broadly (Glasser and Smith 2008). Sex refers to biological differences, either expressed genetically or through particular characteristics, like genitalia and body hair; gender refers to the social practices we understand as masculine and feminine. Even this distinction is questioned by performativity and queer theorists following Judith Butler, who points out that the decision to label primary and secondary characteristics as male or female also involves cultural interpretation. There are also many thinkers who conceptualize both gender and sex as spectrums, often influenced by the rejection of binaries or the experiences of trans, agendered, or gender-nonconforming people. These debates are also bound up in critiques of gender essentialism that equate women or men with particular traits, such as caretaking or violence. Although not all of these insights are applicable to every area of political science research, they are currently rarely considered despite their general utility (Brettschneider 2011). In this volume, too, we found that many contributors struggled because their graduate education conflated sex and gender, and they had few tools to separate them. Ingrid Bego's contribution speaks to this glaring omission, but more concerted efforts across the discipline and the classroom are necessary.

Given our subject, we are particularly interested in how intersectionality, the dominant theoretical apparatus at work in WGS, can be brought to bear on SoTL research in political science. Although it came to prominence in the 1990s through the world of Kimberlé Crenshaw, Patricia Collins, and other feminists of color, and is still dominant today, it was only in the mid-2000s that political science began to respond. There is still too little work on how gender, race, class, and other systematic and historicized oppressions interact in political science teaching. Wilson (2013) offers an edited volume with sharp examples of intersectional political science in action. In essence, our volume continues the work started in Gutiérrez y Muhs et al. (2012), which examines such intersections in the academy at large. In our volume, the challenges of doing intersectional work with tools designed in other paradigms are clear; for example, Alison Staudinger questions the dominant methods in SoTL research for studying complex questions of overlapping and multiple identities.

In short, political science is far from gender-mainstreamed or gender-forward in any but a cursory way. Pioneering work is not effectively diffused across subfields, nor are the threshold concepts or insights of WGS integrated in a meaningful way into the disciplinary curriculum or research paradigms. Although the diversity of methods and fields of inquiry in political science makes it an attractive site to put gender in the forefront, this will be a big task.

Political Science and the Scholarship of Teaching and Learning

To work on the task of putting gender in the forefront in political science, we must first understand how it is currently taught or produced in the classroom. SoTL is an obvious fit for this work. We are using SoTL broadly to refer to a still emerging field that systemically studies teaching and learning, using multiple methods and approaching the classroom as a place for academic inquiry. While instructors have long shared teaching strategies and pedagogy, SoTL looks also for evidence of student learning. This evidence may come in a variety of forms and be analyzed by various methods, but, importantly, it is also shared with a broader audience of peers and reincorporated into the practices of scholarly teaching in the classroom. As a new field, occupied by a variety of disciplinary practitioners, SoTL is full of debates about methods, rigor, and future directions. For example, SoTL tends toward the methods and epistemology of the social sciences, and many arts and humanities instructors seek alternative approaches to what constitutes evidence and rigor.[4] These debates should be linked to concerns about power and hierarchy inside the classroom and academia, particularly around gender, and we hope to contribute to that conversation by example. These concerns should also extend to asking who engages in SoTL; currently, SoTL research is disproportionately carried out by women, either because of gendered norms around the care work of teaching or because of reward structures around tenure and promotion (McKinney and Chick 2010; Myers 2008).

While some political science SoTL projects consider gender, as a whole they have been focused on other questions. *The Political Science Teacher*, a journal published until 1990 and then replaced by *Perspectives on Politics*, has had very few articles on gender during its run, and none are among its most cited or downloaded. *Perspectives on Politics* publishes pieces on pedagogy and SoTL and pays significant attention to gender, but we could not identify any articles on gender and teaching. *The Journal of Political Science Education*, which focuses on teaching and learning, was started in 2005 and has shown significant progress since that time. Although only ten articles, by our count, primarily concern gender, these include substantive treatments of the integration of gender and method (Cassese et al. 2015), online teaching (Pollock, Hamman, and Wilson 2005), American government textbooks (Cassese, Bos, and Schneider 2012; Olivo 2012), and political science's signature pedagogy: simulations (Coughlin 2013; Zeigler and Moran 2008). There are also articles that consider gender as one (bimodal) independent variable among many, concern diversity in a broader sense and include gender, if often briefly, in studies of teaching cultural competence, and so forth. APSA's Teaching and Learning Conference, which is in its fifteenth year, includes a track on "the inclusive classroom" (formerly "diversity, inclusiveness, and equality"), where Danny Mueller presented an early version of chapter 3. This track generally includes some work on gender, as the political or democratic theory track often does, but too little of it ends up published and able to influence the field at large.

There is more space for political scientists to work on gender, and SoTL scholars to work on gender and the political ramifications of it in teaching and learning. Because we argue that SoTL needs more focus on gender in the classroom and the academy at large, particularly at the undergraduate level, our volume contributes to trying to understand gender differences, both experienced and perceived, and potential solutions for the political science classroom and beyond. While there is work in SoTL on feminist study of the classroom, it will only continue if practitioners advance a transformative agenda (Gilpin and Liston 2009). Indeed, there are good reasons to be critical of SoTL from a feminist perspective, particularly as it hardens into a discipline with a set of rules and cannons (Smith 2007). In terms of gender differences in higher education, important work has been done. One interesting new development is that women are now outpacing men as graduates (Ewert 2012). However as women and other previously excluded minorities access college education, the broader culture has also begun to question its value and expense, raising questions about the feminization of higher education. We should study this important question. We can also evaluate when gender is not significant; for example, it appears there are few statistically significant gender-based differences in what faculty include in the syllabus, save that women faculty included more policy details (Doolittle and Lusk 2012). Daisy Rook's chapter takes a justice-based approach to gender and community-based learning, asking how transformational learning and gender intersect when students leave the classroom and engage in service-learning and how we can best equip them to think deeply about gender outside the classroom.

Perceptions about gender matter as well. That gender affects student course evaluations is broadly supported, with many studies suggesting that women and minorities receive lower scores, even in controlled studies (Kogan, Schoenfeld-Tacher, and Hellyer 2010; Young, Rush, and Shaw 2009). Students may also exhibit preferences for teachers of the same gender as themselves (Centra and Gaubatz 2000), or reward professors whose gendered performance matches stereotypical expectations (Fries and McNinch 2003). Ekaterina Levintova's contribution to this volume considers student perceptions about gender, competency, and pedagogy. SoTL scholars can explore how these perceptions are experienced in the classroom by professors and students and what impact they have on student learning. This is particularly important when considering the working lives of women faculty of color, who may be facing multiple misperceptions (Gutiérrez y Muhs et al. 2012). Similarly, the broad debates around active learning in the classroom, which is often opposed to lecturing, have gendered dimensions given the association of traits like collaboration with femininity and authority with masculinity. SoTL scholars who think in an intersectional way about gender will be able to enlighten these debates.

Finally, pedagogical solutions attuned to gender exist, but could be augmented. One promising link between gender and SoTL asks how threshold concepts like patriarchy help illuminate the importance of gender (Hassel, Reddinger, and van Slooten 2011). This echoes work discussed above on "bottlenecks" in the political science classroom (Bernstein 2012). Gender and gender hierarchy could be made so central to political science that the field could not be understood without it. Indeed, if gender (and perhaps other identity-based hierarchies, like race and class) is of primary importance for understanding the political world, it must be included in political science. Given the importance of respect, autonomy, and attention to power that is central to feminist pedagogy and justice-based education, the opportunities to advance gender justice in the classroom fit squarely into SoTL work. In this volume, each contributor suggests research-driven tools for faculty, students, and administrators, which apply in political science and beyond. Each chapter, too, makes a conscious effort to connect political science methodology and problematics with the important debates and research questions in the SoTL literature. The authors of this volume are ultimately interested in what works in the political science classroom, under what conditions, and what improvements can be made to address the effects of gender inequity to make our classrooms more inclusive in political science and beyond. We fully embrace a gender-forward approach that goes beyond gender awareness and sensitivity, making SoTL a potential act of feminist praxis.

Gender in the Disciplinary Socialization of Graduate and Undergraduate Students and Professionals

Along with the need for transformative SoTL and the importance of SoTL as a tool for exploring gender in the political science classroom, this volume is inspired by the continued inequities in both the broader political world and the field that studies it. APSA has already determined that graduate programs in the discipline suffer from a "leaky pipeline," as many female students do not finish their training and drop out due to family obligations and other pressures (APSA 2005). In essence, "women graduate students have markedly different experiences than men in their professional preparation during graduate school, which may affect decisions about entering the profession" (APSA 2005, 3). Unlike the top reasons behind men's departure from graduate school (uncertainty about job prospects), women cite an unfriendly professional environment, inappropriate behavior, and lack of mentoring, professional support, and advising as barriers (APSA 2005, 4). The same sentiments are echoed in the popular press, with female PhD students reporting weak mentoring, more demands placed on them as teaching or research assistants, and the biological constraint of child-rearing age affecting them at the very start of their professional careers as reasons for opting out of the profession, even at the graduate school level (Drezner 2012). These challenges are often multiplied in complex ways for women of color (Agathangelou and Ling 2002). More research on mentoring and professional discrimination is needed for LGBTQ+ colleagues; however, in sociology (Taylor and Raeburn 1995) and in hard sciences and engineering (Bilimoria and Stewart 2009), similar barriers appear, as do risks for studying "gay" topics or engaging in activism.

The problem of gender-marginalized graduate students being subjected to different expectations and professional norms appears to have a systemic character, prompting at least one researcher to isolate four mechanisms through which such subtle and implicit discrimination occurs. Kantola (2008, 202) finds gendered division of labor, gendered interactions, gendered symbols, and gendered interpretations of one's position in the organization in typical political science departments in many advanced industrialized democracies. In particular, the prevalence of men in supervisory roles contributes greatly to this problem. Thus, the gendered image of professional expertise contributes to the feeling of marginalization and professional unworthiness among some female PhD students, and allows masculine presenting men to conform to "true" professional norms and women to see themselves as substandard participants in the academy. In particular, "PhD supervision by men is a... strong structural barrier for women" (Kantola 2008, 204). Moreover, the situation in the twenty-first century has not fundamentally changed from the gendered images identified in the 1990s by Hesli and Burrell (1995) and Sarkees and McGlen (1992 and 1999). The lack of diversity in terms of race, sexual orientation, and identity harms department collegiality and productivity (Hesli Claypool and Mershon 2016). Laura Jenkins and Rina Williams's chapter in this volume, operating with extensive quantitative data on research and methodological training in political science doctoral programs, zooms in on these very problems in the discipline.

There are also issues of gender representation in the political science faculty, whose gender equity is "far from ideal," according to APSA (Tolleson-Rinehart and Carroll 2006). Mirroring prevailing political culture and gender roles, political science as a profession has only slowly become more inclusive. The first woman to serve as president of the APSA, the national professional association, was not elected until 1989, and since then less than a handful of women have headed the organization. In terms of other gender and sexuality differences, we have less data; however, a 2010 survey found that LGBTQ+ individuals have become a larger portion of the individual members of the discipline as have the topics related to LGBTQ+ politics, but experiences of marginalization and discrimination persist (Novkov and Barclay 2010).

As of 2011, women made up about 29 percent of the political science faculty in the United States; less than 2 percent of the total faculty were women of color (Mershon and Walsh 2015). In the early twenty-first century, women constituted about 20 percent of full professors, concentrating at the lower ranks (about 37 percent and 29 percent respectively for assistant and associate professorships) and only about 20 percent of departments are chaired by women. Fewer women get hired as full-time tenure track professors; rather they are relegated to teach as adjunct and visiting faculty with no job security or stability and subpar monetary compensation (Tolleson-Rinehart and Carroll 2006, 511). This precarious labor situation improved only marginally by 2010, with about 22 percent of assistant professors, and about 29 percent of full professors being women, and with roughly 71 percent of all faculty in the field being male (APSA as cited in McMurtrie 2013). In terms of making this data more useful and intersectional, we need more complex findings on which women and which men are remaining in the field.

Gender problems in the discipline cannot be understood through numbers alone. An APSA special report studying institutional culture in political science departments unveiled an academic climate inhospitable to feminized practices, whoever does them. The barriers that women still face include "a culture of research that devalues collaboration, and the chronological overlap between the demanding pretenure years and the years when family responsibilities are greatest" (Tolleson-Rinehart and Carroll 2006, 511). Part of the problem can be directly attributable to the lack of mentors with relevant experience for junior level faculty, since so few women are full professors. Another culprit was excessive service expectations for women that detract from more highly rewarded research productivity (Pyke 2011). This is even more prevalent for women of color or gender minorities, who often serve as a first resource for students struggling with the same issues, therefore bearing higher demands for service commitments that are rarely rewarded in the tenure and promotion process (Sampaio 2006). On the teaching side, women, who are perceived by students as more nurturing, cannot convey this desired quality in a large classroom of two to three hundred students, resulting in lower course evaluations—another important consideration for promotion (McMurtrie 2013). The Committee on the Status of Women in the Profession argues that the "pipeline" is an insufficient metaphor to describe this problem, because adding more women to the pool will not address gender inequality at the top (Monroe and Chiu 2010). While there are proven policies that *do* address this inequity, they are infrequently adopted in political science departments (Monroe et al. 2014).

Among the bright spots in progress toward greater gender equality in the discipline of political science are the increased scholarship on gender and sexuality and additional avenues to publish this work, which is disproportionally written by women. Groups such as "Gendering Political Science" and "The Feminist Theory Workshop," held before the Western Political Science Association, have created productive communities of scholarship and practice. Yet as late as 2013, citations of articles in political science written by women were far less likely than those written by men, especially in the subfield of international relations, traditionally a bastion of male dominance in the profession. Unlike men, women do not cite their own work, one of the reasons behind the discrepancy (McMurtrie 2013). And men still out-publish women by a ratio of nearly two to one, even when considering coedited volumes in political science (Mathews and Andersen 2001).

Another promising development is the growing recognition of women as exceptional classroom teachers, a fact that bodes well for career progression. But even when women are being recognized for their pedagogical mastery and mentorship, once we disaggregate the nuances of data, the picture changes. A recent study from Kennesaw State University, for example, found that even though women tend to win more teaching awards than men do, this trend only applies to research-intensive masters and doctoral degree-granting universities or community colleges. However, teaching awards earned at the universities that privilege research over pedagogy might actually hurt the career progression of women. In fact, when looking at the four-year, teaching-intensive universities (where the majority of academic jobs in political science are), men are more likely to be recognized with teaching accolades, winning awards at the institutions where teaching clearly matters and counts heavily toward tenure and promotion (Butcher and Kersey 2015). These complex reward structures are even more challenging for women of color, who face a double-bind of either conforming to expectations to do more service or rejecting them, either of which can harm their careers (Sampaio 2006). This volume seeks to unpack the nuanced ways in which gender might be impacting the profession, especially one of its essential elements: university teaching. This impact might be especially strong in teaching about and doing research on extremely gendered interdisciplinary topics, like conflict studies in the international relations subfield (Jenkins and Williams's chapter).

Gender, Political Science, and Political Socialization Broadly Defined: Social and Political Implications of Our Volume

Political science departments also need to think consciously about gender as a threshold concept because, especially in the United States, where most of our authors are based, politics is characterized by persistent gender inequality. Although in 2012 women represented 51 percent of the electorate, their participation in other types of political activities, especially elected office, lags behind. In fact, the issue of underrepresentation based on gender is one of the main lines of inquiry in the growing subfield of gender and politics (Fox 2011). Lawless and Fox (2012) indentify seven factors that account for the continued underrepresentation of women in politics, including negative reactions to modern political campaigns, absence of encouragement to run for office, polarizing role models, aversion to hyper electoral competition, lack of self-confidence, risk aversion, and disproportional responsibility for child rearing and household tasks. Other research has found that women hold themselves to a higher standard for political knowledge before venturing into various types of political activities, from voting to working on political campaigns. A knowledge gap that is often merely perceived translates directly into a participation gap (Ondercin and Jones-White 2011). Current scholarship also draws to our attention that gender matters not so much in terms of general elections, but in recruitment and forming political ambition (Fox and Lawless 2005; Lawless and Fox 2010; Sanbonmatsu 2006). Men and women might favor different types of political participation, with women more likely to vote and engage in private activism, and men more likely to engage in direct contact, collective activism, and party membership (Coffé and Bolzendahl 2010). When socioeconomic class is considered, there are even fewer poor and working-class women at all levels of government, although this may also suggest that what we understand as political participation—taking part in elections and governance—is itself a classed and gendered concept. In short, descriptive representation of women, particularly women who are also working-class or racial and ethnic minorities, does not match demographics (Hardy-Fanta 2013).

But the problem goes much deeper than just sheer numbers of women, particularly marginalized women or the ethnic and gender minorities, who participate in the political process. Lovenduski (2005, 48) insists that the very assumptions about the traditional division of labor in politics might warrant a different focus of analysis. Politics remains the realm of masculinity in media narratives and general discourse about politics, resulting in women or, by extension, those who do not perform a dominant mode of masculinity, having very different experiences and challenges when it comes to participating politically (Falk 2008; Lawless and Pearson 2008). "As a result women now constitute 51 percent of electorate during presidential and midterm elections, yet their share in the US House of Representatives and Senate remains consistently in the 17–20 percent range" (Center for Study of Women in Politics, 2018). This gender bias is pernicious and hard to eradicate through quotas and other policy proposals. In this context, the examination of political socialization, including university education, is of utmost importance. Indeed, "early political socialization is particularly important. Several studies of college students suggest that substantial differences in political ambition to run for elective office are already present in college-age citizens" (Lawless and Fox 2010, 169 as quoted in Fox 2011). We hope to address this imbalance by showing how gender biases manifest themselves in political science, the discipline that is purported to give students professional knowledge and understanding of political process. It is essential that we examine gender differences in the classrooms where students are being exposed not only to politics but to political science research and other professional disciplinary norms.

One pressing issue, addressed in Levintova's chapter in this volume, is unpacking the "gender differences in politically relevant perceptions" (Fox 2011). How do students of political science perceive gender in the classroom? Are there specific traits assigned to male and female teachers, advisors, and mentors? In other words, do our classes promote gender equality or do they reinforce already existing stereotypes? In Curtin's chapter, this issue is approached from an international perspective, suggesting that the interactions between the world of politics and political science are complex and differ by country. Curtin suggests that it takes activism as well as teaching to shift these stereotypes. Rinfret and Pautz's chapter asks different questions about politically relevant classroom socialization: Do male and female students participate the same way in our classrooms? And do the patterns of participation mask the division of political labor, in which women are effectively shut out of political conversations, even on the topics important to them? Are women more comfortable in participating in class discussions online or face-to-face? Do women feel empowered and increase their political efficacy by taking political science classes? Do women hold themselves to a higher standard of political knowledge before participating in political science classes, as the scholarship suggests happens in political participation outside the classroom? Already some research (Orenstein 1995; Sadker and Sadker 1994; Sadker and Silber 2006) indicates that girls tend to be shut out of the secondary school classroom discussions by boys who answer teachers' questions faster, raise their hands first, and are, in general, louder, more assertive, and more confident in classroom settings. Does the same hold in higher education?

Yet another way in which political socialization with larger societal implications manifests itself in political science classroom is through consumption of authoritative written sources. Crocco and Libresco (2007) demonstrated that female narratives and problems tend to be excluded from textbook and classroom instruction in secondary education's social studies. Sadker and Zittleman (2002) uncovered gender biases in high school social studies textbooks, which included stereotyping, invisibility, selectivity/imbalance in representation, unrealistic representations, isolation, and linguistic and cosmetic biases. Gendered narratives and images also still permeate political science textbooks at the university level, at least in the American politics subfield (Olivo 2012). But is it as prevalent in the other three subfields? And who writes our textbooks? Mueller's chapter addresses these research questions.

Finally, two chapters consider gender in professionalization practices. Jenkins and Williams's chapter explores the question of professional and political socialization from both the student (doctoral students in this case) and faculty (future political science instructors) perspectives. They consider how our disciplinary methodological divisions stack up against gender differences. Systematically investigating graduate student research allows the authors to tackle important questions about mentoring, professional socialization, and pathways into the academy. They also trace the most recent trends in terms of gender, research methods, and political science subfields (American politics, international relations, comparative politics, and political theory), uncovering gendered trends in the preparation of future political science instructors and practitioners. Curtin takes up these questions in the context of academia in New Zealand, questioning the dominance of the US system while also offering possible solutions for gender inequities in political science drawn from a non-US institutional context.

In terms of the nonacademic professional world of political science, gender looks relatively equal when we consider high-status and elite jobs that attract the college educated or, increasingly, those with graduate degrees, such as lobbyists (Benoit 2007). More work is needed on the gendered nature of campaign consulting, legislative staff, and other political work that is not office-holding. Thus the way that gender and politics interact depends on whether one has a college degree and whether one works professionally in politics or works as a citizen only. The distance between these outcomes leads us to imagine a world in which elite women, even elite women of color or elite nonheterosexual women, achieve a type of parity with elite men, while women with less education, wealth, or the standing that something like citizenship brings might experience significant gender disparity. One mission of the university—arguably yet to be met—is to provide access to class mobility for the formerly marginalized. For this to happen in a way that supports equity, the importance of studying gender and politics from the perspective of the citizen as well as the elected official is important.

Final Thoughts and Thematic Structure of the Book

To put gender first in political science, the Scholarship of Teaching and Learning, or higher education at large, will take the work of teachers and students as well as citizens. We do some of this work in this volume, which we hope also serves as an invitation for the readers to join us in reconsidering gender in their academic and political life. Political science is uniquely positioned as a discipline that links social sciences and the humanities, rich with quantitative and qualitative tools for exploring and explaining the work that gender does in the classroom. At the same time, political science itself needs to respond to the challenges of feminist pedagogy and theory, particularly because the political world at large is still strikingly unequal. Although ultimately this scholarship will need to develop to fully inhabit the threshold concepts adopted from WGS, particularly intersectionality, it must grow toward this connection by starting with the methods and questions of political science. We need to develop passageways into other disciplines and use threshold concepts like gender to link, rather than separate, disciplines and ways of knowing, especially where they are indispensable for studying human life.

Of course, this call for connection occurs in a context where many disciplines are threatened by the politics of higher education and targeted attacks in the service of neo-liberal agenda to destroy public entities. If it has been twenty-five years since the Wahlke report called for the mainstreaming of gender and it has not yet happened, it seems clear that institutional norms and rewards have made such change difficult. Periodic attempts to reform political science, such as the 1960s' caucus for a New Political Science and the 1990s' Perestroika, which advocated for broader methods and more politically relevant political science, included gender in their platforms to varying degrees, and resulted in some changes at APSA at least. Yet, the discipline has, if anything, gravitated toward *less* gender awareness rather than more, and distanced itself from WGS and other politically sensitive programs (and often from normative work). Working toward a change in the discipline as a whole will take more of this revolutionary advocacy, but it will also take the support of citizens themselves for political science and higher education and for their roles in promoting a more just world. Therefore, our volume highlights recommendations for classroom instructors, in hopes of encouraging communities of practice among political scientists and others who put gender first, which can then build instructional change along with their justice-oriented colleagues and students.

Political science methods for studying gender in teaching and learning are necessarily plural, including both classic social science approaches and more interpretative and exegetic practices. Feminist research methods in social science disciplines are "not a series of particular methods ... but a commitment to using a whole range of methods reflectively and critically" and therefore "a way of using and reflecting on methods, and not a particular research design" (Ackerly and True 2010, 6). Although there have been powerful critiques of many social science methods for their gendered assumptions, particularly around the concept of truth as neutral, which is explored in Staudinger's chapter, a multiplicity of methods makes the most sense for getting at gendered concepts in a way that speaks both to the discipline and the other disciplines with which we would like to connect. Feminist methods have had particular importance in the world of international relations, in part through a willingness to integrate and interrogate disparate ways of knowing and fields of scholarship, as in feminist security studies (Wibben 2016). As in this subfield, our authors often discuss men and women as a binary, despite our awareness that this is a thin conception of gender as actually experienced; however, this can be a "political move" (Wibben 2016, 7) in a discipline and a world where gender works in many everyday lives in this fashion. Our authors also consider nonelites, in the classroom and the discipline, and reflect on the role of intersecting identities and social positions throughout.

This volume is split into two thematic blocks. Part 1 considers gender as it matters for political science as an institution and a set of practices, reflecting the discipline's focus on central questions about power, access, and agency. These chapters stick more closely to the gender-mainstreaming promotion of gender equality. In part 2, we shift to understanding gender in the political science classroom itself, building theory through explorations of student learning and offering techniques and pedagogy for responding to gender in political science and beyond. In these chapters, the authors advocate for moving away from gender mainstreaming, or for adding conceptions of gender-forward teaching and learning in addition to efforts toward mainstreaming.

In the institutional section, Ingrid Bego begins in chapter 1, "Gendering the Political Science Classroom While Mainstreaming the Discipline: Understanding the Barriers and Exploring Solutions," by uncovering existing gender barriers in the discipline proper and in our classrooms and offering strategies for creating a gender equitable classroom when controversial topics with gendered dimensions are covered. In chapter 2, "Gender and Methodological Diversity in Recent Political Science Dissertations," Williams and Jenkins argue that male and female graduate students tend to use different research methodologies and that gendered use of methodology is especially pronounced in some subfields, two findings that raise concerns about the recent disciplinary drift toward privileging quantitative methods over their qualitative counterparts. If our field is serious about gender equity, it should consider more intentional incorporation of interpretive, qualitative, and quantitative methods into graduate curricula as a strategy to recruit and retain more female students and future faculty members. In chapter 3, Mueller considers what role gender plays in undergraduate textbooks: Who writes them and what do they depict? How might this authorship and authority gap, if it exists, affect student learning and political socialization? In the last chapter in this section, chapter 4, Curtin expands the scope of our concerns by exploring gender mainstreaming in political science through a case study of New Zealand's higher education institutions offering doctoral studies, connecting the results to the discipline at large and the practice of social scientists everywhere. These institutional considerations are essential for SoTL from a social science perspective, as they consider the context and history in which learning occurs, rather than treating classrooms as independent of the politics of higher education.

In part 2, we move to the classroom and toward a more "gender-forward" approach, framed by part 1's institutional focus. In chapter 5, "Student Perceptions of Gender in Political Science Teaching and Advising," Levintova explores how socialization and stereotypes might matter for student learning. Continuing the theme of analyzing gender difference, Rooks examines the experience of students in service-learning classes in chapter 6. A sociologist of higher education, Rooks analyzes the reflection papers of students in an interdisciplinary course on poverty and homelessness, calls for attention to the legacies of service work by women and some minorities in courses on community-based learning, and recognizes their role in ensuring a transformative experience of civic life for all students. In chapter 7, Rinfret and Pautz seek to understand how gender affects student participation in entry level political science courses, such as American government and politics, in a traditional classroom setting, online format, or hybrid format. Their study also investigates how gendered classroom participation might influence student interest and willingness to engage in political participation outside the college classroom, an important implication to consider.

To suggest how we can respond as teachers to the importance of gender, we look at concrete and theoretical approaches to the classroom. In chapter 8, Staudinger examines the supposed ideal of neutrality in the classroom, and proposes ways that gender can be negotiated as fluid rather than a hypothetically neutral position. She draws on student learning as well as pedagogical theory to progress to greater gender awareness in our classrooms, and to critique dominant methods in SoTL. In chapter 9, Barske offers a solution of "Thinking Through Movement: Embodied Learning as Feminist Pedagogy for the Social Sciences" that pushes us to consider new modes of being in the classroom and advances the goal of gender-forward teaching and learning.

Finally, in our conclusion, we synthesize the insights from this volume and offer some ideas for the future direction of this research in political science, its cognate disciplines, and SoTL. In particular, we return to the notion of integrating threshold concepts such as feminist praxis into political science. Because the volume combines insights from very different institutional contexts, including discussions of private and public schools, research- and teaching-intensive colleges and universities, and regional and national institutions, our concluding chapter also discusses the universals and specifics in the treatment of gender in the classroom. We hope the readers will find here research and strategies that challenge them not only to mainstream gender in their classroom but to advance gender forwardness, and to reconsider the ways in which political science serves as a bridge among disciplines and also between the academic and working worlds of politics.

EKATERINA M. LEVINTOVA is Associate Professor of Political Science, University of Wisconsin–Green Bay, where she teaches comparative politics, political behavior, and international relations courses. Her research on political sociology of post-Communist transitions has been published in *Party Politics*, *Europe-Asia Studies*, *Slavonic and East European Review*, *Journal of Communist and Post-Communist Studies*, and in two edited volumes. Her SoTL-related work has appeared in *The Journal of Political Science Education* and *Canadian Journal for the Scholarship of Teaching and Learning*. She also coedited *From Peasant to Patriarch: An Account of the Birth, Upbringing, and Life of Nikon, Patriarch of Moscow and All Russia*.

ALISON KATHRYN STAUDINGER is Assistant Professor of Democracy and Justice Studies, University of Wisconsin–Green Bay, where she studies democratic theory and practice generally and in the classroom. She regularly teaches courses on gender and the law, American political thought, and social justice. Her SoTL research has appeared in *Teaching and Learning Inquiry*, and her teaching has been recognized by an NEH Enduring Questions Grant. She is a speaker for the Wisconsin Humanities "Shoptalk" series, where she has presented her research on constitutional change in the early twentieth century among other topics.

Notes

1. For example, SoTL in science, technology, engineering, and math (STEM) fields has often lagged behind other areas, prompting some to wonder whether the term has applicability there or whether something like "teaching as research" would be preferable (Connolly, Bouwma-Gearhart, and Clifford 2007). However, in places like the *Journal of STEM Education: Innovations and Research* and within SoTL in the disciplines literature (McKinney 2012), STEM inquiry on learning is growing. We hope to make this so-called difficult journey (Kelly, Nesbit, and Oliver 2012) easier, because political scientists often move between the harder and softer sides of disciplines, engaging in work that ranges from experiments to interpretations of poetry. As a recent report, "Collaborating the

Centers," argues, Centers for Teaching and Learning can also collaborate with centers for STEM education to work on shared projects for the STEM classroom and beyond (Horii et al. 2016).

2. In terms of their relative prominence, employment data is useful. Leanne Sedowski and Michael Brintnall (2006) studied political science job listings in the early 2000s, finding 262 (29 percent) in American politics, 216 (24 percent) in international relations, 180 (20 percent) in comparative politics, and, falling behind, 62 (7 percent) in political theory. The rest of the jobs were listed in smaller subfields, with nearly as many (60 and 57, respectively) in public law and public administration as political theory. See Sedowski and Brintnall (2006) for more nuanced treatment of the data.

3. Joseph Schumpeter, an economist and political scientist (1883–1951), is often credited as one of the foremost theoreticians of the elitist theory of democracy, in which power firmly resides in the political elite and democratic participation is intentionally limited to selections of leaders via elections. On the other side of power continuum, Antonio Gramsci, a neo-Marxist theorist and politician (1891–1937), and later Michel Foucault (1926–84), a social philologist and theorist, contributed insights into power on the level of discursive practices and cultural hegemony. In other words, our discipline's understanding of power ranges from almost crudely objectivist to implicitly normative.

4. For a now classic expression of humanities SoTL, see Chick, Hassel, and Haynie (2009).

References

Ackerly, Brooke, and Liza Mügge. 2016. "Mainstreaming Gender in the Teaching and Learning of Politics." *PS, Political Science & Politics* 49 (3): 541–45.
Ackerly, Brooke, and Jacqui True. 2010. *Doing Feminist Research in Political and Social Science*. Houndmills, UK: Palgrave MacMillan.
Agathangelou, Anna M., and Lily H. M. Ling. 2002. "An Unten(ur)able Position: The Politics of Teaching for Women of Color in the US." *International Feminist Journal of Politics* 4 (3): 368–98. doi: 10.1080/1461674022000031562.
American Political Science Association. (APSA). 2005. *Women's Advancement in Political Science. A Report on the Advancement of Women in Academic Political Science in the United States*. Washington, DC: American Political Science Association. http://www.apsanet.org/Portals/54/files/Task%20Force%20Reports/Womens_Advancement_in_Political_Science_2005.pdf?ver=2015-06-17-105710-443.
American Political Science Association. (APSA). 2011. *Political Science in the Twenty-First Century*. Washington, DC: American Political Science Association. http://www.apsanet.org/portals/54/Files/Task%20Force%20Reports/TF_21st%20Century_AllPgs_webres90.pdf.
Baker, Kelly J. 2015. "Contingency and Gender." *Women in Higher Education*. April 24, 2015. https://chroniclevitae.com/news/984-contingency-and-gender.
Benoit, Denise. 2007. *The Best-Kept Secret: Women Corporate Lobbyists, Policy, and Power in the United States*. New Brunswick, NJ: Rutgers University Press.

Bernstein, Jeffrey L. 2012. "Plowing through Bottlenecks in Political Science: Experts and Novices at Work." *The Scholarship of Teaching and Learning In and Across the Disciplines*, edited by Kathleen McKinney, 74–92. Bloomington: Indiana University Press.

Bilimoria, Diana, and Abigail J. Stewart. 2009. "'Don't Ask, Don't Tell': The Academic Climate for Lesbian, Gay, Bisexual, and Transgender Faculty in Science and Engineering." *NWSA Journal* 21 (2): 85–103. https://muse.jhu.edu/article/316151.

Blanchard, Eric M. 2003. "Gender, International Relations, and the Development of Feminist Security Theory." *Signs* 28 (4): 1289–312. doi: 10.1086/368328.

Blessinger, Patrick, and John M. Carfora. 2015. *Inquiry-Based Learning for Science, Technology, Engineering and Math (STEM) Programs*. Bingley, UK: Emerald Group.

Brettschneider, Maria. 2011. "Heterosexual Political Science." *PS: Political Science and Politics* 44 (1): 23–26. www.jstor.org/stable/40984477.

Butcher, Charity, and Timothy Kersey. 2015. "When Winning Is Really Losing: Teaching Awards and Women Political Science Faculty." *PS: Political Science and Politics* 48 (1): 138–41. doi: 10.1017/S104909651400167X.

Cassese, Erin C., Angela L. Bos, and Monica C. Schneider. 2012. "Whose American Government? A Quantitative Analysis of Gender and Authorship in American Politics Texts." *Journal of Political Science Education* 10 (3): 253–72.

Cassese, Erin C., Angela L. Bos, and Lauren E. Duncan. 2012. "Integrating Gender into the Political Science Core Curriculum." *PS: Political Science and Politics* 45 (2): 238–43. doi: 10.1017/S1049096512000042.

Cassese, Erin C., Mirya R. Holman, Monica C. Schneider, and Angela L. Bos. 2015. "Building a Gender and Methodology Curriculum: Integrated Skills, Exercises, and Practices." *Journal of Political Science Education* 11 (1): 61–77. doi: 10.1080/15512169.2014.985106.

Centra, John A., and Noreen B. Gaubatz. 2000. "Is There Gender Bias in Student Evaluations of Teaching?" *The Journal of Higher Education* 71 (1): 17–33. doi: 10.1080/00221546.2000.11780814.

Center for American Women in Politics, Eagleton Institute of Politics, Rutgers University "Women in Elective Office 2018" Accessed March 19, 2018. http://www.cawp.rutgers.edu/women-elective-office-2018.

Chick, Nancy L., Holly Hassel, and Aeron Haynie. 2009. "Pressing an Ear Against the Hive: Reading Literature for Complexity." *Pedagogy* 9 (3): 399–422. https://muse.jhu.edu/article/361536/pdf.

Coffé, Hilde, and Catherine Bolzendahl. 2010. "Same Game, Different Rules?: Gender Differences in Political Participation." *Sex Roles* 62 (5–6): 318–33. doi: 10.1007/s11199-009-9729-y.

Connolly, Mark R., Jana L. Bouwma-Gearhart, and Matthew A. Clifford. 2007. "The Birth of a Notion: The Windfalls and Pitfalls of Tailoring a SoTL-like Concept to Scientists, Mathematicians, and Engineers." *Innovative Higher Education* 32 (1): 19–34. doi: 10.1007/s10755-007-9034-z.

Coughlin, Richard W. 2013. "Gender and Negotiation in Model UN Role-Playing Simulations." *Journal of Political Science Education* 9 (3): 320–35. doi: 10.1080/15512169.2013.796242.

Crocco, Margaret S., and Andrea S. Libresco. 2007. "Citizen Education for the Twenty-First Century—A Gender Inclusive Approach to Social Studies." In *Gender in The*

Classroom: Foundations, Skills, Methods, and Strategies Across the Curriculum, edited by David Sadker and Ellen S. Silber, 109–63. London: Lawrence Erlbaum.

Dewar, Jacqueline M., and Curtis D. Bennett. 2015. *Doing the Scholarship of Teaching and Learning in Mathematics*. Washington, DC: Mathematical Association of America Press.

Doolittle, Peter, and Danielle Lusk. 2012. "The Effects of Institutional Classification and Gender on Faculty Inclusion of Syllabus Components." *Journal of the Scholarship of Teaching and Learning* 7 (2): 62–78. https://josotl.indiana.edu/article/view/1684/1682.

Drezner, Daniel. W. 2012. "Should Women Get PhDs in International Relations?" *Foreign Policy*. March 11, 2012. http://www.foreignpolicy.com/posts/2012/03/11/should_women_get_phds_in_international_relations.

Elison, Sonja. 1997. "Integrating Women into the Study of European Politics." *PS: Political Science and Politics* 30 (2): 202–4. doi: 10.2307/420494.

Ewert, Stephanie. 2012. "Fewer Diplomas for Men: The Influence of College Experiences on the Gender Gap in College Graduation." *The Journal of Higher Education* 83 (6): 824–50.

Falk, Erika. 2008. *Women for President: Media Bias in Eight Campaigns*. Urbana: University of Illinois Press.

Farganis, Dion, and Jason Kirk. 2012. "A Discipline Divided: Can Threshold Concepts Exist in Political Science?" Panel Presentation, 9th Annual Teaching and Learning Conference. Elon University, Elon, NC.

Fox, Richard L. 2011. "Studying Gender in US Politics: Where Do We Go from Here?" *Politics and Gender* 7 (1): 94–99. doi: 10.1017/S1743923X10000589.

Fox, Richard L., and Jennifer L. Lawless. 2005. "To Run or Not to Run for Office: Explaining Nascent Political Ambition." *American Journal of Political Science* 49 (3): 642–59.

Fries, Christopher J., and R. James McNinch. 2003. "Signed versus Unsigned Student Evaluations of Teaching: A Comparison." *Teaching Sociology* 31 (3): 333–44. http://www.jstor.org/stable/3211331.

Gilpin, Lorraine, and Delores Liston. 2009. "Transformative Education in the Scholarship of Teaching and Learning: An Analysis of SoTL Literature." *International Journal for the Scholarship of Teaching and Learning* 3 (2): 1–8. doi: 10.20429/ijsotl.2009.030211030211.

Glasser, Howard M., and John P. Smith. 2008. "On the Vague Meaning of 'Gender' in Education Research: The Problem, Its Sources, and Recommendations for Practice." *Educational Researcher* 37 (6): 343–50. doi: 10.3102/0013189X08323718.

Greenlee, Jill S., Mirya R. Holman, and Rachel VanSickle-Ward. 2014. "Making It Personal: Assessing the Impact of In-Class Exercises on Closing the Gender Gap in Political Ambition." *Journal of Political Science Education* 10 (1): 48–61. doi: 10.1080/15512169.2013.859083.

Gutiérrez y Muhs, Gabriella, Yolanda Flores Niemann, Carmen G. Gonzalez, and Angela P. Harris, eds, 2012. *Presumed Incompetent: The Intersections of Race and Class for Women in Academia*. Logan, UT: Utah State University Press.

Hancock, Ange-Marie. 2011. *Solidarity Politics for Millennials: A Guide to Ending the Oppression Olympics*. New York: Palgrave Macmillan.

Hardy-Fanta, Carol. 2011. *Intersectionality and Politics: Recent Research on Gender, Race, and Political Representation in the United States*. New York: Routledge.

Hassel, Holly, Amy Reddinger, and Jessica van Slooten. 2011. "Surfacing the Structures of Patriarchy: Teaching and Learning Threshold Concepts in Women's Studies." *International Journal for the Scholarship of Teaching and Learning* 5 (2): 1–19. doi: 10.20429/ijsotl.2011.050218.

Hawthorne, Susan. 2004. "The Political Uses of Obscurantism: Gender Mainstreaming and Intersectionality." *Development Bulletin* 64: 87–91.

Hesli, Vicki, and Barbara Burrell. 1995. "Faculty Rank among Political Scientists and Reports on the Academic Environment: The Differentiated Impact of Gender on Observed Patterns." *PS: Political Science and Politics* 28 (1): 101–11. http://www.jstor.org/stable/420592.

Hesli Claypool, Vicki, and Carol Mershon. 2016. "Does Diversity Matter? Evidence from a Survey of Political Science Faculty." *Politics, Groups, and Identities* 4 (3): 1–16. doi: 10.1080/21565503.2016.1170707.

Horii, Cassandra, Kacy Redd, Mathew Ouellett, Noah Finkelstein, Andrea Beach, Deborah Carlisle, Susan Shadle, and Gabriela Weaver. 2016. *Collaborating at the Centers.* Joint Report from the POD network in Higher Education and the Network of Stem Education Centers. http://podnetwork.org/content/uploads/Collaborating-at-the-Centers-Workshop-Report-20July2016.pdf.

Ishiyama, John, Marijke Breuning, and Linda Lopez. 2006. "A Century of Continuity and (Little) Change in the Undergraduate Political Science Curriculum." *American Political Science Review* 100 (4): 659–65. doi: 10.1017/S0003055406062551.

Kustrar, Dagmar, and Anita Kärner. 2010. "Exploration of Societal Transitions in Estonia from the Threshold Concepts Perspective of Teaching and Learning." In *Threshold Concepts and Transformational Learning*, edited by Jan H. F. Meyer, Caroline Baille, and Ray Land. Rotterdam: Sense Publishers.

Kantola, Johanna. 2008. "Why Do All Women Disappear?: Gendering Processes in a Political Science Department." *Gender, Work and Organization* 15 (2): 202–25.

Kelly, Niamh, Susan Nesbit, and Carolyn Oliver. 2012. "A Difficult Journey: Transitioning from STEM to SOTL." *International Journal for the Scholarship of Teaching and Learning* 6 (1): 18.

Kogan, Lori R., Regina Schoenfeld-Tacher, and Peter W. Hellyer. 2010. "Student Evaluations of Teaching: Perceptions of Faculty Based on Gender, Position, and Rank." *Teaching in Higher Education* 15 (6): 623–36.

Kohli, Atul, Peter Evans, Peter J. Katzenstein, Adam Przeworski, Susan H. Rudolph, James C. Scott, and Theda Skocpol. 1995. "The Role of Theory in Comparative Politics: A Symposium." *World Politics* 48 (1): 1–49.

Kramer, Laura, and George T. Martin. 1988. "Mainstreaming Gender: Some Thoughts for the Nonspecialist." *Teaching Sociology* 16 (2): 133–40.

Krause, Sharon R. 2011. "Contested Questions, Current Trajectories: Feminism in Political Theory Today." *Politics and Gender* 7 (1): 105–11. doi: 10.1017/S1743923X10000607.

Land, Ray, J. H. F. Meyer, and Jan Smith. 2008. *Threshold Concepts within the Disciplines.* Rotterdam: Sense Publishers.

Launius, Christie, and Holly Hassel. 2014. *Threshold Concepts in Women's and Gender Studies: Ways of Seeing, Thinking, and Knowing.* New York: Routledge.

Lawless, Jennifer L., and Richard L. Fox. 2010. *It Still Takes a Candidate Why Women Don't Run for Office.* Cambridge: Cambridge University Press.

———. 2012. *Men Rule: The Continued Under-Representation of Women in US Politics*. Washington, DC: American University: Women in Politics Institute and School of Public Policy. https://www.american.edu/spa/wpi/upload/2012-Men-Rule-Report-web.pdf.

Lawless, Jennifer L., and Kathryn Pearson. 2008. "The Primary Reason for Women's Underrepresentation? Reevaluating the Conventional Wisdom." *The Journal of Politics* 70 (1): 67–82.

Lovenduski, Joni. 2005. *Feminizing Politics*. Cambridge: Polity.

Mathews, A. Lanethea, and Kristi Andersen. 2001. "A Gender Gap in Publishing? Women's Representation in Edited Political Science Books." *PS: Political Science & Politics* 34 (1): 143–47.

McDermott, Rose, and Peter K. Hatemi. 2011. "Distinguishing Sex and Gender." *PS: Political Science and Politics* 44 (1): 89–92.

McKinney, Kathleen. 2012. *The Scholarship of Teaching and Learning in and across Disciplines*. Bloomington: Indiana University Press.

McKinney, Kathleen, and Nancy Chick. 2010. "SoTL as Women's Work: What Do Existing Data Tell Us?" *International Journal for the Scholarship of Teaching and Learning* 4 (2). http://digitalcommons.georgiasouthern.edu/ij-sotl/vol4/iss2/16.

McMurtrie, Beth. 2013. "Political Science Is Rife with Gender Bias, Scholars Find." *Chronicle of Higher Education*. August 30, 2013. http://www.chronicle.com/article/Political-Science-Is-Rife-With/141319/.

Mershon, Carol, and Denise Walsh. 2015. "How Political Science Can Be More Diverse." *PS: Political Science and Politics* 48 (3): 441–44.

Meyer, Jan H. F. 2008. *Threshold Concepts within the Disciplines*. Rotterdam: Sense Publishers.

Meyer, Jan H. F., and Ray Land. 2005. "Threshold Concepts and Troublesome Knowledge: Epistemological Considerations and a Conceptual Framework for Teaching and Learning." *Higher Education* 49 (3): 373–88.

———. 2006. "Threshold Concepts and Troublesome Knowledge: An Introduction." In *Overcoming Barriers to Student Understanding: Threshold Concepts and Troublesome Knowledge*, edited by Jan H. F. Meyer, Ray Land, and Jan Smith, 3–18. London: Routledge.

Monroe, Kristen Renwick, and William F. Chiu. 2010. "Gender Equality in the Academy: The Pipeline Problem." *PS: Political Science and Politics* 43 (2): 303–8.

Monroe, Kristen Renwick, Jenny Choi, Emily Howell, Chloe Lampros-Monroe, Crystal Trejo, and Valentina Perez. 2014. "Gender Equality in the Ivory Tower, and How Best to Achieve It." *PS: Political Science and Politics* 47 (2): 418–26.

Moore, Matthew J. 2011. "How (and What) Political Theorists Teach: Results of a National Survey." *Journal of Political Science Education* 7 (1): 95–128. doi: 10.1080/15512169.2011.539921.

Myers, Carrie. 2008. "College Faculty and the Scholarship of Teaching: Gender Differences across Four Key Activities." *Journal of the Scholarship of Teaching and Learning* 8 (2): 38–51.

Novkov, Julie, and Scott Barclay. 2010. "Lesbians, Gays, Bisexuals, and the Transgendered in Political Science: Report on a Discipline-Wide Survey." *PS: Political Science and Politics* 43 (1): 95–106.

O'Connor, Karen, and Alixandria Yanus. 2009. "The Chilly Climate Continues: Defrosting the Gender Divide in Political Science and Politics." *Journal of Political Science Education* 5 (2): 108–18.

Olivo, Christiane. 2012. "Bringing Women In: Gender and American Government and Politics Textbooks." *Journal of Political Science Education* 8 (2): 131–46. doi: 10.1080/1551 2169.2012.667676.

Ondercin, Heather L., and Daniel Jones-White. 2011. "Gender Jeopardy: What Is the Impact of Gender Differences in Political Knowledge on Political Participation." *Social Science Quarterly* 92 (3): 675–94.

Orenstein, Peggy. 1995. *Schoolgirls*. New York: Anchor.

Perkins, David. 1999. "The Many Faces of Constructivism." *Educational Leadership* 57 (3): 6–11.

Pollock, Philip H., Kerstin Hamann, and Bruce M. Wilson. 2005. "Teaching and Learning Online: Assessing the Effect of Gender Context on Active Learning." *Journal of Political Science Education* 1 (1): 1–15. doi: 10.1080/15512160490921815.

Pyke, Karen. 2011. "Service and Gender Inequity among Faculty." *PS: Political Science and Politics* 44 (1): 85–87.

Sadker, David, and Ellen S. Silber, eds. 2006. *Gender in the Classroom: Foundations, Skills, Attitudes, and Strategies across the Curriculum*. London: Lawrence Erlbaum.

Sadker, David, and Karen Zittleman. 2002. "Gender Biases in Teacher Education Texts: New (and Old) Lessons." *Educational Leadership* 60 (4): 59–63.

Sadker, Myra, and David Sadker. 1994. *Failing at Fairness*. New York: Touchstone.

Sampaio, Anna. 2006. "Women of Color Teaching Political Science: Examining the Intersections of Race, Gender, and Course Material in the Classroom." *PS: Political Science and Politics* 39 (4): 917–92. www.jstor.org.ezproxy.uwgb.edu:2048/stable /20451844.

Sanbonmatsu, Kira. 2006. *Where Women Run: Gender and Party in the American States*. Ann Arbor: University of Michigan Press.

Sarkees, Meredith Reid, and Nancy E. McGlen. 1992. "Confronting Barriers: The Status of Women in Political Science." *Women and Politics* 12 (4): 43–86.

———. 1999. "Misdirected Backlash: The Evolving 'Nature of Academia and the Status of Women in Political Science.'" *PS: Political Science and Politics* 32 (1): 100–9.

Schwartz, Beth M., and Regan A. R. Gurung. 2012. *Evidence-Based Teaching for Higher Education*. Washington, DC: American Psychological Association.

Sedowski, Leanne, and Michael Brintnall. 2006. *Trends in the Political Science Profession: Political Science Job Listings in APSA's eJobs Listing Service*. Washington, DC: American Political Science Association. http://jlewis.huntingdon.edu/Syl /499/APSAJobsGrowthDec06.pdf or www.apsanet.org/imgtest/EJobsWriteUp%20 12%202006.pdf.

Smith, Heather A. 2007. "What We Value about the Scholarship of Teaching and Learning." *Transformative Dialogues: Teaching and Learning Journal* 1 (2): 1–3.

Taylor, Verta, and Nicole C. Raeburn. 1995. "Identity Politics as High-Risk Activism: Career Consequences for Lesbian, Gay, and Bisexual Sociologists." *Social Problems* 42 (2): 252–73.

Tolleson-Rinehart Sue, and Susan J. Carroll. 2006. "'Far from Ideal:' The Gender Politics of Political Science." *American Political Science Review* 100 (4): 507–13.

Wahlke, John C. 1991. "Liberal Learning and the Political Science Major: A Report to the Profession." *PS: Political Science and Politics* 24 (1): 48–60. http://journals.cambridge .org/abstract_S1049096500052926.

Weldon, S. Laurel. 2006. "The Structure of Intersectionality: A Comparative Politics of Gender." *Politics and Gender* 2 (2): 235–48. doi: 10.1017/S1743923X06231040.

Wibben, Annick T. R., ed. 2016. *Researching War: Feminist Methods, Ethics and Politics.* New York: Routledge.
Williams, Paul. 2014. "What's Politic Got to Do with It? 'Power' As a 'Threshold' Concept for Undergraduate Business Students." *Australian Journal of Adult Learning* 54 (1): 8–29.
Wilson, Angelia R., ed. 2013. *Situating Intersectionality.* New York: Palgrave Macmillan. http://link.springer.com/10.1057/9781137025135.
Young, Suzanne, Leslie Rush, and Dale Shaw. 2009. "Evaluating Gender Bias in Ratings of University Instructors' Teaching Effectiveness." *International Journal for the Scholarship of Teaching and Learning* 3 (2). Article 19. http://digitalcommons.georgiasouthern.edu/ij-sotl/vol3/iss2/19.
Zeigler, Sara L., and Sheena M. Moran. 2008. "Revisiting Adam's Rib: Student Performance, Gender Stereotyping, and Trial Simulations." *Journal of Political Science Education* 4(2): 187–204. doi: 10.1080/15512160801998148.

Part One:
National and Institutional Trends

1 Gendering the Political Science Classroom While Mainstreaming Gender in the Discipline: Understanding the Barriers and Exploring Solutions

Ingrid Bego

In 1936, the political scientist Harold Lasswell stated that politics determines "who gets what, when, and how." Particularly, Lasswell (1936) argued that the political science discipline should dedicate itself "to [studying] the influence and the influential," (25) the distribution of power and resources in the society. Almost forty years later, political science as a discipline would acknowledge that perhaps individuals' identities play a role in how they participate and partake in the political process. Prior to the feminist movement of the 1960s, only a few books or articles pertaining to women were written by political scientists[1] and from 1901 to 1966 only eleven dissertations focusing on women were completed (Shanley and Schuck 1974). Thus, political science, not unlike other disciplines within the realm of social science and beyond, has risen out of a legacy of omission and has only a very short history of critically assessing identity politics, and, more particularly, the role of gender in politics.

It is not surprising that like the political institutions it examines, the political science discipline struggles with barriers to equality in representation, pay, prestige, and parity in positions of leadership (American Political Science Association 2004, 2011). Like political institutions, higher education institutions and whole disciplines (including political science) are prone to resisting change and perpetuating the status quo. Historical institutionalists argue that "institutions are sticky" and likely to change only under certain periods of upheaval referred to as "critical junctures." (Hall 1986; Pierson 2000; Thelen 1999; Thelen and Steinmo 1992). Thus, even though gender equality and gender justice are globally accepted standards of human rights, institutional inertia continues to perpetuate the status quo, requiring strong winds of change sweeping a discipline to significantly change norms and practices. Higher education institutions provide ideal conditions for perpetuating existing inequalities: access for the next generation of political scientists is only granted to those who have been successfully taught and mentored by previous generations. Until the axes of inequality are fairly represented in each aspect of political science, we will continue to reproduce a work force of future academics, professionals, and global citizens who will accept and be willing to move forward under the same gender norms and concepts that were either left undiscussed or mirrored inaccurately in our classrooms. This chapter argues that, using the tools political scientists themselves have developed to understand institutions, we can transform our discipline and match the global commitment for a more just and diverse future.

I propose expanding two concepts in political science to ground this change: gender mainstreaming and gendering of a topic or policy. These two underexplored ideas can serve to anchor gender as a threshold concept, as discussed in the introductory chapter. The term *gender mainstreaming* arose out of the United Nations (UN) Conference on Women, in Beijing, China, in 1995. The UN argued that "gender mainstreaming entails bringing the perceptions, experience, knowledge and interests of women as well as men to bear on policy-making, planning and decision-making" (United Nations 2002). This meant that gender would become part of mainstream policies, requiring all policymakers to consider the impact of their actions on women and men. The concept of *gendering* has been mainly used by scholars of public policy, referring to the insertion of language that explicitly makes a distinction between the experiences of men and women during policy debates (Ferree and Merrill 2000; McBride and Parry 2011; True 2003). Gendering the policy discourse recognizes that issues affect different women differently and presents actors and supporters with the opportunity to legitimately participate in the process and affect the policy outcome.

This chapter will lift the concepts of gender mainstreaming and gendering from the feminist policy literature and apply them generally to the political science discipline and more specifically to the classroom. While many topics covered in the classroom have different repercussions for men and women, instructors rarely have any type of guidelines on how to approach the issue from a gender equality perspective. Positive discrimination is looked on as going against neutrality in the classroom, yet so many of the topics discussed in class already affect women differently than men. The process referred to as *degendering* seems to be the status quo for the discipline. The absence of certain content is just as relevant as the inclusion of particular content presented through the concept of the "hidden curriculum" (Jackson 1968). The hidden curriculum refers to the socialization process of schooling, as well as the unspoken, unintentional teaching that takes place in our classrooms. "Until learning states are acknowledged or the learners are aware of them... they remain hidden even if sociologists, bureaucrats, and teachers are all aware of them. Thus a hidden curriculum can be found yet remain hidden, for finding is one thing and telling is another" (Martin 1994, 162). In political science, the hidden curriculum reinforces stereotypes about gender, status, and power (Cassese, Bos, and Duncan 2012). Therefore, there is a need for a conscious effort to critically examine barriers to gendering the classroom and to propose institutional and pedagogical instructions for teaching political science in the twenty-first century.

This chapter introduces the need for mainstreaming and gendering the political science classroom and presents a brief overview of how gender as a construct has entered the discipline. The state of the discipline with regard to gendering the classroom is analyzed using national survey data as well as qualitative data presented in the American Political Science Association Task Force Report prepared in 2011. The concepts of gender mainstreaming and gendering the classroom are discussed and placed in context, explaining how gender can be applied in a way that allows for better understanding of political concepts and how it can open up even larger discussion of power structures and institutional hierarchy. Lastly, the chapter proposes some strategies and solutions for overcoming the gender-blind approach to topics (e.g., war and poverty) and how to instead intentionally insert a gender equity framework into our political science classrooms.

Gender and the Discipline

To understand the need for more systematic efforts toward inclusion in our political science classrooms, we must take a brief journey over the last four decades, during which social movements changed the way scholarship and teaching were conducted. The discipline has experienced a significant degree of change over the past forty years (American Political Science Association 2011). In many cases, political scientists themselves were change agents from within. The study of women and politics within the discipline of political science was stimulated by and has evolved contemporaneously with the feminist movement (Carroll and Zerrilli 1993). The Women's Caucus for Political Science, founded in 1971, began in 1972 to sponsor papers on women and politics at the annual meetings of the American Political Science Association (APSA), and during the early to mid-1970s the first few path-breaking books on women and politics were published.[2] Simultaneously, as illustrated in chapter 4 by Jennifer Curtin's discussion of political science in New Zealand, the discipline was awakened to the need to study women in politics globally. By the early 1990s, the number of papers, articles, and books written by political scientists focusing on women and politics or feminist theory grew considerably. The study of women and politics also became more institutionalized within the discipline throughout the 1970s and 1980s. Two of the most important developments were the establishment in 1981 of the journal *Women and Politics*, today known as the *Journal of Women, Politics, and Policy*, symbolizing the evolution of studies across time, and the formation of an Organized Section on Women and Politics Research within the APSA in 1986. In March 2005, the first issue of *Politics & Gender*, a journal of the APSA's Women and Politics section, appeared in print (Isaac 2014).

The first wave of literature on women and politics critiqued the ways political theory and empirical research in political science have traditionally excluded women as political actors and rendered them either invisible or apolitical. This was a first step toward defining a separate space for gender and politics within the confines of political science. Several important critiques appeared in the 1970s (Boals 1975; Bourque and Grossholtz 1974; Elshtain 1979; Goot and Reid 1975; Iglitzin 1974; Jaquette 1974; Okin 1979; Shanley and Schuck 1974) as well as in the 1990s (Ackelsberg and Diamond 1987; Grant 1991; Halliday 1991; Nelson 1989; Randall 1991; Sapiro 1989). The critiques argued that the foundations of political science, namely political theory and philosophy, have excluded women from politics. Women were invisible in public matters. Feminist scholars were set to bring women back into the picture and examine the reasons women were ignored for so long, as well as how this exclusion has affected our ideas about citizenship, power, and political participation. Feminist scholars pointed out flawed propositions in previous research (Berelson, Lazarsfeld, and McPhee 1954; Campbell et al. 1960; Greenstein 1965) that portrayed women as lacking in political interest and involvement, having low political efficacy, and holding belief systems that lack conceptual sophistication. Early behavioral political scientists accepted unquestioningly the public-private divide and the relegation of women to responsibilities and activities in the private sphere, an assumption evident in much of Western political thought (Elshtain 1979). Having painted women as apolitical, researchers were not interested in asking questions about women's lack of representation in mainstream political institutions, neither were they interested in women's voices or points of view.

In contrast, as the study of women and politics developed, research was conducted that attempted to add women into politics—"add women and stir"—to make them visible as political actors while accepting the existing dominant frameworks of political analysis (Diamond 1977; Eisenstein 1981; Githens and Prestage 1977; Kirkpatrick 1974, 1976; Shanley 1989). These research studies looked at how women were faring on different political issues, including electoral politics. Women were studied as parts of social groups and movements, both anti- and profeminist (Boles 1979; Costain 1982; Freeman 1975; Gelb 1989; Gelb and Palley 1982; Klatch 1987; Mansbridge 1986; Mathews and De Hart 1990), and researchers also assessed their success in affecting public policy. The data showed that women were no different than similarly situated men:

they were just as likely to raise money (Burrell 2005; Fox 2006), participate in political activities, and be interested in following political campaigns. Thus, the myth that women were biologically and unchangeably different than men was debunked. When women acted differently than men it was because of differences in variables such as education, working outside of the home, having children, and other socially constructed differences (Andersen 1975; Baxter and Lansing 1980; Hansen, Franz, and Netemeyer-Mays 1976; Sapiro 1982, 1983; Welch 1977). Some work has found differences between men and women in political ambition within political parties (Constantini 1990; Fowlkes, Perkins, and Tolleson-Rinehart 1979; Kirkpatrick 1974; Sapiro 1982), while other research focusing on women officeholders found no evidence of the discrepancy (Carroll 1985; Diamond 1977; Palmer and Simon 2003). Incumbency also played a large role in women's electoral success (Dolan 2004; Fox 2006). Additionally, cross-national studies demonstrated that women's representation in national legislatures was greater in countries with proportional representation, especially those using party lists, than in countries like the United States that elect representatives based on plurality voting (Lovenduski 1986; Norris 1985). The introduction and implementation of quotas in some European political parties has further enhanced women's representation in these countries (Dahlerup 1988). The literature on women and politics has made a great contribution by demonstrating that *all political subjects are gendered* rather than gender-neutral as previously claimed.

Adding women to existing models of political science research was a step forward in acknowledging the presence of women in political life; however, these efforts did not go beyond attempting to understand how sex characteristics affect political life. Biological differences alone were not what held women back in the history of humanity, rather their socialization according to these sex differences, hence the concept of gender. A major challenge for the study of women and politics was to look beyond surface differences and analyze sex and gender as interrelated but separate concepts. Research has called into question whether our dominant frameworks in political science can accommodate the inclusion of women as political actors and called for a reconceptualization of many of the assumptions and definitions central to political science (Carroll and Zerrilli 1993, 55).

Sex refers to a biological state, while gender is understood in the context of relations between men and women that are embodied in the sexual division of labor, compulsory heterosexuality, discourses and ideologies of citizenship, motherhood, masculinity, and femininity (Orloff 1996). Gender is a larger, more encompassing concept than sex when it comes to understanding politics and its divisions of power. Referring to women alone does not fully capture the modalities of interactions in political institutions and the full dynamics of the political processes. The shift from studying sex to studying gender reshaped the research questions asked and offered important new understanding of how political life has developed and changed.

Young (2002) argues that gender as a concept is necessary to theorize structural processes that position individual subjects in unequal relations of power. Furthermore, she claims that the concept of gender is indispensable for analyzing the institutionalized asymmetries experienced by men and women. Gender is an attribute of social structures more than of persons (Young 2002, 422); it is a form of social positioning of lived bodies in relation to one another. Moreover, Young proposes that gender works along three irreducible axes: the sexual division of labor (or the allocation of productive and reproductive activities by sex), normative heterosexuality (or the presumption that affective partnerships and family units are based on the sexual bond between a woman and a man), and hierarchies of power (an institutionalized valuation of particular associations of maleness or masculinity). Young's approach positions gender and politics well within the scope of political science. After all, studying structures and institutions is a major task of the discipline.

One of the implications of shifting attention from sex to gender is the reformulation of the concepts that underlie our analysis—a refashioning of the discipline (Lovenduski 1998). The reconsideration of the public versus private division has been one outcome of examining gender instead of sex. Susan Carroll found no evidence of the divide, rather public and private in the lives of women officeholders seem to constitute a holistic system of interrelated social relations, where any action taken or choice made has repercussions throughout the system (1989, 63). Therefore, the private is public (Millet 1971). The statement alone did much to position gender and politics in political science, since previously women were seen as private actors and outside of the scope of the discipline. The notion of the public sphere as the sphere of male citizens enjoying rights from that women were excluded has long been central to political theory (Pateman 1983, 1988). Research on this divide (Carroll 1989; Elshtain 1981), however, has demonstrated the value of public and private spheres interacting to affect women's political stances and activities. Private issues such as domestic violence and rape need to be brought forward into the public sphere for women to enjoy full citizenship rights (Phillips 1991). What counts as political must also be reconsidered and expanded. The traditional definition of politics and the public sphere focused narrowly on formal activities within the conventional political arena (Waylen 2007). The definition excludes many of the activities where women's contributions are most prevalent. A wider definition that incorporates informal political activity associated with communities and social movements will give us a different picture of the nature of women's political participation.

The brief overview of the introduction and development of gender as a construct sheds light on some of the barriers, divisions, and skepticism about the utility of a gendered discipline that may remain in mainstream political science. It is not surprising that there is continued resistance to integrating gender into mainstream political science education (American Political Science Association 2011; Baldez 2010; Murphy 2010).

Analyzing National Data

To assess the current situation in the field of political science and in higher education more generally, I make use of the most recent (2013–2015) National Survey of Student Engagement (NSSE) and the Faculty Survey of Student Engagement (FSSE). NSSE annually collects information at hundreds of four-year colleges and universities about first year and senior students' participation in programs and activities that institutions provide for their learning and personal development. The results provide an estimate of how undergraduates spend their time and what they gain from attending college. FSSE is a web-based survey. It is administered nationally to faculty, instructors, and graduate students who teach at baccalaureate degree–granting colleges and universities that are concurrently administering NSSE or have participated in NSSE in the previous year. Among other things, it focuses on the importance instructional staff place on various areas of learning and development. Even though the surveys do not go into details of course content, they pose questions that give us some idea of where we stand in incorporating identity perspectives in our curriculum.

The NSSE utilizes a Diversity Module to survey students and faculty alike on issues of identity. When faculty members across the United States were asked in 2013 and 2014 how often they structured a class session around gender or sexual orientation, as shown in Table 1.1 below, only 7 percent of the faculty responded "very often," 9 and 12 percent, respectively, answered "often." The percentages are a bit higher in 2015, with 11 percent of the faculty responding "very often" and 10 percent "often." Gender and sexual orientation are on average often discussed in about 15 percent of our classrooms in higher education. The most telling result from these surveys is the percentage of faculty members who have never structured a course around gender or sexual orientation, around 55 percent. Thus, more than half of the classes in higher education fail to incorporate gender in the class material. In general, these results suggest a predominance of curricula and higher education classrooms where identity perspectives are seen as irrelevant, and perhaps of degendered classrooms, where neutrality is assumed but instead inherent masculinity is perpetuated. Thus, when we wonder about low numbers of female students in highly male-dominated academic fields, it should come as no surprise. When gender is not problematized, or brought into the classroom comprehensively, it becomes marginalized and an afterthought. Discussions around

Table 1.1. During the Current School Year, about How Often Have You Structured a Class Session around Gender or Sexual Orientation?

	2013			2014			2015		
	Lower Division (%)	Upper Division (%)	Total (%)	Lower Division (%)	Upper Division (%)	Total (%)	Lower Division (%)	Upper Division (%)	Total (%)
Never	58	50	54	56	55	55	54	55	55
Sometimes	24	29	27	25	26	25	25	25	25
Often	9	9	9	14	11	12	11	9	10
Very often	5	8	7	5	8	7	10	11	11

other structures of inequality are also lacking. In 2015, 71 percent of faculty members reported they had never structured a class session around economic or social inequality, and 67 percent report they had never structured a class around issues of race, ethnicity, or nationality. The results provide little promise for an intersectional approach in the classroom.

The FSSE also asked faculty members about how often they had encouraged students to attend events or activities that focused on gender or sexual orientation. I was interested to see whether the lack of emphasis on classroom discussions was matched by the lack of encouragement to understand gender or sexual orientation. Perhaps curriculum framework does not allow for bringing gender to the classroom, but, if the issue is important to faculty members, they would encourage students to attend events outside of the classroom. The survey responses are presented in table 1.2 below. The surveys demonstrate a little bit of difference, but not much. Just as with classroom discussions, around 22 percent of faculty members often encouraged students to attend events, while almost half of the faculty members have never encouraged students to attend an event on gender issues. Furthermore, the problems seem to lie at the level of higher education generally, and were not specific to certain types of institutions. Looking at the data by the type of institution as defined by Carnegie Basic Classification, the survey results do not change much.

One of the most encouraging trends observed in the FSSE survey results is that when faculty members were asked in the most recent survey (2015) how important it is for them that the typical student includes diverse perspectives in course discussions and assignments, an overwhelming 79 percent of social scientists answered "important" or "very important," in comparison to 57 percent of business faculty or an even lower 19 percent of engineering faculty. This trend in the social sciences is positive news for a more comprehensive intersectional approach to inequality. Complete survey responses are presented in table 1.3 below.

Table 1.2. During the Current School Year, about How Often Have You Encouraged Students to Attend Events or Activities That Focused on Examining Their Understanding of Gender or Sexual Orientation?

	2013			2014			2015		
	Lower Division (%)	Upper Division (%)	Total (%)	Lower Division (%)	Upper Division (%)	Total (%)	Lower Division (%)	Upper Division (%)	Total (%)
Never	45	43	44	54	46	50	44	48	46
Sometimes	32	36	34	28	33	31	33	29	30
Often	15	10	13	12	10	11	14	13	14
Very often	8	10	9	7	11	9	10	10	10

Table 1.3. In Your Selected Course Section, How Important Is It to You That the Typical Student Include Diverse Perspectives (Political, Religious, Racial/Ethnic, Gender, etc.) in Course Discussions or Assignments?

Response Options	Social Sciences (%)	Arts and Humanities (%)	Education (%)	Business (%)	Engineering (%)	Health Professions (%)
Not important	6	7	7	20	50	8
Somewhat important	15	14	12	23	31	18
Important	29	30	28	35	12	38
Very important	50	49	53	22	7	36

I was also interested in assessing NSSE student data that may give some more insight on the classroom versus out of classroom identity politics discussions. I was interested to see whether students did deem these issues important for their generation and were having discussions about diversity outside of university classrooms, despite not participating in structured classroom debates. As presented in table 1.4, survey results show that over three years (2013–2015) around 38 percent of college students had discussions about gender or sexual orientation often. These numbers are drastically higher than the numbers of classroom discussions reported by faculty. For example, around 55 percent of the faculty in 2013, 2014, and 2015 reported that they had never structured a class discussion around gender or sexual orientation. Only around 23 percent of students during those same years report to have never had a discussion on the same issues. The situation is similar with regards to class and race. In 2015, around 49 percent of undergraduate students reported having discussions about race, ethnicity, or nationality often, while only 33 percent of faculty members that same year report to have structured a

Table 1.4. During the Current School Year, about How Often Have You Had Discussions about Issues of Gender or Sexual Orientation?

	2013			2014			2015		
	First Year Students (%)	Seniors (%)	Total (%)	First Year Students (%)	Seniors (%)	Total (%)	First Year Students (%)	Seniors (%)	Total (%)
Never	25	28	27	20	19	20	22	24	23
Sometimes	41	37	39	41	39	40	39	37	38
Often	21	19	20	25	25	25	24	21	22.5
Very often	13	16	15	14	18	16	15	18	16.5

class session around these same topics. These results demonstrate the relevance of gender and race issues to our student population: from the students' perspective these are topics that warrant discussion, yet more than half of those discussions are taking place outside of the classrooms in higher education.

There is a clear need for mainstreaming gender not only in political science but in our classrooms across the board. We might expect upper division students to be more likely than lower division students to engage in conversations on the topic of gender and sexuality; however, the consistent lack of faculty inclusion of these topics for both lower and upper division students may explain the lack of difference in student survey responses across years of training. We would like to think that as students leave our institutions of higher education as seniors, they are more likely to have discussions about issues of justice than what they did when they came in as first year students. However, the lacking institutional structure is perhaps hampering the potential for change and defying these expectations, as shown in table 1.4.

American Political Science Association Report

The American Political Science Association's Task Force on Political Science in the Twenty-First Century published its report on the state of the political science discipline in 2011 (hereafter APSA [2011]). The authors recognize that preparing the report is a step forward in understanding the status of the discipline, especially in preparation for large demographic changes already taking place and intensifying even more in the next few decades. It is projected that by 2040 the majority of the United States's population will be made up of equal percentages of people of color and whites/Caucasians (Colby and Ortman 2015, 1). The political science discipline examined the various repercussions of these demographic changes, especially as they relate to concepts that political scientists themselves study, such as citizenship and participatory democracy. While progress with regard to gender equality has clearly been made, the question the APSA report poses is "why research, teaching, and professional development addressing challenges of diversity and inclusion are still perceived by many within the profession to be largely marginalized and often tokenized?" (APSA 2011, 9). The report outlines the progress, identifies the work that still needs to be done, and proposes solutions for addressing issues of diversity in the classroom and curriculum, in many cases discussing mainstreaming gender in the discipline and gendering the classroom.

In 1980, 10.3 percent of full-time faculty were women; in 2010 it was 28.6 percent (American Political Science Association 2011, 41–43). The progress is relatively modest for faculty of color, especially for female faculty of color (García Bedolla 2014; Mershon and Walsh 2014). In 2010, 6.1 percent of female political science faculty were African American, 4.4 percent Asian Pacific Islander, and 3.0 percent Latina (APSA 2011, 42). Thus, in 2010 African American women constituted 1.7 percent of political science faculty nationwide, 161 women in total (Ibid., 41). The growth in the number of female faculty members speaks of efforts to diversify the discipline, stemming from undergraduate education, to graduate studies, and student mentoring. The discipline has also made some incremental systematic changes that have not necessarily reflected a comprehensive strategy but that have constructed supportive spaces and structures for minority faculty members. The report mentions the creation of the Minority Fellows Program in 1969, the Ralph Bunch Summer Institute in 1986, and the creation of various APSA Status Committees, including the Committee on the Status of Women established in 1969.

The APSA (2011) report compared the political science discipline's gender mainstreaming efforts to those of the American Economic Association (AEA) and found some successful AEA programs that that could be replicated in political science. For example, they noted that the AEA provided more intentional professional development opportunities for women and people of color during their early career transitions with substantially more structural and financial support. Data on gender and race representation among economics PhDs and faculty in the United States is gathered and shared systematically. These initiatives were cited as evidence of a committed and focused effort to increase diversity and inclusion in the discipline of economics. The authors of the APSA report also drew comparisons with the American Bar Association (ABA) and the American Association of Medical Colleges (AAMC): both organizations have institutionalized their commitment to diversity in their professions, a policy that APSA could learn from and replicate.

With regard to promoting intersectional teaching methods in the classroom and gendering the curriculum, the APSA (2011) report identifies 2005 as the year when the APSA's Teaching and Learning Conference (TLC) ad hoc

Table 1.5. Percentages of Undergraduate Majors in the Social Sciences in 2009.

	Political Science	Sociology	Anthropology	Economics	Linguistics	History of Science	Ethnic Studies	Total N
African Americans	39.9	37.8	3.2	10.8	0.4	0.1	7.9	12825
Latinos	44.8	27.3	6	12.8	1	0	8.1	12022
Asian/Pacific Islanders	32.3	17.6	5.1	35.2	1.4	0.6	7.8	11309
Caucasians	38.3	30.8	9.4	16.5	1	0.1	3.8	93816

SOURCE: National Science Foundation 2010.

committee on Internationalizing the Undergraduate Curriculum was asked to investigate how to increase cross-cultural awareness in the discipline and collect best practices for teaching sensitivity to the demands of a global context. Also, to improve the quality of teaching and research scholars, in 2004 APSA launched a new conference on "Teaching and Learning in Political Science" (APSA 2011).

The report identifies population shifts in political science classrooms as a result of general population shifts. As demonstrated comparatively in table 1.5 there is more diversity and a much larger population of students of color than we have ever had before in higher education but also specifically in political science. Additionally, data from the NSSE (2009) reveal that a clear majority (57.1 percent) of seniors majoring in political science are women. As shown in figure 1.1, the number of women pursuing bachelor degrees in political science has grown drastically in the last few decades, leading to equal shares of men and women as degree recipients in the 21st century. Noticeable on figure 1.2 is that even the larger gap between male and female students receiving a doctorate degree in political science is closing.

The APSA (2011) report concludes by acknowledging that even though progress has taken place, there is a need for richer, more comprehensive, and systematic data regarding research, teaching and pedagogy, and access and inclusion within the political science profession. The authors praise current best practices of APSA but suggest these need to be institutionalized in political science departments to serve as an effective catalyst for progress in addressing issues of race, ethnicity, gender, and diversity more broadly (APSA 2011, 53). Not noted in the report is the international reach of APSA and its ability to affect change not only in American classrooms, but beyond, as noted by Jennifer Curtin in chapter 4. Institutional inertia on the part of APSA has been a missed opportunity for a global efforts within the discipline as well. In the following sections, we turn to the question of how to overcome these barriers using the concepts that we have developed and discussed.

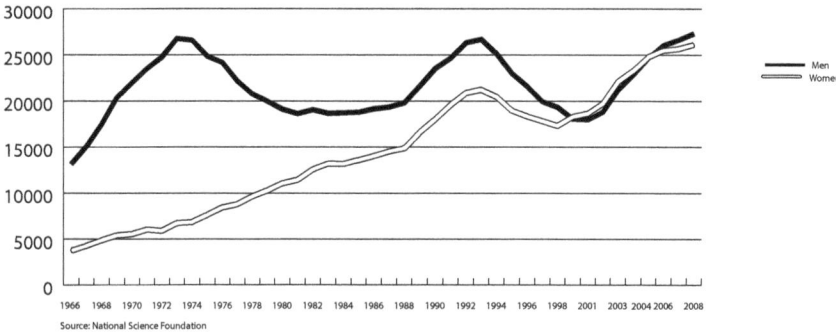

Fig. 1.1 Number of Men and Women Receiving Bachelor's Degrees in Political Science (1966–2008).

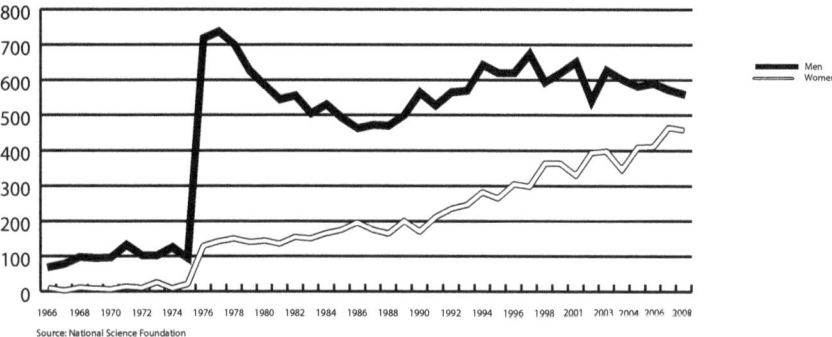

Fig. 1.2 Number of Men and Women Receiving Doctoral Degrees in Political Science (1966–2008).

Gender Mainstreaming and Gendering the Classroom

The concept of gender mainstreaming has been heavily utilized in the gender and development literature. This is particularly important because one of the criticisms of political science as a discipline has been the inability to link academic and theoretical discussions with empirical events and phenomena. In the case of gender mainstreaming, the concept was birthed by the practitioners and activists working for women's rights in the UN and has been heavily used by academia. The concept has served as a bridge between those in the field and the academy, facilitating successful partnerships for common development goals, including gender equality in political and economic spheres, women's empowerment, and guaranteed universal education. Gender mainstreaming has been defined as "the process of assessing the implications for women and man of any planned action, including legislation, policies or programmes, in all areas and at all levels.

It is a strategy of making women's as well as men's concerns and experiences an integral dimension of the design, implementation, monitoring and evaluation of policies and programmes in all political, economic, and societal spheres so that women and men benefit equally and inequality is not perpetuated. The ultimate goal is to achieve gender equality through "transforming structures of inequality" (United Nations Division for the Advancement of Women, 1998, 4).

One of the ways to put gender mainstreaming to work has been through the national gender machineries or Women's Policy Agencies (WPAs). The WPAs emerged as instruments for advancing women's interests after the World Conference of the International Women's Year in Mexico City (1975), but were strengthened in the Platform for Action adopted at the Fourth World Conference on Women in Beijing (1995) (Rai 2003, 17). Whether these institutional structures are capable of mainstreaming gender is still debatable and depends on many factors including their location, resources, and organizational structures. One gender mainstreaming tool is the gender impact assessment. It requires that every planned policy must be assessed as to what influence it might have on women, men, and gendered relations in general (Roth 2008). Monitoring progress also adds to the potential for transformative changes. Finally, change is most likely where actors in civil society push established institutions to take action. Thus, mainstreaming allows for grassroots movements to have an institutionalized role and effect in policy and decision-making.

The gender mainstreaming concept is therefore a perfect fit for analyzing the state of the discipline. Recently, Atchison (2013), Doherty (2013), and Lyle-Gonga (2013) have promoted the use of the term in analyzing political science curricula. For Lyle-Gonga, mainstreaming is a transition from a male-defined curriculum to a more gender-balanced curriculum that better reflects the improved status of women in society (210). Doherty argues that experiential and service-learning can expand gender mainstreaming in the context of political science curriculum. Doherty argues that having an impact leads to feelings of self-efficacy and a broader understanding of political issues (226). Atchison proposes the systemic change that the term embodies be applied in the political science curriculum. Only through discipline-wide initiatives such as revamping textbooks and gaining the support of the most influential among us, she argues, will gender mainstreaming have a chance (233). Daniels (2014) presents an example of what an overhaul of our current structures would look like, sharing a five-point plan that her department developed to address a sex discrimination complaint (465–466). Daniels emphasizes the need for strong support from administration as critical to success in creating a template for equity and diversity in academic departments (472).

The other concept introduced here is that of gendering. Beckwith (2005) argues that in addition to serving as a category, gender also functions as a process. By process, she means behaviors, conventions, practices, and dynamics engaged in by individuals, organizations, movements, institutions, and nations. In gender and politics research, gender as a process is used when looking at the differential effects of structures and policies on women and men (Kittilson 2006; Lovenduski and Norris 1993; Matland and Montgomery 2003; Matland and Studlar 1996; Rai 2003; Studlar and McAllister 2002; Waylen 1994, 2007), as well as examining how masculine and feminine actors actively work to produce favorable gender outcomes (Lovenduski 1998; McBride and Mazur 2010). Htun (2005) argues that gender is better understood as a social position and attribute of social structures. Rather than an attribute of individuals, gender characterizes the large-scale social structures and processes. By studying the gendered nature of political institutions, policies, and norms we are better able to understand the distribution of power and resources.

The concept of gendering has not been directly employed when examining the political science curriculum, but it is an ideal concept to use at the individual classroom level. It allows for tangible pedagogical changes and it challenges the political science curriculum as a whole. As reported earlier in the chapter, the student population in higher education is becoming diverse, which demands diverse tools for teaching and learning. Thus, gendering the classroom can provide opportunities for empowerment, voice, and better representation of all students in discussions.

Is It Only Gender? Intersectional Identities and Power

As we have come to better understand the role of identity in accessing power, efforts to reconstruct our concepts have emerged. The gender difference must also be problematized (Scott 1986). It is necessary to decompose the false binary of men and women and take into consideration the diversity of each group. Women are different depending on class, race, sexuality, disability, and other factors; they do not all experience reality the same way. The concept of *intersectionality* has enriched the study of gender by looking at how different aspects of being a woman have interacted with political institutions and processes. If sex was still the focus of analysis, it would be impossible to capture the diversity and differentiated experiences of women. Gender never really operates independently from other aspects of political life, and so it is misleading to think of gender as an autonomous category of analysis. Instead, gender differences must always be understood within a particular context and in connection with other aspects of identity, both individual and collective. What this means is that even when we are teaching a *Gender and Politics* course, we must take into consideration all vectors of power that have interacted to produce unjust systems. García Bedolla (2014) argues that intersectionality has the potential to build alliances across disciplines in the university context and find common grounds through curricula. She argues that if racial inequality courses also focus on gender issues and gender courses include components on race, faculty members can "see themselves" in these courses and foster a shared sense of inclusivity (450). This is particularly important, as noted above, due to the fact that even though the classroom has become quite diverse in the recent years, the professoriate remains mostly white. Alexander-Floyd (2015, 464) argues that "women of color political scientists are seen as 'space invaders,' that is, individuals outside the 'somatic norms' of political science." She proposes measures designed to achieve gender equity which go beyond the individual to look to changes in departments and other institutions to achieve APSA Task Force diversity goals.

Intersectionality is a concept that describes the interaction between systems of oppression. It refers to a relationship in which social structures combine to create social categories to which certain experiences and forms of oppression are unique (Weldon 2008). Hancock (2007) makes a persuasive argument for reconceiving intersectionality as a research paradigm. Intersectionality does not refer solely to the experiences of African American women, Latinas, or of any specific marginalized group. By envisioning intersectionality as a general approach, Hancock shows how it constitutes a conceptual bridge that can link a wide range of substantive topics in political science. Intersectionality offers a conceptual framework from which to understand and articulate the multiple oppressions that all marginalized groups face. Simien (2007) provides a precise description of the wide range of methods that have been developed to capture and portray intersectionality, methods that transcend the conventional treatment of identity as a dichotomous variable. Weldon (2006) argues that making the case for intersectionality does not mean that we should discard gender or race as analytical categories. If we don't understand how these structures work separately, we will not be able to fully understand their intersections. She further argues that intersectionality is not a multiplicative or additive term, but rather an independent concept.

Including intersctionality as well as gender and race in the classroom demands a global awareness. What constitutes categories themselves is not predetermined but the result of historical processes: identities are what Hancock terms "dynamic productions of individual and institutional factors" (2007). Intersectionality is a strategy for achieving liberation from oppression. By understanding the structures of oppression, we are better able to deconstruct and avoid their perpetuation. Thus, "doing intersectionality" in the classroom is not optional. APSA (2011) argues that if the discipline is to remain relevant, it will have to come to terms with both the diversity of the United States and global interconnectedness. When we speak of gendering the political science classroom, intersectionality should be part of the tool box. We cannot understand or explain structural inequality and its effects on the political process without carefully analyzing the various axes of oppression. The journey of a black woman in the political process is not marked by either her gender or her race but simultaneously by both.

What Does This Mean for Political Science?

In this chapter, I propose gender mainstreaming as an overarching and encompassing strategy for restructuring political science. Gender mainstreaming was recognized as one of eleven recommendations for reforming the undergraduate political science curriculum in the 1991 APSA report "Liberal Learning and the Political Science Major: A Report to the Profession," also known as the Wahlke Report. The Wahlke Report proposed "that the character and implications of ethnic, gender, and cultural diversity and the international and transnational dimensions of particular problems and policies be addressed in all relevant courses—'mainstreamed' in the pedagogical vernacular—not treated as a separate and unique problem to be dealt with in a particular course or two or by a particular faculty member" (Wahlke 1991, 53). Currently, no data exist on the practice of gender mainstreaming in political science and very little evidence demonstrates an emphasis on gender within political science curriculum. Current data suggest only 12.8 percent of political science faculty teach gender and politics courses: 4 percent of male faculty and 10 percent of female faculty. Furthermore, it is usually minority faculty members who feel pressure to teach these courses based on inherent and stereotypical expectations (Nelson Laird 2011; Prieto 2009). In some cases, as demonstrated in chapter 4 on political science pedagogy in New Zealand, the teaching of gender has been passed on to other disciplines, such as sociology or Women's and Gender Studies. A greater awareness of gender in mainstream political science courses is needed rather than limiting the topic to a gender-based course or even confining it to a single lecture or section (Cassese, Bos, and Duncan 2012). The status quo undermines the primary objectives of a diversity-based curriculum: exposing all students to diverse perspectives and experiences (Cassese, Bos, and Duncan 2012, 238). Many times, students self-select out of courses focusing on gender, which reinforces the marginalization of identity politics. Treating the discipline as an institution, barriers exist to achieving equality and a comprehensive agenda is missing. Gender mainstreaming as a concept includes institutional as well as contextual strategies that can lead to systemic transformational changes. Though APSA has used task forces to study the lack of diversity in political science, it still does not have a system of accountability and assessment that can move the discipline forward to realize its mission of transformational change.

Political science classrooms and curricula also need to be gendered. Our classrooms are "a microcosm of the process by which the challenges of democracy can be taught, not only by reading material, but also through thoughtfully staged pedagogical exercises and techniques" (Lyle-Gonga 2013; Matthes

2013, 236). Studying and teaching politics is part of how we learn to participate in political life (Matthes 2013, 236) and understand the practices of "citizenship" and "engagement." Gender is closely linked to key organizing themes in political science, such as power, choice, and inequality (Cassese, Bos, and Duncan 2012, 239), and is a threshold concept. Thus, adjusting our pedagogical approach to teaching—to account not only for gender but also other overlapping identities—is a must. Understanding diversity among women, particularly based on race and ethnicity, has become increasingly relevant issue given demographic trends in student enrollment (APSA 2011). As we will elaborate below, the political science classroom has become highly diverse and requires teaching methods that allow for full participation and empowerment of all students.

Hall and Sandler (1982) described the so-called "chilly classroom climate" where female college students felt left out of discussions and participation in activities. They demonstrated that both male and female professors were more likely to interrupt female students and more likely to call on male students. This type of disempowering classroom experience leads female students to disengage from the topic and either abandon majors as undergraduates or not pursue graduate degrees in those majors. Our teaching and pedagogy are also important in training the future legal work force as most students bound for law school are political science majors (APSA 2011). Disempowering experiences in the classroom can diminish or discourage leadership skills for women in the legal profession. Teaching methods can have a differential effect not only on men and women but also on students with intersecting identities of class, race, and ethnicity. As more first-generation college students are entering our classrooms, our pedagogy needs to be rethought and restructured to keep not only gender but intersectionality in mind as critical considerations for giving students empowerment and voice. While a pedagogical approach of omission by itself might not be the cause of continuous inequality in the discipline, the unintentional, degendered classroom aids in maintaining the masculinist view of power and leadership instead of challenging and critically assessing them.

Where Do We Go from Here?

We lay out some possible solutions for moving the discipline forward in gender equality, teaching methods, and curriculum. This chapter proposes two different solutions for two different levels of analysis: systemic and individual. At the systemic level, mainstreaming gender seems like a plausible plan. Even though there is progress to be made in mainstreaming gender in political life, the concept has brought about a better understanding of the systemic bias that is inherent in institutions. In addition, the concept makes possible to measure desirable institutional outcomes, within the institutional capacity framework, a term that refers to institutional strengths and areas that still need improvement in several key educational areas, including equity in teaching and learning. APSA has the power to lead the way by either making use of existing structures or erecting new ones that serve as catalysts for widely transforming the discipline in the United States and globally. As the case of New Zealand in chapter 4 discusses, APSA maintains the legitimacy to globally affect how political science is transformed in the twenty-first century. The institutionalization of gender initiatives is necessary for the impact to be long-lasting and successful (APSA 2011). Textbooks (chapter 3) have the potential to normalize gender in the discipline (Atchison 2013, 231). A textbook mainstreaming initiative is long overdue (Cassese and Bo 2013). After all, "textbooks are lagged measures of the state of the discipline" (APSA 2011, 37).

The marginalization of gender and intersectional studies as separate areas from mainstream political science must end. Living in an era where we seek to promote human rights, social justice advocacy, and rejection of illiberalism, the discipline cannot afford to ignore identity politics as key to understanding and explaining social reality. Globalization, demographic shifts, and the new ways citizens are accessing power requires some inward analysis of the profession. Thus, along with institutionalization, changing the way gender is approached and taught in political science is vital. Scholars are already incorporating gender in their research agendas, now we just need to incorporate these works into our curricula. For example, human security and violence is now being examined from a feminist perspective (Tripp, Ferre, and Ewig 2013); the prospects for international aggression are examined in relationship to domestic gender equality (Caprioli and Boyer 2001); and all policies can be similarly gendered as demonstrated in a large feminist policy body of work (Mazur 2002). The curriculum selection ought to be intentional and critical. Cassese, Bos, and Duncan (2012) provide examples of activities that can be incorporated in our curricula, making uses of pieces of work that may not yet be part of a textbook but present political science issues from a gendered and multiple identity perspective. While these suggestions are helpful examples of teaching methods, a more systemic effort from the profession is needed to legitimize the practices.

Another area that deserves attention is improving the mentoring programs for marginalized groups entering the political science classrooms as graduate students. We have the privilege to educate the next generation of political science professors and unless we develop a strong commitment to mentoring, we risk alienating marginalized groups from breaking into the profession and further hampering change. Atchison (2013, 233) refers to a "virtuous feedback loop" in which the presence of gender in political science education leads not just to more women in the profession, but to greater acceptance of gender in the discipline. Perhaps gender mainstreaming would be more successful if the political scientist majority, male or female, would be prepared to incorporate gender into their courses. Current instructors may not have been exposed to gender issues in their own education or work (Atchison 2013; Guthrie 1993; Prieto 2009). Focusing on graduate students would ensure a new generation of well-prepared instructors and mentors that together have the potential to change the discipline.

One of the positive outcomes of gender mainstreaming has been setting short and long terms goals for gender equality. Political science as a discipline should do the same. Goal setting forces institutions to change in part through systematic assessments and data gathering. APSA (2011) praised the American Economic Association for their data gathering, their transparency, and the dissemination of their results to the discipline as a whole. Something similar is needed in political science, beyond the scope of a task force. When major institutions and a majority of departments buy into the effort for reporting and accountability, gender and diversity gain legitimacy and move from the margins to the core of the discipline. Only after a large effort of data collection can we truly assess where we stand as a profession on gender equality and other aspects of identity politics.

At the individual level, this chapter proposes gendering the classroom. Scholarship of Teaching and Learning (SoTL) has discussed approaches on how to create equitable and just classrooms (Caro-Bruce et al. 2007; Gay 2002; Mills, Ayre, and Gill 2008; Ruggs and Hebl 2012). The proposed approach in this chapter fits in the framework of this literature. To gender the classroom is to ensure that all topics of political science are assessed with respect to their repercussions for men and women. Furthermore, a gendered classroom allows for intersectional identities, investigating how processes may differently affect not only men and women but men and women of color, men and women of different social class, and so forth. Demographic shifts are taking place in the twenty-first century and our diverse student populations in political science classrooms ought to see themselves reflected in the curriculum. Gendering the classroom is necessary for recruiting and retaining women and other marginalized groups in the major.

A framework that has been suggested for effectively gendering the classroom is that of social justice (Boyer and Davis 2013; Dover 2013). The social justice framework promotes the value of life stories and voices. In this framework, everyone's voice matters, and all students can make contributions in the classroom. Adams, Bell, and Griffin's (1997) emphasis on explicit curricular content related to social identity and injustice; oppression theory; intersectionality, such as the simultaneous analysis of multiple forms of oppression; and reflexive teaching practice is commonly accepted by social justice educators. This teaching approach can eliminate the "chilly classroom effect" and circumvent the "hidden curriculum." Similarly, a feminist pedagogy promotes principles of justice and equity in the classroom. More particularly, feminist pedagogy is a theory about the teaching and learning process that guides our choice of classroom practices by providing criteria to evaluate specific educational strategies and techniques in terms of the desired course goals or outcomes (Shrewsbury 1993, 8). To apply this philosophy to the classroom, instructors must critically engage in dialogue and reflection about both what and how they teach, as well as how who they are affects how they teach (Crabtree, Sapp, and Licona 2009). The framework of teaching changes the classroom dynamics. The classroom is a liberating learning community where each student's voice matters and opportunities for meaningful empowerment and leadership arise.

Thus curriculum changes along with alterations of teaching methods are needed to promote a positive learning environment for all. Based on existing research, we know that more conscious classroom management is needed to ensure that more voices are heard. Rather than waiting for students to respond to discussion questions, perhaps instructors can call students to participate. Service-learning activities and high impact practices also provide opportunities to gender the classroom. Doherty (2013) argues that experiential and service-learning outside of the classroom can further contribute to gendering political science through empowering and hands-on experiences. Diversifying class activities more generally may promote more inclusive and equitable teaching methods. This further emphasizes the value of experience and lived reality. Our classrooms to some degree match social reality, where power is shared and accessed, and privilege lived and demonstrated. It is our role as instructors to address these issues in the classroom through methods that empower rather than diminish students' agency. If we believe that in doing nothing and maintaining the status quo we are taking a neutral stance toward inequality, then we are automatically perpetuating inequality, even if by default. Thus, for gender mainstreaming at the systemic level to be meaningful, educators also have to embrace a pedagogy that is intentional, inclusive, and mindful of the historical past of academia as a whole.

Concluding Remarks

As we assess the value of higher education and learning in the twenty-first-century global economy, principles of citizenship, service, and leadership are all being depicted as valuable in the new world. Political science is "a discipline with a history and obligation of addressing the pressing injustices of our democracy" (Matthes 2013, 238). In an era when the personal is political and the concept of power and how it is shared is being widely explored, academic disciplines such as political science should be at the forefront of revamping institutions, curriculum, and practices nationwide. Particularly for political science, which studies both formal and informal institutions, social movements and change, and public policy adoption and implementation, there should be no shortage of knowledge about how to produce the change necessary to renovate and revamp the discipline. While progress has been made, there is work to be done.

As Jennifer Curtin in chapter 4 points out, APSA has missed the opportunity to reach out globally and set a unified progressive tone in addressing inequality within the discipline and the curriculum. As Curtin suggests, knowledge sharing and transfer between national associations in the Global North and South can certainly positively challenge the North American dominance in political science. For example, as chapter 4 demonstrates, even though New Zealand began from a much lower base in hiring women in the discipline, since the mid-1990s, unlike the United States, where the growth curve has been mostly flat, it has made significant progress.

In this chapter, I have argued that to produce change, a two-pronged solution is needed. First, gender mainstreaming needs to take place at the systemic level. Properly functioning institutions need to be established not only to initiate change but also to set firm goals that can then be properly assessed. Data sharing is also needed for self-evaluation to be properly conducted and assessed. Mentoring programs for graduate students can produce short- and long-term results for mainstreaming. We need to revamp our textbooks to accommodate the changing student body and presented perspectives that have been historically excluded. To achieve these types of changes, a chapter or a discussion module is not sufficient. Centering these undermined experiences in discussions of power and its distribution, war and its disparate effects, and governmental programs and recipient distribution is necessary to fully incorporate gender and other forms of identity into our curriculum.

The second solution proposed in this chapter is the concept of gendering the classroom. Even though the discipline has experienced a drastic change in its demographic makeup, pedagogical tools have been perpetuated and imitated to fit the incentive structure created to succeed. In 1980, female faculty numbered 769 or 10.3 percent of political science faculty, whereas in 2010, that number increased to 2,660 or 28.6 percent (APSA 2011). The strength of a work force stands on the diversity of thought and ideas. Thus, the discipline would benefit from accepting a diversity of teaching methods that take into consideration voice, lived experiences, and the history of marginalized groups in the classroom.

In 2014 *Gender & Politics*, the journal of the Women and Politics section at APSA, published a special symposium on critical perspectives on gender and politics. Mershon and Walsh (2014) advocate for mainstreaming gender in the profession and editors of the special issue put out the same call in "Political Science, Heal Thyself." The contributors to this symposium take on the inequalities that still exist in the discipline and provide some solutions on how to improve gender equality in political science, using scholars and teachers themselves as agents for change. They argue that activism can come from within. Along a similar vein, in 2015 a symposium in *PS: Political Science & Politics* titled "How Political Science

Can Become More Diverse," addressed a timely question of discipline-wide importance: how to diversify leadership and end discrimination in the profession. This symposium applies the tools of the discipline to the discipline itself, amongst other things proposing that political scientists themselves advocate for change and inclusion in political science.

In August 2014, Marcia Chatelain, a professor of history at Georgetown University, challenged her colleagues in academia all over the United States to use the first day of classes as a day to place the racial tensions in Ferguson, Missouri, in context. Furthermore, she developed the Twitter hashtag #FergusonSyllabus for educators to recommend texts, present ways to start a classroom conversation about inequality, and inspire dialogue about the multiple issues that were pouring out of the events in Ferguson. The support was overwhelming: educators from all parts of the country and beyond joined together in a virtual movement to bring Ferguson to the classroom. Chatelain states that "the academy has never owned movements, and youth outside of colleges longed for intelligent questions, honest reflection, and inspiration moving forward" (2014). This was a clear example of twenty-first-century activism entering the academic disciplines in new and innovative ways. This is an opportunity for scholars and teachers to bring voice to the classroom and use current struggles and injustice to funnel explanations of previous establishments of power systems. Thus it could be that the critical junctures we are expecting could arise from below, and political scientists will incorporate innovative social justice movements as platforms for teaching.

INGRID BEGO is Assistant Professor of Political Science and Public Affairs at Western Carolina University. She is author of *Gender Equality Policy in the European Union: A Fast Track to Parity in the New Member States*, examining the effect of gender equality policy changes in reducing the gender employment gap and improving women's equal participation in the labor market.

Notes

1. For an exception, see Duverger 1955.
2. See Amundsen 1971; Kirkpatrick 1974; Jaquette 1974; Freeman 1975.

References

Ackelsberg, Martha, and Irene Diamond. 1987. "Gender and Political Life: New Directions in Political Science." In *Analyzing Gender*, edited by Beth B. Hess, and Myra Marx Ferrée. Newbury, CA: Sage.

Adams, Maurianne, Lee Anne Bell, and Pat Griffin. 1997. *Teaching for Diversity and Social Justice: A Sourcebook*. New York: Routledge.

Alexander-Floyd, Nikol G. 2015. "Women of Color, Space Invaders, and Political Science: Practical Strategies for Transforming Institutional Practices." *PS: Political Science & Politics* 48 (3): 464–68.

American Political Science Association. (APSA). 2004. *Women's Advancement in Political Science: A Report of the APSA Workshop on the Advancement of Women in Academic Political Science in the United States*. Washington, DC: American Political Science Association.

American Political Science Association (APSA). 2011. Task Force on Political Science in the Twenty-First Century. *Political Science in the Twenty-First Century*. Washington, DC: American Political Science Association.

Andersen, Kristi. 1975. "Working Women and Political Participation." *American Journal of Political Science* 19 (3): 439–53.

Atchison, Amy. 2013. "The Practical Process of Gender Mainstreaming in the Political Science Curriculum." *Politics & Gender* 9 (2): 228–35.

Baldez, Lisa. 2010. "The Gender Lacuna in Comparative Politics." *Perspectives on Politics* 8 (1): 199–205.

Baxter, Sandra, and Marjorie Lansing. 1980. *Women and Politics: The Invisible Majority*. Ann Arbor: University of Michigan.

Beckwith, Karen. 2005. "A Common Language of Gender?" *Politics & Gender* 1 (1): 128–37.

Berelson, Bernard R., Paul F. Lazarsfeld, and William N. McPhee. 1954. *Voting*. Chicago: University of Chicago Press.

Boals, Kay. 1975. "Review Essay: Political Science." *Signs* 1 (1): 161–74.

Boles, Janet K. 1979. *The Politics of Equal Rights Amendment: Conflict and the Decision-Making Process*. New York: Longman.

Bourque, Susan C., and Jean Grossholtz. 1974. "Politics an Unnatural Practice: Political Science Looks at Female Participation." *Politics and Society* 4 (2): 225–66.

Boyer, Patricia, and Dannielle Davis. 2013. *Social Justice Issues and Race in the College Classroom: Learning from Different Voices*. Bingley, UK: Emerald Group.

Burrell, Barbara. 2005. "Campaign Financing: Women's Experience in the Modern Era." In *Women and Elective Office: Past, Present, and Future*, edited by Sue Thomas and Clyde Wilcox, 26–40. New York: Oxford University Press.

Campbell, Angus, Philip Converse, Warren E. Miller, and Donald Stokes. 1960. *The American Voter*. New York: Wiley.

Caprioli, Mary, and Mark A. Boyer. 2001. "Gender, Violence, and International Crisis." *Journal of Conflict Resolution* 45 (4): 503–18.

Caro-Bruce, Cathy, Ryan Flessner, Mary Klehr, and Kenneth Zeichner. 2007. *Creating Equitable Classrooms through Action Research*. Thousand Oaks, CA: Corwin Press.

Carroll, Susan. 1985. *Women as Candidates in American Politics*. Bloomington: Indiana University Press.

———. 1989. "Gender Politics and the Socializing Impact of the Women's Movement." In *Political Learning in Adulthood*, edited by Roberta S. Sigel, 306–39. Chicago: University of Chicago Press.

Carroll, Susan. J., and Linda. M. G. Zerilli. 1993. "Feminist Challenges to Political Science." In *Political Science: The State of the Discipline II*, edited by Ada W. Finifter. Washington, DC: American Political Science Association.

Cassese, Erin C., and Angela L. Bos. 2013. "A Hidden Curriculum? Examining the Gender Content in Introductory Level Political Science Textbooks." *Politics & Gender* 9 (2): 214–23.

Cassese, Erin. C., Angela L. Bos, and L. E. Duncan. 2012. "Integrating Gender into the Political Science Core Curriculum." *PS: Political Science & Politics* 45 (2): 238–43.

Chatelain, Marsha. 2014. "Teaching the #FergusonSyllabus." *Dissent.* November 28, 2014. www.dissentmagazine.org/blog/teaching-ferguson-syllabus.

Constantini, Edmond. 1990. "Political Women and Political Ambition: Closing the Gender Gap." *American Journal of Political Science* 34 (3): 741–70.

Colby, Sandra L., and Jennifer Ortman. 2015. "Projections of the Size and Composition of the U.S. Population: 2014 to 2060." https://www.census.gov/content/dam/Census/library/publications/2015/demo/p25-1143.pdf.

Costain, Anne N. 1982. "Representing Women: The Transition from Social Movement to Interest Group." In *Women, Power and Policy,* edited by Ellen Boneparth, 24–67. New York: Pergamon Press.

Crabtree, Robin, David A. Sapp, and Adela C. Licona. 2009. *Feminist Pedagogy: Looking Back to Move Forward.* Baltimore, MD: Johns Hopkins University Press.

Dahlerup, Drude. 1988. "From a Small to a Large Minority: Women in Scandinavian Politics." *Scandinavian Political Studies* 11 (4): 275–98.

Daniels, Cynthia R. 2014. "Transforming a Department, Transforming a Discipline." *Politics & Gender* 10 (3): 464–73.

Diamond, Irene. 1977. *Sex Roles in the State House.* New Haven, CT: Yale University Press.

Doherty, Leanne. 2013. "Gender Mainstreaming in Political Science Experiential Learning Programs." *Politics & Gender* 9 (2): 223–27.

Dolan, Kathleen. 2004. *Voting for Women: How the Public Evaluates Women Candidates.* Boulder, CO: Westview Press.

Dover, Allison. 2013. "Teaching for Social Justice: From Conceptual Frameworks to Classroom Practices." *Multicultural Perspectives* 15 (1): 3–11.

Eisenstein, Zillah. 1981. *The Radical Future of Liberal Feminism.* New York: Longman.

Elshtain, Jean B. 1979. "Methodological Sophistication and Conceptual Confusion: A Critique of Mainstream Political Science." In *The Prism of Sex,* edited by Julia A. Sherman and Evelyn T. Beck, 229–49. Madison: University of Wisconsin Press.

———. 1981. *Public Man, Private Women.* Princeton, NJ: Princeton University Press.

Flaherty, Anne. 2013. "Engaging Issues of Diversity in the Political Science Classroom." Paper presented at the *APSA Teaching and Learning Conference,* Long Beach, CA. http://ssrn.com/abstract=2206024 or http://dx.doi.org/10.2139/ssrn.2206024.

Freeman, Jo. 1975. *The Politics of Women's Liberation.* New York: Longman.

Ferree, Myra Marx, and David A. Merrill. 2000. "Hot Movements, Cold Cognition: Thinking about Social Movements in Gendered Frames." *Contemporary Sociology* 29 (3): 454–62.

Fowlkes, Diane, Jerry Perkins, and Sue Tolleson-Rinehart. 1979. "Gender Roles and Party Roles." *American Political Science Review* 73 (3): 772–80.

Fox, Richard. 2006. "Congressional Elections: Where Are We on the Road to Gender Parity?" In *Gender and Elections: Shaping the Future of American Politics,* edited by Susan Carroll and Richard Fox, 97–116. New York: Cambridge University Press.

García Bedolla, Lisa. 2014. "How an Intersectional Approach Can Help to Transform the University." *Politics & Gender* 10 (3): 447–54.

Gay, Geneva. 2002. "Culturally Responsive Teaching in Special Education for Ethnically Diverse Students: Setting the Stage." *International Journal of Qualitative Studies in Education* 15 (6): 613–29.
Gelb, Joyce. 1989. *Feminism and Politics: A Comparative Perspective*. Berkeley: University of California Press.
Gelb, Joyce, and Marian Lief Palley. 1982. *Women and Public Policies*. Princeton, NJ: Princeton University Press.
Githens, Marianne, and Jewel L. Prestage. 1977. *A Portrait of Marginality: The Political Behavior of the American Woman*. New York: McKay.
Goot, Murray, and Elizabeth Reid. 1975. *Women and Voting Studies: Sage Professional Papers in Contemporary Political Sociology*. London: Sage.
Grant, Rebecca. 1991. "The Sources of Gender Bias in International Relations Theory." In *Gender and International Relations*, edited by Rebecca Grant and Kathleen Newland, 8–26. Bloomington: Indiana University Press.
Greenstein, Fred. 1965. *Children and Politics*. New Haven, CT: Yale University Press.
Guthrie, Robert V. 1993. *Even the Lab Rat Was White: A Historical View of Psychology*. Boston: Allyn and Bacon.
Hall, Peter A. 1986. *Governing the Economy: The Politics of State Intervention in Britain and France*. New York: Oxford University Press.
Hall, Roberta, and Bernice Sandler. 1982. *The Classroom Climate: A Chilly One for Women? Project on the Status and Education of Women*. Washington, DC: Association of American Colleges.
Halliday, Fred. 1991. "Hidden from International Relations: Women and the International Arena." In *Gender and International Relations*, edited by Rebecca Grant and Kathleen Newland, 158–69. Bloomington: Indiana University Press.
Hancock, Ange-Marie. 2007. "Intersectionality as a Normative and Empirical Paradigm." *Politics & Gender* 3 (2): 248–54.
Hansen, Susan B., Linda M. Franz, and Margaret Netemeyer-Mays. 1976. "Women's Political Participation and Policy Preferences." *Social Science Quarterly* 56 (4): 576–90.
Htun, Mala. 2003. *Sex and the State: Abortion, Divorce and the Family under Latin American Dictatorships and Democracy*. Cambridge, UK: Cambridge University Press.
Htun, Mala. 2005. "What It Means to Study Gender and the State," *Politics and Gender* 1 (1): 157–66.
Hurtado, Sylvia. 2003. *Preparing College Students for a Diverse Democracy*. Ann Arbor: University of Michigan Center for the Study of Higher and Postsecondary Education.
Iglitzin, Lynne B. 1974. "The Making of the Apolitical Woman." In *Women in Politics*, edited by Jane S. Jaquette, 25–36. New York: Wiley.
Isaac, Jeffrey. 2014. "Gender and Politics." *Perspectives on Politics* 12 (1): 1–6.
Jackson, Philip W. 1968. *Life in Classrooms*. New York: Holt, Reinhart & Winston.
Jaquette, Jane S. 1974. "Introduction." In *Women in Politics*, edited by Jane S. Jaquette, xxviii–xxix. New York: Wiley.
Kirkpatrick, Janet J. 1974. *Political Woman*. New York: Basic Books.
———. 1976. *The New Presidential Elite: Men and Women in National Politics*. New York: Russell Sage Foundation.
Kittilson, Mikki C. 2006. *Challenging Parties, Changing Parliaments: Women and Elected Office in Contemporary Western Europe*. Columbus: Ohio State University Press.

Klatch, Rebecca E. 1987. *Women of the New Right*. Philadelphia, PA: Temple University Press.
Lasswell, Harold D. 1936. *Politics: Who Gets What, When, How*. New York: McGraw-Hill.
Lovenduski, Joni. 1986. *Women and European Politics*. Amherst: University of Massachusetts Press.
———. 1998. "Gendering Research in Political Science." *Annual Review of Political Science* 1: 333–56.
Lovenduski, Joni, and Pippa Norris. 1993. *Gender and Party Politics*. Thousand Oaks, CA: Sage.
Lyle-Gonga, Marsha. 2013. "A Critical Analysis of Gender Mainstreaming." *Politics and Gender* 9 (2): 209–13.
Mansbridge, Jane J. 1986. *Why We Lost the ERA*. Chicago: University of Chicago Press.
Martin, Jane Roland. 1994. "What Should We Do with a Hidden Curriculum When We Find One?" In *Changing the Educational Landscape: Philosophy, Women, and Curriculum*, edited by Jane Roland Martin, 154–69. New York: Routledge.
Mathews, Donald G., and Jane Sherron De Hart. 1990. *Sex, Gender, and the Politics of ERA*. New York: Oxford University Press.
Matland, Richard E., and Kathleen A. Montgomery. 2003. *Women's Access to Political Power in Post-Communist Europe*. Oxford: Oxford University Press.
Matland, Richard E., and Donald T. Studlar. 1996. "The Contagion of Women Candidates in Single-Member District and Proportional Representation Electoral Systems: Canada and Norway." *Journal of Politics* 58 (3): 707–33.
Matthes, Melissa. 2013. "Conclusion and Rejoinders." *Politics and Gender* 9 (2): 235–38.
Mazur, Amy G. 2002. *Theorizing Feminist Policy*. Oxford: Oxford University Press.
McBride, Dorothy, and Amy G. Mazur. 2010. *The Politics of State Feminism: Innovation in Comparative Research*. Philadelphia, PA: Temple University Press.
McBride, Dorothy E., and Janine A. Parry. 2011. *Women's Rights in the USA: Policy Debates and Gender Roles*. 4th ed. New York: Routledge.
Mershon, Carol, and Denise Walsh. 2014. "Introduction." *Politics & Gender* 10 (3): 432–36.
Millett, Kate. 1971. *Sexual Politics*. London: Granada Publishing Ltd.
Mills, Julie E., M. E. Ayre, and Judith Gill. 2008. "Perceptions and Understanding of Gender Inclusive Curriculum in Engineering Education." Paper presented at *SEFI* 36th Annual Conference, July 2, Aalborg, Denmark.
Murphy, Kate. 2010. "Feminism and Political History." *Australian Journal of Politics & History* 56 (1): 21–37.
Nelson, Barbara. 1989. "Women and Knowledge in Political Science: Texts, Histories, and Epistemologies." *Women & Politics* 9 (2): 1–25.
Nelson Laird, Thomas F. 2011. "Measuring the Diversity Inclusivity of College Courses." *Research in Higher Education* 52 (6): 572–88.
Norris, Pippa. 1985. "The Gender Gap in Britain and America." *Parliamentary Affairs* 38 (2): 192–201.
Okin, Susan Moller. 1979. *Women in Western Political Thought*. Princeton, NJ: Princeton University Press.
Orloff, Ann. 1996. "Gender in the Welfare State." *Annual Review of Sociology* 22: 52–78.
Palmer, Barbara, and Dennis Simon. 2003. "Political Ambition and Women in the US House of Representatives." *Political Research Quarterly* 56 (2): 127–38.

Pateman, Carole. 1983. "Feminist Critiques of the Public-Private Dichotomy." In *Public and Private in Social Life*, edited by Stanley Benn, Gerald F. Gaus, and Croom Helm. London: Croom Helm.
———. 1988. *The Sexual Contract*. Cambridge: Polity.
Phillips, Anne. 1991. *Engendering Democracy*. Pittsburgh: Penn State University Press.
Pierson, Paul. 2000. "Increasing Returns, Path Dependence, and the Study of Politics." *American Political Science Review* 94 (2): 251–67.
Prieto, Loreto R. 2009. "Teaching about Diversity: Reflections and Future Directions." In *Getting Culture: Incorporating Diversity Across the Curriculum*, edited by Regan A. R. Gurung and Loreto R. Prieto. Sterling, VA: Stylus Publishing.
Rai, Shirin. 2003. *Mainstreaming Gender, Democratizing the State?* Manchester: Manchester University Press.
Randall, Vicky. 1991. "Feminism and Political Analysis." *Political Studies* 39 (3): 513–32.
Roth, Silke. 2008. *Gender Politics in the Expanding European Union: Mobilization, Inclusion, Exclusion*. New York: Berghahn Books.
Ruggs, Enrica, and Michelle Hebl. 2012. "Diversity, Inclusion, and Cultural Awareness for Classroom and Outreach Education." In *Apply Research to Practice (ARP) Resources*, edited by B. Bogue and E. Cady. New York: Academic Press.
Sapiro, Virginia. 1982. "Private Costs of Public Commitments or Public Costs of Private Commitments? Family Roles versus Political Ambition." *American Journal of Political Science* 26 (2): 265–79.
———.1983. *The Political Integration of Women: Roles, Socialization, and Politics*. Urbana: University of Illinois Press.
———.1989. "Gender Politics, Gendered Politics: The State of the Field." Paper presented at the *Midwest Political Science Association Meeting*, Chicago, IL.
Scott, Joan W. 1986. "Gender: A Useful Category of Historical Analysis." *The American Historical Review* 91 (5): 1053–75.
Shanley, Mary L. 1989. *Feminism, Marriage, and the Law in Victorian England 1850–1895*. Princeton, NJ: Princeton University Press.
Shanley, Mary L., and Victoria Schuck. 1974. "In Search of Political Woman." *Social Science Quarterly* 55 (3): 632–44.
Shrewsbury, Carolyn. 1993. "What Is Feminist Pedagogy?" *Women's Studies Quarterly* 15 (3/4): 8–16.
Simien, Evelyn M. 2007. "Doing Intersectionality Research: From Conceptual Issues to Practical Examples." *Politics & Gender* 3 (2): 264–71.
———. 2003. "Black Leadership and Civil Rights: Transforming the Curriculum, Inspiring Student Activism." *PS: Political Science and Politics* 36 (4): 747–50.
Sjoberg, Laura. 2007. "Gender and Personal Pedagogy: Some Observations." *International Studies Perspectives* 8 (3): 336–39.
Studlar, Donald T., and Ian McAllister. 2002. "Does a Critical Mass Exist? A Comparative Analysis of Women's Legislative Representation since 1950." *European Journal of Political Research* 41 (2): 233–53.
Thelen, Kathleen. 1999. "Historical Institutionalism in Comparative Politics." *Annual Review of Political Science* 2: 369–404.
Thelen, Kathleen, and Sven Steinmo. 1992. "Historical Institutionalism in Comparative Politics." In *Historical Institutionalism in Comparative politics: State, Society, and*

Economy, edited by Sven Steinmo, Kathleen Thelen, and Frank Longstreth. New York: Cambridge University Press.

Tolleson-Rinehart, Sue, and Susan Carroll. 2006. "Far from Ideal: The Gender Politics of Political Science." *The American Political Science Review* 100 (4): 507–13.

Tripp, Aili Mari, Myra Max Ferree, and Christina Ewig. 2013. *Gender, Violence, and Human Security: Critical Feminist Perspectives*. New York: New York University Press.

True, Jacqui. 2003. "Mainstreaming Gender in Global Public Policy." *International Feminist Journal of Politics* 5 (3): 368–96.

United Nations: Division for the Advancement of Women (UN/DAW). 1998. "National Machineries for Gender Equality," Paper presented at by the United Nations Division for the Advancement of Women and the Economic Commission for Latin America and the Caribbean meeting in Santiago, Chile, August 31–September 4 (see III. Conclusions and Recommendations). New York: United Nations: Division for the Advancement of Women. Accessed February 6, 2018. http://www.un.org/womenwatch/daw/news/natlmach.htm.

United Nations. 2002. *Gender Mainstreaming: An Overview*. New York: United Nations. http://www.un.org/womenwatch/osagi/pdf/e65237.pdf.

Wahlke, John C. 1991. "Liberal Learning and the Political Science Major: A Report to the Profession." *PS: Political Science & Politics* 24 (1): 48–60.

Waylen, Georgina. 1994. "Women and Democratization: Conceptualizing Gender Relations in Transition Politics." *World Politics* 46 (3): 327–54.

———. 2007. *Engendering Transitions: Women's Mobilization, Institutions, and Gender Outcomes*. New York: Oxford University Press.

Welch, Susan. 1977. "Women as Political Animals: A Test of Some Explanations for Male-Female Political Participation Differences." *American Journal of Political Science* 21 (4): 711–30.

Weldon, S. Laurel. 2006. "The Structure of Intersectionality: A Comparative Politics of Gender." *Politics & Gender* 2 (2): 235–48.

———. 2008. "The Concept of Intersectionality." In *Politics, Gender and Concepts: Theory and Methodology*, edited by Gary Goertz and Amy Mazur. Cambridge: New York: Cambridge University Press.

Young, Iris Marion. 2002. "Lived Body versus Gender: Reflections on Social Structure and Subjectivity." *Ratio* 15 (4): 410–28.

2 Divergent? Gender and Methodological Diversity in Recent Political Science Dissertations

Rina Verma Williams and Laura Dudley Jenkins

> [I]f there were more women in various subfields where there are now relatively few, would existing patterns be replicated, altered, or would some of both occur? How might more women in those subfields change them, and the discipline, in terms of questions asked, the posing of new questions, whether and how old(er) questions are asked, the use and/or acceptance of new methods, or altered redeployment of existing ones?
>
> —Rodney Hero, Previous President of the American Political Science Association (2015, 471)

POLITICAL SCIENTISTS CONCERNED about diversity in the field have pursued two streams of inquiry. Some political scientists focus on gender diversity—*who* does political science? Other political scientists focus on methodological diversity—*how* do they do political science? But connecting questions about gender and methodology is rare. This chapter is the first systematic attempt to join these streams.

We focus on graduate education to explore how methodological and gender diversities shape each other, and specifically whether gender shapes methodological choices at the graduate level. For graduate students, writing the dissertation is a pivotal process. Students are both socialized by mentors and striking out on their own. Our study of graduate student research lets us consider questions about mentoring, professional socialization, and pathways into the academy. Gender matters in graduate education more broadly because training graduate students builds the future of the academy. Whether graduate students are broadly or narrowly trained determines how we generate knowledge in the future. Gender is just one dimension of inequity in US political science departments, which also suffer from underrepresentation in terms of race and ethnicity, a dearth of data on other potential forms of inequity (LGBTQ+, class, religious affiliation, nationality, etc.), or sustained examination of how these intersect. The scope of this study is limited to gender and to departments based in the United States, but we hope our work will lead to future intersectional and international analysis.

In academia, the percentage of women students declines from the undergraduate to the master's to the PhD levels. At the PhD level, the decline is more marked in political science than in other social sciences (Hero 2015, 471). The drop-off for women at the PhD level in political science more closely resembles the drop-off in many physical or natural sciences and contrasts with other social science disciplines with more women, such as sociology. The political science gender gap continues beyond graduate school in the form of unequal promotion and citation rates (Voeten 2013). If political science imagines itself as a model discipline that encompasses both humanistic and nonhumanistic approaches, we must examine when, or at what level, the model breaks down and becomes more exclusionary. Perhaps that exclusionary level is when male-dominance in political science starts. Could it begin in PhD programs that emphasize particular research subjects and favor positivist research methods and epistemological approaches or marginalize feminist methodologies, scholarly contributions, or courses?

In the introduction to this volume Levintova and Staudinger discuss threshold concepts and their implications for graduate methods training. Do we provide students with a broad enough methodological tool chest to interrogate political science threshold concepts such as power? Do we expand threshold concepts to include "intersectionality" or "social constructions of gender" as advocated by Launius and Hassel (2014, vii)? If political science offers portals to different areas of inquiry rather than one threshold that all political scientists cross, are some graduate programs nevertheless shutting off portals that might open the discipline to a wider range of students? How might academic socialization during graduate education contribute to methodological hierarchies and gender hierarchies, and are these linked in any way? Could hierarchies contribute to the lower numbers of women political scientists entering and completing PhD programs? If women students feel a decreased sense of efficacy or empowerment with respect to the value of their research or how they do it, their departure from academia can only undermine the attainment of equity—in the broader sense of justice—in the political science (and cognate disciplinary) classroom and the academy as a whole. Our study encompasses both efficacy and empowerment for women in political and other social sciences, and pathways toward justice and equity in their disciplines and the academy.

To begin to unravel these complex issues, we asked: What research methodologies are men and women PhD students in political science departments in the

United States using in their dissertations? To answer the question, we constructed a unique dataset of recent PhD dissertations submitted to *ProQuest*® from US departments of political science from 2012 to 2014. We found that women in our sample were more likely than men to use mixed methodologies in their dissertations; and of the four subfields (American politics,[1] international relations or "IR," comparative politics, and political theory), international relations showed the most significant variance by gender in methodologies used.

Political scientists have been grappling with issues of gender and methodological diversity (or the lack thereof) for some time now. In 2000, an individual or group with the pseudonym "Mr. Perestroika" (Russian for "reconstruction") sent an email to about a dozen recipients—with a request to spread it widely—calling for increased globalization and diversification of US political science. The email sparked what came to be a movement, "perestroika," within the field itself (Monroe 2005; Schram and Caterino 2006; Yanow and Schwartz-Shea 2010). The email demanded recognition of a wider range of political scientists and questioned the growing dominance of statistical and formal modeling approaches within the leading disciplinary journal, the *American Political Science Review* (*APSR*); the leadership of the main professional organization of the discipline in the United States, the APSA; and certain elite PhD-granting political science departments in the United States. Although the critique of the APSA and *APSR* resulted in some limited reforms, including more diverse leadership and a new journal, the critiques of the methodological narrowness and undue clout of a few US PhD programs did not get as much attention.

The original Perestroika email bluntly captured both gender and methods hierarchies in the discipline. On the lack of diverse disciplinary leaders: "Why are the overwhelming majority of Presidents of APSA or editorial board members of *APSR* WHITE and MALE? ... Where is the diversity of United States and the world that APSA 'pretends' to study?" (Perestroika 2000, 10). Turning then to methods, the email continued: "Why are all the articles of *APSR* from the same methodology—statistics or game theory—with a 'symbolic' article in Political Theory ... Where is political history, international history, political sociology, interpretive methodology, constructivists, area studies, critical theory and last but not the least—post modernism?" (Perestroika 2000, 10). Beginning to connect gender and methods, Mr. Perestroika then asked, "Why are a few men ... allowed to represent the diversity of methodologies and areas of the world that APSA 'purports' to represent?" (Perestroika 2000, 9). On PhD programs, the email raised the following question: "Why does a 'coterie' of faculty dominate and control APSA and the editorial board of *APSR*—i [sic] scratch your back, you scratch mine. I give award to your student from Harvard and you give mine from Duke or Columbia" (Perestroika 2000, 10). Notably, the email did not argue that political science as a field lacked methodological diversity—indeed the email noted the diversity of international and even US political science—but the writer(s) contrasted this with the APSA and *APSR*'s lack of both demographic and methodological diversity.

Subsequently, some of the issues were taken up by APSA Presidential Task Forces, including one on *Women's Advancement in Political Science* (APSA 2005) and another on *Political Science in the Twenty-First Century* (APSA 2011). The Task Force on Women's Advancement ultimately advocated the inclusion of more diverse political scientists, research topics, and methods as ways to expand gender diversity in the field. In her contribution, interpretive political scientist Dvora Yanow discussed past experiences of black women political scientists, including the "advice they are being given not to do work of interest to them" (APSA 2005, 44). Six years later, the Task Force on Political Science in the Twenty-First Century considered possible reasons why US political science faculty lack diversity in terms of "race, class, gender, and sexual orientation" (APSA 2011, 13). Some members of the Task Force connected this problem with a lack of methods diversity in the discipline, critiquing "the way that an uncritical emphasis on 'science' allows the discipline to engage in research that is fundamentally exclusive, but still maintain the illusion of 'objectivity'" (APSA 2011, 18).

Political scientists continue to examine gender and methodological diversity largely in separate streams. This separate consideration is exemplified by two symposia in *Perspective on Politics* and *PS: Political Science and Politics*. The first, "Pluralism and the Fate of Perestroika: A Historical Reflection" (Gunnell 2015), includes no articles dealing directly with gender diversity in the field, except for Monroe's brief mention of the APSA's "mixed" progress in diversifying its power structure (Monroe 2015, 424). The second, "How Political Science Can Be More Diverse," examines gender diversity within the field but does not link it explicitly with methodological diversity beyond Rodney Hero's concluding essay (Mershon and Walsh 2015).[2]

Our larger research project seeks to unravel the relationship between methodological and gender diversity in graduate political science education. In this part of the study, we undertake a statistical analysis of our unique dataset of PhD dissertations to expand our understanding of the links between gender and methodological diversity. Two central questions that animate our research explore these links: Do men and female political scientists tend to use different types of methodologies? And can a broader range of methodological training at the graduate level contribute to a more inclusive climate in the discipline and increase retention of women political scientists in graduate programs and through the faculty ranks?

In the next section, we present the literature that led us to our hypotheses and review previous studies to assess what they have covered and what they have missed. In the third section, we summarize our data and methods, and present and analyze our results. We conclude by considering the implications of our analysis and possible directions for future research.

Our Hypotheses—What They Are and Where They Come From

Focusing on research at the dissertation stage—a formative process that reverberates in later professional years—enables us to gain insight into PhD level political science education. The research is significant for gender equity in political science because women continue to be significantly underrepresented among graduates of political science PhD programs, despite the fact that women receive the majority of undergraduate and Master of Arts degrees in political science programs in the United States. According to National Science Foundation (NSF) data (which combines political science and public administration), women consistently comprised just over half of political science Bachelor of the Arts graduates between 2002 and 2012 and an even higher percentage, ranging between 54 and 57 percent, of political science Master of Arts graduates during that same period.

The percentage of women completing PhDs in the discipline continues to lag. In the 1990s, women were getting 30 to 39 percent of the PhDs in political science or government (Brandes et al. 2001; Hall 1998).[3] In our dataset, women wrote about 39 percent of recent (2012-14) political science PhD dissertations from United States institutions. Hesli and colleagues noted that the number of women completing political science PhDs is increasing, but "the progress is neither increasing proportionately to the growing numbers of women admitted to graduate study in the discipline nor increasing as rapidly as in most other social sciences" (Hesli et al. 2006, 317). APSA's review of women in political science included discussion of several "studies stress[ing] the importance of the graduate school experience as one of the most significant sources of 'leaks in the pipeline'" (APSA 2005, 31).

Even the women who complete PhDs in political science may be more likely to move to other interdisciplinary departments or new lines of work after completing the degree, especially scholars of color (Kittilson 2015, 450; Sinclair-Chapman 2015, 455, 457). Could a lack of openness to alternative methodological approaches be a factor behind these demographic trends? Are narrow graduate methods courses in political science PhD programs alienating women students and junior faculty, causing them to leave the discipline and move to broader, interdisciplinary departments? As Hero asks, "Why is it that women comprise a smaller portion of political science than, say, sociology and other disciplines? Is there something about political science as a field of study, the empirical and/or normative questions 'typically' posed, methods employed and/or other reasons?" (Hero 2015, 471).

Writing the dissertation is a pivotal period of give and take, in which mentors socialize students and students set off on their own. Feminist critiques and extant empirical studies of gender and methods raise the question of whether limited methodological options or methodological disconnects between PhD students and their departments, committees, or advisors might have something to do with an underrepresentation of women completing PhDs in political science, compared to their numerical predominance at lower (undergraduate and master of arts) levels. Our own experiences in graduate programs and beyond, as well as those of our women colleagues, many of whom left subfields, political science, or even academia to do research of interest to them, also inspire this project. Our study of PhD dissertations from 2012 to 2014 allows us to trace the most recent trends in methodological choices by men and women at this critical stage.

Struck by the demographic anomalies we had noted in our field, we turned to feminist epistemology studies and prior studies of gender and methodology in political science. We sought insight into the question of whether women, being relatively more marginalized in the discipline, might be more likely than men to use a range and variety of methodologies—or at least be open to using less dominant methodologies—at the sensitive and formative dissertation stage. Taking positivist and particularly quantitative methods as dominant in the field, we asked whether women political science PhD candidates in our sample were more likely than men to use methodologies that were not dominant in their dissertation research. We took nondominant methods to include mixed and interpretive methodologies.

Following Yanow, we defined both quantitative and qualitative methodologies as positivist, hypothesis-driven, and underpinned by realist and empiricist ontologies (Yanow 2003). We defined interpretive methodologies as methods that were subject-centered and concerned with meaning. Rudolph's typology of "scientific" versus "interpretive" modes of inquiry summarizes distinct elements of each approach (Rudolph 2005, 15; see table 2.1). By looking for these key elements we distinguished between "scientific" and positivist qualitative methods and interpretive methods, which have often been folded together in other studies of methodology. Mixed methodologies were those that used any two or more methodologies within the same dissertation: quantitative, qualitative, and interpretive. Thus, in our dataset, we expected to find:

> HYPOTHESIS 1: Women were more likely than men to use mixed methodologies in their political science dissertations.
>
> HYPOTHESIS 2: Women were more likely than men to use interpretive methodologies in their political science dissertations.

We did not hypothesize or assume that women were less likely than men to do quantitative work, nor do we base our hypotheses on essentialist assumptions about women, their preferences or their aptitudes. In our dataset, sex functions

Table 2.1. Susanne Hoeber Rudolph's Ideal Typology of Scientific and Interpretive Modes of Inquiry.

Scientific Mode of Inquiry	Interpretive Mode of Inquiry
Certainty	Skepticism, contingency
Parsimony	Thick description
Cumulative knowledge	Nonlinear succession of paradigms
Causality	Meaning
Singularity of truth	Multiplicity of truth
Universal and homogeneous	Contextual and heterogeneous
Objective knowledge	Subjective knowledge

SOURCE: Rudolph 2005, 15.

as a loose proxy for gender-based marginalization in the discipline. Rather, our hypotheses derived from feminist epistemology and methodology studies, and prior empirical studies of methodologies used by men and women in political science articles, books, and conference presentations.

Feminist Epistemology and Methodology Studies

Sandra Harding (1986) and Joan Scott (1986) use gender as an analytic category. Some feminist political scientists have built on Harding and Scott's pathbreaking work by arguing that research methodologies themselves are gendered, not just political scientists or the topics they choose to study. Mary Hawkesworth notes that methods shape the way political scientists understand the political world and contends that there is a "pervasive androcentrism in the definition of intellectual problems as well as in specific theories, concepts, methods and interpretations of research" (Hawkesworth 2006, 27; 1989, 534). Indeed, an anonymous article in *Politics & Gender* suggests that political science remains a "masculinist discipline" due to methodological hierarchies, despite the increasing representational inclusion of women in political science departments: "What qualifies as good research design, good research methods, and good research are standards that were largely set in the discipline by men and that express masculine values" (Anonymous 2014, 441). Traditional assumptions still embedded in much political science research include the ideal of the objective researcher, the separation of the knower and the known, the rationality of the researcher (and, in certain cases, of those being researched)—all attributes associated with idealized notions of masculinity. If positivist methods are more associated with masculinized traits, might women be more open to using a wider range of (nonpositivist, hence presumably nonmasculinist) methodologies?

To better understand such dynamics, Hawkesworth advocates a focus on "cognition as a human practice," which allows scholars to "investigate the adequacy of the standards of evidence, criteria of relevance, modes of analysis, and strategies of argumentation privileged by the dominant traditions" (Hawkesworth 1989, 551). Many scholars have taken up this call, reconsidering the epistemological and methodological underpinnings of their political science research. Feminist scholars have taken various approaches to knowledge, covering at least "three epistemological phases: rationalist (positivist), anti-rationalist and post-rationalist (interpretive)" (Randall 2010, 119). Although many feminist scholars have embraced the interpretive turn, in Randall's view, feminists in political science "have not called into question their discipline's rationalist foundations or embraced these alternative epistemologies in any wholesale way. Rather they have drawn on them more selectively, in order to problematize specific methodological assumptions and as a source of alternative or supplementary research methods" (Randall 2010, 120). Randall suggests that the feminist political scientists are "drawn to" multiple methodologies, even if they are not adopting interpretive approaches "wholesale."

Ultimately, Hawkesworth advocates a postpositivist approach but also argues for multiple methods, saying that "causal, dialectical, genealogical, hermeneutic, psychological, semiotic, statistical, structural, and teleological explanations may all be important to specific aspects of feminist inquiry" (Hawkesworth 2005, 1989, 552). Randall points out that feminist political scientists advocate combining "different research methods, rather than relying on just one," and she herself promotes methodological eclecticism: "We should certainly not confine our analytical toolkits to methods originating in political science" (Randall 2010, 122). Hawkesworth and Randall's contributions are just a few of the many feminists whose calls for methodological eclecticism and critiques of positivism in political science have led us to want to test these ideas empirically.[4]

Prior Empirical Studies of Gender and Methods in Political Science

Previous studies of women in political science provide further support for our initial hypotheses that women may be more open to using a wide range of methodological approaches—and be especially open to using nonpositivist and nondominant methodologies in their dissertation research. Prior studies of APSA conference presentations, journal articles, and books in the field show that women political scientists remain underrepresented. Some of these studies suggest that women may employ or include a wider range of methodological approaches.

Victoria Schuck recorded women's participation at APSA's annual conferences from 1959 until 1970, a project continued by Martin Gruberg from 1971 to 2008 (Gruberg 2009). Unfortunately, since Gruberg retired, no one has continued the analysis. The number of women chairpersons, paper presenters, and discussants has increased since 1959, when women made up only 1.5 percent of people presenting papers, but it was not until 1972 that women as a percentage of paper presenters at APSA's annual meetings hit double digits (12.1 percent). In 2008, about one-third of chairpersons (33.7 percent), paper presenters (34.2 percent,), and discussants (31.3 percent) were women (Gruberg 2009). Gruberg noticed that when women were the heads of panels or divisions, the number of women participating in these panels or divisions greatly increased.

A similar pattern emerged in studies of political science books. Mathews and Andersen examined seventy-eight edited political science books from 1995 to 1996 (Mathews and Andersen 2001). On average, women authored 22 percent of the chapters in the sample, which is consistent with their levels of APSA membership from 1995 to 1999. However, Matthews and Andersen note that in volumes edited by women, 52 percent of essays were authored by women, as opposed to 15 percent in volumes edited by men.

Studies of journal articles overall find that many major journals publish women's articles significantly less often than men's.[5] During a period in which women's presentations at the APSA and the International Studies Association generally reflected the rate of women's membership in these organizations, women lagged in publishing, according to a study of eight major political science journals. Breuning and Sanders (2007) found that between 1999 and 2004, on average, women made up just over 20 percent of article authors. More recently, Kaba (2013) examined the 2010 volumes of the *APSR* and discovered that nearly nine out of ten of the journal's contributors were men (86.1 percent) over a one-year period.

Turning to studies of methodological diversity, previous work has begun to examine trends in the use of different methodologies. In a 2003 study of 2,207 political science articles from top journals (in some cases going back as far as 1965), the authors discovered that prior to 1998, 49 percent of political science studies employed statistics and 46 percent used qualitative methods. American politics studies, which predominated in the *APSR*, were more likely to employ statistical and formal modeling (Bennett, Barth, and Rutherford 2003). Since 2000, there has been growing interest in incorporating more nonquantitative methods in political science, which has led to an examination of graduate methods training, curricula, and textbooks (Yanow and Schwartz-Shea 2010). In their content analysis of fourteen texts commonly used in political science methodology courses, Schwartz-Shea and Yanow (2002) found an explicit or implied bias toward positivism, such as the assumption that all good research adhered to positivist concepts of validity, reliability, and generalizability. None of the textbooks mentioned nonpositivist research methodologies, and they typically glossed over nonquantitative methods. In a fifty-seven-case sample of US doctoral programs, Schwartz-Shea (2003) found that 66 percent required a quantitative methods course, while only 9 percent required training in qualitative methods. Schwartz-Shea and Yanow (2002) argue that graduate methods training, curricula, and textbooks are becoming *less* diverse methodologically, and that the training shapes the very meaning of what political science is and what it means to *do* political science. Notably, while some journals still heavily feature qualitative work, it is more difficult to find training in qualitative methods (Bennett, Barth, and Rutherford 2003; Maliniak et al. 2011; Schwartz-Shea 2003; Schwartz-Shea and Bennett 2003).

A few studies of political science trends focus on both methods and gender. Some scholars have suggested that women's methodological choices may be connected in some way to findings that they are not being published at the same rate as men, or to their underrepresentation in some political science journals. Evans and Moulder (2011) found that in 2000, 29.3 percent of the articles in four top political science journals included at least one woman, but ten years later that percentage had actually decreased to 26.7 percent. Although they concluded that overall women and men's methodological choices were similar, they discovered that articles with a woman listed as first author (woman-lead) were more likely than man-lead articles to use qualitative methodology (24.3 percent vs. 18.8 percent). Evans and Bucy (2010) found that in two interdisciplinary journals, woman-lead articles were more likely than man-lead articles to use qualitative or mixed methods (66.1 percent vs. 44.6 percent) while men were more likely to do quantitative studies than women (35.6 percent vs. 16.1 percent).

Overall, these studies of women and methods within political science are limited not just to faculty, but to faculty who have published in a narrow range of journals or presented papers at certain conferences. The textbook studies illuminate the state of PhD training but not how it is put to use. Moreover, the studies of publications and presentations do not consider interpretive methods as a distinct category. Our database captures dissertations as distinct from other professionalization processes (paper presentations and publications), sheds light on interpretive methods usage, and gives a comprehensive picture of recent PhD research being done in US political science programs.

Data, Methods, and Results

For this pilot study, we used the conventional social science method of statistical analysis of a unique dataset. We examined two independent variables (gender and subfield) and one dependent variable (methodology). Working with all categorical variables, we analyzed the data using t tests and crosstabulations. Variables were coded as follows.[6]

Gender (M/F). The gender of each PhD recipient was inferred from their name using common conventions. When the name was not readily gendered, we searched online to find more information. A very small number (approximately 0.3 percent, or 4 out of 1,169) of names could not be reliably identified even after searching online, so we eliminated these from the dataset, leaving a final N of 1,165. In the study, we adopted a heteronormative and *cis*-gendered approach to coding gender, with conscious awareness that this is not the only or most accurate possibility. For example, we could not identify transgender persons from *ProQuest* data, nor those who identify as genderqueer. We plan to pursue these refinements to the data in subsequent stages of the project involving surveys and oral histories.

Subfield. We adopted the four traditional subfields of political science: comparative politics, international relations, American politics, and political theory. Subfield was inferred from the dissertation titles and abstracts, and where necessary, from reading into the dissertation itself. American politics indicated a primary focus on US domestic politics. Comparative politics indicated a primary focus on non-US domestic politics. International relations included international political economy and security studies, while political theory indicated a focus on normative theory and political philosophy. In all cases, each dissertation was assigned to one and only one subfield.

Methodologies. The three major methodologies we coded for were quantitative, qualitative, and interpretive. The protocols for coding methodologies are displayed in figure 2.1. For each dissertation we also coded up to three specific methods used. If a dissertation used statistical or mathematical tools or was a large-N study, we coded it quantitative. If a dissertation used in-depth or "thick analysis of rich, dense information concerning specific cases," we classed it as either qualitative or interpretive (Collier and Elman 2008, 781). If it was hypothesis driven, we coded it as qualitative. If a dissertation focused on meaning from the point of view of the actors involved (emic), or focused on the social construction of meaning, we coded it as interpretive. "Mixed methodologies" in our dataset meant dissertations that used any two or more of these methodological approaches—quantitative, qualitative, or interpretive.

In our dataset, dissertations in political theory only infrequently discussed methods explicitly, and the subfield as a whole has been known to have a fraught relationship with research methods. Some ponder whether political theory (in some departments known as political philosophy) has methodology (Robeyns 2007). Considering the distinctions between political philosophy and the rest of political science, Kettler laments the discipline's "intoxication with methodology" and calls on political science to "redefine the interconnection without negating the

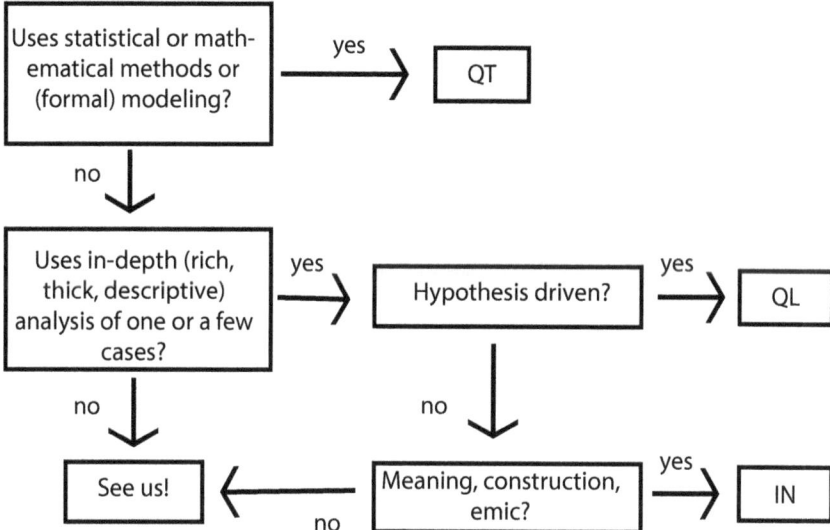

Fig. 2.1 Coding Protocol.

tension" (Kettler 2006, 235). In a similar vein, Shapiro (2002) exhorts political scientists to move from method- to problem-driven research, highlighting the need to bring together normative and empirical theory (597–98). Shapiro's descriptions of what political theorists do (or should do)—ranging from comments on the great normative questions of the day to identifying the assumptions underlying prevailing empirical accounts all fit into our broad definition of "interpretive methods," even if many scholars themselves might not use that label. Likewise, Kettler characterizes contemporary political theorists as largely "intellectual historians, epistemological explorers, or moral philosophers," all of which fall within our definition of interpretive methods (Kettler 2006, 235). Gunnell's take on what political theorists should do—"sensitive textual analysis coupled with historical awareness and conducted with philosophical and political self-consciousness"—also fits our interpretive methods category (Gunnell 1982, 327). Although many political theorists eschew the word method or disagree about its application (as in Gunnell's argument that hermeneutics is not a method), the term "interpretation" seems less repellent; it is at the core of their endeavors (Gunnell 1982, 317). Indeed, "it has become commonplace among political theorists to consider their discipline as a fundamentally interpretive enterprise" (Olesen n.d., 1).

Our dataset yielded the following demographic information about political science PhD recipients with respect to our three variables in the three years

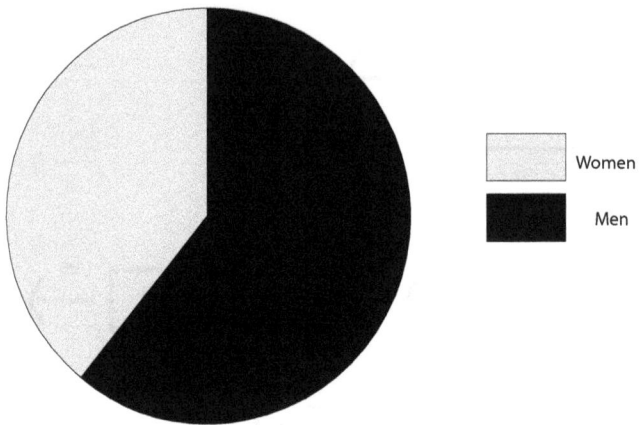

Fig. 2.2 Sample Demographics: Gender.

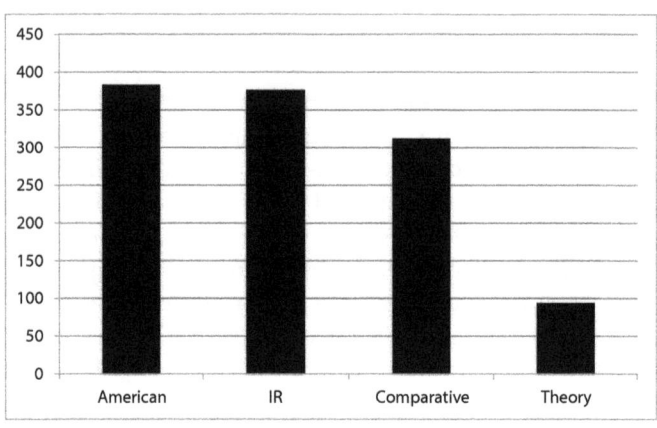

Fig. 2.3 Sample Demographs: Subfield.

studied. In gender terms, the field continues to be male-dominated with 61 percent of the sample men and 39 percent women (figure 2.2; appendix, table 2.4). In subfield terms, American politics and international relations (IR) accounted for almost two-thirds of PhDs, with comparative politics at 27 percent. Theory lagged at under 10 percent (figure 2.3; appendix, table 2.5). The sample was also dominated by quantitative methodologies, used in more than one-third of the

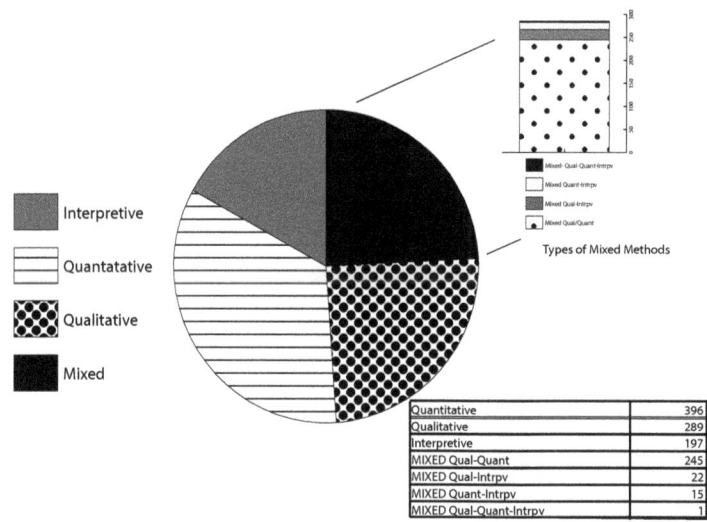

Fig. 2.4 Sample Demographics: Methodologies.

dissertations. Qualitative methodologies were used in a quarter of the sample, followed by mixed (qualitative-quantitative) methodologies at 20 percent. Interpretive methodologies were used in just 17 percent of the dissertations in our sample (figure 2.4; appendix, table 2.6).

Based on t tests and crosstabulation, the sample does support hypothesis 1: women in our sample were more likely than men to use mixed methodologies at a statistically significant level. We included all possible combinations of methodologies in "mixed methodologies": qualitative-quantitative, qualitative-interpretive, quantitative-interpretive, and qualitative-quantitative-interpretive. We did not find support in our sample for hypothesis 2: women were not more likely to use interpretive methodologies than men. Because political theory accounted for the greatest use of interpretive methodologies, we ran these tests both with and without political theory dissertations—in both cases, the relation between gender and interpretive methodologies was not significant at a 95 percent confidence interval (see table 2.2; appendix, table 2.7).

Thus the premise of many feminist epistemology studies—that positivist methodologies (including quantitative and qualitative, as we have defined them) are marked by more masculine traits and characteristics—did not in our sample translate into any greater use by women of nonpositivist methodologies. The finding that women were more likely to use mixed methodologies does not

Table 2.2. *t* Test Results.

	t	Sig. (Two-tailed)
Interpretive methodologies (including theorists)	−0.604	0.546
Interpretive methodologies (without theorists)	1.199	0.231
Mixed methodologies	3.193*	0.001

*Significant at 95 percent confidence interval.

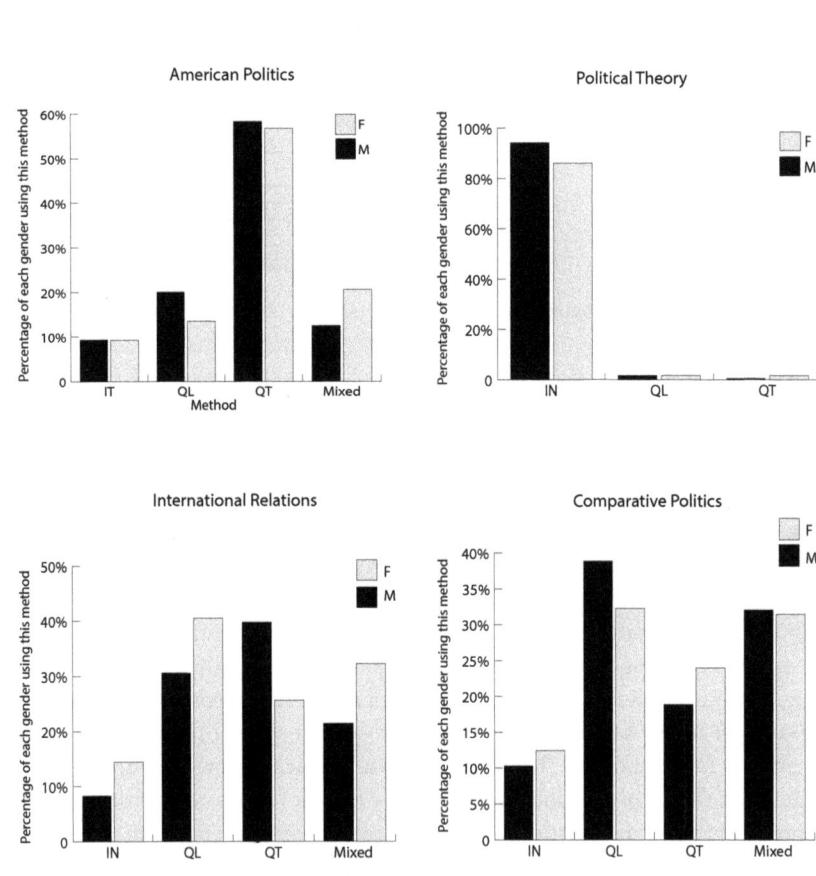

Fig. 2.5 Methodology and Gender by Subfield.

necessarily suggest this either, given that mixed methodologies where themselves dominated by the combination of qualitative/quantitative work, where both were defined as positivist methodologies (figure 2.4). Our study, of course, could not capture the methodological inclinations of those who may have dropped out

Table 2.3. Crosstabulation Results: Gender and Methodology by Subfield.

Subfield	Pearson Chi-Square	Asymp. Sig. (Two-tailed)
American politics	7.349	0.062
Political theory	2.993	0.224
Comparative politics	1.759	0.624
International relations	13.224*	0.004

*Significant at 95 percent confidence interval.

of a political science PhD program or those who might have been steered away from one. We also could not capture other intangibles such as the role of mentoring: Which faculty was available in the departments students were in, and how might the role of a student's dissertation chair and committee members have shaped their methodological choices? Ultimately, we were neither displeased nor surprised to find that women were facile with the range of methodologies; the finding, at a minimum, did not support any potentially essentialist notions of fundamental differences between men and women.

Crosstabulation analysis showed that the following patterns emerged by subfield (figure 2.5; appendix, tables 2.8–2.11). If we set 50 percent as a threshold, then American politics and political theory were the least methodologically diverse subfields. In American politics, over 50 percent of both men and women used quantitative methodologies (55 percent overall); while in political theory, over 90 percent of both men and women used interpretive methods (97 percent overall). By contrast, in comparative politics and IR, no one methodological approach was used by a majority of dissertations, with no one methodology used more than 40 percent in IR or 38 percent in comparative politics. One notable outlier (a woman theorist) was the only person in the entire sample to combine all three methodologies—qualitative, quantitative, and interpretive—in their dissertation.

IR was the subfield that showed the greatest methodological variation by gender, at a statistically significant level (see table 2.3). The only consistency between men and women within IR (as indeed in the sample as a whole) was that interpretive methods were least often used by both. It is unclear why IR might show such significant variation by gender in methodologies used. One might speculate on various factors: The subject matter of the subfield? The evolution and role of gender studies within the subfield? In her article on the dearth of women in international relations, especially at the senior level, Sjoberg highlights the potential impact of gender subordination on scholars' "epistemological assumptions and methodological selections" (Sjoberg 2008, 174). In IR, articles by women get fewer citations than men, a gender gap discussed in at least three recent articles and possibly linked to methods hierarchies in the subfield (Maliniak, Powers and Walter 2013; Mitchell, Lange, and Brus 2013; Østby et al. 2013). Given that IR has taken a leading approach to constructivism (which we classed as an interpretive methodology), we might have expected to see a somewhat greater use of interpretive methodology within IR than we did. Terrell Carver's work points to the particularly dominant role of masculinity in IR and the potential for post-positivist and interpretive methods to challenge it (Carver 2008).[7]

Comparative politics did not show any of these types of patterns: neither did the use of methodology vary significantly by gender (as it did in IR), nor was the subfield dominated by any one methodology (as was the case for American politics and political theory). Comparative politics has long been the largest organized section of the APSA; perhaps its very size and diversity themselves mitigate against the emergence of singular patterns. Beckwith (2010) has noted the subfield's openness to new topics, its methodological pluralism—including qualitative and case study research—and lack of a hegemonic research agenda. Occasionally lamented as weaknesses of the subfield, such openness may be an asset for fostering diversities of various types. Some studies have suggested that comparative politics draws more women and gender-oriented research than other subfields; in 2004 comparative politics scholars, about a fifth of APSA members made up about a third of the Women and Politics Research Section of the APSA (Tripp 2010, 192). Beckwith suggests that such methodological pluralism is one reason for the subfield's appeal for women and scholars doing research on gender (Beckwith 2010, 3). Additional research within the discipline could confirm or disconfirm generalized claims that comparative politics is the most inclusive and gender-friendly subfield.

Conclusions

Our study of gender and methodological diversity in US political science PhD dissertations lends support to the idea that these two forms of diversity may be linked in revealing ways. Our findings—women were more likely to use mixed methodologies, and choice of methodology varied significantly by gender in the IR subfield—call out for further analysis. In subsequent research, we will trace methodological training and methodological decisions during and after graduate school through an online survey of political scientists and oral histories, the latter a project suggested in APSA's report on "Women's Advancement in Political Science" (APSA 2005, 45).

One clear finding confirms the dominant place of positivist and specifically quantitative research methodologies in the field. Quantitative research clearly holds sway among recent PhDs in American politics, and positivist methods more broadly (including quantitative and qualitative research, whether alone or in combination with each other) were overwhelmingly predominant across all the subfields except political theory. With the exception of political theory, the parallel finding to the dominance of positivist methodologies was the marginalization of interpretive methodologies: across gender and subfield, it was never more than 17 percent.

The use of interpretive methodologies in our dataset resided almost entirely with political theory—and political theory together with the interpretive methods predominantly used in that subfield seem both to be subject to parallel or similar marginalization within the discipline as a whole. At the same time, political theory was more male-dominated (70 percent men to 30 percent women) in our dataset than any of the other subfields (consistently about 60 percent men to 40 percent women). The finding surprised us: the more marginalized methodology was actually used most in the most male-dominated subfield. In interpreting our results, we wondered whether it was the case that those who are least marginalized may possess the greater freedom to explore and use methodologies that are most marginal, and vice versa.

Because political theory is akin to philosophy, a discipline with a much higher percentage of men, a recent study about the underrepresentation of women in several fields, including philosophy, offers some possible insight. Leslie and colleagues found that "women are underrepresented in fields whose practitioners believe that raw, innate talent is the main requirement for success, because women are stereotyped as not possessing such talent" (Leslie et al. 2015, 262). Our finding that political theorists rarely specified their method might indicate that the 'innate genius' dynamic occurs in this field too. In other subfields, interpretivists were among the most communicative and reflective about the methods they used.

Schwitzhebel and Jennings (2016) studied the underrepresentation of women in philosophy, which lags other social science and humanities disciplines in gender equity on a variety of indicators. They found that the ethics subfield (defined broadly to include political and social philosophy, and thus perhaps the most akin to what political theorists in political science departments do) was closer to gender parity than other philosophy subfields; nevertheless "ethics remains far from gender parity in junior hiring; and it remains the case that the vast majority of authors of ethics articles in elite Anglophone journals are men" (Schwitzhebel and Jennings 2016, 30). Although they do not consider methods used in philosophy dissertations, further research could consider their findings alongside our examination of gender and subfields in political science, with an eye to possible relationships between methods, assumptions about innate talent, and women's presence in different subfields. In addition to considering what studies of other disciplines, such as philosophy, could tell us about patterns we find in our data, we wonder what our study might mean for other fields. To what extent might our findings about political science PhD programs be common to other social sciences? The question is best answered by further research in other fields, such as sociology and anthropology. If other disciplines are more gender-inclusive and varied in their methodological training, there may be lessons that political science can draw from them.

Although our research focused on graduate education for the reasons specified, it is certainly the case that methodological choice in research seems likely to impact how faculty approach undergraduate teaching. This is an entire research subject in itself, and one that we cannot begin to cover here, but certainly the possible ramifications on teaching and learning at all levels merit further study. Anecdotally, many social science departments grapple with the apparent split between the types of classes undergraduates want and need—in political science, these are often substantive classes on the politics of particular places or on various aspects of civics education—and the formalized training in quantitative approaches that students receive in graduate school. Narrow methods training for PhD students not only shapes the research they go on to do as faculty but is potentially at odds with what their future undergraduate students most need in the classroom and for undergraduate research projects.

One of the most striking aspects of the research was the depth of interpretation required to carry out all phases of a quantitative project: from determining gender from people's names to figuring out what methodology a dissertation used and which subfield it belonged in, to creating dummy variables and recoding data, interpretive work seemed to us to be embedded in the very structure of our dataset and analysis. For this very reason, even as we recognize that positivist quantitative and qualitative research was dominant in our study, we conclude that more systematic training for graduate students in interpretive methods would allow greater reflexivity about methodology even for those who aspire to do strictly positivist work.

We believe a concrete, best practices suggestion that emerges from our study is a recommendation for greater transparency about methodologies and specific methods within political science PhD dissertations. We would encourage the idea that all dissertations, including those in political theory, should explicitly mention methodologies and methods used in the abstract itself. This would enable not only greater transparency for job candidates and search committees, but also greater reflexivity and attention to how the methodologies we choose influence and shape the very questions that we as political scientists seek to ask and answer.

In sum, our findings support broader calls for greater diversity in methodological training for graduate students in US political science departments. We believe our study reinforces a recommendation of the APSA Task Force on Political Science in the Twenty-First Century: "Universities and university systems must be pushed to be more intentional in supporting a fuller range of interests and backgrounds of students who pursue graduate work in political science" (APSA 2011, 2). In terms of the threshold concepts discussed in the introductory chapter, greater diversity in methodological training would open multiple portals into the political science field, rather than the potential bottleneck from a narrow or exclusive methods class or track. The practice of admitting and training graduate students based on matching them with current faculty and potential advisors makes some practical sense, but also replicates existing modes of doing political science. If greater methods diversity in training, advising, mentoring, and research aids in the recruitment and retention of women in political science, thus expanding gender diversity through methodological diversity, then it will have been well worth the effort. We believe such an outcome would be a critical step to achieving both efficacy and empowerment for women and (thereby contributing to) justice and equity in political science, the social sciences, and the academy more broadly.

Over a decade ago, Hawkesworth argued that "feminist 'conjectures and refutations' of dominant paradigms deserve more serious incorporation into undergraduate and graduate curricula" to give students "insights that are not available from other methodological approaches" (2005, 142). Indeed, we envision a future in which training in a range of methodologies is required of all political science graduate students—even if they don't use every methodology in their own research—so that they can work with diverse students and read and follow the major developments in the field. Routine incorporation of interpretive, qualitative, and quantitative methods training into graduate curricula may aid in the recruitment and retention of women scholars in political science, so that gender and methodological diversities can build on each other in reinforcing ways.

Acknowledgements

We gratefully acknowledge the valuable contributions of our graduate research assistants Crystal Whetstone, Kristina Teater, and Anwar Mhajne, and colleague Stephen Mockabee. The staff at *ProQuest*˚ were very helpful and forthcoming. A prior version of this paper was presented at the Annual Meeting of the American Political Science Association, San Francisco, California, in September 6, 2015.

Appendix
Results of Statistical Analysis

Table 2.4. Sample Demographics by Gender.

	N	Percentage of Total Sample (N = 1,165)
Men	711	61
Women	454	39

Table 2.5. Sample Demographics by Subfield.

	N	Percentage of Total Sample (N = 1,165)
American	383	33
IR	376	32
Comparative	312	27
Theory	94	8

Table 2.6. Sample Demographics by Methodologies.

	N	Percentage of Total Sample (N = 1,165)
Quantitative	396	34
Qualitative	289	25
Interpretive	197	17
Mixed qualitative-quantitative	245	21
Mixed qualitative-interpretive	22	2
Mixed quantitative-interpretive	15	1
Mixed qualitative-quantitative-interpretive	1	0.1

Table 2.7. *t* Test Results (Including and Excluding Theorists).

	t	Sig. (Two-tailed)
Interpretive methodologies (including theorists)	−0.604	0.546
Interpretive methodologies (without theorists)	1.199	0.231
Mixed methodologies	3.193*	0.001

*Significant at 95 percent confidence interval.

Table 2.8. Crosstabulations of Methodology and Gender by Subfield: American Politics.

	Crosstabulation: Methodology and Gender				
			Gender		Total
			Male	Female	
Methodology	Interpretive	Count	22	13	35
		% within Gender 1	9.5	8.6	9.1
	Qualitative	Count	44	19	63
		% within Gender 1	19.0	12.6	16.4
	Quantitative	Count	131	81	212
		% within Gender 1	56.5	53.6	55.4
	Mixed	Count	35	38	73
		% within Gender 1	15.1	25.2	19.1
Total		Count	232	151	383
		% within Gender 1	100.0	100.0	100.0

Chi-Square Tests			
	Value	df	Asymp. Sig. (Two-sided)
Pearson chi-square	7.349[a]	3	0.062
Likelihood ratio	7.306	3	0.063
Linear-by-linear Association	4.346	1	0.037
N of valid cases	383		

[a] 0 cells (0.0 percent) have expected count less than 5. The minimum expected count is 13.80.

Table 2.9. Crosstabulations of Methodology and Gender by Subfield: Political Theory.

	Crosstabulation: Methodology and Gender				
			Gender		Total
			Male	Female	
Methodology	Interpretive	Count	66	25	91
		% within Gender 1	98.5	92.6	96.8
	Qualitative	Count	1	1	2
		% within Gender 1	1.5	3.7	2.1

Table 2.9. (Continued).

			Crosstabulation: Methodology and Gender			
				Gender		Total
				Male	Female	
	Mixed	Count		0	1	1
		% within Gender 1		0.0	3.7	1.1
Total		Count		67	27	94
		% within Gender 1		100.0	100.0	100.0

Chi-Square Tests			
	Value	df	Asymp. Sig. (Two-sided)
Pearson chi-square	2.993[a]	2	.224
Likelihood ratio	2.965	2	.227
Linear-by-linear Association	2.621	1	.105
N of valid cases	94		

[a] Four cells (66.7 percent) have expected count less than five. The minimum expected count is 0.29.

Table 2.10. Crosstabulations of Methodology and Gender by Subfield: Comparative Politics.

			Crosstabulation: Methodology and Gender		
			Gender		Total
			Male	Female	
Methodology	Interpretive	Count	17	15	32
		% within Gender 1	9.4	11.5	10.3
	Qualitative	Count	69	41	110
		% within Gender 1	38.1	31.3%	35.3
	Quantitative	Count	33	28	61
		% within Gender 1	18.2	21.4	19.6
	Mixed	Count	62	47	109
		% within Gender 1	34.3	35.9	34.9
Total		Count	181	131	312
		% within Gender 1	100.0	100.0	100.0

Table 2.10. (Continued).

	Chi-Square Tests		
	Value	df	Asymp. Sig. (Two-sided)
Pearson chi-square	1.759[a]	3	0.624
Likelihood ratio	1.765	3	0.623
Linear-by-linear Association	0.133	1	0.715
N of valid cases	312		

[a]Zero cells (0.0 percent) have expected count less than five. The minimum expected count is 13.44.

Table 2.11. Crosstabulations of Methodology and Gender by Subfield: International Relations.

Crosstabulation: Methodology and Gender					
			Gender		Total
			Male	Female	
Methodology	Interpretive	Count	19	20	39
		% within Gender 1	8.2	13.8	10.4
	Qualitative	Count	70	46	116
		% within Gender 1	30.3	31.7	30.9
	Quantitative	Count	89	32	121
		% within Gender 1	38.5	22.1	32.2
	Mixed	Count	53	47	100
		% within Gender 1	22.9	32.4	26.6
Total		Count	231	145	376
		% within Gender 1	100.0	100.0	100.0

	Chi-Square Tests		
	Value	df	Asymp. Sig. (Two-sided)
Pearson chi-square	13.224[a]	3	0.004
Likelihood ratio	13.487	3	0.004
Linear-by-linear Association	0.091	1	0.762
N of valid cases	376		

[a]Zero cells (0.0 percent) have expected count less than five. The minimum expected count is 15.04.

RINA VERMA WILLIAMS is Associate Professor of Political Science and affiliate faculty in Asian Studies and Women's, Gender, and Sexuality Studies at the University of Cincinnati. She is author of *Postcolonial Politics and Personal Laws: Colonial Legal Legacies and the Indian State* and her research and teaching interests focus on comparative Indian politics, religion and nationalism, and gender and identity politics.

LAURA DUDLEY JENKINS is Professor of Political Science and Director of the International Human Rights Certificate Program at the University of Cincinnati. She is author of *Identity and Identification in India: Defining the Disadvantaged* and editor, with Michele S. Moses, of *Affirmative Action Matters: Creating Opportunities for Students around the World*.

Notes

1. We use "American politics" to refer to the specific subfield of political science as it is so known. We recognize the problematic nature of this term, "erasing" as it does the other countries of North and South America. Accordingly, in all other instances we use "US" rather than "American," limiting our use of the latter term only in reference to the subfield of political science.
2. It is worth noting that methodological questions continue to vex the discipline, as witnessed by the most recent (2014–2015) discussions over the "Data Access and Research Transparency" (DA-RT) initiative and the pushback from interpretivists. See www.dartstatement.org/#!response-to-2015-apsa-discussions/bcawm; for a response, see Buthe and Jacobs 2015 and Isaac (2015).
3. Hall's statistics include political science and government PhDs.
4. See also: Haraway 1988; Harding 1991; Breuning and Sanders 2007; Maliniak et al. 2008; Evans and Bucy 2010; Evans and Moulder 2011; Maliniak, Powers, and Walter 2013.
5. See Mathews and Andersen 2001; Breuning and Sanders 2007; McGinty and Moore 2008; Evans and Moulder 2011; Mitchell, Lange, and Brus 2013; Maliniak, Powers, and Walter 2013.
6. We recognize the irony of using quantitative methods to explore the use of methodology in the discipline. While we work from a feminist perspective, we do not use explicitly feminist methods in this study. Subsequent phases of the project—discussed in the conclusion—will employ a broad range of interpretive and feminist methods to explore these questions further.
7. See also chapter 6.

References

American Political Science Association. (APSA). 2005. *Women's Advancement in Political Science: A Report of the APSA Workshop on the Advancement of Women in Academic*

Political Science in the United States. Washington, DC: American Political Science Association.

———. 2011. *Political Science in the Twenty-First Century: Report of the Task Force on Political Science in the Twenty-First Century.* Washington, DC: American Political Science Association.

Anonymous. 2014. "No Shortcuts to Gender Equality: The Structures of Women's Exclusion in Political Science." *Politics & Gender* 10 (3): 437–47.

Beckwith, Karen. 2010. "Introduction: Comparative Politics and the Logics of a Comparative Politics of Gender." *Perspectives on Politics* 8 (1): 159–68.

Bennett, Andrew, Aharo Barth, and Kenneth Rutherford. 2003. "Do We Preach What We Practice? A Survey of Methods in Political Science Journals and Curricula." *PS: Political Science and Politics* 36 (3): 373–78.

Brandes, Lisa, Eloise Buker, Susan Burgess, Constance Cook, Janet Flammang, Shirley Geiger, Susan Okin, Bang-Soon Yoon, and Martha Ackelsberg. 2001. "The Status of Women in Political Science: Female Participation in the Professoriate and the Study of Women and Politics in the Discipline." *PS: Political Science and Politics* 34 (2): 319–26.

Breuning, Marijke, and Kathryn Sanders. 2007. "Gender and Journal Authorship in Eight Prestigious Political Science Journals." *PS: Political Science and Politics* 40 (2): 347–51.

Buthe, Tim and Alan M. Jacobs. 2015. "Conclusion: Research Transparency of a Diverse Discipline." *Qualitative and Multi-Method Research: Newsletter of the American Political Science Organized Section for Qualitative and Multi-Method Research* 13 (1): 52–64. https://www.maxwell.syr.edu/moynihan/cqrm/Newsletters/.

Carver, Terrell. 2008. "Men in the Feminist Gaze: What Does This Mean in IR?" *Millennium—Journal of International Studies* 37 (1): 107–22.

Collier, David, and Colin Elman. 2008. *Concepts and Method in the Social Science: The Tradition of Giovanni Sartori.* New York: Routledge.

Evans, Heather K., and Erik P. Bucy. 2010. "The Representation of Women in Publication: An Analysis of Political Communication and the International Journal of Press/Politics." *PS: Political Science and Politics* 43 (2): 295–301.

Evans, Heather K., and A. Moulder. 2011. "Reflecting on a Decade of Women's Publications in Four Top Political Science Journals." *PS: Political Science and Politics* 44 (4): 793–98.

Gruberg, Martin. 2009. "Participation by Women in the 2008 APSA Annual Meeting." *PS: Political Science & Politics* 42 (1): 173–74.

Gunnell, John G. 1982. "Interpretation and the History of Political Theory: Apology and Epistemology." *The American Political Science Review* 76 (2): 317–27.

———. 2015. "Pluralism and the Fate of Perestroika: A Historical Reflection." *Perspectives on Politics* 13 (2): 408–15.

Hall, Susan T. (1981) 1998. "Political Science/Government Research Doctorates Awarded by Gender and Ethnicity 1981–1998." *Male/Female.* In "Receiving PhDs as a percent Political Science/Government." Science and Engineering Degrees: 1966–1997. NSF 00–310. Arlington, VA: National Science Foundation, Division of Science Resources Studies.

Haraway, Donna. 1988. "Situated Knowledges: The Science Question in Feminism and the Privilege of Partial Perspective." *Feminist Studies* 14 (3): 575–99.

Harding, Sandra G. 1986. *The Science Question in Feminism*. Ithaca, NY: Cornell University Press.
———. 1991. *Whose Science? Whose Knowledge? Thinking from Women's Lives*. Ithaca, NY: Cornell University Press.
Hawkesworth, Mary. 1989. "Knowers, Knowing, Known: Feminist Theory and Claims of Truth." *Signs* 14 (3): 533–57.
———. 2005. "Engendering Political Science: An Immodest Proposal." *Politics & Gender* 1 (1): 141–56.
———. 2006. "Contending Conceptions of Science and Politics: Methodology and the Constitution of the Political." In *Interpretation and Method: Empirical Research and the Interpretive Turn*, edited by Dvora Yanow and Peregrine Schwartz-Shea. New York: M.E. Sharpe.
Hero, Rodney. 2015. "Reflections on 'How Political Science can be More Diverse.'" *PS: Political Science & Politics* 48 (3): 469–71.
Hesli, Vicki L., Jacqueline DeLaat, Jeremy Youde, Jeanette Mendez, and Sang-Shin Lee. 2006. "Success in Graduate School and After: Survey Results from the Midwest Region, Part III." *PS: Political Science and Politics* 39 (2): 317–25.
Isaac, Jeffrey. 2015. "For a More Public Political Science." *Perspectives on Politics* 13 (2): 269–83.
Kaba, Amadu Jacky. 2013. "Profile of Contributors to the American Political Science Review, 2010." *Journal of Politics and Law* 6 (2): 54.
Kettler, David. 2006. "Political Science and Political Theory: The Heart of the Matter." In *Making Political Science Matter: Debating Knowledge, Research and Method*, edited by Sanford F. Schram and Brian Caterino. New York: New York University Press.
Kittilson, Miki Caul. 2015. "Advancing Women in Political Science: Navigating Gendered Structures of Opportunity." *PS: Political Science and Politics* 48 (3): 450–53.
Launius, Christie, and Holly Hassel. 2014. *Threshold Concepts in Women's and Gender Studies: Ways of Seeing, Thinking, and Knowing*. New York: Routledge.
Leslie, Sara-Jane, Andrei Cimpian, Meredith Meyer, and Edward Freeland. 2015. "Expectations of Brilliance Underlie Gender Distributions Across Academic Disciplines." *Science* 347 (6219): 262–65.
Maliniak, Daniel, Amy Oakes, Susan Peterson, and Michael J. Tierney. 2008. "Women in International Relations." *Politics & Gender* 4 (1): 122–44.
———. 2011. "International Relations in the US Academy." *International Studies Quarterly* 55 (2): 437–64.
Maliniak, Daniel, Ryan Powers, and Barbara F. Walter. 2013. "The Gender Citation Gap in International Relations." *International Organization* 67 (4): 889–922.
Mathews, A. Lanethea, and Kristi Andersen. 2001. "A Gender Gap in Publishing? Women's Representation in Edited Political Science Books." *PS: Political Science and Politics* 34 (1): 143–47.
McGinty, Stephen, and Anne C. Moore. 2008. "Role of Gender in Reviewers' Appraisals of Quality in Political Science Books: A Content Analysis." *Journal of Academic Librarianship* 34 (4): 288.
Mershon, Carol, and Denise Walsh. 2015. "How Political Science Can Be More Diverse." *PS: Political Science & Politics* 48 (3): 441–44.

Mitchell, Sara McLaughlin, Samantha Lange, and Holly Brus. 2013. "Gendered Citation Patterns in International Relations Journals." *International Studies Perspectives* 14 (4): 485–92.
Monroe, Kristen R. 2005. *Perestroika: The Raucous Rebellion in Political Science*. New Haven, CT: Yale University Press.
———. 2015. "What Did Perestroika Accomplish?" *Perspectives on Politics* 13 (2): 423–24.
Olesen, Jens. "Methods of Interpretation and Their Significance for Political Theory." PhD diss., Oxford University. www.academia.edu/261070/Research_Proposal_Methods _of_Interpretation_and_their_Significance_for_Political_Theory_.
Østby, Gudrun, Havard Strand, Ragnhild Nordas, and Nils Petter Gleditsch. 2013. "Gender Gap or Gender Bias in Peace Research? Publication Patterns and Citation Rates for Journal of Peace Research, 1983–2008." *International Studies Perspectives* 14 (4): 493–506.
Perestroika. 2000. "The Idea" [a reprint of the original email]. In *Perestroika! The Raucous Rebellion in Political Science*, edited by Kristen Renwick Monroe, 9–11. New Haven, CT: Yale University Press.
Randall, Vicki. 2010. "Feminism." In *Theory and Methods in Political Science*, edited by David Marsh and Gerry Stoker, 119–35. New York: Palgrave Macmillan.
Robeyns, Ingrid. 2007. "Methods in Political Theory/Philosophy Blog." The Crooked Timber Blog, September 4. http://crookedtimber.org/2007/09/04/methods-in-political -theoryphilosophy-bleg/.
Rudolph, Susanne Hoeber. 2005. "Perestroika and Its Other." In *Perestroika! The Raucous Rebellion in Political Science*, edited by Kristen R. Monroe, 12–20. New Haven, CT: Yale University Press.
Schram, Sanford, and Brian Caterino. 2006. *Making Political Science Matter: Debating Knowledge, Research, and Method*. New York: New York University Press.
Schwartz-Shea, Peregrine, and Andrew Bennett. 2003. "Introduction: Methodological Pluralism in Journals and Graduate Education? Commentaries on New Evidence." *PS: Political Science and Politics* 36 (3): 371–72.
Schwartz-Shea, Peregrine, and Dvora Yanow. 2002. "'Reading' 'Methods' 'Texts': How Research Methods Texts Construct Political Science." *Political Research Quarterly* 55 (2): 457.
Schwartz-Shea, Peregrine. 2003. "Is This the Curriculum We Want? Doctoral Requirements and Offerings in Methods and Methodology." *PS: Political Science and Politics* 36 (3): 379–86.
Schwitzhebel, Eric, and Carolyn Dicey Jennings. 2016. "Women in Philosophy: Quantitative Analyses of Specialization, Prevalence, Visibility, and Generational Change." http://faculty.ucr.edu/~eschwitz/SchwitzAbs/WomenInPhil.htm.
Scott, Joan W. 1986. "Gender: A Useful Category of Historical Analysis." *The American Historical Review* 91 (5): 1053–75.
Shapiro, Ian. 2002. "Problems, Methods, and Theories in the Study of Politics, or What's Wrong with Political Science and What to Do About It." *Political Theory* 30 (4): 596–619.
Sinclair-Chapman, Valeria. 2015. "Leveraging Diversity in Political Science for Institutional and Disciplinary Change." *PS: Political Science and Politics* 48 (3): 454–58.

Sjoberg, Laura. 2008. "The Norm of Tradition: Gender Subordination and Women's Exclusion in International Relations." *Politics & Gender* 4 (1): 173–80.

Tripp, Aili Mari. 2010. "Toward a Comparative Politics of Gender Research in Which Women Matter." *Perspectives on Politics* 8 (1): 191–97.

Voeten, Erik. 2013. "Introducing the Monkey Cage Gender Gap Symposium." *Washington Post*, Monkey Cage, September 13, 2013. www.washingtonpost.com/blogs/monkey-cage/files/2013/10/Gender-Gap-Articles.pdf.

Yanow, Dvora. 2003. "Interpretive Empirical Political Science: What Makes This Not a Subfield of Qualitative Methods." *Qualitative Methods Section (APSA) Newsletter* 1 (2): 9–13. https://www.maxwell.syr.edu/uploadedFiles/moynihan/cqrm/Newsletter1.2.pdf.

Yanow, Dvora, and Peregrine Schwartz-Shea. 2010. "Perestroika Ten Years After: Reflections on Methodological Diversity." *PS: Political Science and Politics* 43 (4): 741–45.

3 Gendered Representation in Political Science Textbooks

Daniel Mueller

As an academic discipline, political science tends to have a reputation as both a male-dominated field of study and one which focuses on political actors and their actions that are themselves often dominated by males. It is a reputation explored in detail in several other chapters in this book and a subject that has been investigated by political scientists themselves over the last few decades. The masculine dominance manifests itself in the world of politics outside academia, in faculty statistics like publishing, tenure, and promotion, and in the classroom, where males make up the bulk of political science students. The introductory chapter identified the "leaky pipeline" that leads to a drop-off of females in the discipline and that begins already in undergraduate classrooms. If political science and politics in general absorb these masculinist trends right from the start, it may cause women to feel out of place and unwelcome and make it continuously difficult for women both to enter the political process, in all its forms, and even maintain their current positions and levels of participation.

This chapter explores just one aspect of the male dominance in political science by analyzing images in political science textbooks to shed light on how students taking courses in political science—whether or not they continue in the discipline or in the field professionally—are exposed to the various gender biases that occur in politics and political science. How textbooks depict gender roles can offer hints about how we as academics frame gender in the classroom. While images in these texts may often reflect the state of the world as it is, some might be portraying men and women in ways that reinforce gender stereotypes in politics and may ultimately hold students back as they reflect on what they see in these texts or are taught in the classroom. Whatever students might take away from these images, what they see and how they interpret it does not necessarily have to end with the textbook. If gender is represented in particular ways in political science textbooks, educators can actively engage students in discussions about these stereotypes, directly challenging them to consider how gender is represented versus how it ought to be, or, given the gendered nature of the realities depicted, what certain gender representations in these textbooks ultimately imply about politics around the world. It might also be instructive to uncover, together with students, the social construction of gender roles that are clearly underway in disciplinary textbooks.

In keeping with the important theme of this volume, this chapter seeks not just to identify what gender biases exist in our textbooks, but to explore how educators can utilize a gender-forward approach in the classroom to spur students to think critically about gender and politics. It is our hope that critical discussion of gender representation early in their education, including in introductory and general education courses, may help patch up leaks farther down the pipeline. This kind of approach fits well within the framework of threshold concepts developed by Meyer and Land (2003, 2005). A threshold concept is described by Meyer and Land (2003) as one which is transformative, irreversible, integrative, and potentially bounded and troublesome, which stands in contrast to the more basic core concepts that aid in understanding a subject generally and do not necessarily cognitively challenge students. In other words, when students learn a threshold concept, they are usually confronted with information they do not quickly or easily understand, but that when learned, can lead to a complete and enduring transformation in the way in which students view the subject they are learning and how it relates to other subjects. How gender is represented in political science and politics generally is a threshold concept. Identifying and discussing gender bias in political science textbooks has the potential to challenge students to think about gender and politics in ways they have not before, ultimately transforming their understanding of why gender bias might exist and how to overcome it.

The existence of gender bias in political science is well established in the literature. Breuning and Sanders (2007) carried out a study to determine the gender breakdown of publications in some of political science's most prestigious journals. Their data revealed a striking imbalance between men and women in the academy, with men accounting for 70 to 80 percent of authorship in the majority of the journals Breuning and Sanders reviewed. Similar results are found in edited books in political science (Mathews and Andersen 2001). Maliniak, Powers, and Walter (2013) also demonstrated that there appears to be, especially in the subfield of international relations, a citation gap between men and women. Their findings indicated that not only are women the minority of authors in the subfield, they are also cited far less by both men and women in the discipline. The trend is not just limited to the United States. Internationally, the picture is much the same, with women greatly underrepresented in the disciplinary scholarship in almost every country investigated (Lindroos et al. 2014; Timperley 2013).

The trends are the same in the gender breakdown of graduate students on the job market, with women clearly in the minority and their proportion dropping in recent years (American Political Science Association [hereafter cited as APSA]

2013). Kantola (2008) suggests this marginalization of women in the discipline begins in individual political science departments, where men are usually greater in number and occupy more positions of power, serving as easily accessible role models and mentors to male students. Not surprisingly, this gender disparity might lead to hidden discrimination on the parts of both men and women, which involves the creation of an atmosphere in which the way individuals communicate and the departmental duties they take on help reinforce the male as the stereotypically expert political scientist, an atmosphere that is then internalized by women, leading them to accept the perception of women in political science as outsiders. If this is the case, it would not be surprising, then, to see women publishing less, not advancing in academic ranks, leaving the academy, or not entering it in the first place.

There is also evidence to suggest that political science has followed the trends of the political issues it has studied over the course of the last several decades. Tolleson-Rinehart and Carroll (2006) introduce this very idea, suggesting that while political science has certainly improved in how it values women in the discipline, it still operates with the gendered assumptions and values that underlie many of the very issues and institutions the discipline studies. There seems to be a mutually reinforcing cycle of exclusion, however unintentional and subtle, in which women in both politics and political science are relegated to secondary positions based on the realities of political and academic life.

The issue of gender bias in the discipline may start even earlier—in the undergraduate classroom. Gender in political science has been thoroughly examined at the international, national, and departmental level, but little research exists on the state of gender in the typical political science classroom. It is quite clear that women are underrepresented in political science, both as academics and as students, but there may be some explanation for this found in how men and women in undergraduate classrooms perceive political science—and, by extension, politics itself, how they are introduced to the discipline by their instructors, and the type of learning material students are exposed to. If it is the case that even at the undergraduate level the discipline and its areas of study are skewed in favor of male students, it may indicate a deeper problem, one that lies not necessarily in how academics interact *with one another*, but in how academics *introduce* political science and politics to their students and how these students internalize those gendered assumptions. What instructors say and how they present material likely has some effect on how students perceive political issues, and while this chapter is primarily concerned with how political science textbooks present gender through imagery, discussions about these images in the classroom could and certainly do alter how students perceive gender and politics.

Several cross-cultural studies across a variety of disciplines have explored the relationship between stereotypical gender roles in textbooks and students' performance and have demonstrated that images of stereotypical gender roles are widespread and often help reinforce in students' minds what particular gender roles should be, in public, professional, and private spheres (Bahman and Rahimi 2010; Bazler and Simonis 2006; Eaton and Rose 2013; Ferree and Hall 1990; Foulds 2013; Good, Woodzicka, and Wingfield 2010; Lee and Collins 2008; Rifkin 1998; Sheldon 2004; Sumalatha and Ramakrishnaiah 2004; Táboas-Pais and Rey-Cao 2012; Yanowitz and Weathers 2004). These studies find that images of men are generally more prevalent, and both men and women are overwhelmingly portrayed in their respective traditional gender roles. Good, Woodzicka, and Wingfield (2010) concluded that students' performance can be significantly affected when exposed to stereotypical gender roles. In their study of the science classroom in secondary education, for example, men were more likely to perform better when exposed to male scientists in images than to female scientists, while the opposite was true for women. In other words, the stereotypical gender role of the male as the scientist bolstered male performance, while the same stereotype decreased the performance of female students.

Good, Woodzicka, and Wingfield's (2010) results replicate a well-established literature on the stereotype threat that has linked gender stereotypes and student performance, finding that these stereotypes have a strong negative effect on learning, often implicitly pushing students to conform to them (Davies, Spencer, and Steele 2005; Keller and Dauenheimer 2003; O'Brien and Crandall 2003; Smith and White 2002; Spencer, Steele, and Quinn 1999). The research seems to indicate strongly that traditional gender roles are widespread in classroom material across all ages, numerous disciplines, and countries, and it also demonstrates that these images and texts can lock students into these roles from a very young age.

Given these findings and the fact that most educators utilize textbooks as the core material source for introductory classes, this chapter will explore how gender roles are portrayed in political science textbooks and what this might mean for both men and women, as students and academics, both inside and outside the classroom. I will explore whether men and women are represented differently in political science textbooks by approaching this topic with three research goals in mind: (1) determining what the most common portrayals of men and women in our textbooks are and whether there is a difference between how we represent males and females in the political world; (2) investigating whether the gender of the textbooks' authors has any effect on how men and women are portrayed; and (3) given the findings from these first two examinations, suggesting how we, as a discipline, might address these representations to correct for our own gender biases and ensure that we are not adding to our students' preconceived gender stereotypes in both politics and the discipline of political science.

Methods

To answer the first two research questions, I analyzed images in twenty textbooks from across the various subfields in political science. These textbooks, published between 2011 and 2015, are largely intended for introductory courses. Importantly, introductory textbooks tend to enjoy the widest student readership. Whether or not students continue to pursue political science courses, they are very likely to encounter an introductory political science course at some point throughout their undergraduate career, as either a part of their general educational requirements or as one of the disciplinary major requirements, and it is these introductory textbooks they will most likely encounter. The textbooks analyzed were all published during roughly the same time period to ensure there are no biases related to the date of publication. Comparing modern textbooks to older ones would be a separate research project in its own right.

The textbooks were drawn from the traditional subfields of the discipline, with seven from comparative politics, five from American politics, one from public policy, and seven from international relations.[1] No books were selected from political theory, since most theory courses tend to be upper level, and the texts used in these courses are rarely, if ever, textbooks. It should be noted, however, that most of the theory texts are authored by men, with women greatly underrepresented in this subfield. The public policy subfield reflects the same trends, since its texts either do not follow the standard format of textbooks and do not include images or are simply not textbooks at all, but original research. Consequently, this research relies more heavily on comparative, international relations, and American government textbooks, but it may also be the case that these subfields provide the most popular (and often required) introductory courses for both political science majors and students outside the discipline who take these courses as general education requirements.

Much of this methodology is borrowed from work in the literature cited above that analyzes images in textbooks. Táboas-Pais and Rey-Cao's (2012) analysis served as a primary model for my own methodology. The unit of analysis was an individual image in a textbook, which was coded into one or more of twelve categories. Only images which contained people and in which the gender of the people in the images could be easily determined were used. Cartoons were excluded outright, since I sought to examine real-world images of politics and political issues in these texts rather than their interpretations through commentary and illustrations, although exploring these separately might reveal other interesting viewpoints of the authors themselves. The total number of images available in the textbooks was 2,026. After throwing out unusable images based on the above criteria, n stood at 1,715. The categories and their descriptions are shown in table 3.1.

Table 3.1. Descriptive Categories.

Category	Description
Position of power or influence	Individuals who hold a position of political power, such as world leaders, cabinet members, supreme court justices, ambassadors, heads or representatives of global organizations like the World Trade Organization (WTO); local government officials holding office; high-ranking officials or heads of public or private organizations, such as heads of bureaucratic departments, lobbyists, or chief executive officers (CEOs); and famous celebrities, intellectuals, or activists
Military, police, or emergency personnel	Individuals who are in a military or police force, including nonstate military forces, or other emergency personnel such as firefighters or first responders; and individuals who are being arrested or escorted by military or police forces
Demonstration	Individuals engaging in protests, organized or spontaneous, individual or in groups
Voting	Individuals engaged in the voting process, whether as voters themselves or as officials managing the polling place
Political rally or event	Individuals who are present at an official political rally or event, such as a political convention, a party meeting, an NRA gun show or meeting, a meeting for political movements like the Tea Party, outdoor events with scheduled speakers (while these outdoor events may have people holding signs and look like a protest, they are categorized separately from protests) or high-profile court cases
Daily life	Individuals engaged in activities that fit within the realm of normal, everyday life, such as shopping, riding public transit, cooking, sitting on a laptop, visiting a doctor; this includes images of people not engaged in any particular activity that can be categorized in other groups, such as portraits of unknown individuals, people sitting in a park or in front of a building, people sitting in their homes, people engaging with others in standard, uneventful ways
Refugees	Individuals who are in a refugee camp or are identified as refugees by the image caption; individuals who are engaged in illegal immigration
Violence	Individuals who are engaged in forceful activity with others, directly and indirectly; includes clear violence against other individuals and implied violence, such as someone firing a weapon in a war zone or a protester throwing a Molotov cocktail, with targets out of sight
Labor, business, business, and occupational	Individuals who are depicted in any kind of physical labor, such as removing debris or cleaning a beach; workers in factories; depictions of slavery; individuals engaged in the manufacturing or construction of goods; individuals who are depicted as working in business or white-collar professions; or individuals performing their duties in their official occupational capacities, such as a FEMA worker at a disaster site or a nurse in a hospital

Table 3.1. (*continued*).

Category	Description
Religion	Individuals engaged in any kind of religious ceremony or event related to religion, including a protest, evident through the image itself or the image caption
Education	Individuals engaged in an educational environment, such as a classroom, including both teachers and students

Because individuals in the images could be engaged in several of these categories at once, it is not uncommon for images to be coded multiple times into various categories. Images were also coded by gender, as shown in table 3.2.

Once the images were coded into the appropriate descriptive and gender categories, I also analyzed the individuals in the images. Because categorizing an entire image as predominantly male or female and comparing that to one or several of the twelve descriptive categories wipes out nuances in the images and fails to recognize what individuals of the minority gender in that image are doing, it seemed appropriate to then recode images on a separate level of analysis, focusing on the individuals in the image rather than the image as a whole. For example, several images show German chancellor Angela Merkel surrounded by other world leaders or German politicians, all or most of whom are men. Based on my coding scheme, these images would be classified as "position of power or influence" and "predominantly male," since the image clearly contains more men than women and shows individuals in positions of power. However, Merkel herself is indeed in a position of power, and categorizing the image as predominantly male fails to reflect the woman in power. In other words, looking at individuals after assessing the image as a whole was an attempt to bring more nuance to the research. When coding male and female individuals, the same descriptive categories were used, and images once again could be coded simultaneously into multiple categories. To continue the example, then, when looking at an image at a more nuanced, individual level, I would look at women and men in the image separately from one another and code them into one or more of the twelve descriptive categories. Merkel would be examined separately from others in the image, since she was often the only woman. I would record her as being in a position of power, and then move on to the men in the image, which I would code similarly.

To use another example, many images in these textbooks showed people protesting. One in particular shows protesters and police all in one image, with both protesters and police engaging in violence. When looking at this image as a whole, it was clear that most of the police and protesters were male, so I coded the image as predominantly male. I then coded the image into one or more of the twelve descriptive categories. In this case, the image was coded as

Table 3.2. Gender Categories.

Gender Category	Description
Predominantly male	Males in the image clearly outnumber females
Predominantly female	Females in the image clearly outnumber males
Mix	There is no indication that one sex outnumbers the other; the sexes are split relatively evenly

"military, police, or emergency personnel," "demonstration," and "violence." I then examined females and males in the image independently of one another. In this example, the image showed women in the protest, but only showed men engaged in violence, and the police officers were exclusively male. As a result, I coded female individuals as "demonstration" only, while male individuals were coded as "demonstration," "violence," and "military, police, or emergency personnel." This kind of coding scheme allows for more precision in identifying how males and females are represented in these images, and it emphasizes that while the image as a whole might show people engaged in one or two general activities, men and women in those images might actually be engaged in very different activity from one another.

All coded data was then analyzed through several statistical tests. These consisted of several t tests to determine any link between the gender of the authors and the dominance of any particular gender category by looking for statistically significant differences between means, and to also determine the relationship between the gender categories and the descriptive categories, revealing if gender representations significantly differed from one another given the descriptive categories.

Intercoder Reliability

To ensure validity, two other coders were provided with a sample of the images from the dataset. Initially, the total number of images was 1,550, but increased to 1,715 after more textbooks were added. The intercoder reliability sample was based off the initial total of 1,550 and consisted of 10 percent of this total, or 155. Each image was randomly selected by first assigning a number to each textbook (one to sixteen). I then randomly generated a number selected from this range 155 times. For however many instances a textbook number appeared, I then randomly generated the same number of images based on the appropriate range for each textbook. This ensured randomness throughout the process and guaranteed a sample from each textbook. With three total coders, the average pairwise percent agreement was 83.44 percent, which according to Neuendorf (2002) is acceptable at above 0.8.

Hypotheses

As stated earlier, there are two main research questions in this chapter: (1) What are the most common portrayals of men and women in political science textbooks and is there a significant difference between them? and (2) Does the gender of the authors have any effect on how men and women are portrayed in textbooks? These questions lead me to four hypotheses, largely based on what we would expect from traditional gender roles:

> HYPOTHESIS 1: Men are more likely than women or the mixed group to be shown in the categories of position of power or influence; military, police, or emergency personnel; political rally or event; violence; labor, business, and occupational; and sporting event.
>
> HYPOTHESIS 2: Women are more likely than men or the mixed group to be shown in the categories of daily life, refugees, religion, and education.
>
> HYPOTHESIS 3: The mixed group is more likely than men or women to be shown in the categories of demonstration and voting.
>
> HYPOTHESIS 4: The gender of the authors will have an effect on the predominance of men or women in textbook images, with men favoring men and women favoring women.

Results of Content Analysis

Table 3.3 presents the gender breakdown of images as a whole, followed by an analysis of the individuals within the images (table 3.4) along twelve descriptive categories.

Clearly, political science textbooks are populated predominantly by the images of men—of the 1,715 images analyzed in the twenty textbooks, 1,097 were categorized as predominantly male, 262 were predominantly female, and 356 were mixed. Position of power or influence was by far the most frequent descriptive category. While this is unsurprising, given the nature of the material covered in the textbooks, it is quite telling where each gender group has its main share. Men dominate the share of almost every category, excluding voting and education. In contrast, women dominate nothing and tie with men only in refugees, with the mixed category taking the lead in voting and education. Because there is overlap in the categories, it does not make sense to add up the percentages, but since males are most dominant in position of power and influence and military, police, or emergency personnel, and these prove to be two of the most common descriptive categories, it is safe to say that the textbooks are generally dominated by male images, even without considering the other ten subcategories. Moreover, figure 3.1 (means and their 95 percent confidence intervals calculated from *t* tests) shows that a majority of images categorized as predominantly male (55 percent) show up in position of power or influence.

Table 3.3. Gender Share of Categories.

Category	Male		Female		Mix		Grand Total	
	Total	%*	Total	%*	Total	%*	Total	%**
Position of power or influence	605	79.4	64	8.4	93	12.2	762	44.43
Military, police, or emergency personnel	231	89.53	6	2.33	21	8.14	258	15.04
Demonstration	134	44.67	44	14.67	122	40.67	300	17.49
Voting	14	31.82	12	27.27	18	40.91	44	2.57
Political rally or event	78	51.66	22	14.57	51	33.77	151	8.8
Daily life	72	40.22	67	37.43	40	22.35	179	10.44
Refugees	10	35.71	10	35.71	8	28.57	28	1.63
Violence	55	80.88	3	4.41	10	14.71	68	3.97
Labor, business, and occupational	80	63.49	31	24.6	15	11.9	126	7.35
Religion	15	51.72	10	34.48	4	13.79	29	1.69
Education	11	21.15	16	30.77	25	48.08	52	3.03
Sporting event	10	62.5	3	18.75	3	18.75	16	0.93

*Each percentage is the respective gender category's portion of the descriptive category's total.
**Percentage is a fraction of the total n (1,715).

Table 3.4. Male and Female Individuals.

Category	Male		Female	
	Total	%*	Total	%*
Position of power or influence	699	40.76	216	12.59
Military, police, or emergency personnel	252	14.69	23	1.34
Demonstration	263	15.34	193	11.25
Voting	36	2.1	32	1.87
Political rally or event	134	7.81	102	5.95
Daily life	128	7.46	110	6.41
Refugees	22	1.28	20	1.17
Violence	61	3.56	12	.7
Labor, business, and occupational	97	5.66	56	3.27
Religion	23	1.34	13	.76
Education	43	2.51	46	2.68
Sporting event	14	.82	8	.47

*Percentage is a fraction of total n (1,715).

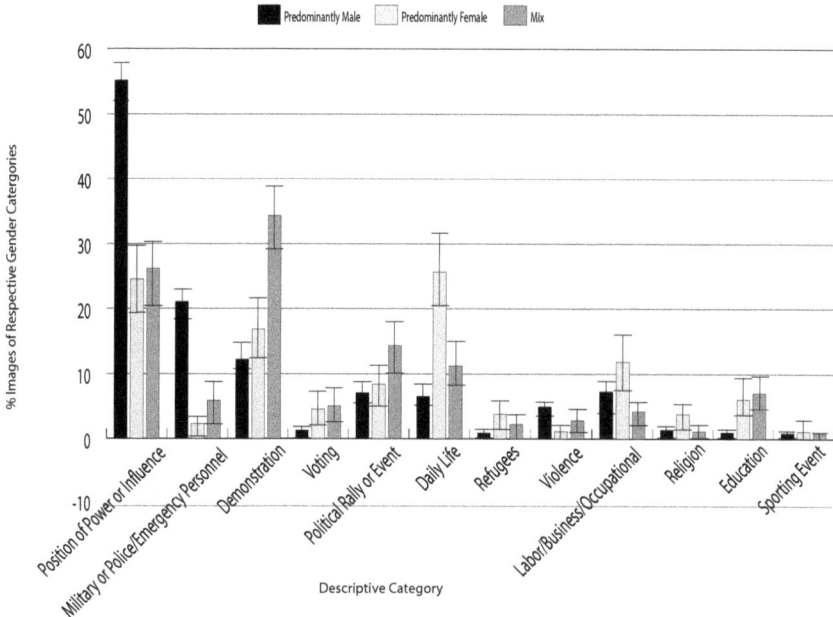

Fig. 3.1 Gender Share of Descriptive Categories.

While at first glance table 3.3 indicates that men dominate every single category (and this is the case because men outnumber women in these texts generally), the actual share that each category represents for male and female images might present a different picture. For example, within the category of daily life, it would appear from table 3.3 that men have the greater share of representation in this category, but when it is broken down by gender (figure 3.1), the picture is reversed. A quarter of all female images are in daily life, while only about 6 percent of male images are categorized this way (figure 3.1). Table 3.4 provides a short summary of the raw data for male and female individuals depicted in selected textbooks.

While table 3.4 reflects the more nuanced approach to the images, it is still clear where men dominate. There are, at least, more women reflected in each category, but there are also more men in each. In fact, where women tied with men before, they now show lower numbers, indicating that in images classified as predominantly female, there was frequently at least one man. In contrast, there were clearly more images classified as predominantly male that had no female individuals at all. Because there is overlap in images, it does not make sense to add up percentages, but even seeing that 40.76 percent of all the images in the textbooks consist of male individuals in positions of power is enough to realize how dominant men are in these images. It is worth noting too that 88 percent of

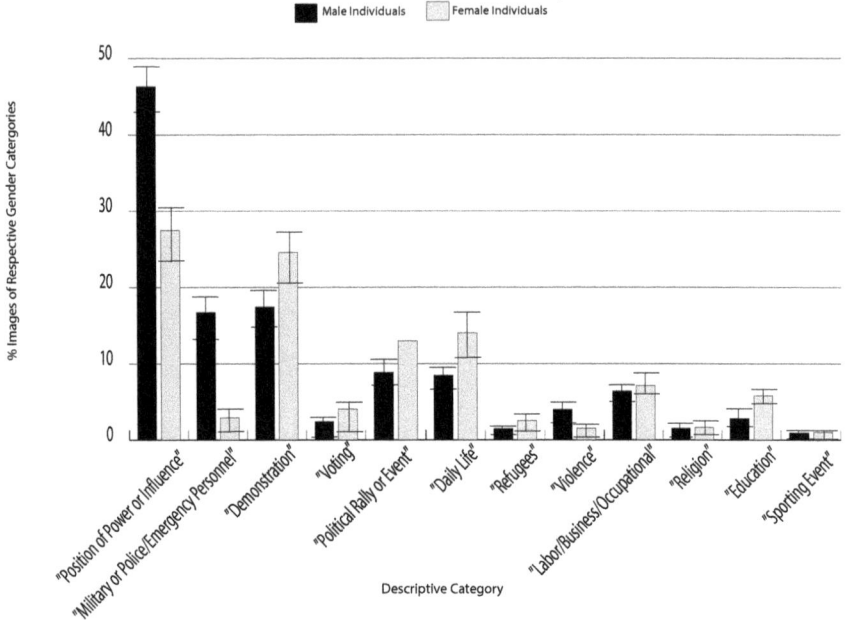

Fig. 3.2 Individuals' Share of Descriptive Categories.

the 1,715 images contain male individuals, while only 46 percent contain female individuals, so it is quite obvious that these textbooks show many more men than women.

Figure 3.2 displays the statistical analysis conducted on individual male and female coded data, displaying means and their 95 percent confidence intervals calculated from t tests.[2] Clearly, male individuals are present in significantly higher percentages than female individuals in the categories of position of power or influence, military, police, or emergency personnel, and violence. Female individuals are represented in significantly higher numbers than males in the categories of demonstration, political rally or event, daily life, and education. There is no significant difference between male and female individuals in the categories of voting, refugees, labor, business, and occupational, religion, and sporting event. Analyzing these images by the individual, rather than by the image as a whole, yields only slightly different conclusions. Men dominate over women in the same categories in which they dominated in the image-level analysis, but women have now been better represented in the political rally or event category. What this reveals is that even when considering female individuals surrounded by men, or vice versa—an approach that actually boosts numbers for each gender in categories in which they did not

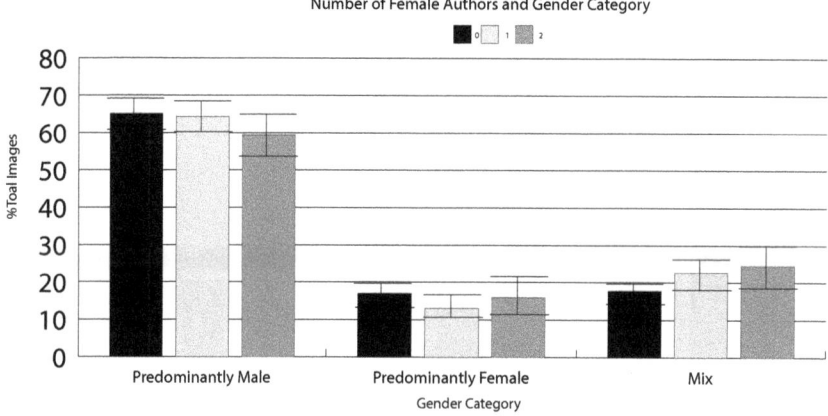

Fig. 3.3 Number of Female Authors and Gender Category.

perform well—the disparities between genders in categories remains largely the same.

In sum, the data show us that within categories, when looking at absolute numbers and raw data alone, images of men dominate almost across the board. When comparing the spread of shares within each gender category across descriptive categories, the picture changes slightly, with images of women dominating demonstration, daily life, education, and refugee or political rally or event, while males dominate position of power or influence, military, police, or emergency personnel, and violence. Voting, religion, labor, business, and occupational, and sporting events are the four categories where neither men nor women seem to dominate. The most common categories for men are position of power or influence, military, police, or emergency personnel, and demonstration, while the most common categories for women are position of power or influence, demonstration, and daily life. The mixed category was most prevalent in position of power or influence, demonstration, and political rally or event.

Finally, figures 3.3 and 3.4 summarize the statistical analysis of the gender of the author (and how many of them there were) compared to the predominance of male, female, or mixed in the images.[3] As there are no overlapping confidence intervals for any of the gender categories, no matter the number of male or female authors, it is evident that there is no significant difference between the sex of the author or the number of authors from either gender related to the predominance of males or females in the images. It is interesting to note, however, that not a single textbook was authored by a majority of women or exclusively by women, which itself reveals much about the gender gap in political science authorship. Table 3.5 provides the actual gender breakdown of authors for each textbook.

102 | *Gendered Representation in Political Science Textbooks*

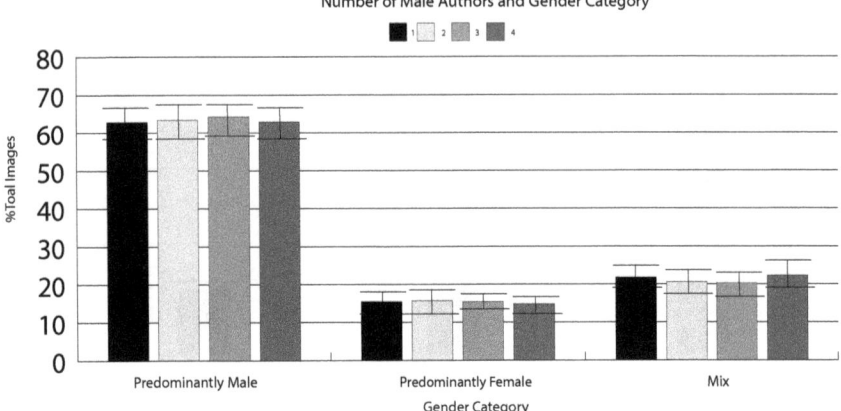

Fig. 3.4 Number of Male Authors and Gender Category.

Table 3.5. Gender Breakdown of Authors.

Authors	Publication Year	Subfield	Number of Authors	
			Female	Male
Dickovick and Eastwood	2013	Comparative	0	2
Hauss	2015	Comparative	0	1
O'Neil, Fields, and Share	2013	Comparative	0	3
O'Neil	2013	Comparative	0	1
Orvis and Drogus	2015	Comparative	1	1
Powell, Dalton, and Strøm	2012	Comparative	0	3
Samuels	2013	Comparative	0	1
Barbour and Wright	2014	American	1	1
Bianco and Canon	2015	American	0	2
Ginsberg et al.	2013	American	2	2
Kernell et al.	2014	American	1	3
Morone and Kersh	2014	American	0	2
Kraft and Furlong	2015	Public policy	0	2
Frieden, Lake, and Shultz	2013	International relations	0	3
Goldstein and Pevehouse	2011	International relations	0	2
Lamy et al.	2015	International relations	1	4
Nau	2015	International relations	0	1
Nye and Welch	2011	International relations	0	2
Robbins	2014	International relations	0	1
Roskin and Berry	2012	International relations	0	2

Interpretation and Discussion

Despite only partial empirical support for each of the four hypotheses, there are very interesting things going on in the selected textbooks. The following discussion will focus on how each descriptive category was represented and whether we, as political scientists writing these textbooks or presenting them to our students, have any control over how gender is represented in each of these categories.

Position of Power or Influence

Position of power and influence was for each gender category the most prevalent descriptive category. This is not surprising: it *is* political science, after all. When we make it our business to study the people in positions of power, then it stands to reason they will feature prominently in our textbooks. However, while this category took the greatest share of each of the gender categories, it is important to note that this was the one most heavily dominated by men. If we consider the research I presented earlier on the stereotype threat, then this is not something we should ignore. It may very well be the case that if female students are consistently confronted with males in positions of power, there might be some hindrance to their own pursuit of these positions. Given the insights of the stereotype threat literature, it appears that our discipline is guilty of perpetuating learning inequities, and looking at this problem from the perspective of political socialization scholarship, it is little wonder women continue to battle widespread societal expectations of not belonging in politics. If the very discipline teaching about politics is rife with gender biases in its depiction of the position of power, we might need to be much more proactive in our classroom discussions of this issue, if political equality is indeed our goal.

Here is where we should ask whether this is something any of us can actually control. Positions of power, especially for world leaders, are limited, and our textbooks are going to show those who are actually holding these positions. For example, if an American politics textbook has a chapter on the presidency, it is obvious, at least at the writing of this chapter, that there will be no images of female presidents. Similarly, if a summit of EU leaders is shown in a comparative or IR book, no political scientist can change the fact that these leaders are overwhelmingly male. In other words, images in position of power or influence may simply be reflecting the reality of the political world, and that reality is male-dominated. There are only so many female world leaders, and even if our textbooks show them all, there will undoubtedly be more men than women represented in positions of political power.

Yet, this does not necessarily mean we have no duty (or agency) to change this image, rooted in reality as it may be. We can at least present a different picture when possible, as many of the textbooks tried to do. For instance, instead of depicting presidents or prime ministers, where female representation might be scant, showing legislatures might make this easier. If a textbook shows the Bundestag, for example, it could make a point to include the female members of that legislative body instead of just male representatives. Even more importantly, the text that the images illustrate should explicitly discuss gender and patriarchy in politics, as many of the current textbooks do not. The conspicuous absence of women in political positions of power, historically and currently, presents a great teaching moment in our own classrooms.

Military, Police, or Emergency Personnel

When considering military, police, or emergency personnel, the situation becomes more complicated. Most of these images in the textbooks showed soldiers or police at protests or various political events. Quite frequently, these images were male, and this may be for reasons just discussed. If these positions are male-dominated in reality and the images included in textbooks attempt to capture a particular event, political scientists will clearly have limited options. Textbook authors have no control over the gender makeup of Brazil's police force or the US military fighting in Iraq. We must choose images that correspond with the events we are discussing, and images depicting gender equity may be unavailable. However, there were many images in the textbooks I reviewed that did include female police officers or military personnel; when images are not concerned with specific events, authors certainly have more options. And when people are shown in isolation, it is entirely possible for political scientists to choose images of female soldiers or police to balance out what might otherwise be a male-dominated category.

Violence

Violence was most often associated with images of soldiers engaged in warfare or with protesters fighting police (or police fighting protesters), and frequently overlapped with these categories. Taking this into account, it is not unusual that men would dominate this category, especially if they are the ones most often depicted in police or military positions. There is some nuance here that I did not explicitly measure when carrying out the research, and that concerns perpetrators and victims. Most images in this category depicted perpetrators, but it would still be interesting to see how men and women split between these. I would expect that men are often represented as perpetrators and women (and children) as victims. Here again, political scientists may come up against the need to represent the reality of a particular situation instead of depicting violence generally. If there is a choice, authors and editors might consciously balance this, but in a category like violence, it is more difficult to see what balancing gender representation might be good for. Perhaps it would help resolve the stereotype threat that male students are confronted with when violence is depicted. Perhaps it might also indicate that women can be just as violent as men. This is not to suggest that we should encourage female students to be more violent, but the stereotype that women are nonviolent or lack aggression might influence passivity in female gender roles. In other words, balancing this category could demonstrate to students that even if there is a societal predisposition for men to be more aggressive than women, males are not predetermined to be violent, nor are females predetermined to be passive.

Demonstration

The demonstration category proved to be an interesting one. Demonstrations, which I classified simply as any instance of protesting, often involved a combination of male and female participants. There were some images that depicted males or females only, and this largely depended on the content of the protest itself. Women's rights protesters, for example, were dominated by women, while farming protesters in the EU were exclusively men. But many of the others, such as those depicting Occupy Wall Street protests, various protests in front of the US Capitol and Supreme Court, or anticorruption demonstrations in Brazil and India, were very frequently a solid mix of men and women. Again, the way in which the data is interpreted will suggest whether this category is truly mixed or actually dominated by females. While this may be one of the most balanced categories in the textbooks, it is relevant to consider whether this reflects reality or is a conscious decision. If protests tend to be a political activity in which both men and women participate together at relatively equal rates, then it might be the case that authors would have to *try* to bias this category in one direction or the other.

Voting

Voting, like the demonstration category, contained mostly mixed images, with a slight bias toward women. Most often, these images depicted lines of voters at polling stations or politicians engaging in a vote in their chambers. The slight bias toward women could be reflected in several images depicting voting in the Global South, especially in India, where images frequently showed lines of largely women voting or women being taught how to use electronic voting devices. In other images, as one would expect in a world where men and women are equally enfranchised (especially in the West, where female turnout is high), the voting lines were almost always mixed with men and women. So, here again, we should wonder whether voting is an inherently mixed political activity and if the images simply reflect that reality.

Political Rally or Event

This category is another confounding one and, admittedly, the most problematic in terms of coding. I decided to separate rallies from protests because oftentimes they are an organized event, such as a party rally at a venue or a more public display of unity around an issue, such as on the National Mall in Washington, DC. Generally, the for and against distinction is what drove these two categories, with rallies being for a position or cause and protests usually against them. However, there were images that did not fit into these categories or any other category so easily, such as a mass citizenship ceremony for new citizens, and these I coded as events. However, "political event," more loosely approached, could really be anything from an election to a bill signing to a mundane speaking engagement. This proved to be a methodological difficulty throughout the process, and may need refinement. Nonetheless, this category often contained mixed images, and seemed to also lean more toward women. Like the demonstration and voting categories, the political event category remains gender-balanced, generally, and might be a reflection of a political activity that is already inherently mixed.

It is here, however, where we should start to consider why the bias toward women in these mixed activities is so prevalent. This might be a reflection of political reality around the world. Where women cannot or do not seek positions of power or influence or do not have a monopoly on force or power in the form of military or police, they can indeed engage in other political activities like voting, protesting, or attending political rallies and events. In this sense, the images of the last few categories might just be reflecting this reality: that men tend to have more power and control and women, therefore, engage in other types of political activities, a finding fully consistent with the political participation literature.

Labor, Business, and Occupational

Originally, I predicted that men would dominate this category, being depicted as high-powered businessmen, doctors, lawyers, or individuals engaged in physically demanding manual labor. The reality was that many images depicted women, especially in South and East Asia, working in places like textile factories or assembling electronics in factories. While the stereotypical male images I just described were present, these were balanced by the female images, and many images depicting work in these factories would show a mix of both men and women. Here again, textbook images may simply be reflecting the reality of the work force rather than gender stereotypes. If textbooks are looking to show images of labor in textile and electronics factories in South and East Asia, they are likely to find these images dominated by women, whether or not that is the goal.

Religion

These images were infrequent, and largely depicted both men and women engaged in various religious activities, like prayer or events related to religion. Most of these were depictions of Islam, such as men in prayer in Tehran, the Ayatollah, or women in Western Europe, particularly in France, wearing the *niqab* or *burqa* in protest of veil bans. As a result, while several images depicted only men in prayer, others depicted only women in protest, which balanced this category out and led to its statistical insignificance, even when comparing men and women to the mixed group. While there was no statistical significance between the three groups of male, female, or mixed, it should be noted that in this category, as well as a few others, the sample size remains far too small to make any meaningful conclusions from statistical analyses, and qualitative interpretations should similarly be approached with caution.

Sporting Events

Of all the categories examined, sporting events yielded the most surprising results. It is frequently the case that sporting events are associated strongly with men, whether as athletes or fans, but the few images that did depict sports in these textbooks actually contained quite a mix to the point that there was no significant difference between any gender category, even when looking at males and females only at the individual level. Much of this can be attributed to the fact that there were so few images related to this category, but the rest can probably be attributed to the types of events being depicted. More often than not, it was not athletes in action, but fans celebrating their team at a rally or impromptu gathering in the streets. Most of these depicted soccer and the World Cup and others showed celebrations for Olympic events. Given the global nature of these events, it might not be as surprising to see images capturing a solid mix of men and women involved in sports, since major global sporting events may attract a significant number of both men and women. As this category stands, given the insignificant results, there is, as with the religion category, little to suggest with regard to how gender is or should be represented, but there may be more going on here, which I address shortly.

Daily Life

Daily life is the category that women dominated at both the image and individual levels, and this is one aspect of textbook images authors may have much control over. Most of these images consisted of women at a market, taking care of children, engaged in everyday activities like riding public transit, cooking, enjoying friends or family, and so forth. Of all the categories analyzed, this one is probably the most stereotypically feminized, and this is one where it is often forgotten or ignored that men engage in daily life activities as well. While several images did depict men and women engaging in these activities together, it is well within the authors' power to change the gender balance in this category. Women might dominate this category many places in the world, but there are also places where males now play a large role in daily life, and images can more easily reflect this new reality.

Education

The education category, while showing no significant difference between males and females, is one that might require a little more unpacking to fully understand. The reason for the insignificant difference, aside from a small sample size, typically falls on depictions of students, who, in a classroom, are largely a strong mix of both men and women, at least in depictions of primary or secondary education. The original hypothesis for this category rested on the assumption that most images would show teachers, who would be predominantly female. In fact, this was the case in the large majority of images. Whenever teachers were presented, it was more likely they were female than male, but the students themselves were most often a mix of genders.

This is perhaps one category where the stereotype can easily be broken. While it may be the case that women are most often depicted as teachers in the classroom, there are obviously many men engaged in this profession as well. There may be differences when we move outside the Western perspective to areas where female educators may predominate; however it would not be difficult to include images that reflect this category as truly mixed, like the students themselves.

Refugees

The refugee category, while significantly gendered when looking at the image as a whole, revealed no significant difference for men and women at the individual level, owing largely to the fact that there were many images in this category that were categorized as mixed. On its surface, this might suggest that refugee images, while biased toward women to some degree, still have a strong balance of both genders. The issue is that the overwhelming majority of images classified as mixed showed women with their children, some of whom were male, thus generating more mixed images.

There is nuance here worth discussing. Certainly, as in most of these categories, the images are reflecting a sad reality. Perhaps these refugees tend to be largely women and their children because the warfare that caused their status in the first place has taken a large portion of the men out of the picture. Regardless, this depiction of women and children consistently shows them in the most vulnerable positions. Of course, depicting this can itself convey to students that while males are certainly affected by warfare and displacement, women bear the brunt of this reality, a realization that serves as another teachable moment.

Conclusion

My analysis suggests that addressing the gender bias in textbook images is much more difficult than simply improving the balance between images of men and women. While it is certainly the case that students may internalize the stereotypes and gender roles portrayed in the textbooks they are using, we must ask ourselves what our role is in addressing this bias. For political science—and indeed, for any social science discipline—the starting point is what the reality of the world around us is and whether we want to reflect it or try to change it, however incrementally. As was shown in this chapter, there is reality—such as male-domination in positions of power—and there is what we want reality to be. Should our role when assembling these texts and other classroom materials be to simply reflect the state of reality and show students that males dominate positions of power and women account for most refugees? Or do we want to correct for stereotypes and show that traditional gender roles can be broken? Is it always appropriate to include more men in a particular category or more women, and if it is, where and how should this be done? As I briefly mentioned earlier, perhaps it is better that we reflect reality in some categories and not in others. If women do suffer from being refugees, it may very well be better that we continue to use images that reflect this, as a way of raising awareness. In other categories, like military, police, or emergency personnel, we may be more effective in breaking gender stereotypes if we present more female images, even if the reality is that men dominate these positions. Whatever the options, we, as a profession, need to have this conversation, as our textbook images clearly contain gender biases.

It is important for educators to be aware of how men and women are depicted in the textbooks they are using, how these images relate to reality, and how these textbooks can be used in the classroom to engage students in critical discussions of gender in politics and political science. There are two approaches to addressing this bias. The first is from the perspective of the textbook author, who can choose which images to include and how to balance out categories. The second is from the perspective of the educator, whose responsibility it is to engage students in critical discussions about what these images depict. For positions of power, for example, educators may want to discuss with their students why males dominate this category so heavily. The textbooks might just reflect reality in this category, but a discussion on *why* this is the reality would bring gender-forward thinking into the classroom, a major theme of this entire book.

In addition to discussing why one gender dominates certain categories, educators may want to discuss why there was a gender balance in some categories, like labor or sports. Are there value judgments to be made here, such as whether it is good or bad that these categories are mixed? Are there deeper mechanisms at work, including governmental policies guaranteeing at least some degree of equality in the workplace or athletic activities, that provide us with this mixed result?

On the other hand, when women were depicted in the workplace, they were often depicted as working in textile or electronic industries in East, South, and Southeast Asia. Educators can use these depictions of working women to start discussions on poverty and economics in these regions. For sports, which in my analysis was a mixed category, educators might point out that while images depict fans as mixed crowds, the way they depict athletes remains male-dominated. This can lead to a discussion on gender in society and the roles we so often assign to one another. In other words, attempting to make all categories mixed and calling it a day is not at all what this chapter suggests as a solution to gender bias in our textbooks. The depiction of gender must go beyond the books themselves. Gender must be brought into discussions in the classroom to determine why some categories might be dominated by one gender, why others are mixed, and, importantly, what the depictions *ought* to be, especially given the reality of gender roles across societies.

Ultimately, I do not claim to know what the best or most appropriate approaches are when designing our textbooks. Much of what is right or good regarding this issue depends on what the authors are trying to depict and what educators in the classroom wish to discuss with their students. It might be good to show more women in positions of power, but it may also be good to simply reflect the male-dominated world of politics and discuss how this could change. There is currently little to no research on the effect political images have on males and females and their perceived gender roles. While analyzing each descriptive category I identified situations where authors might have control over how males and females are represented in images; whether they should exercise that control is beyond the scope of this chapter.

The goal of this research has been to examine the portrayal of gender roles and stereotypes in our textbooks; examine how this might affect our students and, ultimately, the entire discipline of political science; and provide some possible suggestions toward addressing gender bias, both in our textbooks and through critical classroom discussions. This study identifies serious barriers that still exist in our classrooms and have implications for learning through the deleterious effects of the stereotype threat; political socialization; and ultimately the very essence of democratic and equitable political participation.

There are many remaining questions that call for further research. While I mused a little as to why bias might exist in certain categories, establishing causality is another project that would prove useful. Attempting to discover if gender depictions differ by subfield would be another interesting research project, and simply adding more textbooks into the research would yield a richer dataset. As mentioned earlier in the chapter, comparing older textbooks in the discipline to newer ones may reveal interesting trends in gender representation. It would be useful for political scientists to take this research and put forward some strong normative claims about how we ought to represent genders in these categories and how this can be accomplished. Much more research is also needed on how political images actually affect the people who see them. While the literature on stereotypes and student performance reviewed above demonstrates a clear link between what readers see in images and how they define their roles in society, it is far less clear how images affect the way readers construct their own roles and the roles of others in the context of political participation.

While my research was concerned with political science, this issue goes well beyond the discipline. As the research presented at the beginning of this chapter shows, the effects of gender stereotypes and gender roles presented in textbooks and classroom are very real problems for our students and are not confined to one discipline. Whether in the social sciences, the humanities, or the natural sciences, we academics, who create the material our students consume, need to be aware of what we include and how it is presented and discussed. Research examining textbook images and textual content has been done within various disciplines, but the process should continue and expand to even more. Identifying and correcting for our gender biases is very much an interdisciplinary project.

Finally, textbook images remain only a small fraction of the topic that is gender in teaching and learning in political science. As other chapters in this book demonstrate, gender affects how students interact in their classrooms, both with one another and their instructors, how instructors teach or present themselves, and how academics conduct themselves in a research environment. This research raises questions about how to make education in political science inclusive, with a focus on whether the discipline is truly striving to include genders equally. To achieve this goal, the discipline must guarantee more equal distributions of learning opportunities to male and female students, recognize and value gender differences and what they bring to political science and politics, and create more opportunities for traditionally marginalized groups in the discipline, like women, to identify and solve instances of exclusion (Waitoller and Artiles 2013). When educators seek to address gender bias in political science, whether by removing bias in textbook images, discussing those biases in the classroom, or through other methods, maintaining inclusive education should serve as a guiding principle. Meeting the three goals of inclusive education listed above might require a mix of both corrective gender representation in textbooks and classroom discussion, rather than embracing just one of the two approaches. However, regardless of whether textbook authors choose to represent the reality of gender bias or correct for that bias through careful image selection, the instructor in the classroom has an opportunity and perhaps a duty to point out political gender bias when and where it is encountered, compelling students to engage with an important threshold concept that can lead to increased inclusivity in the classroom, the discipline, and politics as a whole.

This chapter identifies gender bias and stereotypes in political science textbooks, but I do not claim that solving this issue is a panacea for gender issues in the discipline. It alone will not solve wider problems. It may, however, help, especially if these gender issues are brought up directly in the classroom in a critical discussion with students. If we become more conscious of the images that we include in our textbooks and work these images into our gender discussions while teaching, we can perhaps prevent at least some of the problems that might arise over time for students and instructors within and outside of the discipline and gradually work toward greater inclusivity and solutions to the gender biases that plague all disciplines at every level.

Acknowledgements

I thank Dr. Mike Salamone for statistical and aesthetic guidance throughout the research process.

DANIEL MUELLER is a PhD candidate at Washington State University in the School of Politics, Philosophy, and Public Affairs.

Notes

1. Table 5 lists each of these books with authors, publication date, and corresponding subfield.
2. The total here is 2,294 instances of both male and female individuals, but this is because there are several images which contain both men and women, so the overlap causes a total beyond the n of 1,715. There were 1,509 images which contained male individuals and 785 with female individuals. Each bar in figure 3.2 represents a portion of its respective individual gender category. In other words, the first bar indicates that 46 percent of the 1,509 images containing male individuals showed these males in positions of power or influence.
3. The values shown are means as percentages with their 95 percent confidence intervals. The first bar in figure 3.3, for example, shows that 65 percent of the images in books with no female authors were predominantly male.

References

American Political Science Association. (APSA). 2013. *Snapshot: Three Years of Political Science Doctoral Student Placement.* www.apsanet.org/files/Snapshot%20Placement%202009%202012_UPDATED%2019%20JUNE.pdf.

Bahman, Masoumeh, and Ali Rahimi. 2010. "Gender Representation in EFL Material: An Analysis of English Textbooks of Iranian High Schools." *Procedia—Social and Behavioral Sciences* 9: 273–77.

Barbour, Christine, and Gerald C. Wright Jr. 2014. *Keeping the Republic: Power and Citizenship in American Politics.* 6th ed. Los Angeles: CQ Press.

Bazler, Judith A., and Doris A. Simonis. 2006. "Are High School Chemistry Textbooks Gender Fair?" *Journal of Research in Science Teaching* 28 (4): 353–62.

Bianco, William T., and David T. Canon. 2015. *American Politics Today.* 4th ed. New York: W. W. Norton & Company.

Breuning, Marijke, and Kathryn Sanders. 2007. "Gender and Journal Authorship in Eight Prestigious Political Science Journals." *PS: Political Science and Politics* 40 (2): 347–51.

Davies, Paul G., Steven J. Spencer, and Claude M. Steele. 2005. "Clearing the Air: Identity Safety Moderates the Effects of Stereotype Threat on Women's Leadership Aspirations." *Journal of Personality and Social Psychology* 88 (2): 276–87.

Dickovick, J. Tyler, and Jonathan Eastwood. 2013. *Comparative Politics: Integrating Theories, Methods, and Cases.* Oxford, UK: Oxford University Press.

Eaton, Asia, and Suzanna Rose. 2013. "The Application of Biological, Evolutionary, and Sociocultural Frameworks to Issues of Gender in Introductory Psychology Textbooks." *Sex Roles* 69 (9–10): 536–42.

Foulds, Kim. 2013. "The Continua of Identities in Postcolonial Curricula: Kenyan Students' Perceptions of Gender in School Textbooks." *International Journal of Educational Development* 33 (2): 165–74.

Frieden, Jeffry A., David A. Lake, and Kenneth A. Schultz. 2013. *World Politics: Interests, Interactions, Institutions.* 2nd ed. New York: W. W. Norton & Company.

Ginsberg, Benjamin, Theodore J. Lowi, Margaret Weir, and Caroline J. Tolbert. 2013. *We the People.* 9th ed. New York: W. W. Norton & Company.

Goldstein, Joshua S., and Jon C. Pevehouse. 2011. *International Relations.* 5th ed. Boston: Longman.

Good, Jessica J., Julie A. Woodzicka, and Lylan C. Wingfield. 2010. "The Effects of Gender Stereotypic and Counter-Stereotypic Textbook Images on Science Performance." *The Journal of Social Psychology* 150 (2): 132–47.

Hauss, Charles. 2015. *Comparative Politics: Domestic Responses to Global Challenges.* Stamford, CT: Cengage Learning.

Kantola, Johanna. 2008. "'Why Do All the Women Disappear?' Gendering Processes in a Political Science Department." *Gender, Work, and Organization* 15 (2): 202–25.

Keller, Johannes, and Dirk Dauenheimer. 2003. "Stereotype Threat in the Classroom: Dejection Mediates the Disrupting Threat Effect on Women's Math Performance." *Personality and Social Psychology Bulletin* 29: 371–81.

Kernell, Samuel, Gary C. Jacobson, Thad Kousser, and Lynn Vavreck. 2014. *The Logic of American Politics.* 6th ed. Los Angeles: CQ Press.

Kraft, Michael E., and Scott R. Furlong. 2015. *Public Policy: Politics, Analysis, and Alternatives*. 5th ed. Los Angeles: CQ Press.

Lamy, Steven L., John S. Masker, John Baylis, Steve Smith, and Patricia Owens. 2015. *Introduction to Global Politics*. 3rd ed. New York: Oxford University Press.

Lee, Jackie, and Peter Collins. 2008. "Gender Voices in Hong Kong English Textbooks—Some Past and Current Practices." *Sex Roles* 59 (1): 127–37.

Lindroos, Kia, Linda Cardinal, Marian Sawer, and Mathieu St-Laurent. 2014. *IPSA Gender Monitoring Report 2013*. Montreal: International Political Science Association. www.ipsa.org/sites/default/files/gender_monitoring_report_2013.pdf.

Maliniak, Daniel, Ryan Powers, and Barbara F. Walter. 2013. "The Gender Citation Gap in International Relations." *International Organization* 67 (4): 889–922.

Marx Ferree, Myra, and Elaine J. Hall. 1990. "Visual Images of American Society: Gender and Race in Introductory Sociology Textbooks." *Gender and Society* 4 (4): 500–533.

Mathews, A. Lanethea, and Kristi Andersen. 2001. "A Gender Gap in Publishing? Women's Representation in Edited Political Science Books." *Political Science Politics* 34 (1): 143–47.

Meyer, Jan, and Ray Land. 2003. "Threshold Concepts and Troublesome Knowledge: Linkages to Ways of Thinking and Practicing within the Disciplines." In *Improving Student Learning: Theory and Practice—Ten Years On*, edited by C. Rust, 412–24. Oxford: Oxford Centre for Staff and Learning Development.

———. 2005. "Threshold Concepts and Troublesome Knowledge (2): Epistemological Considerations and a Conceptual Framework for Teaching and Learning." *Higher Education* 49 (3): 373–88.

Morone, James A., and Rogan Kersh. 2014. *By the People: Debating American Government*. New York: Oxford University Press.

Nau, Henry R. 2015. *Perspectives on International Relations: Power, Institutions, and Ideas*. 4th ed. Los Angeles: CQ Press.

Neuendorf, Kimberly A. 2002. *The Content Analysis Guidebook*. Thousand Oaks, CA: Sage Publications.

Nye, Joseph N., and David A. Welch. 2011. *Understanding Global Conflict and Cooperation: An Introduction to Theory and History*. 8th ed. Boston: Longman.

O'Brien, Laurie T., and Christian S. Crandall. 2003. "Stereotype Threat and Arousal: Effects on Women's Math Performance." *Personality and Social Psychology Bulletin* 29 (6): 782–89.

O'Neil, Patrick H. 2013. *Essentials of Comparative Politics*. 4th ed. New York: W. W. Norton & Company.

O'Neil, Patrick H., Karl Fields, and Don Share. 2013. *Cases in Comparative Politics*. 4th ed. New York: W. W. Norton & Company.

Orvis, Stephen, and Carol Ann Drogus. 2015. *Introducing Comparative Politics: Concepts and Cases in Context*. 3rd ed. Los Angeles: CQ Press.

Powell, G. Bingham, Russell J. Dalton, and Kaare Strøm. 2012. *Comparative Politics Today: A World View*. 10th ed. Boston: Longman.

Rifkin, Benjamin. 1998. "Gender Representation in Foreign Language Textbooks: A Case Study of Textbooks of Russian." *Modern Language Journal* 82 (2): 217–36.

Robbins, Richard H. 2014. *Global Problems and the Culture of Capitalism*. 6th ed. Boston: Pearson.

Roskin, Michael G., and Nicholas O. Berry. 2012. *IR: The New World of International Relations*. 9th ed. Boston: Longman.

Samuels, David J. 2013. *Comparative Politics*. Boston: Pearson Education.
Sheldon, Jane P. 2004. "Gender Stereotypes in Educational Software for Young Children." *Sex Roles* 51 (7–8): 433–44.
Smith, Jessi, and Paul White. 2002. "An Examination of Implicitly Activated, Explicitly Activated, and Nullified Stereotypes on Mathematical Performance: It's Not Just a Woman's Issue." *Sex Roles* 47 (3): 179–91.
Spencer, Steven J., Claude M. Steele, and Diane M. Quin. 1999. "Stereotype Threat and Women's Math Performance." *Journal of Experimental Social Psychology* 35 (1): 4–28.
Sumalatha, K., and D. Ramakrishnaiah. 2004. "Sex Bias in Secondary School Social Studies Textbooks: A Case Study in India." *American Journal of Applied Sciences* 1 (1): 62–63.
Táboas-Pais, Maria, and Ana Rey-Cao. 2012. "Gender Differences in Physical Education Textbooks in Spain: A Content Analysis of Photographs." *Sex Roles* 67 (7–8): 389–402.
Timperley, Claire. 2013. "Women in the Academy: Key Studies on Gender in Political Science." *Political Science* 65 (1): 84–104.
Tolleson-Rinehart, Sue, and Susan J. Carroll. 2006. "'Far from Ideal': The Gender Politics of Political Science." *American Political Science Review* 100 (4): 507–13.
Waitoller, Federico R., and Alfredo J. Artiles. 2013. "A Decade of Professional Development Research for Inclusive Education: A Critical Review and Notes for a Research Program." *Review of Educational Research* 83 (3): 319–56.
Yanowitz, Karen L., and Keven J. Weathers. 2004. "Do Boys and Girls Act Differently in the Classroom? A Content Analysis of Student Characters in Educational Psychology Textbooks." *Sex Roles* 51 (1–2): 101–7.

4 Gender Mainstreaming and Political Science Teaching in New Zealand: Still a Work in Progress

Jennifer Curtin

THE CONCEPT AND practice of gender mainstreaming, while contested, have been taken up as potentially transformative mechanisms for the promotion of gender equality and for "making visible the gendered nature of assumptions, processes, and outcomes" (Walby 2005, 321; Bacchi and Eveline 2003). In chapter 1, Ingrid Bego provided a comprehensive review of the history of gender mainstreaming globally, but it is also useful to recognize that before Beijing, feminists in some countries had made considerable strides integrating gender into the policy making environment. Australia was a world leader in the pursuit of gender mainstreaming through its "femocrat" (feminist bureaucrat) strategy in the early 1970s. New Zealand followed suit in the mid-1980s, creating a gender analysis tool to support government agencies' consideration of gender in policy formulation, with a dedicated Ministry of Women's Affairs to guide and support this work (Curtin and Teghtsoonian 2010; Sawer 1990).

It is unsurprising that the concept of gender mainstreaming might be considered transferable to teaching political science, where masculine understandings of power, institutions, and the international abound. Arguably, the early influence of femocrats in New Zealand had the potential to result in a contagion effect on the teaching of political science in New Zealand directly, or through the Women's and Gender Studies (WGS) departments that had been established in the 1970s and 1980s. We raise this possibility because the discipline in New Zealand appears at first glance to be fluid and flexible and informed by an eclectic range of epistemological, theoretical, and methodological traditions. Unlike its United States counterpart, there has not been a heavy emphasis on large *N* studies and game theoretic approaches in either the research or teaching of political science in New Zealand. Indeed, the *science* in political science has been the subject of some debate in New Zealand and only three out of eight departments currently include the term in their title. Nor is there a discipline-wide agreement as to what must be offered as foundational courses in politics and international relations.

Thus, the discipline in New Zealand might be seen to epitomize the "messy center," albeit at the geographical margins of the political science teaching and research community, presenting itself as potentially open to gender mainstreaming and integrating gender as a threshold concept.

Yet there is evidence to suggest that the study of politics in New Zealand has been slow to recognize the contributions of women as political actors and scholars, and even slower to engage with gender as an analytical category of import or feminism as an analytical lens. The resistance is not unique to New Zealand, as is evidenced by previous chapters in this book. It does suggest that feminist disruptions to the discipline may prove difficult to embed even in a geographical region where strict disciplinary norms are absent and where the US political science hegemony of the scientific for studying the political is less entrenched. These questions arise then: What can the New Zealand case tell us about institutional ambivalence to women's presence as faculty and to the inclusion of gendered content in the curriculum? Does the case of New Zealand reveal that the success of gender mainstreaming is dependent on certain conditions, in a way that is similar to gender mainstreaming in the bureaucracy? For example, to what extent does it require political and bureaucratic will, an activist classroom pedagogy, the revival of gender studies' programs and the involvement of feminist entrepreneurs or change agents? And how does gender mainstreaming take account of intersectionality, indigeneity, and diversity?

These questions are addressed through a brief introduction to politics in New Zealand followed by an investigation of three interrelated dimensions of teaching and learning; first, the extent to which political science departments nationally incorporate gender across the curriculum; second, where gender can be found in core texts and in scholarship on New Zealand political science; and third, whether the discipline nationally is normalizing women's presence in the discipline as faculty. The final section concludes with an analysis of whether the conditions and capacities of the political science discipline are sufficient to produce a more substantial and critically aware turn toward gender mainstreaming in teaching and learning.

Political Science in New Zealand

The first political science department in New Zealand was established in 1939 at Victoria University College, Wellington. Courses were offered in the areas of history of political thought, comparative political institutions, and modern democracies. As staff numbers grew, courses were expanded to cover the study of parliament, New Zealand politics, and international relations. Over the next thirty years, political science departments were established in other universities around the country. Although the nature of the discipline in New Zealand has not been fixed over time, some general trends are apparent. From the 1950s, a growing scholarly interest in elections, government formation, and the voting behavior of New Zealanders developed, as was the case elsewhere. Political theory and the history of political thought have an established presence, while comparative politics, media politics, Māori politics, and international relations (and its various theoretical traditions) have also been well-represented, as evidenced by scholarship published in the New Zealand journal *Political Science*. However, articles on or by women, historically at least, have appeared less frequently (Curtin 2013).

Despite less of a focus on the scientific, in recent times, the evaluation of New Zealand political scientists' research outputs has become more explicitly tied to citation levels, the relative rankings of the discipline's journals, and assessment through peer review. That it is the quantitatively oriented US journals which feature at the top of the international impact factor lists—and which remain male-dominated—is a point not lost on New Zealand academics, with much energy spent arguing for greater domestic recognition of regional and thematically oriented journals (Curtin 2013).

The eight major public universities in New Zealand are research-led teaching institutions, meaning the research of faculty members feeds into curriculum design. In practice, although students are required to complete a certain number of subjects and points at each level to obtain a bachelor's degree majoring in political science, there is seldom a requirement for students to undertake core or foundational courses in the discipline or in methodology. As such, the discipline in New Zealand has not been bound by the same rules or norms as the United States in terms of what constitutes political science. For example, the dominant subfields are more loosely applied and American politics is unlikely to feature except as a single upper level undergraduate course or as a case study of "presidentialism" within a more generic comparative politics course. By contrast, New Zealand politics sits alongside international relations and political theory as a common specialization. Few politics departments teach methodology at the undergraduate level, while students who wish to pursue quantitative methods may elect to do so at upper levels, often by taking courses in other disciplines such as sociology.

We might imagine, then, that political science as taught in New Zealand could, theoretically at least, be amenable or open to feminist thought, pedagogical methods, and gender mainstreaming because of its eclectic traditions and pluralistic approaches. However, the discipline is comparatively small in size (less than one hundred tenured academic staff) and, as a consequence, the New Zealand Political Studies Association has limited resources to monitor, evaluate, and instigate gender and diversity specific measures similar to those taken up by its US counterpart.[1] More generally, the New Zealand tertiary education sector is largely self-regulated, and allows individual institutions to set their own curriculum. This degree of autonomy is valued, but it also means there is little likelihood of implementing an external requirement to mainstream gender into the curriculum.[2]

Nevertheless, the political sphere in New Zealand has a long history of being a site of feminist engagement. New Zealand women were the first in the world to win the national right to vote in 1893, although women were voting in local government earlier that this (from 1867), and New Zealand was the first country in the British Empire to see a woman mayor elected in 1894. It was not uncommon for early feminist activists to view the state as a provider of welfare and social services, and feminist demands on the state continued throughout the twentieth century in a range of forms: indigenous and imported; pragmatic and radical (Curtin 2015). Women's representation reached 21 percent in the national parliament by 1993—a comparatively unusual political feat. Since then, two women have become Prime Minister, and the national election of 2011 was the first time since 1993 that neither of the two major parties was headed by a woman. Thus, by their presence alone, women as political actors are a subject worthy of study.

How best to incorporate gender politics and feminism into the teaching of core political science and international relations at the undergraduate level has long been an important focus for feminist politics' scholars in New Zealand, in part a result of watching and learning from their feminist sisters in Australia (Sawer and Curtin 2016). The Australian Political Science Association Women's Caucus was pioneering in its efforts to mainstream gender content, sponsoring a resolution at the Association's Annual General Meeting in 1981 that the study of women should be incorporated in all politics courses. The motion was passed, and various audits of course guides and textbooks followed, demonstrating mixed results (Sawer 2004).

As noted elsewhere in this volume, in 1991 the American Political Science Association (APSA) argued that the practice of gender mainstreaming was necessary to reform the undergraduate political science curriculum. However, while there exists good data on diversity of faculty in the United States, there has been little systematic data collected on the implementation of building gender as a threshold concept across the subfields, there or elsewhere around the world. This has made it difficult to assess whether departments have developed mechanisms and guidelines to support the integration of gendered content (Cassese, Bos, and Duncan 2012). Papers presented at a one-day International Political Science Association World Congress workshop in 2012 indicated that there had been little progress in terms of mainstreaming gender in teaching across the discipline.

In New Zealand, several women established an informal women's caucus in 1986, which has continued to meet during the New Zealand Political Studies Association (NZPSA) annual conference. These pioneers expressed concern about the discipline's lack of openness to feminist-informed research and teaching in politics. The disestablishment the year before of a position where the female incumbent had taught feminist political theory and gender politics reinforced the sense that a women's network within the association was necessary for survival (Sawer and Curtin 2016). Over time, the caucus has helped to build a sense of solidarity among women political science scholars and prompted the establishment of the *Women Talking Politics* publication, which continues to this day (https://nzpsa.co.nz/women-talking-politics/). However, there is no record of any formal resolutions being brought to the NZPSA executive regarding the need to mainstream gender in the teaching of the discipline. Recent workshops and publications have focused primarily on the status of women within the discipline and the opportunities and barriers facing female postgraduate and doctoral scholars looking to enter the academy (Al Janabi, McMillan, and Lam 2014).

A website survey of the first-year course summaries in political science and international relations was undertaken in June 2012 (Curtin 2013). Of the twenty-five first-year courses on offer across eight New Zealand universities, only three of the summary course descriptions visible to students online made any mention of gender, sexuality, or women; two of these were courses taught by women, and two were political theory courses. No mention of gender as an analytical construct or feminism as a social movement or ideology appeared in any of the summaries outlining the introductory courses on New Zealand politics. Three years later, the picture remained gloomy. Of the five stand-alone political science programs in New Zealand in 2015, only two had first year courses featuring gender or feminism (three courses in total), two in political theory and one in international relations.[3] At the upper undergraduate level, several programs offered distinct courses in feminist theory, gender politics, and international relations, while a few also included references to feminist ideas in courses dedicated to political theory, development studies, and global politics. However, no area or regional studies course summaries included references to women or gender, and of the two international relations theory courses dedicated to the study of critical perspectives neither included a mention of feminist international relations. In total, only 10 percent of all upper level undergraduate course summaries offered in these five New Zealand political science programs referred to gender, feminism, or women and politics.[4]

Questions about gender mainstreaming the political science curriculum go beyond traditional classroom-based teaching. In New Zealand, there is an increasing demand for students to exhibit employability as a graduate attribute, and this has become a key objective laid out in the government's tertiary education strategy (Ministry of Business, Innovation, and Education (MBIE) 2014). To date there has been no explicit gender analysis of what might count as or represent employability, but there is a general consensus that service-learning and for-credit internships should feature in political science programs. A long-standing graduate level parliamentary internship is offered at one university, potentially providing students with the opportunity to pursue a feminist or gendered directed study. However, the course guide does not provide incoming students with cues as to whether a gendered analysis would be appropriate. Two other universities offer for-credit internships (one at undergraduate and the other at graduate level), and placements include local government offices and organizations from the private and nonprofit sectors. Although not advertised to students as such, one internship course includes three feminist organizations that host interns who work on gendered audits of contemporary public policy. In summary, while several individual academics have sought to include gendered perspectives in their teaching, this is by no means common practice.

Reviewing Students' Source Materials

Textbooks are an important indicator of the state of gender mainstreaming in the discipline, given that faculty will select materials that reflect their preferred mode of teaching core ideas and empirical cases. These preferences convey to the students, particularly those in their first year, the theories, evidence, and methods that "should" be given prominence immediately and in their future studies and research decisions. While no comprehensive gender analysis of New Zealand political science textbooks exists, two texts were included in the Australasian textbook review undertaken by Elizabeth Harman and Janice Dudley in 1996 (Dudley and Palmieri 1999). At that time, no books were rated highly in terms of their discussion of the women's movement, feminist theory, and women's political representation. Richard Mulgan's (1994) book *Politics in New Zealand* fared better than most (and was used by three of the six New Zealand departments surveyed in 2012), with his chapter on the composition of New Zealand society, including some discussion of gender as a distinctive and significant cleavage (Dudley and Palmieri, 1999). Mulgan identified competing feminist perspectives and referred to women's issues and their political "interests."

Since this time, the presence of chapters on women, gender, and feminism has fluctuated. Early editions of Raymond Miller's *New Zealand Government and Politics* featured a range of chapters authored by women on the women's movement, feminist ideology, and women and politics, but over time, these have disappeared (Roper 2011). Indeed, the index to the 2010 edition of the textbook features fewer references to feminism, gender, or women than does Mulgan's earlier text. By contrast, as the subject of gender politics has decreased in visibility, the number of women contributors to the Miller volume has levelled out; 28 percent in the fifth edition (Miller 2010) compared to 29 percent in the fourth edition (Miller 2006). In 2015, a new edition of the volume was released with a new (female) editor (Hayward 2015). Two chapters are dedicated to feminism and the women's movement and women make up 33 percent of authors. However, if the objective is to go beyond token chapters or pages on women or feminism—recognizing gender as a construct as well as a "cleavage" and feminism as offering critical perspectives on traditional understandings of ideas, interests, and institutions—then current texts do not measure up. Although the Treaty of Waitangi and issues related to Māori have a strong presence, with three pages dedicated to Māori women; discussion of gender, feminism, and women is limited to thirty pages scattered through the six hundred plus page volume. Even at the most minimal level, there is no reference to the gender gap in voting behavior, the gendered impact of electoral system choice, the reasons why women might be underrepresented in parliament and cabinet, nor to the contemporary debates around gender quotas that have featured in the public domain in New Zealand in recent years.

Another recent addition to the New Zealand textbook scene is a single-authored work titled *Democracy in New Zealand* (Miller 2015). The book provides figures on women's representation, and Māori representation is discussed throughout, but there is only one mention of feminism and no discussion of gender. This is despite the plethora of New Zealand feminist political science scholarship published over the past fifteen years, little of which features in Miller's 2015 volume (Curtin 2015). For example, unlike in Mulgan's work, there is no discussion of gender as a social cleavage and its relationship to gender gaps in voting behavior, no mention of the claims made on the state by feminist organizations in civil society over time, and gender differences in parliamentary and executive representation are described but not interrogated. The reference list includes few of the well-known New Zealand feminist political science scholars who have addressed many of the points above and more.[5] Inclusion of these topics would amount to a minimal level of gender mainstreaming in the study of domestic politics. That such analysis does not appear to any significant extent in the primary textbooks set for first year courses in New Zealand politics is stark evidence that gender as a threshold concept remains at the margins of the discipline.[6]

The textbooks and readers utilized in first year international relations, comparative politics, and political theory courses are varied in terms of their attention to gender mainstreaming and critical feminist perspectives. Feminist international relations is taken up explicitly in one department's first year course and is linked to a textbook that is authored by two female scholars. The text focuses less on traditional international relations and more on contemporary global questions where the answers invoke attention to gender (although, as with the texts above, the subject index offers few clues to readers that gender, feminism, or women are significant subjects in their own right, with only twenty relevant pages quoted). Political theory readers are more inclusive of women, often including reference to Mary Astell, Mary Wollstonecraft, and other more contemporary feminist theorists. However, there is a strong correlation between feminist political theory teachers and the degree of gender mainstreaming in the curriculum.[7] A similar correlation is evident in the teaching of international relations, New Zealand, and comparative politics.

A discussion of the presence of female and feminist faculty as teachers features in more detail below. Before turning to this, it is important to investigate two more "authorities" that students access in learning the discipline. The first are the discipline's journals and the second are the now-popular handbooks that provide relatively short summations of the major themes, methods, and subfields, directing students and other readers to further sources. These handbooks are an international publishing phenomena, and reach New Zealand through their availability to students online and in libraries.

The profession in New Zealand prides itself on being located in a university environment where research-based teaching is the norm; teaching-track positions are rare in the eight leading universities, in part because of the government's research-funding framework, but also because of the requirement to supervise postgraduate research students at both the master's and doctorate level.[8] Theoretically, good teaching that is research-led would look to contemporary scholarship being produced by political scientists, feminist and otherwise, local and international, for inclusion in the curriculum.

In New Zealand, from the outset, the discipline has been supported by a peer reviewed journal. *Political Science*, while not a highly ranked international journal, publishes quality research and conveys an image of the profession, identifying to the readers and students what constitutes good and valuable political science (Moloney 1998, 5). Elsewhere I have provided a comprehensive gender audit of the journal; here it is sufficient to note a few key points (Curtin 2013). Prior to the 1980s, women constituted a small percentage of authors (on average around 6 percent prior to 1979, replicating their presence in the discipline around that time); commissioned manuscripts for special issues rarely featured women authors; and no women were appointed to the first editorial advisory board established in 1975, despite that year being designated International Women's Year by the United Nations.[9] Thus, from its outset, the journal reflected and reinforced the perception of New Zealand political science as a predominantly male community.[10] Since the 1980s, there has been an incremental increase in the number of gendered articles—although this is partly a result of four special issues either dedicated to women and politics or edited by women—indicating that gender mainstreaming is yet to be demonstrated through the journal's contents. *Political Science*'s record on reviewing books on women, feminism, or gender has proved less positive until very recently. Since the 1970s, research on the women's movement, feminist political theory and methodologies, gendered institutions, and gender as a central analytical construct in understanding political power (as opposed to sex as a variable in electoral behavior) has become increasingly relevant to a large number of primarily women political scientists in their teaching and research.[11] For example, the journal *Politics & Gender*, launched in 2005 and endorsed by the APSA, was ranked sixth among the 139 political science journals included in the Institute for Scientific Information (ISI) ranking of journals by impact factor in 2010.

This suggests that research scholarship on feminist politics, theory, and international relations is thriving as a subfield. Less clear is the extent to which mainstream political science engages with this research. In the New Zealand case, Moloney was being optimistic when he noted that the special issue of *Political Science* on "Women and Politics in New Zealand" (Catt and McLeay 1993) signaled the importance with which gender is regarded in the academy in New Zealand (Moloney 1998, 36). The visual representation of the journal's contents produced by Tan, Buck, and Schrader (2009) underscores this point. Although the term "women" appears in the word cloud portraits between 1980 and 1989 and again, alongside the word "gender" between 1990 and 1999, (periods that featured special issues), neither "women" nor "gender" appeared in the cloud portrait for the period between 2000 and 2008 (Curtin 2013, 79).

In the United States, audits of disciplinary journals indicate a tendency to separate out research on women from "core" political science research, labeling it as "women's studies" or categorizing the subject as "miscellaneous" (Miller, Tien, and Peebler 1996). Thus, the categorization of political science into traditional subfields, perhaps unwittingly, has reinforced the trend for political scientists to ignore the contribution of feminist political science. It also conveys a negative message to students, undergraduate and graduate, who work on politics and gender or feminism—and the associated methodological and epistemological tools on offer—that such scholarship is marginal to the broader direction and development of the discipline.

A cursory review of the *Oxford Handbook of Political Science* indicates a similar ambivalence. In his introduction to the state of the discipline, Robert Goodin argues that political science is primarily interested in how power can and should be exercised and constrained, giving particular emphasis to checks and balances, separation of power, political accountability, and political competition. Within the discipline, practitioners recognize a set of "shared codes, traditions, standards, and practices" that enable us to channel our collective energies and undertake "collaborative attacks on common problems" (Goodin 2009, 10–11). It is interesting that in this relatively recent ten-volume handbook, feminism is dealt with primarily in a chapter in the *Law and Politics* volume. The chapter focuses on Western debates concerning the "woman question" and feminist legal positions. There is some discussion of philosophy, jurisprudence, and psychology, but the chapter's source materials are drawn primarily from North American scholarship (Baer 2009). There is little recognition in the remaining volumes of the influence of feminist political science thinkers on the traditional subfields of institutionalism, voting behavior, political economy, public policy, or political theory. The latter subfield does feature several women as scholarly leaders and a few are noted on the leader-boards in other subfields. However, the number of women listed pales to insignificance in comparison to the extensive list of male scholars. Of the nine key texts Goodin lists that political scientists should become more familiar with, none are authored by women. Making the leader-board is most often dependent on citations, and elsewhere there are indications that this process is in itself gendered (Curtin 2013).

If this ten-volume handbook is a fair representation of the state of the discipline, it is unsurprising that feminist political scientists have produced a separate *Oxford Handbook of Gender and Politics* (Waylen et al. 2013). The downside of this outcome is that while feminist political scientists now view gender and politics as a legitimate subfield within the discipline, traditional political science scholars are yet to see it as such, despite the manifestly evident (and observable) gender, queer, and intersectional inequalities in the exercise and constraint of social and political power (Smith 2015). There also remains the risk that compartmentalization of feminist politics as a subfield may reinforce the marginalization of such work within the discipline as a whole. Feminist political scientists have recognized this tension, and have increasingly sought mainstream outlets for their research, but how we convert this to gender mainstreaming the curriculum remains a challenging prospect.

It is necessary to recognize that encyclopedic-like handbooks, textbooks, and the discipline's journals as publications help to construct the gendered nature of research norms and practices and the culture of the profession. These publications are critical mechanisms by which we may challenge or maintain a curriculum that privileges masculine understandings of what constitutes threshold concepts and core knowledge within political science. Moreover, "performance" of and within the discipline implicitly signals to female students and students from indigenous, diverse, and minority groups whether they can expect to "find themselves" in political science courses (Cassese, Bos, and Duncan 2012, 239).

It is evident that new challenges have arisen with the adoption of new forms of research governance and quality assessment to identify and reward research excellence. In New Zealand and Australia there is concern that these research quality frameworks may reinforce existing and highly gendered hierarchies of knowledge that privilege the traditional approaches associated with political science in the United States, which will have implications for both textbook content and research-led teaching (Johnson 2014, 127–28; Sawer and Curtin 2016). The political science landscape in New Zealand remains pluralistic and eclectic, but the academic performance of feminist scholars within this landscape continues to be measured against the norms of the discipline in the United States. Political science in the United States is considered the founding branch of the discipline, but it is one that is geographically distant and often appears uninterested in the extent to which its influence, in part by virtue of its size, might be interpreted as stifling regionally and qualitatively different knowledges of local institutions and politics (Foster et al. 2013). As a result, the opportunities to transform the discipline in New Zealand in a way that recognizes gender, intersectionality, and indigeneity may prove dependent on the successes of feminist scholars in the United States.

Women's Presence as (Feminist) Teachers

Does it matter then, who teaches political science in New Zealand, and is there a need for more feminist scholars? If good teaching and learning in political science is student-centered and responsive to students' needs, *who* the teacher is should be inconsequential. Feminist political scientists have asked the same question of parliamentary representation for a number of decades now, and provided a variety of responses that can be applied to universities and political science programs as institutional spaces. Anne Phillips offers several convincing reasons why the descriptive presence of women matters. These will be well known to many, but they are worth reiterating here. The first reason relates to the idea of justice. If no systemic structural discrimination existed, faculty positions in political science programs would be randomly distributed between both sexes, relative to the proportion women and men completing their PhDs. Second, Phillips takes up the fraught issue of the representation of women's interests. She suggests that while there is no fixed set of interests, women's experiences are sufficiently different from men to warrant representation; particularly given they are seldom addressed adequately in a politics dominated by men. Moreover, Phillips argues that it is precisely because interests are varied, fluid, influenced not just by sex or gender, and often created through the process of articulation that a case can be made for more women being present (Phillips 1991, 1998). Building on this view, the concept of substantive representation of women has received considerable scholarly attention, with explorations of when and how women representatives might speak and act for women.

Applying these ideas to curriculum development, we know political science paradigms and perspectives evolve over time, and what we choose to teach will be influenced by who we are and how we experience the discipline. Diversity in perspectives, genders, ethnicities, and so on amongst faculty is thus necessary to construct and produce a diverse curriculum that has the potential to be more open to gender (plus) mainstreaming. However, while women's representation in the discipline may be a necessary condition for the implementation of gender mainstreaming in political science teaching programs, it is unlikely to be sufficient. In other words, gender mainstreaming may remain elusive if women and indigenous and LGBT people are not present to insist on change, to articulate the knowledge interests of young women and other students keen to learn about how gender as a threshold concept shapes and is shaped by politics, institutions, and power relations. Symbolically, their presence reminds colleagues that politics need not be wedded to masculine norms and concepts.

So what do we know about the presence of women in the discipline in New Zealand? Juliet Lodge (1976) conducted what appears to be the first report on the status of women in 1974. She found that the political science profession consisted of forty-four men and only three women at the level of lecturer or above (6.8 percent). Twenty years later, research by Nicholl and Cousins (1998) indicated there were approximately ten women political scientists employed full-time, compared to around seventy men, that is, 12.5 percent. By 2012 this had increased to 32.6 percent of teaching faculty, with women spread relatively evenly across the levels, comprising one third of those at the lecturer, senior lecturer, and associate professor or professor positions (Curtin 2013).

The data in table 4.1 give a contemporary view of where women are located in the discipline in the five New Zealand universities that have stand-alone politics departments or programs in 2017. We see that women make up around a third of the tenured teaching faculty, in three of the five universities, and half at a fourth. Around 45 percent are in senior positions. The incremental increase of women in the profession in New Zealand is similar to patterns evident elsewhere. Data from the United States reveal that there has been a twenty-five-point increase over the past thirty years, most of which occurred between 1980 and 2000. Since that time there has been a more gradual improvement, with gains described as "small and glacial" (APSA 2005). This replicates trends in Australia, Canada, and the United Kingdom, where progress has also stalled over the past ten years. By contrast, New Zealand began from a much lower base and took longer to address the hiring of women, but since the mid-1990s has made significant progress.

However, it is sobering to note that at the time of writing there were only three women professors in political science across all universities, and only two women professors out of a total of fourteen political science professors (14 percent) at the five universities listed here. Prior to this there had been only three women appointed to the level of professor in the history of discipline in New Zealand. Moreover, the proportion of women represented in the teaching faculty does not appear to reflect the student body studying the social sciences. Table 4.2 demonstrates that in terms of domestic enrolments, women outnumber men at the undergraduate level, and there is gender parity at the doctoral level.

In the New Zealand case, we do not know whether women's presence as faculty within the discipline (or lack thereof) matters to young women studying and researching politics. However, evidence from the Teaching, Research, and International Policy (TRIP) project suggests that in the United States there is a

Table 4.1. New Zealand Universities Ranked by Female Academics in Political Sciences (2017).

Rank	University Department	% Female (n)	Number of females at senior level*
1	University of Canterbury; School of Social and Political Sciences	50.0 (4)	3
1	University of Auckland; Politics and International Relations, School of Social Sciences	38.5 (5)	3
3	Victoria University of Wellington; Political Science International Relations Programme	36.3 (8)	1
4	University of Otago; Politics Department	33.3 (4)	2
5	University of Waikato; Political Science and Public Policy	12.5 (1)	1

*Associate professor and professor are counted in the New Zealand system as senior levels (the former is equivalent to reader); the other levels are lecturer and senior lecturer and are the equivalent of tenured or tenurable positions.

Table 4.2. New Zealand Domestic Students Completing by Qualification Level and Gender in Political Science and Policy Studies (2015).

	Students Completing by Qualification Level 2010			
	Bachelors	Honors	Masters	PhD
Female	385 (59.2%)	80 (53.3%)	120 (48.9%)	10 (50%)
Male	265 (40.8%)	70 (46.7%)	125 (51.1%)	10 (50%)
Total	650	150	245	20

Department of Education website, www.educationcounts.govt.nz/statistics/tertiary_education/retention_and_achievement, accessed January 1, 2017.

relationship between women as faculty and diversity in what is taught. Maliniak et al. (2008) reveal that female international relations scholars tend to research different topics than their male colleagues and "in noticeably different ways" (123). Moreover, these differences are reflected in curriculum content: female IR scholars spend more time than their colleagues teaching nontraditional theoretical frameworks such as constructivism and feminism, and they are more likely to consider human rights, environmental politics, and international organizations.

The 2014 TRIP data for New Zealand indicate that no IR scholars nominate gender as their primary area of research and only nine percent nominate gender as their secondary area. However, of the nine faculty who indicated they taught international security to undergraduates (39 percent of total respondents), 44 percent include gender and inequality or poverty in their syllabus. This seems promising in terms of gender mainstreaming (although we do not know the sex of these four out of nine respondents). We do not have similar data for the other subfields of political science in New Zealand, but we do know that of those who publish on feminism and politics in New Zealand, approximately nine teach political science or political theory courses at the undergraduate level in four of the five universities examined here (Curtin 2013). From this we might assume that at least some undergraduate students are exposed to gendered perspectives both within and outside international relations.[12]

How feminist scholars teach politics and feminist content was the subject of a plenary session at the New Zealand Political Studies Association conference in 2014, and one of the questions addressed was whether integrating feminist perspectives and gender questions across the political science curriculum was effective or desirable. The six panelists (four of whom were New Zealand–based scholars) agreed that mainstreaming was an important strategy, but argued that this approach alone was insufficient. From their perspective, "gender weeks" and courses dedicated to feminist perspectives on politics remained essential to ensure students are exposed in some depth to feminist theoretical frameworks, ideas about intersectionality, and texts that seldom appear in traditional textbooks or reading lists (Lacey and Smits 2015).

There is visible progress in terms of the percentage of women within the profession in New Zealand—there has been a significant increase over time, particularly over the past fifteen years, and the proportion of women political scientists is similar to rates in comparable countries. However, it is important to recognize that women are a heterogeneous group: not all will identify as feminist, and not all are in sufficiently senior or administrative positions to encourage or cajole nonfeminist faculty to undertake gender mainstreaming or include material relevant to understanding intersectionality in course curricula. Even if they were, the fact that choices around curriculum content are most often left to individual academics makes the task of mandating gender mainstreaming impossible. Although feminist scholars may actively embed gender as a threshold concept in their own teaching, to date there has been little explicit evidence of a contagion effect across courses.

Prospects for Gender Mainstreaming in New Zealand and Beyond

The APSA Task Force on Political Science in the Twenty-First Century argues that the discipline's pedagogical practices and content need to diversify and become more comprehensive given the increasing diversity of the student body. If they do not, a focus solely on "great men," leaders, or thinkers that does not recognize the gendered dimensions associated with the interpretation of such "greatness" may reinforce a sense of marginality already experienced by female political science majors, and potentially harm recruitment, retention, and completion of degrees.

In addition, the relevance to the discipline of gender as an analytical construct (rather than simply sex as a variable in electoral behavior) is intellectually important in its own right. Incorporating gender perspectives asks students to consider how institutions and policies are constructed as gendered; how gender has informed the distribution of political power; and how theoretical and empirical questions emerge from a particular standpoint that is informed by one's subjective (and gendered) position.

New Zealand has made some progress, in ways not dissimilar to the last four decades of change evident in the United States. New Zealand has exhibited the same institutional inertia noted in the United States by Ingrid Bego in chapter 2, despite the increasing presence of women in the New Zealand Political Studies Association (NZPSA) and on faculty. Although the NZPSA approved the establishment of a formal gender politics section and helped to fund the 2012 "Women's Advancement in the Discipline" workshop, these have not proved to be focusing events leading to institutional change (Jensen 2011). The profession (as represented by the NZPSA) does not feature a "chilly climate," but neither has it taken up the issue of gender mainstreaming within the curriculum, unlike its US counterpart. This is despite the New Zealand state having a history of incorporating a feminist bureaucratic model of working from the inside to mainstream gender analysis.

In terms of recognizing the contribution of feminist political science and international relations scholars, transformation remains a long way off. The teaching of gender, feminism, and intersectionality has been left largely to sociology or WGS programs in New Zealand, notwithstanding the burgeoning and highly respected feminist political science scholarship available locally and internationally in both books and journals. And although *Political Science* is a journal where women scholars are choosing to send their work, it is not evident that it is considered a "natural" outlet for research on gender politics and policy.

Nevertheless, there have been steady increases in the number of women entering the political science profession over the past twenty years. Women make up a third of tenured staff across the country, and have begun to reach senior levels within the discipline, although promotion to full professor remains rare. How significant women's faculty presence is to gender mainstreaming remains unclear. For example, Beckwith and Cowell-Myers (2003) maintain that increasing the numbers of women will not necessarily challenge what remains deep-seated male domination in both politics and political science. Yet scholarship by feminist political scientists reminds us that in politics, the election of (feminist) women who undertake critical acts, as individuals or collectively as a "critical mass," can create new spaces and opportunities for change. Moreover, as Kelly Dittmar (2015) argues, gendered institutional rules may be influenced by who holds positional power in politics. In the case of New Zealand, we know feminist-oriented ministers in the Cabinet have made a difference to gender mainstreaming and to the production of policies aimed at addressing gender inequalities (Curtin 2008).

Applying Dittmar's arguments to gender mainstreaming in teaching and learning, we may need to view the curriculum as a gendered institution characterized by "gendered relations of power, gendered culture and symbolism, and a pattern of gender arrangements" that inform our behavior as teachers and maintain accepted or traditional understandings not only of what constitutes the curriculum but also the processes associated with curriculum construction. Dittmar (2015) goes on to suggest that shifting the balance of power to include and empower women (as political professionals has the potential to create conditions for institutional disruption that benefits all actors, in our case faculty and students. If so, then the employment and promotion of more women within the discipline may be critical for descriptive and substantive reasons.

As such, a number of challenges remain. Although disciplinary norms around curriculum content are perhaps less rigid in New Zealand than in the United States, and although the New Zealand political science community is comparatively small (not much larger than a community of practice), there is no means by which gender mainstreaming can be mandated. Feminist political scientists in New Zealand are "doing it for themselves" and for their students, often through a combination of mainstreaming; "gender weeks": offering separate courses on feminism, gender, and intersectionality; and bringing feminist experiential learning opportunities into the classroom and external internships. These feminists are a very small minority of the discipline in New Zealand, and few are professors with sufficient positional power to influence their program's curriculum. Furthermore, in an environment where research audits are becoming increasingly common and research continues to be valued more highly than teaching in terms of promotion, it seems unfair to ask the feminists to be the only agents of change around gender mainstreaming.

Gender monitoring processes, such as those recently conducted by women in the New Zealand political science community, help to raise awareness of the need for the inclusion of gender as a core construct in the curriculum. However, gendering policy analysis research tells us that successful gender mainstreaming requires more than evaluation, but also intervention and institutional buy-in at the formulation stage. Thus, input is required at the point of curriculum review or rejuvenation, overseen and encouraged by supportive heads of departments, directors of teaching and learning, and college or faculty deans. Gender mainstreaming requires political will and administrative investment, as well as feminist entrepreneurs on faculty. New Zealand has feminist faculty, but currently lacks the other necessary conditions to make further progress. If all these conditions come into alignment, then perhaps a window of opportunity will open, and feminist political scientists will be able to further the gender mainstreaming project in New Zealand and elsewhere.

I would suggest that transformation requires a global perspective. Bego notes the importance of a mixing microlevel changes (taking a social justice, intersectional, inclusive approach to teaching and thinking about gender in the classroom), with more systemic strategies around textbook content and institutional goal-setting. However, I argue that this strategy needs to become a three-pronged approach that goes beyond the national. There needs to be a greater recognition that the discipline in the United States has significant global reach and impact, through textbook production, journal impact factors, and higher education institutional rankings, as well as the increasing use of MOOCs and other online teaching and learning forums. As such, there needs to be more knowledge sharing and transfer between national associations in the Global North and South to identify the challenges and opportunities associated with gender mainstreaming that exist in smaller disciplinary communities. If gender mainstreaming is our collective goal as feminist political scientists then our pedagogy needs to be historical, intersectional, and global, if it is to be truly transformational.

JENNIFER CURTIN is Professor of Politics and Public Policy and Director of the Public Policy Institute at the University of Auckland, New Zealand. She teaches courses in comparative politics and public policy at the graduate and undergraduate levels.

Notes

Parts of this chapter have appeared in Jennifer Curtin. 2013. "Women and Political Science in New Zealand: The State of the Discipline," *Political Science* 65 (1): 63–83; and Jennifer Curtin. 2015. "Feminist Contributions to New Zealand Political Science," *Women's Studies Journal* 29(1): 4–20.

1. For example, the APSA has relatively good data on the slow increase in African American, Latina/o, and Asian Pacific Islander faculty and has also had committees on the Status of Blacks in the Profession since 1969, on Latinas/os since 1970, on LGBT Americans since 1992, and Asian Pacific Americans since 2003 (American Political Science Association [hereafter cited as APSA] 2011, 9).

2. New Zealand has eight research-led universities, which are all publicly funded. The government of the day provides broad policy objectives in terms of matching inputs (funding) with preferred outputs (employability, research outputs). Levels of tuition fee increases are subject to maxima specified by the Minister of Tertiary Education. The universities have collective self-regulatory control over academic qualifications. New

programs, and significant changes to existing programs, are subject to approval by Universities New Zealand, a board made up of the vice chancellors (presidents) of the eight universities, with detailed scrutiny being carried out by its Committee on Academic Programs. Ongoing approval of programs is subject to a review within five years of initial offering. Quality assessment is undertaken through peer expert reviews conducted by scholars at other universities; revisions or exclusion of new courses cannot be requested on the basis of competition or overlap, only on the basis of quality of curriculum, assessment mechanisms, dedicated resources, and external professional interest. It is unlikely that the lack of a feminist lens or the inclusion of gender as a threshold concept in courses has caused concern during the review process. By contrast, recognition of obligations under the Treaty of Waitangi (a founding governing document originally signed between Māori and the Crown in 1840) by higher education institutions ensures an indigenous lens has been applied to the process of review and new programme development.

3. Politics courses are also taught as part of social science programs in the three other public universities (see Sawer and Curtin 2016).

4. Upper level undergraduate and graduate courses in gender and feminist politics are listed on four political science program websites, but it is not clear that all are offered on a regular basis.

5. A list of gender and feminist contributions to the subfield can be found in Curtin (2015). The scholarship on that list is easily accessible to any political scientist and many have been published in New Zealand.

6. There are of course a range of other New Zealand politics edited volumes that are used by scholars in their teaching, including the election books series published by Auckland University Press and Victoria University of Wellington Press, which feature chapters by female authors but seldom address topics directly related to gender politics (for a recent exception see Curtin 2014).

7. The author's audit of course websites in 2015 shows that course coordinators who research and publish on feminist political theory are those that advertise the inclusion of these feminist theorists in their syllabi.

8. Research productivity and impact has always been a significant component of career promotion in New Zealand, although the demand for research outputs has intensified with the six-yearly national audit exercise that was adopted in 2003. The research productivity of the individual researcher is the largest component of this exercise, although research supervision and PhD completions also count. Although the scores of individual academics are released to the institutions, they are officially anonymous, thereby precluding a gender analysis of results.

9. Although Margaret Clark was appointed to the Editorial Advisory Board in 1977.

10. This perception was not helped when women were absent as authors in special issues celebrating the jubilees of two prominent New Zealand political science departments; Issue 40 (1) July 1988 and Issue 41 (2) in 1989.

11. As evidenced by the fourth biennial European Conference on Politics and Gender, which attracted over 400 scholars from around the world. The International Political Science Association includes two research committees dedicated to gender, which together hosted the second largest number of panels at the conference in 2012.

12. My thanks to Anita Lacey, who is the New Zealand country partner contact in the TRIP project, for drawing my attention to this data which is available here: https://trip.wm.edu/reports/2014/rp_2014/index.php. See also Curtin 2013, 140.

References

Al Janabi, Aysser Kate McMillan, and Carla Lam. 2014. *Advancing the Status of Women in Politics and International Relations in New Zealand*. https://nzpsa.co.nz/womens-caucus.

American Political Science Association. (APSA). 2005. *Women's Advancement in Political Science*. Washington, DC: APSA. www.apsanet.org/portals/54/Files/Task%20Force%20Reports/Womens_Advancement_in_Political_Science_2005.pdf.

———. 2011. *Political Science in the Twenty-First Century: Report of the Task Force on Political Science in the Twenty-First Century*. Washington, DC: APSA. www.apsanet.org/portals/54/Files/Task%20Force%20Reports/TF_21st%20Century_AllPgs_webres90.pdf.

Bacchi, Carol, and Joan Eveline. 2003. "Mainstreaming and Neoliberalism: A Contested Relationship." *Policy and Society* 22 (2): 98–118.

Baer, Judith A. 2009. "Feminist Theory and the Law," In *Oxford Handbook of Political Science*, edited by Robert Goodin. Oxford, UK: Oxford University Press.

Beckwith, Karen, and Kimberley Cowell-Myers. 2003. "Sheer Numbers: Critical Representation Thresholds and Women's Political Representation." *Perspectives on Politics* 5 (3): 553–65.

Cassese, Erin C., Angela L. Bos, and Lauren E. Duncan. 2012. "Integrating Gender into the Political Science Core Curriculum." *PS: Political Science and Politics* 45 (2): 238–43.

Catt, Helena, and Elizabeth McLeay, eds. 1993. "Women and Politics in New Zealand." Special issue, *Political Science* 45 (1). http://journals.sagepub.com/toc/pnzb/45/1.

Curtin, Jennifer. 2008. "Women, Political Leadership and Substantive Representation: The Case of New Zealand." *Parliamentary Affairs* 61 (3): 490–504.

———. 2013. "Women and Political Science in New Zealand: The State of the Discipline." *Political Science* 65 (1): 63–83.

———. 2015. "Feminist Contributions to New Zealand Political Science." *Women's Studies Journal* 29 (1): 4–20.

Curtin, Jennifer, and Katherine Teghtsoonian. 2010. "Analyzing Institutional Persistence: The Case of the Ministry of Women's Affairs in Aotearoa/New Zealand." *Politics and Gender* 64 (4): 545–72.

Dittmar, Kelly. 2015. "Change Agents? Female Political Professionals as Gender Equity Entrepreneurs." Paper presented to the European Conference on Politics and Gender, June 11–14, Uppsala University.

Dudley, Janice, and Sonia Palmieri. 1999. *"'Can Ladies Work Here Too, Nanna?' Gender and Politics Australasian Textbooks."* Canberra. Paper presented to the Australaian Political Science Association Conference, Australian National University. https://pdfs.semanticscholar.org/94de/eb9fc4592964a5e467d6d7ee4b208612cfc6.pdf.

Foster, Emma, Peter Kerr, Anthony Hopkins, Christopher Byrne, and Linda Ahall. 2013. "The Personal Is Not Political: At Least Not in the UK's Top Politics and IR Departments." *British Journal of Politics and International Relations* 15 (4): 566–85.

Goodin, Robert. 2009. "The State of the Discipline, the Discipline of the State." In *Oxford Handbook of Political Science*, edited by Robert Goodin. Oxford: Oxford University Press.

Hayward, Janine, ed. 2015. *New Zealand Government and Politics*. 6th ed. Melbourne: Oxford University Press.

Jensen, Carsten. 2011. "Focusing Events, Policy Dictators and the Dynamics of Reform." *Policy Studies* 32 (2): 143–58.

Johnson, Carol. 2014. "Hard Heads and Soft Hearts: The Gendering of Australian Political Science." *Australian Feminist Studies* 29 (80): 121–36.

Lacey, Anita, and Katherine Smits. 2015. "Teaching Feminism/Teaching as a Feminist in Politics Departments." *Women's Studies Journal* 29 (1): 56–63.

Lodge, Juliet. 1976. "New Zealand Women Academics: Some Observations on their Status, Aspirations, and Professional Advancement." *Political Science* 28 (1): 23–40.

Maliniak, Daniel, Amy Oakes, Susan Peterson, and Michael J. Tierney. 2008. "Women in International Relations." *Politics and Gender* 4 (1): 122–44.

Miller, Arthur H., Charles Tien, and Andrew A. Peebler. 1996. "The American Political Science Review Hall of Fame: Assessments and Implications for an Evolving Discipline." *PS: Political Science and Politics* 29 (1): 73–83.

Miller, Raymond, ed. 2006. *New Zealand Government and Politics*, 4th edition. Melbourne: Oxford University Press.

Miller, Raymond, ed. 2010. *New Zealand Government and Politics*, 5th edition. Melbourne: Oxford University Press.

Miller, Raymond. 2015. *Democracy in New Zealand*. Auckland: Auckland University Press.

Ministry of Business, Innovation, and Education (MBIE). 2014. *Tertiary Education Strategy (TES) 2014–2019*. www.education.govt.nz/further-education/policies-and-strategies/tertiary-education-strategy/.

Moloney, Pat. 1998. "Political Science in Retrospect." *Political Science* 50 (4): 4–37.

Mulgan, Richard. 1994. *Politics in New Zealand*. Auckland: Auckland University Press.

Nicholl, Rae, and Margaret Cousins. 1998. "Brief Encounter? Women and *Political Science*. The First Fifty Years." *Political Science* 50 (1): 38–52.

Phillips, Anne. 1991. *Engendering Democracy*. Cambridge: Polity Press.

———. 1998. *The Politics of Presence*. Oxford: Oxford University Press.

Roper, Brian. 2011. "Extended Review. The Transition of New Zealand Government and Politics." *Political Science* 63 (2): 244–46.

Sawer, Marian. 1990. *Sisters in Suits. Women and Public Policy in Australia*. Sydney: Allen and Unwin.

———. 2004. "The Impact of Feminist Scholarship on Australian Political Science." *Australian Journal of Political Science* 39 (3): 553–66.

Sawer, Marian, and Jennifer Curtin. 2016. "Organizing for a More Diverse Political Science: Australia and New Zealand." *European Political Science* 15 (4): 441–56.

Smith, Nicola. 2015. "The Queerness of Political Science: Challenging and Destabilizing the Discipline's Boundaries." London School of Economics and Political Science, June 30. http://blogs.lse.ac.uk/politicsandpolicy/the-queerness-of-political-science/.

Tan, Alexander C., Jessica Buck, and Erik Schrader. 2009. "Portraits of New Zealand Political Science, 1980–2008: A Picture is Worth Eighty Words." *Political Science* 61 (1): 81–83.

Walby, Sylvia. 2005. "Gender Mainstreaming: Productive Tensions in Theory and Practice." *Social Politics* 12 (3): 321–43.

Waylen, Georgina, Karen Celis, Johanna Kantola, and Laurel Weldon, eds. 2013. *The Oxford Handbook of Gender and Politics*. Oxford: Oxford University Press.

5 Student Perceptions of Gender in Political Science Teaching and Advising

Ekaterina M. Levintova

WHILE POLITICAL BEHAVIOR research in the political science discipline has already identified the impact of gender on political participation and public attitudes—including a gender gap in partisanship and ideology—gender effects in the teaching and learning of political science remain unexamined. Yet, gender is one of the most important sources of political socialization, especially for college-educated citizens, who continue to outperform other social strata in voting and other forms of political participation. In fact, increased levels of education among women have been linked to closing the voting gap that traditionally existed between men and women, to the point that in the 2012 presidential elections, women accounted for 51 percent of all voters casting their ballots. While gender clearly matters in the US politics, does it matter in political science education?

This question is important, given the prescribed moral imperative of teaching political science on a university level, namely, our discipline's direct responsibility for fostering civic engagement, political tolerance, and active citizenship. These learning outcomes are intrinsically related to issues of equity, of which gender is one of the most essential and persistent components. From this perspective, political socialization that happens in our classrooms, by students observing gender relationships and perceiving gender roles in the context of an academic discipline charged with examining political power, is extraordinarily important. Who is studying political power and political inequalities, and who is doing the teaching? Do political science classroom experiences empower or weaken political participation by gender? Are we aware of how perceptions of gender in a classroom might contribute to civic and political engagement and active, equitable exercise of our citizenship rights and responsibilities?

The subject of the chapter speaks to the big picture view of higher education in which democratic citizenship, much like literacy and writing, can be fostered "across curriculum" (Smith, Nowacek, and Bernstein 2010), but especially so in political science. In fact, this strand of the Scholarship of Teaching and Learning (SoTL) literature is booming, and its canon now includes works from a variety of disciplines—that is, history, environmental studies, literary studies, sociology, natural and applied sciences, communication, and computer science—as chapters in *Citizenship across the Curriculum* and other recent publications illustrate (Fleury 2005; Liss and Liazos 2010; Marino and Hayes 2012; Murphy 2004; Smith, Nowacek, and Bernstein 2010). Learning about citizenship and acquiring the citizenship-supporting skills of civic engagement, political efficacy, cultural empathy, respect for diversity, and the ability to reconcile conflict and reach consensus through peaceful means are also currently recognized as liberal education goals, essential beyond narrow disciplinary confines (Braskamp, Trautvetter, and Ward 2008; Colby et al. 2007; Colby et al. 2003; Ehrlich 2000; Farrah and O'Connor 2008; Mendel-Reyes 1998; Nussbaum 2002; Reisch 2012; Rhoads 2000, 2003). Yet, there are specific issues explored in this chapter that political science as a discipline continues to grapple with.

As many who teach political science courses know, at least anecdotally and impressionistically, there are pronounced differences in classroom behavior, levels of efficacy and participation, and general comfort with the political science curriculum between male and female students. Routinely, female students in general education political science classes abstain from classroom discussions, express lack of knowledge of the subject matter, and exhibit more ambivalence about the application of political knowledge beyond the classroom. Yet, their academic output, measured through written work, exams, and course projects, matches or surpasses that of their male counterparts.

For a variety of reasons, political science as a discipline remains deeply gendered and relatively unaffected by larger trends in higher education, which is witnessing increasing numbers of female students and faculty and is moving toward gender mainstreaming in curriculum and research (see the introductory chapter in this book). The problem is by now fairly well-documented. In 2006, *American Political Science Review*, the premier scholarly outlet for political science, published a groundbreaking article on the gendered character of the profession (Tolleson-Rinehart and Carroll 2006). In the following years, the problem did not disappear from public discussions, as evidenced by recent articles in the *Chronicle of Higher Education*, the *Washington Post*, and an acclaimed professional blog, *The Monkey Cage* (McMurtrie 2013; Voeten 2013a, b). Another recent article in the *Chronicle of Higher Education* described the grievances felt by female faculty members and graduate students in the political science department at Rutgers University, including financial and promotional discrimination, concluding that "political science has been one of the most male-dominated disciplines among social sciences" (Moser 2008, A14).

At the university where the author of this chapter works, with its 65:35 female to male ratio in the student population, political science classes usually have a reversed gender breakdown, irrespective of the course. In the courses ranging from the lower level, general education *Global Politics* to highly specialized upper level courses on *US Foreign and Defense Policies*, *Comparative Politics*, and *Political Behavior* required for political science majors, the gender dynamics remains almost constant. The majority of the students are men, and it is the male students who do the bulk of talking and participating in the class. Breaking the gender barriers in the political science classroom remains challenging and requires awareness of various gender-sensitive pedagogical approaches, classroom management techniques, and tailored feedback even on the part of female faculty members. To date, the research on this topic, with important implications for social justice, gender equality, and closing the gender gap beyond voting behavior, has been limited and relegated to other social science disciplines. Yet, based on recent findings, our discipline is unique in remaining relatively unaffected by progress in professional gender equity. My study fills the existing gap by looking at the effect of the instructor's gender on student perceptions of teaching and learning in the political science classroom.

The normative motivations that animate this study align more with equity and social justice, rather than efficacy and female empowerment central to other chapters in this book. Obviously, female instructors who have risen to positions of authority already have a high degree of self-efficacy and empowerment, but they still might face gendered barriers in teaching and gendered student perceptions of their role in facilitating learning. Without a closer look at this topic, we might not be able to adequately assess male and female teaching and might be rewarding people (with merit raises and promotions) without a nuanced understanding of what role an instructor's gender plays in student evaluations. This study is also implicitly about the messages that our female students might be getting by seeing female professors inside and outside the classroom and speaks to issues of empowerment, efficacy, and socialization into professional fields in general and our field in particular. Either way, this chapter and other chapters in this book add to our understanding of inclusive education and education for inclusive citizenship.

Existing Scholarship of Teaching and Learning on the Gender of Instructor and Student Evaluations and Perceptions of Teaching

This chapter is interested in gender, not biological sex, and its effects on teaching and learning of political science, as they manifest themselves in student perceptions. Since the emphasis of this study is on classroom relationships and social and cultural characteristics, as opposed to biological differences, I am less interested in how physical and biological characteristics of teachers might affect student perceptions of teaching and learning. Rather, I am interested in what psychological, attitudinal, and behavioral traits students assign to instructors of different genders. Do people see female professors as more nurturing, approachable, emphatic (all culturally constructed traits associated with female gender) as opposed to more knowledgeable, efficient, and professional male professors (typical cultural and social constructs assigned to males in our society and our profession)? To be clear, there is a difference between sex (biological) and gender (cultural and social) as concepts, of which I am keenly aware, but teaching and learning are themselves cultural and social (if not outright political) processes and so my focus is on gender, not sex. I believe that students who responded to my surveys were fully aware of this distinction, despite that gender might still be a threshold concept in higher education (Launius and Hassel 2014). In short, in this chapter, I fully subscribe to the American Psychological Association's definition of gender as "the attitudes, feelings, and behaviors that a given culture associates with a person's biological sex" (APA 2011).

What is less clear and studied is gender as a threshold concept for our own discipline (see the introductory chapter in this book). Political science instructors are not fully aware of all the different—often implicit and unexamined—ways in which gender manifests itself in their own training, teaching, and learning of their students. Nor do instructors systematically examine how they are affected by gender expectations of students, and how, in turn, students see gender in the political science classroom. Does gender matter beyond the standard gender-related subjects we teach (i.e., gender in political participation and socialization)? Does it matter in pedagogy that teachers employ? In the textbooks that we use? In the classroom methods that teachers practice? In the courses that are taught? In the topics that instructors cover in their research and teaching? In their relationships with students? While other authors in this book give answers to these questions, this chapter is predominantly on the issue of how students see gender in the classroom, which has implications for classroom discussions, merit evaluations, faculty promotions, and faculty development.

Although this chapter investigates unique dynamics of the gender perceptions in a political science classroom, it speaks to a larger *problematique* of gender in the social sciences and the academy in general. It continues the cross-disciplinary SoTL dialogue on this topic, both substantively and methodologically. Substantively, it adds to the exploration of what gender differences in teaching and learning are by looking at a particular discipline. While some of the elements of student perceptions of gender differences in political science teaching, advising, and mentoring might be unique, the overall findings have general applicability beyond our own discipline. Essentially, I am asking the broadest, most fundamental SoTL research question: What is the role of gender in teaching and learning, and why might it matter?

Methodologically, I use indirect observations of learning context by relying on student self-reported perceptions of how men and women differ as political science teachers, advisors, and mentors, and what classroom challenges women are observed to face. A part of SoTL analytical apparatus, this chapter departs from previously used methodologies of pre- and post-intervention measurements (i.e., surveys, course evaluations, or analysis of student work) by using experimental research design. Yet, it adds to the growing body of research by using real empirical evidence, a must for any SoTL work. Understanding student responses from an experimental setting gives us a different view of classroom environment in which actual learning takes place. In essence, this chapter provides a link between national and international trends in gender in political science (chapters 1–4), and on-the-ground, classroom SoTL research (chapters 6–9).

Previous research has already dealt with the issue of the instructor's gender in social sciences. For example, Saunders and Saunders (1999) investigated the effects of instructor's gender on knowledge acquisition and course evaluations in introductory economics courses at Indiana University, finding only limited support for the gender-matching theory, according to which female students learn better from female instructors and rate their female professors higher than male ones. A similar conclusion, uncovering only a minor effect of gender on student achievement, was found by Hoffmann and Oreopoulos. That study concluded that "a same-sex instructor increases average grade performance by at most 5 percent of its standard deviation and decreases the likelihood of dropping a class by 1.2 percentage points" (Hoffman and Oreopoulos 2009, 479).

Admittedly, it is difficult to isolate the effect of gender on student ratings of a professor. After all, how do we know that lower evaluations are only a function of gender biases, and how can we control for it, if gender can be so easily observable? Online education provided a first opportunity to really test the theory that the instructor's gender drove some of the numbers in course evaluations. The most recent study by McNell, Driscoll, and Hunt (2015) as well as research by Mulhere (2014) and Zaino (2015) demonstrated that in online sociology and anthropology classes where gender information could be manipulated, "the male instructor had lower ratings when students were told their instructor was female. The female instructor had higher ratings when students were told their instructor was male," controlling for all other factors.

Other qualitative studies have already identified that students did recognize gender of the instructor in their classroom experience, expecting female instructors to be "ladylike," friendlier, and less assertive than their male counterparts (Anderson and Miller 1997; Basow 1998; Kierstead, Agostino, and Dill 1988). Closer to this study, Anderson and Smith's (2005) investigation of student perceptions of a professor's warmth, political bias, and professional capabilities (based on gender, race, and ethnicity) yielded some interesting results. For instance, based on student reactions to a collection of syllabi indicating varying teaching styles, instructor genders, and ethnicity, Latina professors were viewed as warmer when they had a lenient teaching style and less warm when they had a strict teaching style when compared with Anglo female professors with similar styles. That study, like the previous ones (Saunders and Saunders 1999; Hoffman and Oreopoulos 2009), did not find much support for the matching-gender theory. However, the main thrust of Anderson and Smith's research was on ethnicity and it used a different methodology to tease out gendered differences. Bennett (1982a, b) determined that men were rated as more effective teachers than women, but that study should be updated, considering the increased number of female professors who have entered the workforce since the early 1980s. An important conclusion about the differences in student evaluations of instructors based on the latter's gender appeared in the recent article by Zivkovic et al. (2012). The theory that female instructors tend to be rated lower than their male counterparts due to gender stereotypes and biases, selective perceptions, and contrast effect was tested in the American University located in Nigeria. The evidence confirmed that students evaluated male faculty more favorably than female ones, not only on the course attributes but also on individual traits, including teaching skills, enthusiasm, clarity, and rapport. The same conclusions are echoed in the work of Collings, Chrisler, and Quina (1998, 151–152), who uncovered that female professors struggle with establishing their professional expertise and are held to different standards as far as knowledge and nurturing are concerned. These findings suggest that men are perceived by students as more organized, knowledgeable, and suitable for teaching, perpetuating the implicit gender stereotypes. The persistent gendered expectations of female teachers to be nurturing and approachable likely stem from the inherent trope of a teacher as a moral mother which originated in the gradual feminization of the teaching profession at the turn of the twentieth century and simply transferred a traditional gender role from the family to the educational sphere (McCormick 2007). Does this stereotype still exist in the field of political science?

Given the inconsistency of the previous studies, with most quantitative investigations uncovering only a minor (at best) effect of gender and more qualitative analyses confirming existence of the gender biases in college education, which camp is more correct? Does gender matter in teaching and learning of political science? Do female faculty in our discipline face the same gender expectations as the ones identified in the research on social sciences broadly defined? How did the recent changes in higher education, with more female faculty and female students entering universities in general and political science in particular, affect this process? Perhaps the best way to solve this puzzle is through research design that combines both qualitative and quantitative approaches to test the old hypothesis that the gender of the instructor does color student perceptions of teaching and learning (instructor–student relationship) with the most up-to-date data. This is exactly what I undertake in this chapter.

Previous studies used gender as an independent variable in explaining learning outcomes via analysis of differences in course evaluations, exam scores, and GPA (all dependent variables). This study's methodology treats gender as the primary focus of investigation. Through experimental design, it reveals that students do indeed recognize gendered differences in instruction, including classroom management and preferences for assignments, as well as in advising, mentoring, and academic relationships with students. To my knowledge, no other study applied this methodology to investigate how gender matters in teaching and learning. Additionally, no study asked students about gender in the classroom directly; until now any conclusions have largely been inferences from quantitative or qualitative data obtained almost accidently, as part of other assessments. Even though this investigation does not operate with classroom evidence proper, it does supplement the existing body of knowledge on the role of gender in teaching and learning, with implications beyond political science.

Ironically, the methodology employed in this chapter is firmly within the realm of the traditional social science methodological apparatus, highlighting the difficulties that even those most sympathetic to the cause of gender equity in the classroom might be experiencing. Although I am aware of the existence of feminist methodologies and theories, I myself was neither trained in them nor given a chance to collaborate with feminist experts, as is the case for many of my political science peers, making this book (especially its chapter on graduate methods training and chapters that do employ feminist methods of analysis) timely and compelling. Many chapters in this book reflect the problem identified in the introduction: we continue to shun gender-sensitive pedagogy, methodology, and epistemology in favor of traditional behavioralism, objectivism, and social science methodologies. Gender is indeed a threshold concept in our own discipline that we need to illuminate, not least of all through graduate and professional training in feminist methodology, epistemology, and pedagogy.

Research Problem

In this chapter, I investigate the effect of instructor's gender not on the test scores or course evaluations, but on the student-instructor relationship in the classroom. Does gender matter in how students perceive the knowledge and expertise of an instructor? Do they see differences in pedagogies? In types of course work that male and female faculty assign? Do students find female instructors more relatable? Do they themselves behave differently in the classrooms of male and female instructors? I suspect that students, consciously or subconsciously, react to the gender of their instructor and such reactions might have effects on the success of traditionally underrepresented groups in the classroom (e.g., female and ethnic/racial minority students in political science). Such reactions might offer an explanation for the gender-matching theories described above.

The research design employed in this study is experimental versus control group. In this research design, two equal groups of students from upper-level political science classes offered in the Spring 2014 semester were given teaching scenarios identical in wording, with the exception of gendered names

Table 5.1. Demographic Characteristics of Two Groups Answering the Surveys after Being Presented with Male and Female Faculty Scenarios.

	Male Faculty Scenario Surveyed Group	Female Faculty Scenario Surveyed Group
Total number of completed survey respondents	33	26
Gender breakdown (%)	Male: 23 Female: 77	Male: 56 Female: 44
Partisanship breakdown (%)	Democrats: 65 Republicans: 24 Independents: 4 Greens: 8	Democrats: 68 Republicans: 16 Independent: 4 Third Party (Socialist and Libertarian): 12
Age breakdown (%)	18- to 20-year-olds: 20 21- to 23-year-olds: 40 24- to 26-year-olds: 23 30- to 39-year-olds and older: 6 40+ year-olds: 3	18- to 20-year-olds: 44 21- to 23-year-olds: 24 24- to 26-year-olds: 16 30- to 39-year-olds: 8 40+ year-olds: 8
Class standing breakdown (%)	Seniors: 63 Juniors: 20 Sophomores: 10 Graduate: 7	Seniors: 36 Juniors: 16 Sophomores: 36 First year students: 12
Listed major breakdown (%)	Political science: 57 Public administration: 53 Environmental policy: 33 Democracy and justice studies: 23 History: 7 Human development: 7	Political science: 52 Public administration: 32 Environmental policy: 8 Democracy and justice studies: 28 History: 8 Environmental science: 8

and pronouns referring to political science professors. In survey 1, the faculty member involved was male; and in survey 2, the faculty member was female (see appendix A). After reading the short description of a teaching situation (scenario), students in each group were given a short survey questionnaire, asking identical questions (see the questions in appendix A). The survey was administered through Qualtrics software from March to April 2014.[1] Sample sizes in each group differed—fifty-one students took part in the survey featuring the male faculty member in its script; forty students took the female faculty-centered survey. However, only thirty-three and twenty-six respondents actually finished their respective surveys, making the subsamples more equal in size (see table 5.1).

Analysis of Results

In addition to size, there were other appreciable differences between the groups The first group, where respondents reacted to the male faculty script, was overwhelmingly female (77 percent). Sixty-six percent of respondents identified with the Democratic Party; 24 percent with the Republican Party; 8 percent with the third parties (mostly Green Party); and 4 percent reported being Independent. This group was a bit older with 40 percent of respondents ages 21 to 23; 23 percent were in the 24 to 26 age bracket; 20 percent were in the 18 to 20 age bracket; 10 percent being older than 30; and 7 percent being between ages 27 and 29. Sixty-three percent of the subsample comprised of seniors; juniors, 20 percent; sophomores, 10 percent; and graduate students taking undergraduate classes, 7 percent. Fifty-seven percent of the subsample were political science majors, with 53 percent also being public administration majors; 33 percent were environmental policy majors; 23 percent were democracy and justice majors; and 7 percent each were human development and history majors.[2]

On the other hand, 56 percent of the second group were male respondents and 44 percent were female respondents. Sixty-eight percent of respondents reported being affiliated with Democratic Party; with only 16 percent the Republican Party; 12 percent being supporters of third parties (Libertarians and Socialists); and four percent Independents. Forty-four percent of that subsample was ages 18 to 20; with 24 percent ages 21 to 23; 16 percent ages 24 to 26; and eight percent each, ages 30 to 39 and older than 40. Sophomores and seniors made up 36 percent of the subsample each, followed by juniors (16 percent), and first year students (12 percent). Most were political science majors (52 percent), with public administration (32 percent), democracy and justice studies (28 percent), environmental policy, environmental science and history (8 percent each), and business administration majors also represented in the subsample. Results of the quantitative survey questions are summarized in table 5.2.

In general, students in both sub-samples rated hypothetical instructors as adequate, albeit not excelling along many indicators used to measure teaching effectiveness and mastery. Evidently, in some areas gender played no discernible part. For instance, class management techniques were viewed similarly. However, gender variance of instructors resulted in several noticeable differences. The most pronounced ones were recorded in students' respect for an instructor and instructor's relatability, with the hypothetical female instructor garnering substantially more respect and relatability than her male counterpart in their respective scenarios. The female instructor was also perceived as a more effective, professional, and competent teacher, who was more approachable and respectful of students. Students also recorded a higher level of enjoyment of a

Table 5.2. Sample Descriptives Using *t* Tests for Equality of Means.

	Male Instructor Scenario		Female Instructor Scenario		
	M	SD	*M*	SD	*t* test
Teaching effectiveness	7.70	1.33	7.88	1.24	ns
Knowledge of subject matter	7.57	1.38	7.50	1.79	ns
Level of professionalism	7.39	1.66	7.62	1.55	ns
Instructor's treatment of students in class	8.36	1.69	8.65	1.65	ns
Nurturing ability	7.36	2.36	7.19	1.79	ns
Level of competence	7.97	1.49	8.08	1.52	ns
Level of approachability	8.03	1.99	8.12	1.71	ns
Relatability of instructor	7.39	2.11	8.27	1.81	−1.65*
Student's level of respect for Professor	8.00	1.98	8.42	1.63	ns
Instructor's ability to manage class	7.55	2.12	7.50	2.24	ns
Enjoyment of class as taught by instructor	7.69	2.16	7.85	2.07	ns
Willingness to participate in classroom discussions	7.92	2.47	8.12	1.76	ns

*$p < 0.1$.
Note: M = Mean. SD = Standard Deviation. Teaching effectiveness through willingness to participate in classroom discussions range from 1 (not at all) to 10 (completely).

class as taught by the female faculty and a greater comfort with class discussions. Yet, students also saw the female instructor as less knowledgeable and, surprisingly, less nurturing than the hypothetical male professor. In general, quantitative responses reveal a higher ranking of the female instructor on all but three questions of the quantitative part of the survey (see means for each question in table 5.2).

Statistical analysis of data from the two surveys that followed the male and female faculty scenarios did uncover statistically significant differences in student perceptions of gender differences in the classroom, despite the relatively low numbers of responses. An independent-samples *t* tests were performed to compare student perceptions of the level of professionalism, classroom effectiveness, approachability, knowledge (see table 5.2) in the male or female instructor scenarios. There was a statistically significant difference between male instructor scenario ($M = 7.39$, SD = 2.11) and female instructor scenario ($M = 8.27$, SD = 1.91),

t (57) = −1.65, p = 0.1 for the student perception of the instructor demeanor and relatability. Therefore, instructor gender does matter for student perception of gender differences in teaching. Specifically, female instructors are perceived by students as more relatable.

One more statistically important relationship was found between student gender and student perceptions of female instructor treatment of students in the second survey that followed the female faculty scenario. Male students perceived the hypothetical female instructor as more respectful of students. An independent-samples t test was performed to compare male and female student perceptions of the level of professionalism, classroom effectiveness, approachability, and knowledge in both male and female faculty surveys. The only statistically significant difference was found between male students (M = 9.21, SD = 1.19) and female students (M = 8.09, SD = 1.97), (t (23) = 1.77, p < 0.1) for student perceptions of the treatment of students by the instructor in the female faculty scenario. Specifically, male students saw female instructors as more respectful of students. Although this finding does not explicitly deal with the gender of the instructor in classroom, it shows that male students might feel more respected by female teachers.

Even more differences were reported in the third part of both surveys, dealing with reasons why students select political science or closely related fields of public administration, democracy and justice studies, or environmental policy (table 5.3).[3] Essentially, students were asked to rank reasons for choosing political science as their major on a ten-point scale. There, contact with female faculty members, be it through taking classes, having a female role model, or receiving mentoring or advising from female professors, seemed to make a bigger difference in influencing student choice for political science as a major, as female-centric reasons outperformed male-centric ones in each gendered category. However, in both surveys, faculty-related factors were not the most important decision-making factors, trailing behind more professional and student-centered reasons for choosing the field (personal interest in politics, desire to work in this field, or desire to pursue graduate training). Yet, it is also clear that classroom relationships matter and matter profoundly, trampling the influence of friends and family.

Even more importantly, the instructor gender effects emerged from performing a chi-square statistical tests. A chi-square test of independence was performed to examine the relation between gender and various reasons for choosing political science major in both surveys. The relationship between student gender and taking an inspiring class from a female faculty as a reason for choosing political science was significant, X^2 (2, N = 45) = 23.03, and p < 0.01. Therefore, gender of the instructor matters in inspiring the female

Table 5.3. Reasons for Choosing Political Science as a Major (Combined Results from Both Surveys).

Factors influencing choice of political science or closely related field (from most important to less important)	N	Mean	Standard Deviation
1. Personal interest in politics	53	8.00	2.55
2. Desire to pursue career in politics or closely related field	52	7.88	2.42
3. Desire to pursue graduate training in political science or closely related field	48	7.02	2.96
4. Taking an inspiring and interesting class taught by a female faculty	45	6.42	3.12
5. Taking an inspiring and interesting class taught by a male faculty	44	5.84	3.31
6. Having a female faculty as a role model	45	5.71	3.26
7. Having a mentoring relationship with female faculty	45	5.47	3.35
8. Having a male faculty as a role model	45	5.20	3.04
9. Having a mentoring relationship with male faculty	44	4.86	3.55
10. Friend's recommendation	41	4.61	3.42
11. Desire to teach political science or closely related field in secondary or postsecondary education	43	4.35	3.05
12. Family suggestions	39	3.54	3.01

students to major in political science. Specifically, female students were statistically more likely to choose political science as a major after taking an inspiring class by the female professor. And since taking an inspiring class from a female instructor was consistently identified as one of the important reasons for majoring in political science and its cognates, this finding suggests that gender of instructor does matter for the future of our discipline and more gender empowerment and equity.

The quantitative analysis, however, only gets us so far; because of the small N, even closed-ended, scaled response options from my surveys are closer to qualitative data. The true qualitative data from open-ended questions (see appendix A) that were also included in the survey paint a more nuanced and somewhat different picture, giving more credence to the gender effect in the teaching camp.

Results of open-ended questions from both surveys are presented in appendix B (table 5.4). In the second part of the surveys, students were asked to self-report any gender differences they might have observed during their political science education through the open-ended questions. Only responses containing these self-reported gender differences were recorded and presented in table 5.4 (appendix B). They are grouped by questions (four in total), asking students about their perceptions of differences in (1) teaching styles, (2) course assignments, (3) advising styles, and (4) mentoring styles of male and female instructors. Each comment represents one survey response; no coding other than reporting of direct quotes from students was performed, as it was important to leave student comments to speak on their own. Nonetheless, some interesting gender-related themes did emerge.

The qualitative responses reveal that the students are indeed more aware of the gender differences in teaching political science than what the quantitative data would suggest. The female faculty are perceived as more empathetic, open, personable, approachable and punctual and less arrogant, yet subject to more classroom challenges, especially from male students. On the other hand, male faculty members are portrayed as more easy-going, laid back, and organized, yet taking less interest in students. Likewise, students noticed differences in classroom assignments, reporting that female faculty tend to favor more group projects, more class discussions, and other forms of participation, as well as homework and in-class exercises (suggesting higher frequency of learning assessment), while male professors tended to gravitate toward papers and exams with multiple-choice questions. On some level, it also suggests that students realize how much harder female faculty work to be perceived as effective and good teachers.

The most pronounced differences were recorded in the answers to questions dealing with gender differences in advising and mentoring styles and techniques, with students reporting much more individualized, patient, flexible, and caring approaches by female advisors as well as more nurturing, open-mindedness, approachability, empathy, and sensitivity by female mentors. Female mentors and advisors appear to students to be more emotionally invested in student success. They are also perceived as more available (outside office hours) and as valuing personal interaction with students.

Who is more likely to see effects of instructor's gender in the classroom? Another interesting finding of the survey was the disaggregation of qualitative results by gender. In other words, who is more likely to comment on gendered differences in the classroom instruction, mentoring, and advising—the male or female respondents? It might also speak to the matching gender theory discussed in the section on existing literature on gender effects in teaching social sciences. Does having an instructor of the same gender matter for student perceptions? Here, I found an interesting effect. In the survey for the male faculty scenario, most gender specific remarks were made by the female students, who dominated that survey sample (eleven relevant responses were made by female students, only one by a male student). However, in the survey for the female faculty scenario, male students wrote the majority of gendered qualitative remarks (three out of four responses) even though that survey was taken by almost equal numbers of male and female students. This suggests that mismatching gender in the classroom activates a greater awareness of the role of gender in the classroom. In other words, mismatching gender in the classroom does not necessarily lead to a difference in academic performance (confirming previous findings); rather it makes the students see gender differences more clearly and be more sensitive to it. It is a different, but probably also valuable, learning outcome.

All in all, the quantitative results of the survey were interesting and, on occasion, confirmed my hypotheses, but in general, they were not always conclusive. The qualitative data was more definitive in teasing out the gendered differences, but it was not necessarily generalizable. Before we can safely claim that gender perceptions matter in a classroom through quantitative data analysis, more data should be collected and from more disciplines. Perhaps with more data and adding the open-ended answers as ordered variables in the future studies, we will see stronger effects. So far, we do know that the relationship between gender and student perceptions of teaching and advising exists (based on the comments students made in the open-ended section of the survey); it is just not being captured in surveys with few respondents, or the effect is so small that we might need more data to see it.

Conclusions

This study confirms that the gender bias in student perceptions of political science faculty exists and is easily detectable. In the eyes of students, female faculty differ from their male counterparts not only in their personal dispositions (more empathetic, approachable, interested in student success), but also in their pedagogy and classroom assignments. The students also see female and male faculty as facing different levels and types of challenging student behaviors.

These insights only emerge when one looks at the qualitative data, endorsing previous findings offered by more qualitative approaches to the study of this issue. It turns out that the quantitative investigations might overlook the existence of gender biases, thus necessitating a heavier reliance on qualitative studies of this particular topic. The students tend to mask their gendered stereotypes behind numerical responses or our samples might be too small to capture gender biases more accurately.

Seen another way, this study also calls for more and different quantitative data. The experiential scenario research design employed in this study can be easily replicated, not only for political science, but also in other disciplines, to get a larger N. In the future, it would also be important to do comparison between private and public schools, first year students and seniors, and different majors. With a larger N the results of the statistical testing will become even more compelling. Another way to bolster the value of quantitative analysis is to use the responses from the open-ended questions and turn those into multiple-choice response options in the future. Doing so will enable the researchers to collect more data to analyze and compare.

This chapter also found another lens to use when looking at the gender-matching theory of learning. Although the use of qualitative data in this study limited the ability to perform statistical analyses, qualitative results suggest that instead of directly affecting academic performance, student-teacher gender mismatches makes students more aware of gender in the classroom.

These findings also demonstrate that female faculty conforming to the additional (gendered) expectations of compassion, empathy, and nurturing should do well in the classroom and will receive fair course evaluations. Those not exhibiting these traits might act at their own risk. Yet, male faculty are not really expected to perform (or be perceived as performing) these additional tasks, creating implicit inequality and unfairness in teaching evaluations and the political science profession.

Knowing that gender biases exist, how should students and faculty approach teaching and learning in the political science classroom, and what should be the reaction of departmental chairs and other members of academic administrations? It would seem advisable to expose students to even more scholarship on persistent gender stereotypes in large societal and political contexts and to practice uncovering implicit gender biases present in these spheres. It might help correct enduring assumptions of what women are expected to do in and outside the classroom. It appears that not only are they expected to work harder in the classroom, grading more frequent assignments that require more supervision and management (group projects) and are more time-consuming (homework assignments and in-class exercises as opposed to multiple-choice exams), but they are also expected to set aside time to nurture and reach out to students as advisors and mentors, another laborious and hard-to-recognize-and-reward task. Until we realize that these gender differences do exist, we will not be able to achieve true fairness, not only in the workplace, but in a true sense of democratic academic citizenship that is predicated on equality.

What might be even more important is sharing this information with both students and faculty. Both groups would be served well to have their awareness raised about the realities of student perceptions as they relate to gender. Gender inequities are real. The results of surveys like this *should* be shared with political science classes and presented at faculty development events in a way that stimulates discussions of gender issues.

These results are especially important in light of equity/social justice normative lens that this chapter adopted. Equity starts with unpacking our assumptions, in this case about both male and female instructors' teaching, advising, and mentoring being evaluated fairly, in a gender-sensitive manner. It should not end with a resigned acceptance that female faculty are expected to perform more (and more traditional) roles in their teaching, mentoring, and advising. We should include gender of instructor and students on student evaluations and test for any gender biases that might pop up. Inclusive education, at the very minimum, should be about fairness in performance evaluation. It is also imperative to think about gender of instructors in our hiring practices and teaching assignments for the sake of our students and the future of the profession, if we are ever to achieve a fair and inclusive educational environment.

If our classrooms remain the channels of political socialization into traditional views on gender roles, the ideal of political gender equality might remain a lofty but distant goal. Student expectations of a certain degree of domesticity in the professional setting—applied only to female faculty—might be the biggest unintended learning outcome that we, as a discipline, need to be cognizant about. Our students will be bringing these experiences and assumptions, however implicit, to the voting booth and other types of political participation, and it is incumbent on our discipline to help students (and ourselves) see the subtle ways in which gender biases exist and have effect on democratic politics in and outside educational context. In the future, political science classrooms, as microcosms of politics in general, need to better instill ideals of democratic fairness, including gender equity. This is food for additional thought for the entire system of higher education, since it transcends the borders of our discipline and the academy itself.

Acknowledgements

I am very grateful to Terri Johnson, a former University of Wisconsin–Green Bay colleague, for her helpful suggestions on analysis and interpretation of my data. Funding for this research was provided, in part, by the University of Wisconsin–Green Bay Teaching Scholars Program. Big thanks to David Voelker, its former director, for research design ideas.

Appendix A

Script 1 (Scenario 1: Male Faculty Teaching)

Professor Mark Zane gives a lecture on the role of media in politics. In the beginning of class, students are still talking to each other, complaining about the lack of time to do everything they need to accomplish this week. Professor Zane looks at the class, waiting for the conversations to die out, and then mentions that he is likewise overwhelmed with work and family obligations. Students stop talking and start paying attention. That day, Professor Zane discusses issues of agenda-setting, framing, and priming, giving students examples of each. For instance, he asks students if they noticed anything interesting in the phrases "political race," "campaign ticker," and "battleground states." Students correctly identify military references and conflict captured by such phrases. He then asks if politics in general is framed by the media as a competitive game. Students respond in the affirmative and give their own examples of "front runner," "challenger," and "election bowl."

He proceeds with questions about important issues that dominated media coverage a couple of months ago. After some silence, a student volunteers an answer of Syria. Professor Zane asks how many students heard about Syria this week, as opposed to Affordable Care Act. Students nod their heads in agreement. "What about US negotiations with Israel?" he asks. "You mean Iran?" corrects a student. Professor Zane thanks a student for correcting him and jokes that he should watch even more news to get his facts straight. He finally makes his point that the media elevates certain stories and angles and neglects others, even if they are very important ones. He gives example of George Bush Sr. whose strong foreign policy record was rarely touted, while his inability to get US out of recession was often emphasized. He shows a clip from Jon Stewart's *Daily Show* to illustrate his points and closes the lecture with the quote from Bernard Cohen: "The media ... may not be successful in telling its consumers what to think, but it is stunningly successful in telling the audience what to think about."

Script 2 (Scenario 2: Female Faculty Teaching)

Professor Marilyn Zane gives a lecture on the role of media in politics. In the beginning of class, students are still talking to each other, complaining about the lack of time to do everything they need to accomplish this week. Professor Zane looks at the class, waiting for the conversations to die out, then mentions that she is likewise overwhelmed with work and family obligations. Students stop talking and start paying attention. That day, Professor Zane discusses issues of agenda-setting, framing, and priming, giving students examples of each. For instance, she asks students if they noticed anything interesting in the phrases "political race," "campaign ticker," and "battleground states." Students correctly identify military references and conflict captured by such phrases. She then asks if politics in general is framed by the media as a competitive game. Students respond in the affirmative and give their own examples of "front runner," "challenger," and "election bowl."

She proceeds with questions about important issues that dominated media coverage a couple of months ago. After some silence, a student volunteers an answer of Syria. Professor Zane asks how many students heard about Syria this week, as opposed to Affordable Care Act. Students nod their heads in agreement. "What about US negotiations with Israel?" she asks. "You mean Iran?" corrects a student. Professor Zane thanks a student for correcting her and jokes that she should watch even more news to get her facts straight. She finally makes her point that the media elevates certain stories and angles and neglects others, even if they are very important ones. She gives example of George Bush Sr. whose strong foreign policy record was rarely touted, while his inability to get US out of recession was often emphasized. She shows a Jon Stewart's *The Daily Show* clip to illustrate her points and closes the lecture with the quote from Bernard Cohen: "The media ... may not be successful in telling its consumers what to think, but it is stunningly successful in telling the audience what to think about."

Survey Questionnaire (Following Either Script 1 or Script 2)

QUESTION 1: On a scale of 1 (completely ineffective) to 10 (extremely effective) how would you rate professor's teaching effectiveness?

QUESTION 2: On a scale of 1 (not at all knowledgeable) to 10 (extremely knowledgeable), how would you rate professor's knowledge of this subject?

QUESTION 3: On a scale of 1 (extremely unprofessional) to 10 (extremely professional), how would you rate professor's professionalism?

QUESTION 4: On a scale of 1 (extremely disrespectful) to 10 (extremely respectful), how would you rate professor's treatment of students in this class?

QUESTION 5: On a scale of 1 (extremely indifferent) to 10 (extremely nurturing), how would you rate professor's nurturing ability?

QUESTION 6: On a scale of 1 (not at all competent) to 10 (extremely competent), how would you rate professor's level of competency?

QUESTION 7: On a scale of 1 (not at all easy) to 10 (extremely easy), how would you rate professor's approachability?

QUESTION 8: On a scale of 1 (not at all relatable) to 10 (extremely relatable), how would you rate professor's demeanor?

QUESTION 9: On a scale of 1 (no respect at all) to 10 (a great deal of respect), how much would you respect a professor who taught this way?

QUESTION 10: On a scale of 1 (extremely poor) to 10 (outstanding), how would you rate the professor's classroom management techniques?

QUESTION 11: On a scale of 1 (not at all likely) to 10 (extremely likely), how likely are you to enjoy a class with this professor?

QUESTION 12: On a scale of 1 (not at all comfortable) to 10 (extremely comfortable), how comfortable would you be to participate in discussions in this professor's class?

QUESTION 13: Have you ever noticed any differences in teaching between male and female faculty members? If so, please describe them below:

QUESTION 14: Have you ever noticed any differences in the types of classroom assignments that male and female faculty members assigned in their classes? If so, please describe them below:

QUESTION 15: Have you ever noticed any differences in advising styles of male and female faculty members? If so, please describe them below:

QUESTION 21: Have you ever noticed any differences in the mentoring styles of male and female faculty members? If so, please describe them below:

QUESTION 22: On a scale of 1 to 10, how important was each of these factors in choosing political science or a closely related field as your minor or major?

> Mentoring relationship with male faculty
> Mentoring relationship with female faculty
> Having a female faculty as a role model
> Having a male faculty as a role model
> Taking an inspiring and interesting political science class taught by a female instructor
> Taking an inspiring and interesting political science class taught by a male instructor
> Friend's recommendation
> Family suggestion
> Personal interest in politics
> Desire to pursue a career in politics or closely related field
> Desire to pursue graduate training in political science or closely related field
> Desire to teach political science or closely related field in secondary or higher education
> Other, please explain below

QUESTION 23: What is your gender?

QUESTION 24: What is your partisanship?

QUESTION 25: If you are a third-party supporter, which third party do you support?

QUESTION 26: What is your age?

QUESTION 27: What is your class standing?

QUESTION 28: What is your major? Please select all that apply.

Appendix B

Table 5.4. Direct Student Quotes Capturing Gendered Differences in Teaching, Classroom Assignments, Advising, and Mentoring (Each Quote Represents One Student Response).

Open Ended Survey Questions	Male Instructor Scenario Open-Ended Questions Responses	Female Instructor Scenario Open-Ended Questions Responses
Have you noticed any differences in teaching between male and female political science instructors?	• Male professors try to push their own beliefs onto us as students more than our female professors. • Female professors are better at connecting with students in some ways. They are more open compared to males. Some of the male instructors I have had are like "my door is always open," but then they are not very helpful at all. My experience with female professors have been pretty positive. • Female faculty members are more effective in their teaching styles and knowledge. • The males are a lot more laid back and easier to relate because of that. • Male faculty are more relaxed and easy going as compared to female faculty. • Speaking very generally, females tend to be quiet during lectures, tend to make the connections for students rather than ask students to make them themselves. In terms of classroom management, females tend to stop things like whispering and other distractions more than their male counterparts. • Male faculty members tend to be more likely to show up late and be unprepared whereas my female professors are always	• There is quite a difference I feel with men and women as teachers. First, I find the women to be more personable, but I find men to be more organized. • In my experience, the female professors I have had have been more nurturing and approachable. • I have noticed that female professors are more likely to try to get students involved in discussions while male professors seem more focused on lecture. • Female professors tend to be more reserved. • I find that male teachers are a little less approachable. I have not really had this problem, but I have observed other students having difficulty speaking with a male instructor.

Table 5.4. (*continued*).

Open Ended Survey Questions	Male Instructor Scenario Open-Ended Questions Responses	Female Instructor Scenario Open-Ended Questions Responses
	present and ready to begin class right on time. • I am more comfortable approaching female faculty members because I believe they are more empathetic. I believe some of the male faculty members hold a sense of arrogance to themselves. • I find that specifically male students will exemplify more obnoxious (texting/talking) behavior during lesson plans of female professors.	
Have you noticed differences in classroom assignments that male and female instructors give their classes?	• Male professors tend to assign more papers and tests compared to female professors who seem to have more group assignments. • I have seen male students be blatantly disrespectful toward female professors (tell them they are wrong or debate with a bipartisan professor). I have never seen this behavior toward male professors. • Female: homework assignments and in-class exercises; males: no homework. • In general, males give tougher assignments. • Male faculty members give more lecture-based education, while female faculty prefer more discussions and class participation. • I noticed that in most of my classes, I don't think I have ever had a female professor give me an exam that required scantron.	• Men teachers I had tend not to give out any homework assignments, while women give them with extra credit. • Males assign less homework and require less discussion. • Female professors tend to lean more toward group work for assignments. • Male professors have had more readings; however, I do not feel this is related to their gender ... maybe it is though.

Table 5.4. (continued).

Open Ended Survey Questions	Male Instructor Scenario Open-Ended Questions Responses	Female Instructor Scenario Open-Ended Questions Responses
Have you noticed any differences in advising styles of male and female faculty members?	• Most of the female faculty are more open to suggesting internship ideas and advisor really being an advisor and mentor to you. • Female professors that I have worked with are not only more patient and understanding of life complications, but they seem more flexible. • Female instructors are more hands on, they want to be updated, whereas with some of the male faculty members I sometimes wonder if they even care if I am progressing with a project or work. It feels so nice to be cared about sometimes. • In general, females are easier to approach. • Female faculty members are better communicators, in general. • I have two advisors for my two different majors, one female, one male. The female advisor reaches out to me more to ensure I am on the correct path to graduation. Additionally, she spends time asking about other things in my life, such as graduate school applications, other courses I am taking, my involvement on campus, and so forth. My male advisor is good, but I was never reached out to. Any meetings we had were initiated by me, which is not a bad thing. When we did meet, it was very professional, no fluff added, and he would use tools like SIS to figure out what classes	• Sometimes male instructors are harder to approach. • Male professors usually seem to have a slightly more relaxed style. • Female faculty do tend to talk out situations more. • Women make themselves more available and have been more willing to help me with questions. They have promoted coming to see them where male faculty have given out office hours availability but left it at that.

Table 5.4. (continued).

Open Ended Survey Questions	Male Instructor Scenario Open-Ended Questions Responses	Female Instructor Scenario Open-Ended Questions Responses
	I have taken/needed to take. By contrast, my female advisor always knew that information prior to our meeting and would suggest classes that would fulfill requirements but that she also knew I would enjoy. • Females tend to be more open to suggestions whereas males are more straight forward and would rather direct you to someone who knows more rather than discuss. • Male advisors provide only the answer to direct questions instead of making recommendations about opportunities.	
Have you noticed any differences in mentoring styles of male and female faculty members?	• More female faculty are encouraging for students who lack self-confidence in their own abilities and will often suggest opportunities for them. • I find female professors more able to listen and encourage class discussions or be more sensitive if students aren't totally grasping concepts. I have a male professor who is a great guy, but when I have said things in class and it's not the exact answer he was looking for, he kind of ignores what was being said. It just feels less encouraging and now I feel less inclined to speak in class, whereas female professors I have worked with will use what seems like gender terminology ("I see what you are getting at but what about this?" or "that's a valid point, but …").	• No responses in the second, female scripted scenario survey

Table 5.4. (continued).

Open Ended Survey Questions	Male Instructor Scenario Open-Ended Questions Responses	Female Instructor Scenario Open-Ended Questions Responses
	• I think that female professors become a little more emotionally invested/care a bit more than male professors in some ways. My current advisor is male and I sometimes feel like he thinks his working with me is a chore and a hassle. It does not have the same camaraderie I have received working with female instructors here on campus. • Females are easier to approach. • Females are *much* more approachable. That's not to say that males are bad at mentoring, it is just more difficult to get close to them and make connections. Once that connection is made though, I feel the same level of respect and care from my male instructors as I do from my female mentors. • Female faculty are more accepting; male faculty have been more straight-forward and to the point. Neither (qualities) are negative; just different. • Females seem more nurturing, males seem more dominant and "do it your own way." • Female advisors are more willing to offer opportunities for me to get more involved and explore my future options for career via internships and suggesting graduate school.	

EKATERINA M. LEVINTOVA is Associate Professor of Political Science, Global Studies, and Democracy and Justice Studies at the University of Wisconsin–Green Bay, where she teaches courses on comparative politics and international relations. She is co-editor (with Kevin Kain) of *From Peasant to Patriarch: An Account of the Birth, Upbringing, and Life of Nikon, Patriarch of Moscow and All Russia*.

Notes

1. IRB approval was granted for this project and both surveys. University of Wisconsin–Green Bay IRB approval number is # F_13-28.
2. Our university actively promotes double or even triple majoring, by adding interdisciplinary major requirements to traditional disciplinary majors, such as political science. Therefore, most students also opt to pursue interdisciplinary majors in public administration, democracy and justice studies, environmental policy and planning, and human development, a fact reflected in the major distribution of respondents in both subsamples.
3. Students could choose all reasons that applied.

References

American Psychological Association, (APA). 2011. *The Guidelines for Psychological Practice with Lesbian, Gay, and Bisexual Clients*. Available at: http://www.apa.org/pi/lgbt/resources/guidelines.aspx.
Anderson, Kristin, and E. D. Miller. 1997. "Gender and Student Evaluations of Teaching." *PS: Political Science & Politics* 30 (2): 216–19.
Anderson, Kristin J., and Gabriel Smith. 2005. "Students' Perceptions of Professors: Benefits and Barriers According to Gender and Ethnicity." *Hispanic Journal of Behavioral Sciences* 27 (2): 184–201.
Basow, Susan A. 1998. "Student Evaluations: The Role of Gender Bias and Teaching Styles." In *Career Strategies for Women in Academe: Arming Athena*, edited by Lynn H. Collins, Joan C. Chrisler, and Kathryn Quina, 135–56. Thousand Oaks, CA: Sage.
Bennett, Sheila K. 1982a. "Student Perceptions of and Expectations for Male and Female Instructors: Evidence Relating to the Question of Gender Bias in Teaching Evaluations." *Journal of Educational Psychology* 74 (2): 170–79.
———. 1982b. "Undergraduates and Their Teachers: An Analysis of Student Evaluations of Male and Female Instructors." In *The Undergraduate Woman: Issues in Educational Equity*, edited by Pamela J. Perun, 251–73. Lexington, MA: Lexington Books.
Braskamp, Larry A., Lois Calian Trautvetter, and Kelly Ward. 2008. "Putting Students First: Promoting Lives of Purpose and Meaning." *About Campus* 13 (1): 27–32.
Colby, Anne, Elizabeth Beaumont, Thomas Ehrlich, and Josh Corngold. 2007. *Educating for Democracy: Preparing Undergraduates for Responsible Political Engagement*. San Francisco: Jossey-Bass.

Colby, Anne, Thomas Ehrlich, Elizabeth Beaumont, and Jason Stephens. 2003. *Educating Citizens: Preparing America's Undergraduates for Lives of Moral and Civic Responsibility.* San Francisco: Jossey-Bass.

Collings, Lynn H., Joan C. Chrisler, and Kathryn Quina, eds. 1998. *Career Strategies for Women in Academe: Arming Athena.* Thousand Oaks, CA: Sage Publications.

Ehrlich, Thomas. 2000. *Civic Responsibility and Higher Education.* Phoenix, AZ: Orynx Press.

Farrah, Jeffrey, and Patrick O'Connor. 2008. "Promoting Political Engagement through American Government Classes." *Peer Review* 9 (Spring/Summer): 31–34.

Fleury, Anthony. 2005. "Liberal Education and Communication against the Disciplines." *Communication Education* 54 (1): 72–79.

Hoffman, Florian, and Philip Oreopoulos. 2009. "A Professor Like Me: The Influence of Instructor Gender on College Achievement," *Journal of Human Resources* 44 (2): 479–94.

Kierstead, Diane, Patti Agostino, and Heidi Dill. 1988. "Sex Role Stereotyping of College Professors: Bias in Students Ratings of Instructors." *Journal of Educational Psychology* 80 (3): 342–44.

Launius, Christie, and Holly Hassel. 2014. *Threshold Concepts in Women's and Gender Studies: Ways of Seeing, Thinking, and Knowing.* New York: Routledge.

Liss, Jan R., and Ariane Liazos. 2010. "Incorporating Education for Civic and Social Responsibility into Undergraduate Curriculum." *Change: The Magazine of Higher Learning* 42 (1): 45–50.

Marino, Matthew T., and Michael T. Hayes. 2012. "Promoting Inclusive Education, Civic Scientific Literacy, and Global Citizenship with Videogames." *Cultural Studies of Science Education* 7 (4): 945–54.

MacNell, Lillian, Adam Driscoll, and Andrea Hunt. 2015. "What's in a Name: Exposing Gender Bias in Student Ratings of Teaching." *Innovative Higher Education* 40: 291.

McCormick, Theresa. 2007. "Strong Women Teachers: Their Struggles and Strategies for Gender Equity." In *Gender in the Classroom: Foundations, Skills, Methods, and Strategies Across the Curriculum,* edited by David Sadker and Ellen S. Silber, 1–31. London: Lawrence Erlbaum.

McMurtrie, Beth. 2013. "Political Science Is Rife with Gender Bias, Scholars Find." *Chronicle of Higher Education.* http://chronicle.com/article/Political-Science-Is-Rife-With/141319/.

Mendel-Reyes, Meta. 1998. "A Pedagogy for Citizenship: Service Learning and Democratic Education." *New Directions for Teaching and Learning* 1998 (73): 31–38.

Moser, Kate. 2008. "Women Accuse Rutgers Political-Science Department of Bias and Hostility." *Chronicle of Higher Education* 55 (8): 14.

Mulhere, Kaitlin. 2014. "Students Praise Male Professor." *Inside Higher Ed.* www.insidehighered.com/news/2014/12/10/study-finds-gender-perception-affects-evaluations.

Murphy, Troy A. 2004. "Deliberative Civic Education and Civil Society: A Consideration of Ideals and Actualities in Democracy and Communication Education." *Communication Education* 53 (1): 74–91.

Nussbaum, Martha. 2002. "Education for Citizenship in an Era of Global Connection." *Studies in Philosophy and Education* 21 (4): 289–303.

Reisch, Jacqueline C. 2012. "Global Learning as General Education for the Twenty-First Century." *Educational Research and Reviews* 7 (21): 464–73.

Rhoads, Robert A. 2000. *Freedom's Web: Student Activism in an Age of Cultural Diversity.* Baltimore, MD: The Johns Hopkins University Press.

———. 2003. "Now Civic Engagement Is Reframing Liberal Education." *Peer Review* 5 (3): 25–28.

Saunders, Kent T., and Phillip Saunders. 1999. "The Influence of Instructor Gender on Learning and Instructor Rating." *Atlantic Economic Journal* 27 (14): 460–74.

Smith, Michael B., Rebecca S. Nowacek, and Jeffrey L. Bernstein. 2010. *Citizenship Across the Curriculum.* Bloomington: Indiana University Press.

Tolleson-Rinehart, Sue, and Susan J. Carroll. 2006. "'Far from Ideal:' The Gender Politics of Political Science." *American Political Science Review* 100 (4): 507–13. www.apsanet.org/imgtest/APSRNov06Tolleson-Rinehart_Carroll.pdf.

Voeten, Eric. 2013a. "Gender Bias in Political Science." *The Monkey Cage*, August 31, 2013. http://themonkeycage.org/2013/08/31/gender-bias-in-political-science/.

———. 2013b. "Concluding the Gender Gap Symposium." *Washington Post*, October 6, 2013. www.washingtonpost.com/blogs/monkey-cage/wp/2013/10/06/concluding-the-gender-gap-symposium/.

Zaino, Jeanne. 2015. "Gender Bias in Student Evaluations." *Inside Higher Ed*, February 23, 2015. www.insidehighered.com/blogs/university-venus/gender-bias-student-evaluations.

Zivkovic, Jelena, Apkar Salatian, Fatima Ademoh, and Lawrence Oborkhale. 2012. "Perceptions of Male and Female Lecturers at an American Style University in Nigeria." *International Journal of Academic Research in Business and Social Sciences* 2 (5): 43–52.

Part Two:
Classroom Evidence and Solutions

6 Getting to No: The Need for Gender-Conscious Pedagogy in Service-Learning Courses

Daisy Rooks

MANY ASPECTS OF teaching and learning in the social sciences are gendered. As Rinfret and Pautz point out in chapter 7, gender shapes college students' participation in online and in-person courses. In chapter 5, Levintova demonstrates that students' perceptions of instructors are informed by the gender of instructors as well as students. This chapter explores gendered dynamics in service-learning courses in the social sciences.

Political scientists have a keen interest in service-learning. Some political scientists focus on students' motivation to participate in service-learning, linking it to astronomical growth in volunteerism in the United States over the past three decades (Galston 2001; Walker 2000). For many young people, service-learning is a credible alternative to participation in mainstream politics (Owen 2000; Walker 2000). As young adults have grown skeptical about the political process in the United States, they have become increasingly enthusiastic about "localized activities where" they "can 'get things done' and immediately see results" (Walker 2000, 647). Service-learning is one of these activities. Other political scientists examine the institutionalization of service-learning. As service-learning courses have become ubiquitous in US high schools and colleges, scholars have raised questions about whether and how the pedagogy influences young adults' civic and political values (Galston 2001; Hepburn, Niemi, and Chapman 2000). Other political scientists attend to the benefits of service-learning. Some explore the tangible benefits of service-learning for students, namely, its positive impact on students' confidence, critical thinking skills, tolerance, and appreciation of diversity (Dicklitch 2003; Galston 2001; Hepburn, Niemi, and Chapman 2000; Hunter and Brisbin 2000; Owen 2000). Others examine the broader impacts of service-learning, such as its ability to produce knowledgeable, engaged citizens. These scholars explore whether service-learning is an effective tool for "increasing students' limited knowledge about democratic politics and general sense of civic responsibility" (Hunter and Brisbin 2000, 623).[1]

Despite the ample anecdotal evidence that service-learning benefits students (Dicklitch 2003; Hepburn, Niemi, and Chapman 2000; Owen 2000), it is less clear whether service-learning courses facilitate students' understanding of gender, race, class, and sexual orientation. This is an important concern for political scientists in light of Levintova and Staudinger's assertion in this volume that the discipline should integrate threshold concepts from Women's and Gender Studies (WGS). This chapter explores gender dynamics in service-learning courses by answering two related questions: How does gender influence students' experiences with service-learning, and how can instructors help service-learning students think deeply and critically about gender? By going beyond pedagogical concerns, this chapter also illuminates the political and social implications of this approach to teaching and learning.

Literature Review

Gender-Neutral Service-Learning Pedagogy

According to the National Service-Learning Clearinghouse, service-learning is "a teaching and learning strategy that integrates meaningful community service with instruction and reflection to enrich the learning experience, teach civic responsibility, and strengthen communities." The scholarly research on service-learning has identified several common pedagogical approaches of these courses: topical content, active and experiential learning, and structured reflection.[2]

Many service-learning courses include readings, lectures, and discussions about the communities, social issues, organizations, and policies that are relevant to the course. For example, a service-learning course in which students work with low-income adolescents might contain readings about child development, low-income families, and poverty. Topical content helps prepare students for their service; it also helps them make sense of their volunteer experiences later in the semester. For example, articles about low-income families could help students in the course described above understand the challenges confronting the youth and organizations that they are working with.

Service-learning courses engage students in experiential learning, active learning, or both. Students engaged in experiential education learn by doing instead of by reading or listening to lectures (Myers-Lipton 1998). Community service is integrated into most service-learning courses, in order to provide students with opportunities to "do" (Delve, Mintz, and Stewart 1990; Green 2001). While learning from their volunteer service, students gain knowledge, skills, empathy, and civic values (Burns 1998; Cohen and Kinsey 1994; Hunter and Brisbin 2000). Active learning sounds similar, but is actually quite different. In courses that emphasize active learning, the instructor rejects the assumption that her primary role is to impart knowledge to students (Mitchell 2008; Mooney and Edwards

2001; Smirles 2011), and instead assumes that students and instructors can, and should, learn from each other. To facilitate active learning, instructors encourage students to work independently, pursue lines of inquiry that interest them rather than passively receiving knowledge, and demonstrate their knowledge in creative ways (Smirles 2011). While some service-learning courses combine active and experiential learning, not all do. Some service-learning instructors rely on traditional instructor-centered pedagogy.

The third, and perhaps best documented, component of service-learning pedagogy is structured reflection (Bringle and Hatcher 1996; Felten, Gilchrist, and Darby 2006; Honnett and Poulsen 1989; Potter, Caffrey, and Plante 2003). Service-learning reflection can take multiple forms, from interactive to individual, and from verbal to written. Interactive verbal reflection typically happens in small group discussions, whole-class discussions, or virtual discussions in online courses. Individual written reflection can take the form of journaling, blogging, free-writing during class time, and formal academic writing. While reflection typically explores students' service experiences, it can also cover other topics, such as privilege, guilt, and discomfort.

Scholarly articles about service-learning often refer to structured reflection to emphasize the importance of careful planning and execution (Keen and Hall 2009). Structured reflection does not have much in common with casual discussion in seminar-style courses; instead instructors pose specific questions or problems for students to consider. Well-designed reflection exercises help students tie their service experiences back to the topical content of the course. When planned and executed well, structured reflection facilitates all other learning in service-learning courses.

Despite sharing these three components, service-learning courses do not offer identical approaches to teaching and learning. Depending on its treatment of privilege, power, and social change, a service-learning course could be considered either traditional or critical (Catlett and Proweller 2011; Mitchell 2008). Instructors of traditional service-learning courses focus their attention on students, and are most concerned about the impact of service and learning on students. They reference students' acquisition of knowledge, skills, empathy, and civic values as evidence of the transformative potential of service-learning. Instructors of critical service-learning courses strive to "redistribute power amongst all participants in the service-learning relationship, [develop] authentic relationships in the classroom and community, and [work] from a social change perspective" (Mitchell 2008, 50). While they are concerned about impacts on students, they are equally, and in some cases, most concerned about impact on community partners. They cite the empowerment and capacity-building of community partners as evidence of the transformative potential of service-learning.

Literature about service-learning often describes approaches to teaching and learning that are gender-neutral (as well as race-neutral and class-neutral). First, service-learning courses often push students outside of their comfort zones. One way that instructors do this is by having students serve in communities with racial, ethnic, religious, or class compositions that are different from their own (Green 2001; Keen and Hall 2009; Keller, Nelson, and Wick 2003; Marullo 1998; Vogelgesang 2004). The discomfort that often results from this pedagogical decision has been well-documented in the scholarly literature (Catlett and Proweller 2011; Dunlap et al. 2007; Green 2001). If the students' gender, race, and class backgrounds influence the extent and type of discomfort that they experience, gender-neutral (as well as race-neutral and class-neutral) pedagogy, further critiqued in chapter 8 in this book, would be inadequate to help them navigate this unease.

Student discomfort is especially pronounced in critical service-learning courses. In these courses, instructors encourage students to think about the structural causes of clients' situations, as well as the individual causes. When students in critical service-learning courses confront the "unjust structures that create differences" they can often feel anxious and overwhelmed (Mitchell 2008, 56). These courses also encourage students not to distance themselves from clients but instead to recognize that if not for one or two factors, they could have ended up in a similar situation. While this creates awareness about precariousness and the importance of safety nets, it can also cause significant stress for students.

Second, differences between women and men's experiences inside educational institutions have been well-documented. At the K–12 level, girls and boys in the same classroom often have divergent educational experiences (Adler, Kless, and Adler 1992; Ferguson 2001; Pascoe 2011). The same is often true in college classrooms. If female and male college students have divergent experiences in service-learning courses, gender-neutral pedagogy would be inadequate for these settings as well. One explanation for the gendered nature of education is gender socialization.

Gender Socialization and Education

Men and women receive very different messages about how to act, what to think, how to look, and what to aspire to. In the United States, boys are regularly encouraged to be assertive, unemotional, and outspoken, while girls are encouraged to be demure, accommodating, and nurturing. The messages that girls and boys receive about "gender typical behavior" vary somewhat by race, ethnicity, and class (Risman 2004, 436). For example, Hill (2002) demonstrates that African American girls receive more messages about gender equality than their white counterparts. Raffaelli and Ontai argue that the opposite is true for Latino families, who tend to espouse "gender role traditionality" (2004, 298). Ferree (1980) contends that working class girls receive messages about gender that are less traditional than is often assumed.

Families, schools, and other institutions promote traditional gender roles in a variety of ways. Some compel girls to conform to gender typical behavior by convincing them that these behaviors are natural and/or inevitable. Others motivate girls to conform to these messages by warning them about the "social punishments for flouting gender expectations" (Hollander 2002, 490). These penalties include inability to attract a spouse, make friends, or be viewed positively at work.

Deutsch and Saxon argue that the family is "often the locus of the creation of gender" in the United States (1998, 359). Hill agrees that much of the "gender role training" that girls receive happens in the family (2002, 495). However, the family is not the only place where girls receive messages about gender. Mass media, peer groups, churches, and schools are also important sites of gender socialization. Scholars have examined the prevalence of gendered messages and gendered behaviors inside schools. For example, while conducting research about peer subcultures in elementary schools, Adler, Kless, and Adler (1992, 170) observed many boys adopting "active postures" and many girls adopting "passive postures." This passivity, they explain, reflects gendered expectations that girls be pleasant, friendly, and accommodating. But schools are not only arenas in which gender socialization plays out; they are also sites of production for gendered messages and ideologies. As Ferguson (2001) demonstrates in her study of African American middle-schoolers, teachers and schools often motivate and discipline children differently depending on their race and gender. Through their actions, Ferguson (2001) argues, teachers communicate their preconceived notions of African American boys as disruptive, distracted, and in need of strict discipline.

These trends have been observed at all levels of the US education system. For example, gendered messages from teachers and administrators can shape high school girls' and college women's career and academic choices. For example, young women who accept the gendered messages that they received at home and at school often seek out occupations that emphasize caring and nurturing.[3] Given the low wages and low prestige of pink-collar occupations, these choices can adversely affect women's earning potential over their lifetimes. Young women who succumb to gendered expectations that they be accommodating and deferential might eschew leadership opportunities available on their high school and college campuses. This decision can have long-term consequences. Limited leadership experience can undermine young women's ability to secure internships and acceptance to graduate programs and national service programs such as AmeriCorps and Peace Corps. Women's underrepresentation in high levels of business, government, and the nonprofit sector in the United States has also been attributed to girls' hesitance to lead.

Although education is an important site of gender socialization, it can also facilitate resistance to espouse "gender role traditionality" (Raffaelli and Ontai 2004, 298). For example, single-sex high schools and colleges often encourage female students to adopt "active postures" and question the "gender role training" they received at home (Adler, Kless, and Adler 1992, 170; Hill 2002, 495). Elementary school teachers can encourage girls and boys when they defy the "gender role training" that they received at home (Hill 2002, 495). High school teachers can encourage girls to lead and boys to follow. College faculty can persuade female students to pursue male-dominated occupations, and male students to pursue pink-collar occupations. In these and many other ways, schools can help girls and boys resist gendered messages about how to act, what to think, how to look, and what to aspire to.

Despite this potential, too many educational institutions ignore gender socialization or attempt to create gender-neutral learning environments. The gender-neutral pedagogy commonly found in service-learning courses is an example of this. However, this is a mistake. As I illustrate below, gender socialization shapes students' experiences in service-learning courses in profound ways, creating a need for gender-conscious service-learning pedagogy.[4]

Data and Methods

My thinking about gender and experiential education is influenced by my experience teaching service-learning courses for over a decade. In order to examine this topic empirically, I analyzed data from an interdisciplinary service-learning course about hunger and homelessness that I have taught at the University of Montana for the past six years.[5] Even though it is not a political science offering, the course deals with several subjects that concern political scientists, especially those in the public policy subfield. My analysis of data collected from students in the course offers insights about service-learning which will be relevant to many political scientists, especially those committed to helping students develop their citizenship skills.

The course has three main components. First, students explore the complexity of the topic through required readings, lectures by the instructor, and guest lectures by local practitioners. Second, students volunteer thirty-six hours at the Poverello Center, a local homeless services agency, and reflect on their service. Finally, students learn about qualitative research design and practice qualitative data collection techniques, such as ethnographic observation and in-depth interviewing.

Data

In my course, students' reflections about their volunteer service take the form of ethnographic fieldnotes. Ethnographic fieldnotes are much less speculative and impressionistic than the written reflections that students produce in many other service-learning courses. In their ethnographic fieldnotes, students describe their service in great detail including the tasks that they completed, and the clients, volunteers, and staff whom they worked with. They also capture emotional experiences by documenting how they felt during each volunteer shift and exploring why. In their fieldnotes, students also describe their interactions with clients, volunteers, and staff; often by reconstructing dialogue to the best of their ability. Every claim in students' fieldnotes must be backed up with observational evidence. For example, instead of simply mentioning that they had an uncomfortable interaction with a client, a student would describe every aspect of the interaction, including tone of voice, body language, and dialogue.

During the semester, students' fieldnotes serve as a venue for reflection. They also provide my community partner and me with insights about students' volunteer experiences. Finally, they are a data source for students' term papers. Since they are so rich and detailed, the utility of the fieldnotes extends beyond the end of the semester. After securing their consent, over the years I have used the students' fieldnotes to enliven volunteer trainings, prejudice reduction workshops, qualitative research lectures, and a journal article.[6] In this chapter, I use these fieldnotes to explore how gender influences students' service-learning experiences.

Analysis

As table 6.1 demonstrates, sixty-two students completed my service-learning course, and generated 535 sets of ethnographic fieldnotes in the process. These sets range in length from one single-spaced page to eight or nine double-spaced pages. After gaining permission from fifty-five students to use their fieldnotes for this project, I assembled a dataset of 469 sets of ethnographic fieldnotes.[7] I changed all names that appear in the dataset to pseudonyms before analyzing the data.

Gender was an important theme in the dataset. The students who volunteered with the shelter's outreach team reflected on how gender shaped peoples' experiences living on the streets. While anyone living on the streets confronts harsh weather, uncertainty, and the potential of violence, women face the additional threat of sexual assault. In their fieldnotes, the students who volunteered inside the shelter reflected on how gender shaped clients' experiences. Since the Poverello Center serves many more men than women, dozens of male clients

Table 6.1. The Dataset.

Year	Number of Students Enrolled	Number of Fieldnote Sets Required	Number of Fieldnote Sets Generated by Students	Number of Student Permissions	Number of Fieldnote Sets with Permissions
2010	10	8	80	6	48
2011	12	~9	113	11	102
2012	11	~10	118	10	105
2013	8	~9	77	7	67
2014	10	7	70	10	70
2015	11	7	77	11	77
Total	62	~8	535	55	469

Table 6.2. Analyzing the Dataset.

Type of Gendered Interaction	Key Word Searches
Client comment about student's appearance	Face, hair, teeth
Client comment about student's attractiveness	Pretty, beautiful, lovely
Client comment about student's relationship status	Boyfriend, husband, married
Client asking student out	Go out, going out, date

sleep together in large dorms while female clients sleep in a smaller, more intimate room. These students also had gendered interactions with clients, volunteers, and staff; these are the focus of the findings section below.

As table 6.2 illustrates, I used key word searches to identify gendered interactions between students, clients, volunteers, and/or staff in the dataset. First, I searched the dataset for the words "face," "hair," and "teeth" to locate clients' comments about students' appearances. I then searched the dataset for the words "pretty," "beautiful," and "lovely" to identify clients' comments about students' attractiveness. I then searched the dataset for the words "boyfriend," "husband," and "married" to locate comments about students' relationship status. Finally, I searched the dataset for the phrases "go out," "going out," and "date" to identify clients' requests for dates.

Although key word searching is typically a deductive analytical technique, I used it inductively for this project. I identified the four types of gendered interactions after reading 535 sets of fieldnotes; I did not derive them from existing empirical or theoretical studies. This analytical technique has several benefits. First, it moves the study beyond an anecdotal discussion of the gendered nature of service-learning. Second, it made it possible to identify examples of gendered client interactions from the past six years; without a systemic scan of the dataset I might have relied heavily on examples that were most recent, or that I remembered most vividly. Finally, it helped me understand the prevalence of each theme. Key word searching made it possible to locate each instance of a particular theme in the dataset.

How Gender Shapes Students' Experiences with Service-Learning

Gendered Interactions with Male Clients

The dataset contained many examples of gendered interactions with male clients. Below, I describe the four most common: comments about students' appearances, questions about students' relationship status, requests for dates, and inappropriate touching.

COMMENTING ON STUDENTS' APPEARANCES

In their fieldnotes, many students described conversations that they had with male clients about their appearance. Jeanne had this type of interaction during a food service shift in 2011.[8] As she explained, "I dyed my hair a very rich (fake, not auburn) red this weekend. I've had my hair this color many times before, but not in over a year. I forgot that it garners quite a bit of attention from children and friendly adults. People often comment on it, and today was no exception. At least half a dozen people complimented me, from staff to clients. One man came in and said, "Your hair is badass. Everybody's been talkin' about it." This was not an uncomfortable interaction for Jeanne. In fact, she noted in her fieldnotes that "the compliment made me smile."[9] For many female students in my service-learning course, though, clients' comments about their appearance were disconcerting.

This was certainly the case for Elaine. During a volunteer shift in the shelter's front office in 2012, a male client came in and asked her for a bottle of Listerine. "I reached up, grabbed it, and handed it to him. He smiled warmly, nodded, and said, "Thank you very much." I smiled and he said sounding a little pained and a little jealous, "Wow you have really white teeth. I wish I had white teeth like yours." When reflecting on the interaction in her fieldnotes, Elaine noted that she "felt a little bit uncomfortable" during and after the interaction. The interaction was clearly gendered, given the client's unsolicited commentary about Elaine's appearance. But it also highlights the class and status differences that exist between clients and students in the course. White, straight teeth are often the result of consistent access to dental work, something that few clients at the Poverello Shelter have had during their lives.

Inquiries about Relationship Status

In their fieldnotes, many students described conversations with clients about their relationship status. In 2015, near the end of a food service shift, Carissa interacted with

> a man perhaps in his 40s or 50s ... who I've not seen before ... [His] biker-esque look is completed by a partially exposed chest or should[er] tattoo and a large 'Sterling' that is tattooed in blue on his neck ... [He] goes quietly through the line while I try not to smile too much or ask him questions about the pin on his vest or be overly zealous as I normally am with bikers. He's gone before I have too much time to annoy him. Ten minutes later, [he] is back. He stops in front of me, leaning slightly over the barrier of food warmers. I smile and he asks "are you married?"

Feeling extremely uncomfortable, Carissa responded in the negative. A few seconds later, the client returned and told her "well, you have beautiful eyes" and then walked away again. As I discuss below, Carissa worried about her role in the interaction later in this set of fieldnotes.

In their fieldnotes, many students described conversations with clients about their relationship status. Male clients tended to use these comments as precursors to date requests, while female clients tended to use them to as lead-ins to relationship advice.

Asking Students Out

A third type of gendered interaction that appeared frequently in the dataset was clients' requests for dates. During a food preparation shift in 2012, a male client who was roughly Constance's age "turned his attention to me. He asked if I was a student and I told him I was." After brief discussion of Constance's major and the service-learning course, the client

> then made a quick switch of topics and asked if I've ever seen a play at the university. I told him I used to watch plays all the time, but haven't been in a year or so. The man nodded his head and all his attention was on me. I got the feeling that he could hardly wait for me to finish my sentence because he was so excited to agree with me ... He was extremely friendly, but something just was not connecting. I [couldn't] really put my finger on it. The man then began exaggerating [about] how great the plays are. He then stammered out "do you want to go with me sometime?"

Constance was surprised by the question, but not immobilized like many of the female students in my course. As I describe below, many female students were taken aback by gendered interactions with clients.

Tiffany had a similar experience during a volunteer shift in the shelter's clothing room in 2012. A male client in his thirties with "bleach blonde shoulder length hair" wearing "an unbuttoned Hawaiian style shirt and shorts" engaged her in light banter about his impressions of the town.[10] After a while "he pulls out a wad of money (a five-dollar bill and a couple of ones) and asks if he can leave a donation" for the shelter. When Tiffany responded "'I think so, but I'm not sure where. You should probably go down to the main office and ask someone there.' He said 'well, how about I just take you out for coffee instead?'" After Tiffany rebuffed him several times, he finally gave up.

Inappropriate Physical Contact

Sometimes students' gendered interactions with clients move out of the verbal realm and into the physical one. These interactions are often prefaced by clients' comments about students' appearance or questions about students' relationship status. During a food service shift in 2015, a male client initiated physical contact with Marion. She explains that during her shift, the client who was working beside Marion turned to face her, put "his wet hands on my shoulder, and said 'you know who you remind me of? That girl who plays on *That 70s Show*' ... I laughed and told him I get that quite often and told him that her name on the show was Donna. He exclaimed 'Donna!' quite loudly and rubbed my shoulder. He had maintained contact throughout our short conversation." Despite the fact that Marion felt "slightly weird about" the shoulder rub, her physical interaction with the client did not end there. As she "was getting ready to leave, [the client] called out from the kitchen 'hey Donna, are you leaving?' I told him I was, and he reached to shake my hand, but instead of simply shaking it, he held my hand between both of his and rubbed his thumb over the back of my hand." Nearly every student who described these interactions in their fieldnotes shared Marion's discomfort. Their uneasiness was influenced by two things: the fact that it was nearly always initiated by clients (and not the students), and formal and informal prohibitions against physical touch at the shelter.[11]

While the pervasiveness of gendered interactions in the dataset is interesting, even more striking is the gender composition of these interactions. They almost always involved a female student and a male client. This is compelling evidence that gender shapes students' experiences with service-learning. These interactions do not comprise the only evidence of the gendered nature of service-learning that my analysis uncovered, however.

Struggling to Navigate Gendered Interactions

Female students in my course were not only more likely than male students to have gendered interactions with clients; how they navigated them was also qualitatively different. While female students in my course struggled to respond in direct and confident ways, male students did not. My analysis uncovered three ways that female students commonly responded to gendered interactions with male clients: ignoring, downplaying, and deflecting.[12] As I argue below, these responses are highly consistent with women's gender socialization.

Ignoring

The most common way that female students in my service-learning course responded to gendered interactions with clients was to ignore them. Previously, Marion ignored the client who compared her to Donna from *That 70s Show*. During a food service shift the next week, the client "walked up to me ... and put his hand on my waist and said when he leaves tomorrow (assuming he's getting his new place) that he could get my number. I just laughed nervously and he walked away.... When he came back he put his hand on me again and said well since you didn't say anything I'll take that as a no? He phrased it as a kind of playful question; his voice rose noticeably at the end and he chuckled a bit afterward." As Marion and many other female students in my service-learning course have learned over the years, ignoring gendered interactions with clients is ineffective. While reflecting on the interaction in her fieldnotes, Marion "realized I should have just told him "no" but I was in the middle of stirring the carrots and figured if I ignored him he wouldn't press the matter. He did." If this strategy is so unsuccessful, why do so many female students in my course employ it? As I explain below, ignoring is consistent with women's gender socialization. So, too, is another response employed by many female students in my course: downplaying.

Downplaying

Many of the female students in my course downplayed gendered interactions with clients. In her fieldnotes, Rebecca described another student, Annette, downplaying a gendered interaction with a male client. During both students' food service shift in 2015, a male client who "works in the kitchen during dinner service, asked [Annette] if he could give her his number." When the client left the kitchen to take a break Rebecca noticed that Annette "was blushing a deep shade of red," indicating her discomfort with the situation. A little while later, the client returned from to the kitchen and "apologized to [Annette] for what he did and she said it was okay."[13]

My analysis suggests that female students tend to downplay when clients' behavior is mildly inappropriate, and when clients apologize directly to them. Key word searching uncovered a few instances when students downplayed behavior that was highly inappropriate, such as highly sexualized comments from clients and sexualized physical contact. Like ignoring, this response is also consistent with women's gender socialization.

Deflecting

Many of the female students in my course deflected gendered interactions using humor, information, and misinformation. Constance used humor to deflect a gendered interaction during a food preparation shift in 2012. In response to a client's inquiry about her marital status, Constance remembered that "on my right hand I had on a giant heart-shaped 'I love JB' ring. The JB stood for Justin Beiber [sic]. I diverted the conversation by saying 'well no, but I am engaged.' Instead of flashing my real ring, I flashed my giant plastic JB ring and we all laughed. I told the guys good-bye and they said they'd see me next week." Constance's use of humor deflected attention from her and lightened the mood in the kitchen. However, it did not address her discomfort. When reflecting on the interaction in her fieldnotes, Constance remembered feeling "a little uncomfortable" by the question, especially since it "came out of left field." Constance's use of humor is interesting. She also could have used information to deflect the situation, since she was recently engaged.[14]

A few female students in my service-learning course used facts to deflect gendered interactions with male clients. This was how Elaine responded to the male client's compliments about her teeth (see above). "All I do is brush my teeth," she said, to which the client responded with "something like 'your teeth are beautiful.' I shrugged again. He looked down again. He tapped his feet for a minute or so" and left the room after making a self-deprecating comment about himself. However, it was much more common for female students to use misinformation to deflect gendered interactions with male clients. The most common type of misinformation that students offered was their relationship status. After a male client asked Marion for her phone number, she "laughed nervously again and said, 'maybe if I didn't have a boyfriend.' I lied completely, but I didn't know how else to tell him no after my explanation of the [shelter] rules on the twentieth didn't work. He reeled back and said, 'a boyfriend!' in disbelief. Without skipping a beat, he moved over to [Rebecca], put his hand on her hip, and said, I don't suppose you have a boyfriend? [Rebecca] faced him and looked him in the eye while she told him that she did have a boyfriend." At first glance, Rebecca's response appears direct and confident, something that occurred very infrequently in the dataset. However, as she revealed in her own fieldnotes, Rebecca did not actually have a boyfriend.

It is understandable why so few female service-learning students, such as Constance, used accurate information to deflect gendered interactions. Sharing personal information might pique the client's interest more or invite more personal questions. What is curious, though, is why so few female students simply explained that they were not interested or cited shelter prohibitions against dating clients. The gender-conscious pedagogy that I developed for my service-learning course prompts female students to reflect on their responses to gendered interactions with male clients. As I explain below, it also compels both female and male students to think deeply and critically about gender in general, including gender socialization.

Gender-Conscious Service-Learning Pedagogy

The previous section provided empirical evidence that gender influences students' experiences with service-learning. My anecdotal awareness of this phenomenon convinced me to develop a gender-conscious pedagogy for my service-learning course. As I explain below, this pedagogy has three main components. First, it examines female students' indirect and passive responses to gendered interactions with male clients. Then, it explores the conflicts between the demands of service-learning and gender socialization. Finally, it provides female and male students with tools to overcome gender socialization. My gender-conscious service-learning pedagogy relies heavily on excerpts from students' ethnographic fieldnotes.

The Roots of Reticence

As I mentioned above, female service-learning students' typical responses to gendered interactions are rarely effective. Not only do they not discourage clients in the moment, but they rarely prevent future overtures from the same client. The female students are acutely aware of this, reflecting on it often in their ethnographic fieldnotes. For example, after watching Rebecca deflect a male client's attention effectively, Marion remarked "I wished I had been more direct with him; maybe then he would have taken me more seriously." Despite their awareness of the problem, many struggle to become more direct and confident. A key component of the gender-conscious pedagogy that I have developed over the years is helping female students identify the causes of their hesitation.

When I first broach the topic of female students' reticence, I ask students why so many of them struggle to confront or report inappropriate behavior in their personal lives. Students respond that they do not want to be rude, that they are uncomfortable with conflict, and that they are often confused about their role in the situation.[15] Then we move into a discussion of why many students ignore, downplay, or deflect gendered interactions with clients. I purposively frame this in a gender-neutral way, although this is a gendered phenomenon in my course. I do this to keep male students engaged in the discussion. Students repeat all of the reasons mentioned above, as well as several factors specific to the shelter. Students explain that they are often unsure about the clients' understanding of shelter rules. Like many other homeless shelters, the Poverello Center has a long list of rules for clients, volunteers, and staff. Many students struggle to master the list during the semester, and wonder if perhaps the client simply was not familiar with the shelter rule prohibiting dating relationships between clients and volunteers.[16] Students also mention concerns about consequences for clients. Like many other homeless shelters, the Poverello Center has a graduated discipline policy. While minor infractions, such as not completing their daily chore, can earn a client twenty-four hours out of the shelter, more serious violations, such as sexually harassing or striking a volunteer or staffer, can result in a client being banned from the shelter for a week, a month, or permanently. The students fear feeling responsible if a client is removed from the facility. This is especially true in the winter months, when sleeping outside in Montana can be quite dangerous.

Next, we transition into a brief lecture about gender socialization. I take the lead, introducing what gender socialization is and how it works. I explain the gendered expectation that women be pleasant, friendly, and accommodating at all times. I then ask all students to reflect on examples of gender socialization from their own lives. This discussion of gender socialization does not happen just once; most semesters I return to the topic several times. This lecture dovetails nicely with discussions about rules, which comprise the second component of my gender-conscious service-learning pedagogy.

Underscoring the Need for Rules

At the beginning of the semester, the shelter staffers introduce the most important shelter rules, those focusing on mandatory chores, onsite substance use, and disrespecting or threatening staffers. The staffers briefly explain how these rules are necessary to keep the shelter clean, organized, and safe. While most of my students are vigilant about following shelter rules themselves, many hesitate to report rule violations to staffers when they witness them. This is equally true of the female and male students in my course.

There are several reasons for the students' hesitation. Two reasons are gender-neutral: some students fear conflict, and others dread the negative consequences for the clients. One reason is gendered: reporting rule violations contradicts gendered expectations of a female student. While discussions about shelter rules are sensitive to gender, they do not focus intently on female students, the way that the first component does.

To increase the likelihood that students will report rule violations, these sessions explore the underlying logic of the most important shelter rules: those about personal relationships with clients, interactions with clients outside of the shelter, and gift-giving. I begin these sessions by presenting a fieldnote excerpt describing a rule violation, and then have students brainstorm about what is at stake if the violation is not reported.

Many of these sessions focus on shelter prohibitions on gift exchanges between the clients and volunteers (and clients and staff, for that matter). In her fieldnotes, Jeanne illustrates the rationale behind this rule. During a volunteer shift in the shelter's food pantry in 2011, Jeanne had an uncomfortable interaction with a male client. As she recalled in her fieldnotes, earlier in the semester, just outside of the shelter, she had "bummed a cigarette from him in exchange for my peanut butter. He sat and talked to me for a long time, and gave me a dream catcher that he had found." During the shift in question, the client came into the pantry looking for peanut butter. Jeanne asked a shelter staffer whether she should serve him, since he had already visited the pantry that week. The staffer told Jeanne "that even though he had been in several times that week and was not eligible for shelf items, that it was up to my discretion, and I could give him the peanut butter. When he heard me ask her if he was allowed to have it, [the client] interrupted her answer and said, 'I know I'm not allowed to have it. I'm asking if I can talk you into giving it to me.' I found his statement to be rude, but I gave him the peanut butter anyway." As Jeanne's excerpt illustrates, the client knew that he was asking Jeanne to bend a shelter rule. While it is possible that he would have asked any volunteer to do this, it is probable that he asked Jeanne because of their previous interaction. If he thought that he had done her a favor by giving her the cigarette and a dream catcher, he might believe that she owed him special treatment. The fieldnote excerpts that I select for these sessions illustrate the short- and long-term ramifications of rule violations at the shelter.

The shelter staffers often participate in these sessions. When they do, they emphasize that the clients often have radically different interpretations of interactions than the volunteers and staffers involved in them. Recall, for example, when the male client apologized to Annette for asking for her phone number, and she assured him that it was all right (see above). Even if the request was acceptable to Annette on a personal level, which I am not convinced that it was, it was unacceptable on an institutional level. His behavior was a clear violation of a shelter rule. As staffers would explain, downplaying the interaction could inadvertently communicate to the client that it was all right that he broke a shelter rule.

These sessions tend to make a stronger impression on male students than female students. When male students in my course understand the underlying logic of shelter rules, they become more comfortable reporting clients' violations. In contrast, female students continue to struggle with this and with navigating gendered interactions with male clients directly and confidently.

Undoing Gender Socialization

The third component of my gender-conscious service-learning pedagogy explicitly addresses female students' challenges. At first glance, it appears to focus on how to navigate awkward interactions with clients, but it is designed to help female students challenge gender socialization.

Like the rest of my gender-conscious pedagogy, this component draws heavily on excerpts from the students' ethnographic fieldnotes. For most of the semester, students read and discuss fieldnote excerpts, some written by their classmates and some by students in previous years. In the beginning of the semester, these exercises focus on the mechanics of writing ethnographic fieldnotes, but as the semester progresses they shift to personal and professional issues, such as managing awkward or inappropriate interactions with clients.

I assemble several excerpts describing awkward conversations with clients, gendered interactions with clients, rule violations, and so forth. Appendix A contains one of these exercises, entitled "managing uncomfortable client interactions." After the students read the excerpts, I ask them to jot down their thoughts about how they would respond in the same situation, and then discuss their ideas with a partner. I then provide the students with the remainder of the excerpt, which describes how each author handled the situation, and the clients' response. I ask the students to evaluate, first in pairs and then in a large group, each authors' response and compare it to the ideas that they jotted down. I always invite shelter staffers to participate in these exercises, and over the years they have made important contributions. Most years they explain what the best response to each scenario would be from the shelter's perspective. This helps students understand the institutional impact of rule violations.

It is not a coincidence that most of the excerpts in these exercises describe gendered interactions between clients and students. This makes it possible for me to circle back to gender, and gender socialization in particular. When discussing scenarios in which the student failed to respond directly or confidently, I ask students what they think prevented the student from doing so. While students often mention individual personality, I return to the topic of gender socialization. I explain that pressures to be pleasant, friendly, and accommodating shape many female students' hesitancy and indecision during gendered interactions with clients. They also make it challenging for many female service-learning students to meet shelter staffers' expectations of them, I continue.

The shelter staffers who are present for these exercises underscore the importance of direct communication, enforcement of rules, and maintenance of professional and personal boundaries for the volunteers (as well as the shelter staffers). I wrap up by exhorting all students, female and male, to critically examine the negative impacts of gender socialization in their lives. Doing so, I argue, will make it possible for them to resist gender socialization, or at least the aspects that hold them back in professional settings.

Discussion

On one level, the forty-one women and twenty-one men who have completed my service-learning course had very similar experiences. They read the same articles and books about hunger and homelessness, dissect them verbally and in writing, produce ethnographic fieldnotes, and synthesize the qualitative data contained in their fieldnotes. The analysis of students' ethnographic fieldnotes that I have presented in this chapter, however, strongly suggests that gender influences students' experiences with service-learning.

First, I found that the female students in my service-learning course had qualitatively different interactions with clients than the male students. In their ethnographic fieldnotes, the female students described gendered interactions with male clients that ranged from comments about their appearance to inappropriate physical contact. Although the male students occasionally had gendered interactions with clients, they did so much less often than their female classmates. The dataset reflects this.

Second, my analysis suggests that gender shaped how the students in my course navigated gendered interactions with clients. I identified three ways that the female students typically responded to gendered interactions with male clients: ignoring, downplaying, and deflecting. My analysis uncovered very few examples of female students directly and confidently responding to these interactions. I offered an explanation for this: the fact that directness and confidence are inconsistent with women's gender socialization. Since this is not the case for men, gender socialization might also explain why male students in my course struggle less with client interactions than female students.

The fact that so many female students in my course internalized the messages about "gender typical behavior" that they received as girls (Risman 2004, 436) suggests the robustness of gender socialization. So too does the female service-learning students' tendency to adopt "passive postures" during their volunteer service (Adler, Kless, and Adler 1992, 170).

The female service-learning students' compliance with gender socialization is curious because so many of them have strong, outspoken personalities. Many identified as feminists, and some actively challenged gender norms outside of the classroom. One explanation for their compliance is service-learning's tendency to push the students outside of their comfort zones (Catlett and Prowrller 2011; Dunlap et al. 2007; Green 2001; Keen and Hall 2009; Keller, Nelson, and Wick 2003; Marullo 1998; Vogelgesang 2004). Could female service-learning students' acquiescence to gender norms be related to this stress and discomfort? Further research could explain whether women are more likely to comply with gender socialization when they are uncomfortable or under pressure.

The persistence of "passive postures" among female students is also interesting given the lack of "social punishments for flouting gender expectations" (Hollander 2002, 490; Adler, Kless, and Adler 1992, 170) in my course. In fact, my course actively encourages female students to challenge the messages about gender and femininity that they received as girls. As I described above, an important component of my gender-conscious pedagogy is educating students about how gender typical behavior complicates many of their interactions with male clients. Despite the lack of penalties for rebuffing gender norms, many of the female students in my course hold onto them for dear life. Could the female students be receiving additional messages that contradict or undermine the gender-conscious pedagogy that I developed for the course? It is possible that clients, shelter staffers, local practitioners, or other students in the course are sending implicit or explicit messages that the female students should comply with traditional gender expectations. It is also possible that I am somehow unconsciously encouraging "passive postures" while explicitly encouraging the female students to be direct and confident communicators. Future research could identify implicit and explicit messages received by the female service-learning students, including the sources and impact of these messages.

In response to the gendered nature of service-learning, the pedagogy that I developed for my service-learning course promotes deep and critical thinking about gender. After exploring how gender socialization informs female students' responses to gendered interactions with clients, I help the students think critically about, and ideally undo, gender socialization. The integral role that ethnographic fieldnotes play in my pedagogy underscores the importance of structured reflection in service-learning courses (Bringle and Hatcher 1996; Felten, Gilchrist, and Darby 2006; Honnett and Poulsen 1989; Keen and Hall 2009; Potter, Caffrey, and Plante 2003).

Even though my course had a modest amount of gender content, it created numerous opportunities for the students to think deeply and critically about gender. For example, in their fieldnotes and during class discussions, many students have reflected about how women, families, and children experience hunger and homelessness differently than single men. Service-learning courses with even less emphasis on gender, such as those focusing on school children, animals, or the natural environment, might provide fewer opportunities for students to think about gender. In these courses, gender might exert a weaker influence on the students' service-learning experiences. Research on a broader range of service-learning courses could elucidate whether, and to what extent, gender shapes the students' experiences in courses with little or no gender content.

As table 6.3 illustrates, my findings reflect the social and demographic context of the course. My course took place in Western Montana, a part of the country where a high value is placed on politeness. This complicated my efforts

Table 6.3. Demographic Composition of the Course.

Year of the Course	Number of Students Enrolled	Students of Color	Female Students	Out-of-State Students
2010	10	1 (10%)	5 (50%)	5 (50%)
2011	12	0 (0%)	8 (67%)	3 (25%)
2012	11	2 (18%)	9 (82%)	5 (45%)
2013	8	1 (13%)	6 (75%)	4 (50%)
2014	10	0 (0%)	5 (50%)	6 (60%)
2015	11	3 (27%)	8 (73%)	3 (27%)
Total	62	7 (11%)	41 (66%)	26 (42%)

to understand how gender influences students' service-learning experiences. Above, I argued that the female students' struggles to respond directly and confidently to gendered interactions with male clients largely reflect gender socialization. However, female students who grew up in Montana could experience an additional conflict between their cultural values and shelter staffers' expectations that they be direct communicators. Conducting similar research in other parts of the country, or systematically comparing the experiences of Montana natives and out-of-state service-learning students, could generate interesting insights about the complex interplay between individual personality, cultural values, and gender socialization.[17]

Western Montana is also extraordinarily racially homogeneous. According to the 2010 census, 89.5 percent of the state's population was white and 92.4 percent of the population of Missoula County, where my course takes place, was white. This explains the paucity of discussion about race in this chapter. The client population of the Poverello Center is overwhelmingly white; so are the students who have completed my course.[18] Both reflect the demographic context of the course. As a result, race was not a robust topic of discussion in the course, despite my best efforts and despite my enthusiasm for intersectionality and intersectional pedagogy. While I encouraged students to attend to race when describing client interactions in their fieldnotes, the small number of people of color using shelter services made that hard. If gender-neutral service-learning pedagogy is insufficient, as I argued above, the same is likely to be true of race-neutral service-learning pedagogy. Research on service-learning courses in more diverse locations, and courses with more diverse student populations, could yield evidence about the need for race-conscious service-learning pedagogy (Marullo 1998). Despite these limitations, this project offers several important insights into the gendered nature of service-learning.

Conclusions

In this chapter, I have demonstrated that gender shapes students' service-learning experiences in profound ways. I have also argued that gender-neutral pedagogy inadequately prepares students for, and does not help them navigate, their service-learning experiences. If this is true in service-learning courses with a modest amount of gender content, like mine, it is certainly the case in service-learning courses with more explicit foci on gender. While some instructors use materials from their own disciplines to infuse gender, race, class, and sexual orientation into their service-learning courses, I argued for a more comprehensive approach. I proposed that gender-neutral service-learning pedagogy be replaced with a pedagogy that is gender-conscious (and race-conscious, class-conscious, and sexual orientation-conscious, for that matter). This pedagogy relies heavily on written reflection, and makes that reflection visible to all students in the course and the community partner.

Making written reflection visible can inspire service-learning students to think deeply and critically about gender. When female students read excerpts of other student's fieldnotes, they learned that they were not alone, and specifically that other female students were having gendered interactions with clients and were struggling to navigate these interactions. When male students read other students' fieldnote excerpts, they gained a deeper understanding of how gender influenced female students' interactions with clients, and how gender socialization shaped many female students' responses to those interactions.

Making written reflection visible can also deepen instructors' relationships with their community partners. When Poverello Center staffers read excerpts from my service-learning students' fieldnotes, they learned a great deal about volunteers' experiences.[19] This was especially useful for the volunteer coordinators and other shelter staffers who work closely with volunteers. Sharing the students' fieldnotes with my community partner also improved the quality of reflection discussions, especially those about gender and gender socialization. In years when they read students' ethnographic fieldnotes, shelter staffers helped me identify inappropriate behavior and rule violations that I surely would have missed because I am less familiar with shelter rules than they are. In years when staffers were unable to read students' fieldnotes, I shared fieldnote excerpts with them.[20] These excerpts informed their presentations to students about the importance of shelter rules and reporting rule violations.

After reading the fieldnote excerpts presented in this chapter, especially those describing gendered interactions with male clients, a reader might conclude that settings like the Poverello Center are a poor match for service-learning courses. These community partners, readers might conclude, simply make students too uncomfortable, causing distress for the students and creating additional work for the instructor. However, as I explained above, discomfort and distress are common features of the students' service-learning experiences (Catlett and Proweller 2011; Dunlap et al. 2007; Green 2001). Although scholars often celebrate this discomfort, service-learning courses generate a number of different kinds of discomfort, some of which are not beneficial for students. For example, service-learning courses should not create ethical discomfort for students by requiring them to participate in volunteer service that violates their core beliefs. Service-learning instructors should also not construct scenarios where students are knowingly and repeatedly exposed to racism, sexism, homophobia, and other types of discrimination. Finally, service-learning courses should not expose students to physical harm or danger. The discomfort that would arise from these kinds of courses is not and should not be considered to be positive for service-learning students. While it is not necessary for instructors to select community partners and settings that will keep students inside their comfort zones, they must develop service-learning pedagogies that help students understand and overcome their own discomfort in complex and dynamic settings such as the Poverello Center. As I have demonstrated in this chapter, the gender-conscious pedagogy that I developed for my course is capable of doing this. I am confident that other service-learning pedagogies that are gender-conscious (and race-conscious, class-conscious, and sexual orientation-conscious) can do the same.

Despite significant gains in the arena of gender equality over the past few decades, gender socialization is alive and well in American society. Gendered messages shape how many women and men act, what they think, how they look, and what they aspire to. While this is detrimental to both women and men, it is especially problematic for women. The "gender role training" that girls receive at home and in other institutions convinces many to adopt "passive postures," eschew leadership opportunities, and pursue low wage, low prestige pink-collar careers (Adler, Kless, and Adler 1992, 170; Hill 2002, 495). It has also contributed to women's underrepresentation in the upper echelons of US business, government, and nonprofit sectors.

However, this chapter has demonstrated that higher education, and service-learning in particular, can be important sites of production for resistance to these messages. Service-learning courses can help students think deeply and critically about "gender role traditionality," and develop aspirations and senses of self that are not limited by, or to, their genders (Raffaelli and Ontai 2004). However, this will not happen as long as the service-learning courses employ gender-neutral pedagogy, not even in courses with significant gender content. In order to harness service-learning's potential for resistance, instructors must adopt pedagogies that are gender-conscious (and race-conscious, class-conscious, and sexual orientation-conscious, for that matter). Doing so will certainly benefit students, as I have illustrated in this chapter. But it will also benefit political scientists and other social scientists who are striving to integrate threshold concepts from WGS into their disciplines.

Appendix A

"Managing Uncomfortable Client Interactions" Exercise

In each of the fieldnote excerpts below the author describes an uncomfortable interaction between themselves and a client. After you have read each excerpt, write down a few ideas about how you would react if you were in the same situation. Then discuss your ideas with a partner. Try to focus on the positives and negatives of each option before deciding which response you think is best for each scenario.

Excerpt 1

S walked back to the other side of the kitchen and the younger gentleman drying dishes turned his attention to me. He asked if I was a student and I told him I was. He asked what I was studying to be at the Pov. This is a tricky question. I feel rude or guilty or something telling him I'm there to study poverty and homelessness, but I am there to study poverty and homelessness and so that is what I told him. To my surprise that man seemed interested instead of insulted. His eyes widened and he nodded his head, as if thinking, "That is interesting." He then made a quick switch of topics and asked if I've ever seen a play at the university. I told him I used to watch plays all the time, but haven't been in a year or so. The man nodded his head and all his attention was on me. I got the feeling that he could hardly wait for me to finish my sentence because he was so excited to agree with me. At that moment I began thinking the man may have a disability. He was extremely friendly, but something just was not connecting. I can't really put my finger on it. The man then began exaggerating on how great the plays are. He then stammered out, "Do you want to go with me sometime?"

Excerpt 2

A client that K knew came in and was talking with her. S said to me, "Can you pass me that Listerine?" At first I didn't know what he said, and asked him confused, "What are you looking for?" The Listerine would normally be with the toothpaste so that was an odd place for it too. I turned around and seeing the large bottle realized what he was asking for. "Oh yeah for sure," I told him. I reached up, grabbed it and handed it to him. He smiled warmly, nodded, and said, "Thank you very much." I smiled and he said sounding a little pained and a little jealous, "Wow you have really white teeth. I wish I had white teeth like yours." One, I thought that my teeth aren't that white, I do drink coffee every day and I wasn't looking, but I didn't notice that he had bad looking teeth. Thinking about it, I think that he has about the same color as mine. So I felt a little bit uncomfortable.

Excerpt 3

The man with the dyed (?) black hair and intriguing face stops by the office. He slowly approaches the door and states "you make me happy when you come here but you make me even happier when you leave" very flatly. I laugh but I am totally confused. This is only the second time I've seen him so I don't think it is directed at me, but maybe just to whoever was going to be in the office when he decided to do this. I laugh but before I can ask him anything about it he turns around and leaves. It wasn't uncomfortable at all, just unusual. The tall woman who left when R stopped by came back into the office sans nutroll. I'm glad she is done eating. The first thing she does is leans over the desk and says "I left so you could flirt!"

Below are fieldnotes excerpts that explain how each author responded during their uncomfortable interaction with a client. After you have read each excerpt, discuss their reaction with your partner.

- *What did you think that each author did well? Why?*
- *What did you think that each author did poorly? Why?*
- *Would you do the same thing as the author, or something else? Why?*

Excerpt 1

This question took me completely off guard. I paused for a second trying to think of the appropriate response. There was no threatening manner about him and I don't even know if he was inappropriately asking me out or just wanted to go see a play. After getting my thoughts together I responded with a simple, "No, I don't think so." The man smiled and nodded his head and returned to drying the dishes. Disconnect was still there and I was not sure where to go with the conversation, so I just kind of smiled and awkwardly walked out of the room.

Excerpt 2

Shrugging it off literally and metaphorically, I said, "All I do is brush my teeth." He said something like, "Your teeth are beautiful." I shrugged again. He looked down again. He tapped his feet for a minute or so. Then he stopped tapping, raising his head, straightened his back and said hopefully, "Well there are married guys who are bald right? Maybe it can still happen for me." He left the room with large, slow steps with hands in his pockets. At the door he turned around and waved goodbye to K and I, saying something like, "Have a good day ladies."

Excerpt 3

I let out an unintentional "ugh!" which was probably incredibly rude and I scramble quickly to recover the situation. I figure it would be a little too much personal information for me to give to someone who I don't know their name to say that I am in a long term relationship … "He's so old!" I say, which is half true. He's probably much older than me. She responds with a shrug "I would have flirted with him when I was your age." It doesn't seem like she was offended by my first comment. That's good. "He is probably umm at least 20 years older than me!" "Well maybe when I was his age, ha ha!" She seems to be comfortable and we chat back and forth some and she leaves when the conversation dies.

DAISY ROOKS is Associate Professor of Sociology at the University of Montana. She teaches in her department's Inequality and Social Justice option area, and conducts research on rural homelessness, labor-environmental coalitions in rural areas, and public education.

Notes

1. Much of this research starts from the assumption that factual knowledge "is a prerequisite for becoming an educated and engaged citizen" (Carpini and Keeter 2000, 636).

2. Pedagogy is not the only, or main, focus of the research about service-learning. For example, numerous articles have measured the impact of service-learning on students, namely how service-learning courses shape students' professional, ethical, and civic outlooks.

3. In their article about gender and service-learning, Keller (2003) provide compelling evidence that educational institutions often influence women's decisions to enter pink collar occupations. They argue that higher education, and service-learning courses in particular, often reinforce "a self-sacrificial ethic of care already too prevalent in feminine gender training" (Keller, Nelson, and Wick 2003, 39).

4. As Connell (2005) has demonstrated, men have gender too. As such, gender-conscious service-learning pedagogy does not focus exclusively on women, but explores how gender shapes the experiences of female and male students in service-learning courses.

5. Over the years, shelter staffers have played a critical role in my service-learning course. They have helped me recruit and screen students, assess students' volunteer service, deliver guest lecturers, and facilitate class discussions. Using the term "my course" in this paper, rather than "the course that I teach in collaboration with the shelter," helps keep the prose lean, but is not entirely accurate.

6. This project received approval from the University of Montana's Institutional Review Board (218–309).

7. Of the seven students who did not grant me permission to use their fieldnotes, three were graduate students planning to use their fieldnotes for their Master of Arts thesis projects, and four were students who failed to return the permission form to me.

8. All names in this chapter are pseudonyms.

9. In this same set of notes Jeanne exemplified the deep learning that is often facilitated by service-learning reflection. After describing the attention that her dyed hair and tattoos garner, she "began to ponder the question, 'Am I an attention-seeker?!' The answer was 'I have a bunch of black ink on my arms and neon red hair. Yes. Yes, I am.' I'm learning so much about myself—I'm not sure if I like it."

10. One thing that is unique about Constance's and Tiffany's experiences is the age of the clients who asked them out. Although clients in their twenties and thirties sometimes appear in students' descriptions of these interactions, over the years many more male clients in their forties, fifties, and sixties have solicited female students for dates.

11. Marion reflected on these prohibitions in the same set of fieldnotes. "Most of the clients that work in the kitchen are friendly with me" she noted, "but none ... go out of their way to initiate touch with me." She remembered that during her first volunteer shift at the shelter she "attempted to shake" the hand of a client "but he instead awkwardly bumped fists with me, inadvertently teaching me my first lesson about initiating contact with residents."

12. On rare occasions, the female students responded confidently and directly to gendered interactions. Constance did this during a food preparation shift in 2012. As she reports, the male client's request for a date, which I described above in the section called "Asking Students Out": "[T]ook me completely off guard. I paused for a second trying to think of the appropriate response. There was no threatening manner about him and I don't even know if he was inappropriately asking me out or just wanted to go see a play. After getting my thought[s] together I responded with a simple 'no, I don't think so.' The man smiled and nodded his head and returned to drying the dishes ... I was not sure where to go with the conversation, so I just kind of smiled and awkwardly walked out of the room." Constance simply told the truth, that is, she was not interested in dating the client, and went about her business. Although the interaction was somewhat awkward, the client did not get angry, push the issue, or demand an explanation, as other the female students feared.

13. Although Rebecca did not criticize Annette's response to this gendered interaction, a second male client who witnessed it, did. After Annette told the first client that everything was fine, the second client turned to her "and stated quite firmly 'no, it's not okay and you should tell him that!' before turning back to [the first client] to let him know that it wasn't okay." The second client was so concerned about the interaction that he ended up reporting it to a shelter staffer.

14. Later in the same set of fieldnotes, Constance mentioned her discomfort revealing personal information about herself. "Wearing my engagement ring makes me feel a little uncomfortable at the Poverello," she explained, "because it is a nice ring and I almost feel undeserving of it, especially when so many of the clients are at least double my age."

15. Carissa mused about this when reflecting on her interaction with the middle-aged biker who asked her about her marital status (see above). "I wonder," she wrote "if I maybe smiled more at him than I did the other clients? Or maybe I was checking out his biker garb too intently and I gave him the wrong idea? Or maybe my eyes just really are that beautiful? (I know you can't see it, but I winked when I wrote that)." This response is not unique to my students; it is a common response to sexual harassment among women.

16. This certainly influenced Marion's decision to ignore and deflect a male client's advances, described above. After one interaction with the client in question, Marion turned to Rebecca, a fellow student volunteer and said "it's ok? and shrugged. [Rebecca] reminded me that [clients] could get an out for hitting on us if we were to report it. When I told her

I felt [bad] about not telling him no in the first place she reminded me that the clients know the rules, and the sanctions for their actions weren't our fault.

17. As table 6.3 demonstrates, twenty-six of the sixty-two students (42 percent) who have completed my service-learning course grew up outside of Montana. Almost half of these students grew up in states with cultures that are similar to Montana's, though. For example, eight students grew up in nearby states, Idaho, North Dakota, Wyoming, and Colorado with similar cultures. Three more students grew up in Midwestern states, Illinois, Minnesota, and Ohio, which also place a cultural value on politeness. These cultural similarities would make the comparison mentioned above challenging.

18. As table 6.3 illustrates, just seven students of color have completed my course; four American Indian students, two Asian American students, and one Latino student. This reflects the racial demographics of the University of Montana; in 2014 87.9% of students at the university were white (University of Montana 2014).

19. It is critical to get students' permission before sharing their fieldnotes with community partners, since they often are quite personal.

20. Each year, one or two shelter staffers have been involved in course preparation, student recruitment, and applicant screening for my service-learning course. Although these staffers often express interest in reading students' ethnographic fieldnotes, this has happened in just three of the past six years. Reading student fieldnotes requires a formidable time commitment; students generate roughly seventy-five double-spaced pages of writing when they submit fieldnotes. Like many underfunded nonprofit organizations, the Poverello Center struggles to provide basic services, and cannot always spare the staff time necessary to read students' fieldnotes.

References

Adler, Patricia A., Steven J. Kless, and Peter Adler. 1992. "Socialization to Gender Roles: Popularity among Elementary School Boys and Girls." *Sociology of Education* 65 (3): 169–87. doi: 10.2307/2112807.
Bringle, Robert G., and Julie A. Hatcher. 1996. "Implementing Service Learning in Higher Education." *The Journal of Higher Education* 67 (2): 221–39.
Burns, Leonard T. 1998. "Make Sure It's Service Learning, Not Just Community Service." *Education Digest* 64 (2): 38–41.
Carpini, Delli, Michael X., and Scott Keeter. 2000. "What Should Be Learned through Service Learning?" *PS-Political Science & Politics* 33 (3): 635–37. doi: 10.2307/420870.
Catlett, Beth S., and Amira Proweller. 2011. "College Students' Negotiation of Privilege in a Community-Based Violence Prevention Project." *Michigan Journal of Community Service Learning* 18 (1): 34–48.
Cohen, Jeremy, and Dennis F. Kinsey. 1994. "'Doing Good'and Scholarship: A Service-Learning Study." *Journalism & Mass Communication Educator* 48 (4): 4–14.
Connell, R.W. 2005. *Masculinities*. 2nd ed. Berkeley, CA: University of California Press.
Delve, Cecilia I., Suzanne D. Mintz, and Greig M. Stewart. 1990. "Promoting Values Development through Community Service: A Design." *New Directions for Student Services* 1990 (50): 7–29.

Deutsch, Francine M., and Susan E. Saxon. 1998. "Traditional Ideologies, Nontraditional Lives." *Sex Roles* 38 (5/6): 331–62.
Dicklitch, Susan. 2003. "Real Service = Real Learning: Making Political Science Relevant through Service-Learning." *PS-Political Science & Politics* 36 (4): 773–76.
Dunlap, Michelle, Jennifer Scoggin, Patrick Green, and Angelique Davi. 2007. "White Students' Experiences of Privilege and Socioeconomic Disparities: Toward a Theoretical Model." *Michigan Journal of Community Service Learning* 13 (2): 19–30.
Felten, Peter, Leigh Z. Gilchrist, and Alexa Darby. 2006. "Emotion and Learning: Feeling Our Way toward a New Theory of Reflection in Service-Learning." *Michigan Journal of Community Service Learning* 12 (2): 38–46.
Ferguson, Ann Arnett. 2001. *Bad Boys: Public Schools in the Making of Black Masculinity*. Ann Arbor, MI: University of Michigan Press.
Ferree, Myra Marx. 1980. "Working Class Feminism: A Consideration of the Consequences of Employment." *The Sociological Quarterly* 21 (2): 173–84. doi: 10.2307/4106149.
Galston, William A. 2001. "Political Knowledge, Political Engagement, and Civic Education." *Annual Review of Political Science* 4: 217–34. doi: 10.1146/annurev.polisci.4.1.217.
Green, Ann E. 2001. "'But You Aren't White': Racial Perceptions and Service-Learning." *Michigan Journal of Community Service Learning* 8 (1): 18–26.
Hepburn, Mary A., Richard G. Niemi, and Chris Chapman. 2000. "Service Learning in College Political Science: Queries and Commentary." *PS-Political Science & Politics* 33 (3): 617–22. doi: 10.2307/420867.
Hill, Shirley A. 2002. "Teaching and Doing Gender in African American Families." *Sex Roles* 47 (11/12): 493–506.
Hollander, Jocelyn A. 2002. "Resisting Vulnerability: The Social Reconstruction of Gender in Interaction." *Social Problems* 49 (4): 474–96. doi: 10.1525/sp.2002.49.4.474.
Honnett, Ellen Porter, and Susan J. Poulsen. 1989. *Principals of Good Practice for Combining Service and Learning*. Racine, WI: The Johnson Foundation, Inc.
Hunter, Susan, and Richard A. Brisbin Jr. 2000. "The Impact of Service Learning on Democratic and Civic Values." *PS-Political Science and Politics* 33 (3): 623–26. doi: 10.2307/420868.
Keen, Cheryl, and Kelly Hall. 2009. "Engaging with Difference Matters: Longitudinal Student Outcomes of Cocurricular Service-Learning Programs." *The Journal of Higher Education* 80 (1): 59–79.
Keller, Jean, Sheila Nelson, and Rachel Wick. 2003. "Care Ethics, Service-Learning, and Social Change." *Michigan Journal of Community Service Learning* 10 (1): 39–50.
Marullo, Sam. 1998. "Bringing Home Diversity: A Service-Learning Approach to Teaching Race and Ethnic Relations." *Teaching Sociology* 26 (4): 259–75.
Mitchell, Tania D. 2008. "Traditional versus Critical Service-Learning: Engaging the Literature to Differentiate Two Models." *Michigan Journal of Community Service Learning* 14 (2): 50–65.
Mooney, Linda A, and Bob Edwards. 2001. "Experiential Learning in Sociology: Service Learning and Other Community-Based Learning Initiatives." *Teaching Sociology* 29 (2): 181–94.
Myers-Lipton, Scott J. 1998. "Effect of a Comprehensive Service-Learning Program on College Students' Civic Responsibility." *Teaching Sociology* 26 (4): 243–58.
Owen, Diana. 2000. "Service Learning and Political Socialization." *PS-Political Science & Politics* 33 (3): 639–40.

Pascoe, C. J. 2011. *Dude, You're a Fag: Masculinity and Sexuality in High School.* Berkeley, CA: University of California Press.
Potter, Sharyn J., Elizabeth M. Caffrey, and Elizabethe G. Plante. 2003. "Integrating Service Learning into the Research Methods Course." *Teaching Sociology* 31 (1): 38–48.
Raffaelli, Marcela, and Lenna L Ontai. 2004. "Gender Socialization in Latino/a Families: Results from Two Retrospective Studies." *Sex Roles* 50 (5/6): 287–99.
Risman, Barbara J. 2004. "Gender as a Social Structure: Theory Wrestling with Activism." *Gender & Society* 18 (4): 429–50. doi: 10.1177/0891243204265349.
Smirles, Kimberly Eretzian. 2011. "Service Learning in a Psychology of Women Course: Transforming Students and the Community." *Psychology of Women Quarterly* 35 (2): 331–34. doi: 10.1177/0361684311403660.
University of Montana. 2014. *Data Digest.* Missoula, MT: University of Montana.
Vogelgesang, Lori J. 2004. "Diversity Work and Service-Learning: Understanding Campus Dynamics." *Michigan Journal of Community Service Learning* 10 (2): 34–43.
Walker, Tobi. 2000. "The Service/Politics Split: Rethinking Service to Teach Political Engagement." *PS-Political Science and Politics* 33 (3): 647–49.

7 Class Format, Gender, and Student Attitudes toward Political Participation

Sara Rinfret and Michelle Pautz

ACTIVE LEARNING STRATEGIES and learner-centered teaching have increasingly gained prominence in college classrooms as faculty across disciplines endeavor to incorporate more student engagement and involvement in their classrooms (Weimer 2013). In the political science classroom, engagement and participation is of particular interest as we attempt to model and encourage citizen engagement and political participation for our students. One question of interest about participation is whether there are differences in the ways that men and women participate. Understanding participation rates, both in the classroom and public square, is essential in a democracy. In this chapter, we focus on different participation rates of men and women by class format (e.g., traditional, online, hybrid). This exploratory research can be used for future considerations about gender identification and participation in the classroom.[1]

In particular, we conducted student pretest and posttest surveys across two universities during the 2014–2015 academic year with approximately one hundred students in a range of political science courses. The student surveys included questions that ranged from political knowledge, democracy, and political efficacy, to students' comfort level discussing politics by class format. Although research to date has offered noteworthy insights into what can drive classroom participation (Cohen 1991; Rocca 2010), we offer a different perspective—how a student's sex and class format affect changes in attitudes toward political science. Put succinctly, we offer insights into the attitudes and opinions about political participation more broadly through student classroom experiences.

The chapter begins with a review of the literature about how students participate in the college classroom. Then, we turn to the focus of our study—how male and female student attitudes about classroom discussions differ by classroom format in political science classes. Although we know a great deal about participation in American society more broadly (i.e., party preference, voting record), we understand less about any connections between participation in college classes and political participation in subsequent years (Lawless and Fox 2012). Ultimately, our findings suggest student perceptions are impacted by class format and slight differences are apparent for male and female students, which have implications not only for political participation more broadly, but how faculty design their courses.

Nonetheless, this research helps to engender fruitful conversations about how instructors can design their courses to encourage student political participation and promote citizen engagement by taking the time to allow students to discuss politics in a variety of forms (e.g., semester pause, pair/share, group circle, current events, simulations) to meet different student learning styles. By understanding how students perceive discussions about politics in various classroom settings as a function of sex, we can better meet the needs of all our students and ensure—to the best of our abilities—a dynamic and engaging learning environment. Simply put, we can create an environment that not only promotes self-efficacy and empowerment to participate in the classroom, but encourages political participation more broadly.

Political Engagement and the Classroom

For decades, political scientists have studied the role and practice of political participation. Broadly speaking, political participation encompasses activities such as voting, working on a campaign, participating in a protest, or contacting a local official. In political science classrooms across universities, we suggest faculty should play a significant role in cultivating basic knowledge about our government in an effort to foster a desire in our students to participate in the political process and be engaged citizens for the rest of their lives. This is because, as John Dewey among many others noted, a democracy's institutions are only as good as its citizens, and we have a basic responsibility to educate citizens to ensure the survival and legitimacy of our institutions. Indeed, a "culture of responsible participation ... can engender and sustain fair, trustworthy, and appropriately accountable political institutions" (Colby et al. 2007, 25). The faculty have long sought to encourage political participation and engagement. Colby and colleagues (2007), in *Educating for Democracy*, note extensive discussions about the political skills, that stretch far beyond voting, which faculty strive to develop in students to prepare them as engaged citizens. Their *Political Engagement Project* provides a carefully crafted effort at revamping political science curriculum to these ends. Despite this vital role, faculty continue to find their students disengaged in the subject matter and with waning political efficacies (Colby et al. 2007). For many of us, this is deeply distressing. Accordingly, we turn to an array of prescriptions to understand student attitudes about participation.

Classroom Participation

Of particular importance for political science instructors is classroom participation because it can serve as a gateway for civic engagement more broadly. Although we are interested in how student perceptions about politics are affected by different class formats, we begin by defining what we mean by classroom participation before turning to a review of student perceptions about the topic.

Class participation is a widely used term to describe an array of activities in the classroom. Rocca notes that "[p]articipation can be seen as an active engagement process" (2010, 187). According to Dancer and Kamvounias (2005), classroom participation includes five dimensions: classroom preparation, contribution to discussion, group skills, communication skills, and attendance. The benefits of these aforementioned participation dimensions are easily discernible for both seasoned faculty and newcomers: they include bringing students actively into the educational process (Cohen 1991), increasing student motivation (Junn 1994), promoting better learning (Daggett 1997; Weaver and Qi 2005), improving critical thinking skills (Crone 1997), and fostering character development and improvement (Kuh and Umbach 2004). With these benefits from participation, our attention turns to existing research about students' inclinations to participate.

Numerous studies investigate student participation in the classroom and Rocca's (2010) meta-analysis provides a strong synthesis of the factors that influence the participation of students. More specifically, five categories of factors are offered: (1) course logistics, (2) confidence levels of students, (3) classroom environment, (4) student personality traits, and (5) differences by sex. First, the logistics of the course matter. The number of students in a class, what time of day the class meets, the seating arrangements, course policies, and the use of media and technology are all part of the course logistics that affect student participation. Additionally, Fritschner (2000) noted differences in participation based on the level of course—introductory versus upper-division. Faculty generally have a sufficient amount of control over classroom design and can do much to encourage participation by simple alterations such as seating arrangements or course policies, for example.

Second, the confidence levels and apprehension of individual students matter for participation. We know from our own classrooms that students have a panoply of their own fears, such as feelings of inadequacy, nerves, or struggles of confidence, that affect their participation. These dimensions often leave faculty with little obvious means of changing the dynamics of class participation. Nevertheless, faculty can and do have control over some aspects of the classroom environment that might encourage participation. For example, faculty can reconfigure the physical space of the classroom to be more inviting and encourage conversation.

Third, the instructor and the classroom environment can also influence student participation. More specifically, how faculty members communicate with students, the level of respect conveyed, eye contact, and a supportive classroom environment can all have major effects on participation levels. Perhaps this category of factors is the one faculty members have the greatest control over. Fourth, the individual personality traits of students matter. Students' self-esteem and level of assertiveness factor into participation levels. The final category of influences that affects classroom participation is differences between men and women, which is our focus (Rocca 2010).

Men, Women, and Class Participation

Although numerous factors affect classroom participation, our primary interest is the influence a student's gender has on his/her opinions about classroom participation and whether these perceptions change from the beginning to the end of the semester. To date, the literature yields mixed results, despite the common perception that the college environment is "chilly" for women (Heller, Puff, and Mills 1985). Some studies (Crawford and MacLeod 1990; Crombie et al. 2003; Krupnick 1985; Peters 1978) find that male students participate more in class than females, whereas other studies find no discernible difference in classroom participation (Boersma et al. 1981; Cornelius, Gray, and Constantinople 1990; Howard and Henney 1998).

However, common perceptions indicate a difference in participation between men and women, and numerous explanations abound as to why differences in participation have been observed. Tannen (1992) concludes that male students participate more in class than female students because they have had more practice at it during their education. Wade (1994) found male students were more likely to see their own participation as important relative to female students' views on their own participation. In addition to individual student perceptions, instructional environment is also offered as an explanation. Wright and Kane (1991) note that female students spoke up more when they were encouraged to speak out. The sex of the instructor has also been shown to have an effect on participation—male professors tend to interrupt students more often versus female professors who are interrupted or challenged by male students (Brooks 1982; Canada and Pringle 1995; Crawford and MacLeod 1990; Krupnick 1985). Many of these investigations into participation were conducted before online courses were commonplace, which leads us to wonder whether or not course format is an important variable as we consider participation.

Course Format

A component of our study is the format of the course (in-person, hybrid, or online); therefore, existing research on classroom format and participation merits consideration.

In-Person Format: Under the traditional classroom setting, Krupnick (1985) suggests that male students speak in class more than their female peers because female students are more likely to be interrupted, and once interrupted female students tend to refrain from contributing further in the day. As noted previously, Rocca (2010) suggests confidence plays an important role in classroom participation—males are more confident than females and therefore more likely to participate and find their participation to be valuable.

Online Format: It seems there are differences in the participation rates of male and female students in online courses. Caspi, Chajut, and Saporta (2008) report female students post more than male students during online discussion forums. In a similar fashion, Barrett and Lally (1999) suggest online discussion behaviors between male and female students in the online learning format differed; male students wrote more frequent and shorter responses, while female students wrote lengthier, less frequent responses. Within a similar vein, Koenig (2015) found that when both male and female students participated in online science, technology, engineering, and mathematics (STEM) courses, women asked more questions than men; but in humanities and social science online courses, there was more parity between men and women.

Hybrid Format: Recall, a hybrid course offers both in-person format and online components. Jackson and Helms contend that "blended learning is expanding," and therefore this area of research is ripe for investigation (2008, 7). The rationale for growth in this course format is manifold. For instance, Gould (2003) demonstrates that hybrid-learning experiences compel increased student-to-student and student-to-professor interactions due to a less-intimidating environment, and help to support the supposition that the "chilly" classroom barriers females face in traditional classrooms may be mitigated by this teaching format. Nonetheless, we use this research as building blocks to better understand how students perceive their own role in classroom discussions.

With this foundation, we designed a study to explore if the type of classroom format affects how male and female students participate in the political science classroom. We are particularly interested in the participation rates of male and female students in the traditional, hybrid, and online formats. We hypothesize that female students are more apt to participate in online discussions, whereas male students participate at higher levels during traditional in-person or hybrid classes. The data collected here use a pretest and posttest methodology to determine if there were any mean differences in responses.

Study Overview

As noted, we want to understand how class format affects changes in attitudes toward political science by sex. Further, we are also interested in any observable differences between the beginning and the end of the semester.

Building on the work of Levintova et al. (2011), we used a quantitative political science research methodology. We created a pretest and posttest for introductory and upper-level political science courses at two universities.[2] The pretest and posttest survey was used to determine if participation differences exist by class format (hybrid, online, in-person). The pretest and posttest survey contained basic demographic questions (e.g., sex, age, class standing, etc.) and eleven statements for students to respond do with a five-point Likert response scale:[3]

1. I consider myself informed about US politics.
2. US politics plays only a small part in everyday life.
3. Democracy requires citizens to regularly participate in government.
4. Democracy requires citizens to be knowledgeable about their government.
5. I feel comfortable discussing US politics and government.
6. I feel more comfortable discussing US politics and government in online discussions.
7. I enjoy having discussions with people whose ideas and values are different from my own.
8. Learning about people from different cultures is a very important part of my college education.
9. I feel comfortable discussing US politics and government during face-to-face discussions.
10. I feel that I can influence my own government.
11. I feel that I can contribute to my community.

Based on the student responses for the pretest and posttest survey, we hypothesize that women are more likely to discuss politics via online and hybrid courses, whereas men participate more during in-person college classes. These hypotheses are in concert with research that suggests men are more assertive than women are in answering teachers' questions in the secondary school classroom (Orenstein 1995; Sadker and Sadker 1994).

Before turning to our findings, we recognize there are limitations to our research. First, we were not able to teach the same class across class formats; put differently, we do not have data from US government courses in each course format. Second, the students were not matched with the pretest and posttest surveys due to university research protocol. Despite these limitations, we believe the data presented here contributes to our understandings about the relationships between class format, gender, and participation in political science courses and will encourage ongoing conversations on the subject.[4]

Differences and Class Format

In each of our courses, we strongly encourage and promote active discussions. For instance, in our in-person courses, the approach to classroom discussions is to foster conversation throughout the entire class period, in each class. Numerous active learning strategies are incorporated, including discussion circles and think, pair, and share activities. In the hybrid course, the class was set up so that students would discuss, in class, a topic (e.g., political parties, campaigns) during particular class days (Mondays and Wednesdays). Then, on each Friday, the class would meet synchronously online to reflect on the readings and materials for the week. More specifically, two to three students per week would serve as discussion leaders to pose questions they might have about the weekly readings and discussions. Our online courses took a similar pathway, assigning weekly discussion leaders to provide an environment of active participation in which to digest weekly readings. Our pretest and posttest findings provide some intriguing results concerning differences between male and female students across formats.

Before delving into the mean differences between our pretest and posttest results, we start by reporting demographic data and overall results for the entire sample (tables 7.1–7.3). For the sake of brevity, we report statistically significant findings ($P \leq .05$) between pretest and posttest surveys, which are illustrated by sex and class format (tables 7.4–7.7). In order to determine the significant differences between pretest and posttest, we ran independent sample t tests comparing the means.[5]

Overview of Sample

Our data consists of one hundred pretest and posttest survey responses across four political science courses (see table 7.1), which offered variance in format (e.g., hybrid, online, or in-person). The class size ranged from fourteen to twenty-five students per class. We opted to examine smaller classes because students participate less in larger classes. The pretest and posttest survey was administered in courses during the 2014–15 academic year. The traditional, or in-person, course was an upper-level public administration elective course; the hybrid course was an introductory course on US government and politics; and the online courses were an introduction to American government and politics course and an upper-level elective course on film and politics.[6] These courses were selected to represent different formats and based on what each professor was teaching. We also conducted instructor observations to document the different classroom experiences, and provided students the opportunity to engage in written reflections on their classroom experience at the end of each survey.

Table 7.1. Respondents.

Type of Course	Course Format	Pretest and Posttest Sample Size (N = 100)
US government and politics	Hybrid	37
US government and politics	Online	15
Film and politics	Online	25
Introduction to public administration	In-person	28

Table 7.2. Demographic Data.

	Sample (N)	Male (N)	Female (N)
	100	43	57
Age			
18–21 years old	51	20	31
22–25 years old	49	23	26
Class Rank			
Freshmen	19	8	11
Sophomore	18	9	9
Junior	24	7	17
Senior	39	19	20

As table 7.2 indicates, of the one hundred participants in our study, forty-three were male and fifty-seven were female. Moreover, fifty-one students were between the ages of eighteen and twenty-one years old; forty-nine students fell between the ages of twenty-two and twenty-five years old. The class standing distribution included nineteen freshmen, eighteen sophomores, twenty-four juniors, and thirty-nine seniors who completed the pretest and posttest surveys. Respondents were also asked, "Have you ever taken a class similar to US government and politics?" Unsurprisingly, a vast majority of students ($N = 68$) responded they had taken a similar course. From instructor observations, we know the majority of students enrolled in each of these courses were likely to be a political science major or minor, or a student pursuing an emphasis in government for a degree in education.

In addition to demographic data, table 7.3 illustrates the overall mean differences for each of the eleven questions asked on the pretest and posttest survey. Recall, that a five-point Likert scale was used (1 = strongly disagree; 5 = strongly agree).

Although table 7.3 depicts slight changes and reveals predicted directions (mean score increased from pretest to posttest), students in our sample

Table 7.3. Overall Mean Differences between Pretest and Posttest Surveys.

Question	Pretest or Posttest	N	Mean
I consider myself informed about US politics*	Pretest	46	3.3043
	Posttest	54	3.9444
US politics plays a small part of everyday life	Pretest	46	2.1957
	Posttest	54	2.0370
Democracy requires citizens to regularly participate in government*	Pretest	46	3.8478
	Posttest	54	4.0185
Democracy requires citizens to be knowledgeable about their government	Pretest	46	3.6304
	Posttest	54	4.0000
I feel comfortable discussing US politics and government*	Pretest	46	3.6739
	Posttest	54	4.1296
I feel more comfortable discussing US politics and government in online discussions	Pretest	46	2.9783
	Posttest	54	3.2778
I enjoy having discussions with people whose ideas and values are different from my own	Pretest	46	4.1087
	Posttest	54	3.9630
Learning about people from different cultures is a very important part of my college education	Pretest	46	4.2826
	Posttest	54	4.4444
I feel comfortable discussing US politics and government during face-to-face discussions	Pretest	46	3.8696
	Posttest	54	3.7593
I feel I can influence my own government	Pretest	46	3.3913
	Posttest	54	3.5185
I feel that I can contribute to my community	Pretest	46	4.2609
	Posttest	54	4.3148

*Statistically significant findings.

indicated moderate levels of comfort discussing US politics more broadly. The following questions showed statistically significant differences between pretests and posttests. (1) *I consider myself informed about US politics*; (2) *Democracy requires citizens to be knowledgeable about their government*; and (3) *I feel more comfortable discussing US politics in online discussions*. It is not surprising that students demonstrated increased levels of knowledge about US politics across each of the courses from the beginning to the end of the semester.

For example, there was a slight increase from "neutral" to "agree" in the student mean score ($M = 3.30$ to $M = 3.94$) indicating students felt more informed about US politics at the end of the semester. Moreover, students also agreed ($M = 4.02$) "democracy requires its citizens to be knowledgeable about their government." By the end of the semester, across formats, our students "felt more

Table 7.4. Significant Male and Female Differences.

Question	Male or Female	Pretest or Posttest	N	Mean
Democracy requires citizens to be knowledgeable about their government	Male	Pretest	20	3.7500
	Male	Posttest	23	4.0000
I feel more comfortable discussing US politics and government online	Male	Pretest	20	2.8500
	Male	Posttest	23	3.4348
	Female	Pretest	26	3.0769
	Female	Posttest	31	3.1613
I feel that I can contribute to my community	Female	Pretest	26	3.8077
	Female	Posttest	31	4.1935

comfortable discussing US politics" ($M = 4.13$). Thus, the question becomes whether these differences vary by gender or course format. Accordingly, tables 7.4 to 7.7 offer additional statistically significant findings.

Table 7.4 demonstrates the statistical differences by gender. Collectively, the male and female respondents were somewhat neutral that they "feel more comfortable discussing US politics and government online." In a closer examination of this shared similarity, male students were more comfortable with online discussions ($M = 3.43$) by the end of the semester than female students ($M = 3.16$).

By comparison, our male respondents were more likely to agree that "democracy requires citizens to be knowledgeable about their government" ($M = 4.00$). Yet female students were more likely to agree they "can contribute to their community" ($M = 4.1935$). In examining these differences, it seems male students felt more compelled to be knowledgeable about their government, whereas female students may have a stronger political efficacy for their own communities. On one hand, this might be indicative of more traditional gender roles in which women are more apt to volunteer in their local community and serve in various community service capacities. To investigate these findings further, we turn to an additional analysis of the data categorized by gender and class format.

Table 7.5 offers a snapshot into the statistically significant factors driving our data for the hybrid course. We find a very slight change in both male and female students' comfort level discussing US politics and government from the beginning to the end of the semester in a hybrid course format (male students have mean score of 3.4 and females have a mean score of 3.8). Thus, the male and female students are still somewhat neutral in their responses to the statement: "I feel comfortable discussing US politics." However, differences do

Table 7.5. Significant Male and Female Differences for Hybrid Format.

Question	Male or Female	Pretest and Posttest N	Mean
US politics plays a small part of everyday life	Male	Pretest = 6 Posttest = 9	2.3333 1.5556
I feel comfortable discussing US politics and government	Male and Female	Male Pretest = 6 Male Posttest = 9 Female Pretest = 12 Female Posttest = 10	3.3333 3.4444 3.5000 3.8000
I feel more comfortable discussing US politics and government in online discussions	Female	Pretest = 12 Posttest = 10	3.1667 3.3000

exist between the male and female students within the hybrid classroom. For example, we find a decrease in the mean for male students when provided with the statement: "US politics plays a small part of everyday life." More specifically, the decrease in the mean from 2.3 to 1.5 indicates male students disagree with this statement. In comparison, the female students presented a slight increase ($M = 3.3$) in that they "feel more comfortable discussing US politics and government in online discussions."

Table 7.6 examines results for in-person course formats. The driving explanatory factor for male respondents is that we found an increase in affirmation of the following statement: "I consider myself informed about US politics" ($M = 3.77$). Somewhat surprisingly, the female students had a strong level of agreement that they felt more comfortable discussing US politics and government by the end of the semester. We posit this could be because their instructors were both females, which is in concert with the aforementioned literature (Brooks 1982; Canada and Pringle 1995; Crawford and MacLeod 1990; Krupnick 1985). Recall, male professors often interrupt students, discouraging participation, whereas female professors are more apt to provide a positive environment for classroom discussions.

We also found female students changed their opinions from a neutral response (3.00) to disagreement (2.75) that online discussions are a more conducive environment to discuss US politics. Based on our own qualitative observations, this finding is explainable. In one of the online classes, we had a male student who would often dominate the classroom discussion board during the midpoint of the semester, which could have contributed to a lower level of comfort when discussing politics online for the female students.

Table 7.6. Significant Male and Female Differences for In-Person Format.

Question	Male or Female	Pretest and Posttest N	Mean
I consider myself informed about US politics	Male	Pretest = 9 Posttest = 9	3.4444 3.7778
I feel comfortable discussing US politics and government	Female	Pretest = 8 Posttest = 12	4.3750 4.7500
I feel more comfortable discussing US politics and government in online discussions	Female	Pretest = 8 Posttest = 12	3.0000 2.7500

Table 7.7 offers important insights into the driving factors that explain differences between men and women in the online course format. However, we are cautious about these particular results due to the low level of student completion rate for the pretest and posttest surveys. Regardless, the differences between male and female students warrant an explanation.

For male students who took the online courses, we find several significant changes between pretest and posttest survey responses. For instance, the males consider themselves more informed about US politics at posttest (4.00); believe more strongly that citizens should be knowledgeable about their government (4.00); report a stronger level of enjoyment in having discussions with people whose ideas and values are different from their own (5.00); and agree more strongly that learning about people from different cultures is important for their college education (5.00). Yet, what was most surprising from our male respondents is the decreased response to: "I feel comfortable having face-to-face discussions" ($M = 3.00$).

In delving deeper into the online course responses, the shared statistical findings between the male and female students should also be explained. Although we find statistical support from students of both genders for the statement "US politics plays a small part of everyday life," differences for the male and female students are present. As the means suggest, the response for the males decreased—male students "strongly disagree" (1.00) that "US politics plays a small part of everyday life." With this same statement, we find an increase response from the females—female students are neutral ($M = 3.11$).

Additional differences warrant consideration. In our examination of the statement: "I can influence my own government," with both male and female students, we find a slight decrease in support over time. The male students fell

Table 7.7. Significant Male and Female Differences for Online Format.

Question	Male or Female	Pretest and Posttest N	Mean
I consider myself informed about American politics	Male	Pretest = 5 Posttest = 5	3.4000 4.0000
American politics plays a small part of everyday life	Male and Female	Male Pretest = 5 Male Posttest = 5 Female = 6 Posttest = 9	2.6000 1.0000 2.1667 3.1111
Democracy requires citizens to be knowledgeable about their government	Male	Pretest = 5 Posttest = 5	3.6000 4.0000
I enjoy having discussions with people whose ideas and values are different from my own	Male	Pretest = 5 Posttest = 5	4.2000 5.0000
Learning about people from different cultures is a very important part of my college education	Male	Pretest = 5 Posttest = 5	4.6000 5.0000
I feel comfortable discussing American politics and government during face-to-face discussions	Male	Pretest = 5 Posttest = 5	3.4000 3.0000
I feel I can influence my own government	Male and Female	Male Pretest = 5 Male Posttest = 5 Female Pretest = 6 Female Posttest = 9	3.6000 3.0000 3.1667 3.1111

from a mean score of 3.60 to 3.00. The female students also presented a very slight decrease in their level of support of this statement ($M = 3.11$).

Discussion and Conclusion

By way of summary, our research provides a glimpse into student attitudes about class format and whether differences exist between genders. When examining our entire sample, we found expected increases between pretest and posttest surveys. Recall that students are somewhat supportive of discussing politics in the online format and believe being informed about democracy requires a person to be knowledgeable about politics.

In comparison, the male students felt more comfortable and knowledgeable about politics, and felt more strongly that politics is an important aspect of our everyday lives. As a result, our findings provide some important implications not only for the political science classroom, but political participation more broadly.

Implications

Although this analysis was exploratory, it does provide some important implications for the political science classroom. First, in this study, male and female students offer different perceptions about their level of comfort when discussing politics. As instructors, recognizing these differences do exist is important to meet the diversity of student learning styles. As noted, our male students seem to feel more comfortable discussing politics across most formats, but this was not the case for our female students.

It is important that we understand the cause of these differences, because if female students do not feel comfortable discussing politics, this could decrease their chances to engage in politics outside of the classroom (e.g., running for office, voting, or working on a campaign). As faculty, we need to be able to engage students in a multitude of discussions to increase their comfort level, regardless of the format. Thus, venues for participation should provide a range of opportunities for classroom discussion—partner activities, group discussions, or presenting current events. Another viable option is to set up a mid-semester pause by which students meet with the professor one-on-one about course materials. This is a great opportunity for the faculty member to discuss potential future opportunities within the profession with students and for the students to ask questions they may not feel comfortable posing during class. Varying the methods to stimulate class participation should help reach students with different preferences and comfort levels. Also, class participation does not have to imply verbal participation. The students can write, draw, or use technology (i.e., clickers) to participate.

Second, regardless of course format, course design must engage students in the material. All too often faculty members believe they can easily recreate their in-person class for other formats. For instance, during our in-person classes, students are often asked to share current events to connect the readings to real life. This same assignment could be used for the hybrid or online classroom. Faculty members should work with campus instructional web developers to ensure what is used in person is not lost online. For example, there are ample opportunities to simulate political participation online for students, such as the gerrymandering or redistricting game. Nevertheless, it is important to be intentional in our course design and think about how participation can be encouraged.

Third, as political science professors we need to think about how we want to use the classroom to foster political participation for the longer term. The classroom is part of a student's political socialization, and how we design a course and the materials we use contribute to whether or not a student will vote, volunteer for a campaign, or even run for office (Lawless and Fox 2012). However, classroom experiences may also affect students' behavior and political participation more broadly (Krain and Lantis 2006; Martin, Tankersley, and Ye 2012). What is often most important about understanding student attitudes or perceptions is that they are "learning to become more comfortable with ambiguity and complexity, how to disagree without being disagreeable, and perhaps, above all, how to be more empathetic" (Smith, Nowacek, and Bernstein 2010, 2). This is important because students can leave the political science classroom with more knowledge and as "more skilled political actors, able to reach political opinions and able to express themselves better than they previously had" (Bernstein 2010, 29).

Put simply, the political science classroom is a sphere that should encourage ways to enhance political efficacy, so our students participate in politics. For example, in our own classroom evaluations and instructor observations, many students thanked us for providing a classroom environment in which all students could talk. Recall, the online class had a male student who dominated the discussion board. As the instructor, this student was contacted (via telephone) to discuss his performance and how it was impacting his classmates. This student was unaware of his behaviors and apologetic. Again, this stresses the importance of course design. More specifically, the question becomes whether such occurrences could be prevented in the future. We posit that by discussing the role of gender in politics in our courses it may raise levels of student self-awareness.

With these insights, however, there are still challenges to note. First, this pretest and posttest survey was only conducted across two universities with a relatively small sample of students and courses. Data from more classes are needed.

Second, our subset of students who completed the pretest and posttest survey was relatively small. In particular, many of the students did not fully complete the eleven questions at the beginning or end of the semester surveys. Thus, their results were not included in our overall sample. We posit that in order to increase the response rate for online students, incentives might be necessary. One of the downsides of online learning is you do not "see" these students on a daily basis and email reminders often cannot replace having an instructor in front of the room asking students to complete the survey.

Third, the question becomes whether student perceptions about political subjects would differ across disciplines. The vast majority of students in our sample were either a political science major or minor. But, if the same pretest and posttest survey was provided in courses in education, environmental studies, or history, we could engender a greater appreciation for the study and practice of politics.

The goal of this chapter was to provide building blocks for future research investigating how student perceptions are affected by teaching format. As faculty we can use multiple approaches to meet a diversity of learning styles, so our students have the appropriate skills to participate in the many facets of political life. We should remember that "inculcating such an expansive capacity for citizenship is beyond the reach of a single instructor or a single course. To be most effective, the themes and practice of citizenship should be conveyed throughout the college experience" (Smith, Nowacek, and Bernstein 2010, 2). We need to be cognizant of the differences among our students and do our best to encourage participation by using formats suitable for all learners.

MICHELLE PAUTZ is Associate Professor of Political Science and Assistant Provost for the Common Academic Program at the University of Dayton. She is author of *Civil Servants on the Silver Screen: Hollywood's Depiction of Government and Bureaucrats* and co-author with Sara Rinfret of *The Lilliputians of Environmental Regulation: The Perspective of State Regulators* and *US Environmental Policy in Action: Practice & Implementation*.

SARA RINFRET is Associate Professor of Political Science, Director of the Master of Public Administration Program and Codirector of the Social Science Research Laboratory at the University of Montana. She is author with Michelle Pautz of *The Lilliputians of Environmental Regulation: The Perspective of State Regulators* and *US Environmental Policy in Action: Practice and Implementation*.

Notes

1. The hybrid classroom is often referred to as blended learning, where part of the class is offered in-person while the other portion is offered online.
2. A few notes are needed about the two university settings. The University of Dayton is a private, Catholic university located in Dayton, Ohio, with approximately eleven thousand students. It is predominately an undergraduate institution, but has robust graduate programs in STEM fields. Hartwick College is a private, liberal arts school with approximately fifteen hundred undergraduate students located in Oneonta, New York.
3. 1 = strongly disagree; 2 = disagree, 3 = neutral, 4 = agree, and 5 = strongly agree.
4. Data collection was IRB approved.
5. We would have conducted a multiple regression on the overall sample followed by separate models for our relevant subsamples. However, given our small sample size, subsample-specific regression analyses were not feasible.

6. Missing data: if a student did not complete the pretest or posttest survey, we did not include their responses in the analysis. The total for missing responses was eighteen (thirteen for online; one in person; four hybrid).

References

Barrett, E., and V. Lally. 1999. "Gender Differences in an Online Learning Environment." *Journal of Computer Assisted Learning* 15 (1): 48–60.
Bernstein, Jeffrey. 2010. "Citizenship Orientated Approaches to the American Government Course." In *Citizenship across the Curriculum*, edited by Michael B. Smith, Rebecca S. Nowacek, and Jeffrey L. Bernstein. Bloomington: Indiana University Press.
Boersma, P. Dee., Debora Gay, Ruth A. Jones, Lynn Morrison, and Helen Remick. 1981. "Sex Differences in College Student-Teacher Interactions: Fact or Fantasy?" *Sex Roles* 7 (8): 775–84.
Brooks, Virginia R. 1982. "Sex Differences in Student Dominance Behavior in Female and Male Professors' Classrooms." *Sex Roles* 8 (7): 683–90.
Canada, Katherine, and Richard Pringle. 1995. "The Role of Gender in College Classroom Interactions: A Social Context Approach." *Sociology of Education* 68 (3): 161–86.
Caspi, Avner, Eran Chajut, and Kelly Saporta. 2008. "Participation in Class and in Online Discussions: Gender Differences." *Computers & Education* 50 (3): 718–24.
Cohen, Mel. 1991. "Making Class Participation a Reality." *PS: Political Science & Politics* 24 (4): 699–703.
Colby, Anne, Elizabeth Beaumont, Thomas Ehrlich, and Josh Corngold. 2007. *Educating for Democracy: Preparing Undergraduates for Responsible Political Engagement*. San Francisco: Jossey-Bass.
Cornelius, Randolph R., Janet M. Gray, and Anne P. Constantinople. 1990. "Student-Faculty Interaction in the College Classroom." *Journal of Research and Development in Education* 23 (4): 189–97.
Crawford, Mary, and Margo MacLeod. 1990. "Gender in the College Classroom: An Assessment of the 'Chilly Climate' for Women." *Sex Roles* 23 (3/4): 101–22.
Crombie, Gail, Sandra W. Pyke, Naida Silverthorn, Alison Jones, and Sergio Piccinin. 2003. "Students' Perceptions of Their Classroom Participation and Instructor as Function of Gender and Context." *Journal of Higher Education* 74 (1): 51–76.
Crone, James A. 1997. "Using Panel Debates to Increase Student Involvement in the Introductory Sociology Class." *Teaching Sociology* 25 (3): 214–18.
Daggett, Luann M. 1997. "Quantifying Class Participation." *Nurse Education* 22 (2): 13–14.
Dancer, Diane, and Patty Kamvounias. 2005. "Student Involvement in Assessment: A Project Designed to Assess Class Participation Fairly and Reliably." *Assessment & Evaluation in Higher Education* 30 (4): 445–54.
Fritschner, Linda Marie. 2000. "Inside the Undergraduate College Classroom: Faculty and Students Differ on the Meaning of Student Participation." *The Journal of Higher Education* 71 (3): 342–62.
Gould, Thomas. 2003. "Hybrid Classes: Maximizing Institutional Resources and Student Learning." Proceedings of the 2003 ASCUE Conference.
Heller, Jack F., C. Richard Puff, and Carol J. Mills. 1985. "Assessment of the Chilly Climate for Women." *The Journal of Higher Education* 56 (4): 446–61.

Howard, Jay R., and Amanda L. Henney. 1998. "Student Participation and Instructor Gender in the Mixed-Age College Classroom." *The Journal of Higher Education* 69 (4): 384–405.

Jackson, Mary Jo, and Marilyn Helms. 2008. "Student Perceptions of Hybrid Courses: Measuring and Interpreting Quality." *Journal of Education for Business* 84 (1): 7–12.

Junn, Ellen. 1994. "'Pearls of Wisdom': Enhancing Student Class Participation with an Innovative Exercise." *Journal of Instructional Psychology* 21 (4): 385–87.

Koenig, Rebecca. 2015. "In STEM Courses, a Gender Gap in Online Class Discussions." *The Chronicle of Higher Education*, January 6. http://chronicle.com/blogs/wiredcampus/in-stem-courses-a-gender-gap-in-online-class-discussions/55399.

Krain, Matthew, and Jeffrey S. Lantis. 2006. "Building Knowledge? Evaluating the Effectiveness of the Global Problems Summit Simulation." *International Studies Perspective* 7 (4): 395–407.

Krupnick, Catherine G. 1985. "Women and Men in the Classroom: Inequality and Its Remedies." *On Teaching and Learning* 1 (1): 18–25.

Kuh, George D., and Paul D. Umbach. 2004. "College and Character: Insights from the National Survey of Student Engagement." *New Directions for Institutional Research* 122: 37–54.

Lawless, Jennifer L., and Richard L. Fox. 2012. "Men Rule: The Continued Under-Representation of Women in US Politics." *Women in Politics Institute*. https://www.american.edu/spa/wpi/upload/2012-Men-Rule-Report-web.pdf.

Levintova, Ekaterina, Terri Johnson, Denise Scheberle, and Kevin Vonck. 2011. "Global Citizens Are Made, Not Born: Multiclass Role-Playing Simulation of Global Decision Making." *Journal of Political Science Education* 7 (3): 245–74.

Martin, Pamela, Holley Tankersley, and Min Ye. 2012. "Are They Living What They Learn? Assessing Knowledge and Attitude Change in Introductory Politics Courses." *Journal of Political Science Education* 8 (2): 201–23.

Orenstein, Peggy. 1995. *Schoolgirls*. New York: Anchor.

Peters, Ruth A. 1978. "Effects of Anxiety, Curiosity, and Perceived Instructor Threat on Student Verbal Behavior in the College Classroom." *Journal of Educational Psychology* 70 (3): 388–95.

Rocca, Kelly A. 2010. "Student Participation in the College Classroom: An Extended Multidisciplinary Literature Review." *Communication Education* 59 (2): 185–213.

Sadker Myra, and David Sadker. 1994. *Failing at Fairness*. New York: Touchstone.

Smith, Michael B., Rebecca Nowacek, and Jeffrey Bernstein, eds. 2010. *Citizenship Across the Curriculum*. Bloomington: Indiana University Press.

Tannen, Deborah. 1992. "How Men and Women Use Language Differently in Their Lives and in the Classroom." *The Educational Digest* 57 (3): 3–6.

Wade, Rahima C. 1994. "Teacher Education Students' Views on Class Discussion: Implications for Fostering Critical Reflection." *Teaching and Teacher Education* 10 (2): 231–43.

Weaver, Robert R., and Jiang Qi. 2005. "Classroom Organization and Participation: College Students' Perceptions." *The Journal of Higher Education* 76 (5): 570–601.

Weimer, Maryellen. 2013. *Learner-Centered Teaching: Five Key Changes to Practice*, 2nd ed. San Francisco: Jossey-Bass.

Wright, Richard A., and Catherine C. Kane. 1991. "'Women Speak This Week': Promoting Gender Equality and Awareness in Class Discussions." *Teaching Sociology* 19 (4): 472–76.

8 Beyond Gender Neutrality in the Scholarship of Teaching and Learning and the Classroom

Alison Kathryn Staudinger

MANY STUDENTS CRY in my office. I tell myself this is a sign that they feel safe, but worry that I am just mean. Only one student has ever cried about the syllabus on the second day of class. This student, a young woman whose first-day freewrite on why she was taking a political science class (she argued that art must be protected by the political guarantee of freedom) was impressive, came to my office hours thin-lipped, determined to be calm. She told me that she was planning to drop my class because of the 15 percent of her grade that would be based on participation. I began my standard speech about the importance of active learning, and even pulled out the instrumentalist claim that public speaking would be good for her future. She began to weep, and, in retrospective, this was fair enough. Did I have any proof that participation was good for her? Was I doing anything more than imposing my own experiences as a loud undergrad and competitive graduate student on my classroom? I asked her why she was sure she would not participate, expecting the standard "I'm shy." But she responded by telling me, shakily, that she had been bullied in high school and college, including mockery of her speaking voice in class. Later in the year, at a meeting of an on-campus feminist group, she would make clear that this bullying resulted from gossip after she was sexually assaulted—gossip which blamed her for the encounter. I had a neutral policy of grading for participation, and it applied to all my students fairly, and yet I had nearly driven away this student and perhaps others who, for gendered reasons, were terrified to speak. Fairness was not enough.

Fairness, ensconced in our legal system in notions like the "rule of law" or "one person one vote," is an important core of liberalism. However, it is not without internal contradictions, both in the legal and political sense, where there is unequal access to rights. There is also the powerful fact that initial distributions, particularly related to class and race in the United States, matter for this sort of access, and these contradictions suggest the concept itself is lacking as a principle of justice. However, classrooms premised on the idea of a meritorious system of education where the best will succeed are modeled as spaces of "fairness" where all students receive equal treatment (Rodabaugh 1996). The syllabus, for example, sets out rules which apply to every student in more or less the same way. This means that the students like the one I discussed above will be harmed by seemingly neutral policies; in my classroom, I suspect that the students who have the easiest times are those who happen to share my intellectual proclivities and habits. But fairness assumes a world that is postidentity, where equality has been achieved and there is no need for feminist, antiracist, or LGBTQ+ politics or policies. Structural inequality hides in the ideology of color, gender, or other "blindness" that informs our shared world and demands a neutral treatment of all students conceived as fairness. It rejects overt and personal discrimination only. However, a lack of bigotry does not free a classroom from bias, and a gender-neutral approach may in fact leave broader structural inequalities in place. This insight applies to our Scholarship of Teaching and Learning (SoTL), too.

Political theorists and scientists study power, democratic voice, and education; they should more carefully import these notions into the classroom and cultivate methods of teaching that are not gender-neutral, but gender-forward. To do this, we also can better engage with Women's and Gender Studies (WGS) scholarship and pedagogy, especially central insights about power and intersectional identity. A neutral or nondiscriminatory approach, particularly given the association of many traits valued in academia with masculinity, can instead be a hegemonic one. It also has complex implications for students who do not perform their gender as expected (nonbinary or genderqueer), or who are otherwise marginalized on account of identity. College students come to campus, at whatever their age, with multiple, evolving identities which matter for how we teach and learn together, and we honor these identities by recognizing their complexity.

I came to a concern with gender neutrality through a project that initially sought to explore student understanding of inequality and intersectionality. My initial research question, firmly in the category of "what is?" in the typology of SoTL questions, was whether students could transfer intersectional knowledge about one type of structural inequality (class) to another (race). As I worked on the project, I engaged a second question, at the more meta-level, about how SoTL researchers could best approach identity in their work. From examining both questions, I hope to present not only a substantive discussion of the gendered classroom, but also a humanistic approach to SoTL that still speaks to disciplinary audiences in political science and beyond.

Methods in SoTL Research

SoTL is a broad and interdisciplinary field with contributing scholars from all areas of academia; it has been rightly called a "trading zone" where disciplinary methods, concerns, and concepts can intermingle, and scholars can stretch themselves to learn from other disciplines (Mills and Huber 2005). However, some disciplinary ways may take up more space than others. As the field cohered, many agreed that "the quantitative and qualitative research methods with which social scientists are most familiar are more obviously adaptable to the study of teaching and learning than are the typical methods of scholars in the humanities and sciences" (Huber and Morreale 2002, 11). Methodological pluralism has continued to develop, such that researchers often choose the method best suited to their question and its scope (Hubball and Clarke 2010). Yet, it has been hard to shake "a pervasive belief that educational research is restricted to empirical, if not quantitative, generalizable studies such as those found in educational psychology" and that there is a danger of social science hegemony (Miller-Young and Yeo 2015, 38; Grauerholz and Main 2013). Chick notes that in a study of recent SoTL work, "half of the projects drew solely on numerical evidence, a breakdown that again mirrors much of what I've seen in the broader field" (2014, 8). She expands on the notion of "methodological soundness" in part to advocate for collecting and analyzing multiple types of "rich" evidence of student learning to aid in representing complexity.

It would be an oversimplification to argue that all rich data is qualitative, and all poor data is quantitative, or to link richness with gender-forward SoTL and paucity with its opposite. However, there are powerful and consistent feminist critiques of dominant research methods which might prompt us to consider the limits of some methods for asking certain types of questions, particular in light of intersectionality. The prominence of psychology as a discipline which historically has conducted pedagogical research has meant that its methods are common in SoTL work, including in programs like the Wisconsin Teaching Fellows and Scholars that train instructors to systematically study learning. Wilson-Doenges and Gurung establish "benchmarks" for rigorous SoTL rooted in part on the "gold standard" in psychology research, which is the double-blind experiment with randomly assigned test subjects (2013, 64). This gold standard is "longitudinal research on multiple dependent variables, randomized experiments, double-blind tests, large-sample sizes and advanced and multivariate statistical analysis" (2013, 64–65). Although they also mention "mixed methods," they only (briefly) describe qualitative work using NVivo and other software that integrates qualitative and quantitative data, leaving out the array of alternatives drawn from the arts and humanities. These methods are one way of understanding truth and rigor, perhaps particularly appropriate to psychology where they can readily be found (Wilson-Doenges, Troisi, and Bartsch 2016), but they also train us to look for what can be measured and quantified, and turn us from the "swampy lowlands" (Schön, quoted in Chick 2014, 6) where learning can be messy.

Gender and identity are swampy lowlands. In both qualitative and qualitative work, intersectionality, or the notion that identity is neither mutually exclusive nor additive, is difficult to represent (Bowleg 2008). It is perhaps most difficult to represent in studies which attempt to approximate the scientific method through the paired comparison of two courses, because necessarily the students become fungible, so that they can be compared. A research design using multivariate analysis may even want to control for the effects of gender, race, or class, often treating them as bivariate measures. Beyond the common difficulty of controlling the many external variables or comparing two like classrooms, this sort of experimental research design makes it difficult to reflect on identity itself, or the process of learning about deeply contested and political issues, such as structural violence or inequality.

Political science is broadly committed to the same positivist "gold standard" mentioned above, but, as discussed in the introduction, there are many alternative research traditions, both qualitative and interpretative. In cases where there is large-N data available, as in Williams and Jenkins's chapter in this book, quantitative analysis is warranted. Even in smaller scale surveys, such as chapter 5, mixed methods are appropriate. In cases where the investigator is studying the process of identity formation and worldviews, in one classroom with all its particularity, interpretative methods make more sense.

To illustrate why this might matter, I share here two different ways of analyzing a SoTL project: first, through quantitative social science methods and second by drawing on multiple types of evidence. There are tradeoffs to doing a study each way, and I hope to show that as well—but, ultimately, gender analysis is aided through drawing on pluralistic data and methods. I also reflect on how the movement from gender neutrality in SoTL might connect to critiques of the universal subject and citizen in political theory and the classroom.

Intersectionality is a threshold concept in WGS, and we argued in the introduction that it should also become a portal into political science. Not without its detractors, intersectionality emerges from the critiques of feminists of color who argue for the importance of understanding the mutual construction of identity among multiple axes, all at once, such that difference, whether in terms of class, race, gender, ability, age, or immigration status must be considered together, as they mutually inform and construct identities. I teach about intersectionality in many different courses, both in political science and interdisciplinary programs: democracy and justice studies and WGS. I also notice that students involved in campus activism around gender and sexuality are well versed in the term, and even employ it to critique other students or texts in classes. But, I wanted to understand how students processed intersectionality and what they really mean by it. I admit that this motivation emerges in part from my own struggle with the concept and desire to teach it well. I worry that it can accidentally end up producing the famous "oppression Olympics" (Hancock 2011), or providing excuses for students who are highly privileged on one axis but disadvantaged on another to reject the idea of their privilege—as in "#NotAllMen."

To better understand the students and how learn about intersectionality, I intended to test whether insights on intersectionality in relation to one type of identity, class, would transfer to how students perceived and interpreted another type of inequality, in this case gender, race, or ability. Knowledge transfer is an important marker of deep learning, but students cannot always apply prior knowledge (Ambrose et al. 2010, 108–109). I first needed to measure their initial understanding of intersectionality and inequality, then teach a module on class in an intersectional frame, and then measure their intersectional understanding of class as well as gender, race, and ability. If their understanding of class as an intersectionally constructed identity or subject position improved, but class, race, and ability did not, then it would suggest a low level of knowledge transfer between these identity dependent concepts. Of course, this is a complicated type of knowledge transfer, since these types of identity cannot be analogized—yet it was for understanding the intersectional nature of each identity, a similar concept despite its particularized application. Variation between the improvement in the various categories might tell me something interesting about ideology related to hierarchy or the transferability of these concepts. To explore intersectional understanding, I used four video clips (described in appendix 1) and asked students to freewrite for fifteen minutes to describe and explain what they saw, giving them credit for completion, at the beginning and end of the one-semester class. My primary goal was to answer a "what is?" question about student understanding of intersectionality in this class, but I also hoped to speak a bit about "what works?" or, as Biesta (2007) helpfully corrects, "what worked?" for these particular students in this context.

There were thirty-five students in American Political Thought (APT), a 300-level elective in both political science and democracy and justice studies, with students, mostly sophomores and juniors, nearly evenly split between these majors. Thirty-three completed the course. Like many APT courses, this one features historical speeches, treatises, and other writing from liberal thinkers like James Madison and Thomas Jefferson, conservatives like John C. Calhoun and Ronald Reagan, and radicals like Emma Goldman and Thomas Paine, but also contemporary writings on prison abolition, whiteness, settler colonialism, and sexuality. We began the course with the first set of freewriting on the video clips, framed as an introduction to the type of visual analysis students might want to do for their blogs. Then, in the first module on the debates over the US Constitution, I introduced the notion of class as a key factor for analysis, but in relation to other types of difference. Although, like Beard's ([1913] 2012) famous class-based analysis, some approaches to the implications of late eighteenth-century politics focus on one type of hierarchy; putting them in dialogue with other authors who consider gender (Ritter 2006), women (Schwarzenbach and Smith 2012), race (Waldstreicher 2010), and new evaluations of class and democracy (Levinson 2006) allows us to consider what these authors did not, as do intersectional approaches to constitutionalism (Baines, Barak-Erez, and Kahana 2012). Although at this point I explicitly discussed intersectionality, and did not hesitate to ask prompting questions throughout the semester that might lead to intersectional insights, I did not explicitly thematize it again. There were moments—reading Sojourner Truth, Orestes Brownson, and Elizabeth Cady Stanton—when the question of intersecting identities was begged by the author's own attention (or lack thereof) to them. On the last day of the course, we did another set of video clip freewriting. I then compared the thirty-three paired sets of pre- and postwritings. (Three students had left the course, and one joined late and had no initial writing).

To measure student perceptions of intersectionality in their analysis of the video clips, I developed a measure adapted from a typology designed to help researchers develop intersectional analysis in psychology; the typology focused on how research addressed issues of inclusion, inequality, and similarities between diverse social categories (Cole 2009). The prompting questions Cole provided apply to all stages of the research process, so I choose those related to "analysis" and "interpretation of findings" because those best fit the task my students were performing (172). Each of these two measures had three embedded questions, adapted as shown in table 8.1. For this, I coded each response in relation to each of the four clips, answering either "yes" or "no" to each of the six dimensions of the measure and ending up with an intersectionality score for each response (1–6), for each of the four clips, as shown in table 8.2. I conducted a paired-samples t test to evaluate the impact of the class-based intersectionality teaching on the student's perception of intersectionality in the four areas. There was a statistically significant increase in Intersectional concepts for all four from Time 1 to Time 2 ($p < 0.05$). However, the effect size differed greatly, with class (eta squared 8.54645), gender (eta squared = −0.3288), race (eta squared = −0.19) and ability (eta squared = −0.238) as shown in table 8.3. In short, the students improved somewhat in every category, and since their initial means were so very low, all of these improvements were statistically significant. However, the magnitude of these gains was very low, except in relation to class (which was taught as part of the class). It seemed like lessons about intersectionality were not transferring well to other domains. I also examined the statistics using a Wilcoxon signed-rank test, which showed that race *did not* change in a statistically significant way, although class, ability, and gender did. This test was better able to work with the very small data set and magnitude of changes. This Wilcoxon signed-rank test showed that a teaching unit on class and intersectionality did not elicit a statistically significant change in intersectional understanding of race ($Z = -1.613$,

Table 8.1. Relevant Measures of Intersectionality.

Research Stage	Who Is Included within This Category?	What Role Does Inequality Play?	Where Are the Similarities?
Analysis	Attends to diversity within a group and may be conducted separately for each group studied	Tests (or discusses) for both similarities and differences	Interest is not limited to differences
Interpretation of findings	No group's findings are interpreted to represent a universal or normative experience	Differences are interpreted in light of groups' structural positions	Sensitivity to nuanced variations across groups is maintained even when similarities are identified

Table 8.2. Representative Student Data.

STUDENT	CLASS		GENDER		RACE		ABILITY	
	Pretest	*Posttest*	*Pretest*	*Posttest*	*Pretest*	*Posttest*	*Pretest*	*Posttest*
718183	3	4	2	2	1	2	4	5

Table 8.3. t Test for Student Pretest and Posttest.

CLASS				GENDER			
Pretest		*Posttest*		*Pretest*		*Posttest*	
M	SD	M	SD	M	SD	M	SD
0.2727	0.71906	1.7576	1.50063	0.7576	1.22552	1.1212	1.34065
$t(99) = -6.020$				$t(99) = -2.814$			
$p = 0.000$				$p = 0.008$			

RACE				ABILITY			
Pretest		*Posttest*		*Pretest*		*Posttest*	
M	SD	M	SD	M	SD	M	SD
0.2121	0.3939	0.5455	0.86384	0.2424	0.56071	0.4848	0.87039
$t(99) = -2.268$				$t(99) = -2.484$			
$p = 0.030$				$p = 0.018$			

$p = 0.107$), but did for class ($Z = -4.015$, $p = 0.000$), gender ($Z = -2.588$, $p = 0.010$), and ability ($Z = -2.271$, $p = 0.023$). Again, the effect is greatest for class and least for race, although this test suggests that race does not even reach the level of statistical significance.

Although these findings were interesting, they left me uneasy. I had taken hundreds of pages of student writing and reduced it to a few numbers per student. And, although a student research assistant and I worked together to read and code the papers, most of our best insights were in conversation over them rather than the emerging data. As a political theorist, who uses interpretative methods of textual and historical analysis in research, it felt odd to do work this way, although it is important that SoTL is place where scholars stretch themselves methodologically. I wondered—what other levels of "richness" can I explore and how can I, as a political theorist, do work in SoTL that speaks to my conception of rigor? My research assistant and I had also noticed that a few students seemed, in his words "woke": nuanced in their perception of intersectionality and the politics of inequality. Others seemed anxious to avoid any mention of identity. We wondered just who these students were and lamented the study design that had led us to leave out this information. I knew I would have to change my approach to learning about this problem.

SoTL study design, along with the dominance of social science methods, taken from psychology in particular, is shaped by the expectations of Institutional Review Boards (IRB) which evaluate research done on human subjects. Given the power dynamics inescapable in a classroom, where professors have both material and social advantage over students, it is imperative that students are protected from coercion and unequal treatment. However, some typical methods to prevent coercion and unfairness can limit the ability of researchers to gather and analyze the "richness" they seek. For example, it is often recommended that faculty anonymize data to avoid the appearance and practice of favoring students who choose to participate, or punishing those who do not. Unless a study is specifically studying a demographic question—for example, "does student gender change the perception of instructor competence?"—students are treated as fungible or without qualities. The drive for "generalizable findings implicitly assumes that students in one university setting are substantively like students in other ones. Indeed, one of the challenges of a discipline-focused book like this is to provide inspiration for other disciplines without claiming that all good teaching is identical.

Some of the best SoTL work, also IRB approved, does not anonymize students. Bloch-Schulman (2016) actually includes videos of the paired think aloud he completed with a student and professional philosopher in a work published as part of *Thinking and Learning Inquiry*'s symposium on arts and humanities SoTL. Partnering with students is another way to improve this work (Cook-Sather, Bovill, and Felten 2014). However, these types of projects are difficult, in fact seemingly impossible, to find in political science SoTL work. Although my research assistant was not able to participate in coauthoring, we did redesign the study together, and in the future I will begin from the goal of partnership in studying student learning and reflecting on my own teaching.

Ultimately, I decided to reframe my study by answering the provocative question that Easton and Hewson argue we should add to standard SoTL questions of what is, what works, and what could be: "[f]or whom does this practice and pedagogy work?" (2012, 78). I also wanted to use methods that preserve and engage with identity rather than cover over it. Treating "students" as one coherent population and measuring them as such did not work well in my study above, or rather it stripped my findings of some of the potential meaning they could have. Gilpin and Liston (2009) argue for the centrality of recognizing the power of identity to shape our learning experiences, and power is also shaped by the sort of data and results we present as compelling. Similarly, Bloch-Schulman et al. (2016) suggest that we must ask "bigger questions" in the context of our SoTL work, including when we debate about methods. For me, the bigger question is whether our liberal commitments to neutrality create deeply unfair classrooms. The seemingly neutral "student" in many SoTL projects is also a projection and production of power, and to understand the implications of that I turned to political theory and its approach to other seemingly neutral subjects.

Liberalism and Neutrality

Neutrality is a goal of political liberalism; a system of liberal equality is one in which all persons, regardless of status or identity, are equal before the law. This understanding of justice as blind is not without emancipatory heft, given that it must entertain the claims of those who are not receiving such equality. However, these claims are not always heard, in part because one of the inequalities produced by actually existing liberalism is access to both political spaces and to the status of political subject who has the right to speak there. The liberal state aims for neutrality toward attributes like gender, race, and status. In the terms of US Constitutional law, there are particular groups, called "suspect classes," whose status requires that the state provide a "compelling reason" if it intends to discriminate on the basis of membership in such a class. However, this Fourteenth Amendment jurisprudence, although initially developed in support of the equality of black citizens and extended, somewhat, to cover women as a "semiprotected class" in the 1970s, has also enforced the claims of the dominant classes, including whites and men, because it favors equal treatment. At the same time, "conservatives and liberals alike now view the US's racial hierarchy as an unfortunate historical fact that now has no bearing on contemporary society," perhaps because racism and neoliberalism work together to privatize racial discourse such that it appears only a form of individual bigotry, while institutional racism is unmentioned (Giroux 2003, 192). This same dynamic, with different specificity, is gendered because students start from postfeminist and neoliberal ideologies that understand feminism—and gender inequality—as passé (Weber 2010). As many feminists have shown, neutrality does not function well under systems of deep and structural inequality, because it treats a challenge from a disadvantaged group as the same as one coming from an advantaged one. It also compares people on one axis only, such as men or women, or straight or gay, occluding the way in which both gay men and straight women might, albeit in different ways, need particular adaptations for entering workplaces dominated by a hegemonic masculinity that privileges heteronormativity; this complexity is one reason why the judicial system, and the public, has struggled on issues of gender expression.

Liberal neutrality is central to two key conceptions of the public political space, and they too are vulnerable to challenges. Jürgen Habermas and John Rawls, two of the most prominent theorists of the late twentieth and, in Habermas's case, the twenty-first century, explored and defended theories of political action and communication, and garnered critiques in particular on the nature of the political subject in these theories. Their theories depend both on a seemingly neutral subject who turns out to have gendered expectations and qualities, as well as a public/private divide that places gendered issues outside of the political space and therefore depoliticizes them. These critiques parallel the issues with the SoTL subject, and also the classroom.

Critiques of the liberal subject have been applied to the social contract figures who form early liberalism, particularly John Locke, through the argument that beneath each "social contract" sits the sexual contract which subsumed women to men through the assumed marriage contract (Pateman [1988] 2014). Rawls's ([1971] 1999) *A Theory of Justice* develops a social contract narrative for the twentieth century, arguing that, if we imagine a person "behind the veil of ignorance" where they have no idea where they will end up in society, they will choose what he calls "justice as fairness." Pateman identifies in Rawls's famous "original position," a place where individuals imagine themselves without qualities and are necessarily without sexual difference, a place of such abstraction that it cannot possibly produce theories sensitive to the subjugation of women expressed in the social contract, especially in relation to care labor ([1988] 2014). Many critiques of Rawls came from his own students, such as Susan Moller Okin, who offered a friendly amendment rooted in the lived experiences of women as vulnerable legal subjects. Okin argues that "gender-neutral terms frequently obscure the fact that so much of the real experience of 'persons,' so long as they live in gender-structured societies, does in fact depend on what sex they are" (1991, 11). Rawls, in insisting on the gender neutrality of the "head of household" he imagines in the "Original Position," presents a nongendered model of citizenship that is implicitly gendered. Okin, argues that despite Rawls supposed focus on "basic structures" as matters of justice, he does not include the family as a basic structure that might need to be made just, and that in this he ends up reproducing the public/private dichotomy that plagues liberalism. Rawls defended himself against this charge by saying that "the primary subject of justice is the basic structure of society understood as the arrangement of society's main institutions into a unified system of social cooperation over time. The principles of political justice are to apply directly to this structure, but they are not to apply directly to the internal life of the many associations within it, the family among them" (Rawls 2001, 163). Yet, if Okin is right that the family is a central place for learning democracy and experiencing injustice, this does not satisfy. If Rawls's notion of justice as fairness depends on a seemingly neutral subject who turns out to be a "head of household," and if the family is shielded from the considerations of justice in private, then gender equity is unlikely.

Even in Rawls's (2005) reformulation of his theories, *Political Liberalism*, there are troubling assumptions about the power of neutrality. In this book, he takes up the problem of radical pluralism in a contemporary democratic society, noting that we cannot expect citizens to agree at the level of their comprehensive doctrines, and yet they live in the same political space and must find a way to communicate and even collaborate. Rawls' argument for what makes a plural *and* stable democracy possible are norms of public reason, which require that citizens make arguments in the public space, articulated without resorting to one's comprehensive doctrine. Although in some ways this removes the concerns that the assumed subject is a man, in that the subject is now pluralized, feminists still criticized the idea that an antisexist position might be relativized as just one among many, and that sexist arguments, if they accord with "public reason," would need to be accepted. They also worried that, in a world where families educate children differently depending on gender, boys and girls would grow up with different capacities and this position would be accepted as "reasonable" (Okin 1994, 29). Even more worrisome for Okin is the lack of restrictions on comprehensive doctrines which proscribe "considerable gender inequality" (1994, 31). Here, although the playing field is theoretically made even for all but the most objectionable doctrines, for liberal tolerance is the norm, this seeming equality again makes invisible gendered and other hierarchies.

Habermas's public sphere arguments also involve a political space where gender and other inequalities can be masked. Habermas describes a communicative space in which identity is bracketed and deliberation over public purposes produces a check on the power of elites; in his case the model is rooted in eighteenth-century salon culture and the circulation of shared texts. He does not, however, explicitly put forth the "bourgeois" public sphere as a contemporary model and is quite clear that, despite the "bracketing" of identity, the members are all men of a certain class with shared national identity. "These societies ... excluded women and forbade gambling and exclusively served the need of bourgeois private people to create a forum for a critically debating public: to read periodicals and discuss them" (Habermas 1991). He is also hesitant to suggest that the public sphere could be a model in the age of mass politics. Nonetheless, his "public sphere" has become a major line of research and critique.

Feminist thinkers allege that Habermas's portrayal of an identity-bracketed subject denies the importance of identity for our experiences as social and political beings. However, because of his focus on communication, they also feature concerns about how gender figures into experiences of voice and power. Historically, the notion that public spheres were "identity-bracketed" and not masculine ones is unlikely. Joan Landes explores the historical realities of the "public sphere" model and argues that it was a more gendered place than his work or other theorists had previously considered, and was "essentially, not just contingently, masculinist" (1988, 7). Others contest that actual existing public spheres as "salons" were facilitated or dominated by women in a practical sense, although this leaves the normative conception of a gender-free public sphere in place (Cowan 2001).

Habermas's concepts have been expanded to fit a more complex and gendered world, but not in a way that privileges neutrality. Nancy Fraser (1990) argues that we should look for many public spheres, rather than one, although these subaltern political spaces or "counter-publics" are sometimes "weak" because of their relationship to hegemonic modes of politics. The implications of Fraser's arguments are that identity matters for the construction of and participation in public spheres; indeed, they may cohere around particular identities. Seyla Benhabib (2013) modifies Habermas with attention to gender concerns; shifting his commitment to the generalized and universalist position of the other into one toward concrete others. Here too is a movement beyond neutrality to "perspective taking."

There are conceptions of a political subject and of public spheres more thoughtful about the need to be non-neutral or gender forward. Iris Marion Young offers an alternative conception of a public sphere sensitive to difference, and a critique of deliberative democracy that applies to both thinkers; it is her arguments that I think have direct bearing on a gender-forward classroom and SoTL. For Young, deliberative democracy fails to recognize that "ordinary politics" produce "deep wrongs" and thus they must be challenged and changed to achieve social justice, using the tools of direct action rather than deliberation (2001, 673). In Young's dialogue, the deliberative figure criticizes the activist for advancing a particularist position that benefits their group's interest, for considering activist politics as unreasonable or noncommunicative and, most importantly, for the potential exclusivity of deliberation in the world as we know it, when "deliberation" may often provide political cover for powerful elites who manage these settings. Even when the marginalized are included, Young's activist worries that unspoken norms about communication structure deliberations in a way that privileges elites. She shows how "[e]xisting social and economic structures have set unacceptable constraints on the terms of deliberation and its agenda" (Young 2001, 682). Instead, she argues for a model of inclusive communication, arguing that: "[w]e can conceive the exchange of ideas and processes of communication taking place in a vibrant democracy as far more rowdy, disorderly, and decentered, to use Habermas's term" (Young 2001, 688). In contrast to Rawls and Habermas, Young (1994) conceives of identity as unbracketable yet, as she expresses elsewhere, this is not identity as a biological essentialism, but one built on contingent coalitions or "sets" that are built through political struggle. Groups should be given particular representation and support in the political space, such that they can resist some of the cultural and economic hegemony (1990, 185). This non-neutrality, always open to revision, recognizes the plural and always "in process" nature of our world.

Returning to SoTL and Method

If the neutrality in SoTL studies, and neutrality in public spheres, privileges the already hegemonic and naturalizes it with ideology, how should we proceed? I decided first to go back to my evidence of student learning. First, I redesigned my study to be more thoughtful about the identity of students in my analysis, and the implications of the more careful study, both in terms of the evidence of student learning and in terms of my own development as a teacher, suggests what a gender-forward classroom could look like.

To reconsider my class's experience with intersectionality and identity, I turned to the tools of the political theorist. There are many branches of political theory, including a venerable tradition of analytic political philosophy that is an "argument-based and issue-oriented, rather than thinker-based and exegetical, approach that emphasizes logical rigour, terminological precision, and clear exposition" (List and Valentini 2016, 525). However, my approach hews more closely to the thinker-based and exegetical, with the exception that I am treating my students' work as worthy of exegesis. This aligns with the interpretative approach in political theory that understands meaning as rooted in part in the very contested nature of political concepts and their involvement in ideologies, and of the way that meaning can outstrip an author's intention and tell us something about the way politics are understood in the world. To know "[w]hich typical things go through people's minds when they think about politics ... must be a major research objective of political theorist" (Frazer 2008, 205). This work requires us to carefully interpret (some might say over-interpret) all political texts, including the work of students. Akin to the method that literary scholars employ, political theorists read closely and with attention to the families of political ideas in which arguments fall, as when identifying a way of studying the classroom with a theory of legitimate government such as liberalism. My core commitments as a political theorist in the classroom are to recognizing students as political speakers and actors in their own right, not only once they have learned the "expert moves," but in their initial conceptualizations of the world. At the same time, I want them to develop a healthy critical response to their own initial political views, identifying which family they fall into and interrogating their logics and sources. I thus want to share my initial analysis of the class overall and then dial down on three specific authors to explore their positions as expressing common political positions.

As I noted above, my class had thirty-three students by the end, and I had two sets of four short essays (typically 100–500 words) per student, comprising the pre- and postwriting, both interpretations of video clips. The pre- and postwriting fell into general patterns which mostly mirror the quantitative analysis above, with some interesting exceptions. In the prewriting, nearly all students shied away from commenting in particular on raced, disabled, or otherwise marked bodies in the video clips, instead referring to "people" or sometimes "he" or "she." A few students (six) did speak directly about these features, and it was these students who were most likely to interpret situations as having a structural basis in institutions rather than individual effort. Four of them expressed an intersectional insight about identity; only one student spoke about intersectionality and not structures. In general, they seemed to be carefully guarding their language on the controversial subjects of race and gender; a student who criticized black character and work ethic, for example, prefaced the comment with "I know this isn't politically correct, but ..." This concern with an assumed norm of "political correctness," which certainly has broader implications, flowed throughout the precourse writing.

Indeed, the students stuck very closely to a view of color-blind, liberal tolerance in the classroom and written work. The University of Wisconsin–Green Bay, where I teach, has a student body that is over 85 percent white, although we have more diversity of socioeconomic class and age and growing populations of African American, Hmong, and American Indian students, mostly from Oneida and Menominee Nations.[1] Many white students have little experience with people of color, although their writing and in-class discussion tends to reflect some a variation of liberal neutrality toward the various differences. This was clearly shown in their precourse responses to a video clip which showed a young black man pulled over by the police for driving in the "wrong" neighborhood; over half of the class attempted to explain this situation without discussing race at all. Similar struggles were at issue with the depictions of gender and ability, with the exception that there seemed to be a general sympathy toward the disabled person, even though few students named them as such. The clip that showed class-based discrimination or struggle, in this case to pay a copay for a prescription, was the most directly discussed, albeit in terms of "poverty." No students commented on the interlocking aspects of the "poor" character's identity; it is interesting that class seems to be understood in a different way from the other identities, perhaps as a nonessential one. Not only does this mirror the way that social class and socioeconomic status are not protected classes in the United States' liberal jurisprudence, it also reflects the notion that identity or difference is for nonwhites.

In direct comparison, the postcourse writing was notably much longer, even though the same time period for writing was offered in each case. This also meant there was more room for interesting U-turns or reconsiderations in the posttest, which felt much more exploratory and less anxious about my approval. There were fewer words crossed out in the second set. Many students had a more complex conceptualization of identity across the board in the posttest of readings, although few articulated this in either test without signaling their uncertainty or ambiguity, using words such as "perhaps," "seems," "kinda," and "sometimes." In the posttest, questions about sexuality, perhaps prompted by the then concurrent Supreme Court ruling on marriage, were raised about a clip with two women.

After the course, race, class, and gender were named more directly, although not as uncontested terminology, such that students wrote "black, african mmerican [sic], rich, man, woman" to describe people. In this later writing, the terminology "working class" appeared in five student's responses, and not always referring to the clip depicting the (most obviously) working-class character. While the term "intersectionality" was only used by three students, the notion or practice of looking for more than one identity, or reading between the lines for potential meaning was more frequent. For example, a student wrote about the two women mentioned above: "[w]hile there was no physical touching, it seemed as if they might be in a relationship, and perhaps this meant that they approached the situation with fear. It could also mean that, being together, they felt more confidence." This was a nuanced attempt to think through the identities of the characters.

Student responses expressed coherent ways of thinking about inequality, with relative consistency over the two tests, even as their writing became more complex in many ways. They expressed both the coherency of contemporary thinking about difference and a nascent self-reflective critique about them. To highlight this and show what richness there can be in close reading of student work. I decided to focus on three of these interviews because they offered linkages to prominent "families" of conceptualizing inequality and justice in the world of political theory, and also express, implicitly, some key critiques of these areas. I here situate them in relation to political traditions and ideas. One student, I think, expresses a variant of critical race theory, a second student, liberal feminism, and the third student is a strong defender of liberal neutrality. These particular students had stable positions through the two writings, with the exception that their questions became more complex in the second round.

Three Student Approaches to Intersectionality and Inequality

The first student interpreted a postcourse clip, from *Orange Is the New Black*, dramatizing the relationship between prisons and poor communities of color, as illustrative of the broader hierarchies of society. She wrote, "this is ... why when we talk about incarceration rates we need to talk about what ... jobs there are in the inner city, what sort of opportunity," and also police violence. She did not distinguish between the clip and the world at large, and she commented in particular on the fact that this story is not always told. I associate both of these traits with critical race theory, because she was conscious that media is part of the unquestioned naturalization of our ideas about race and inequality. "Critical Race Theory questions the very foundations of the liberal order, including equality theory, legal reasoning, Enlightenment reasoning, and neutral principles of Constitutional Law" (Delgado and Stefancic 2012, 3). This student developed her argument in relation to her own experience, reflecting this theory's emphasis on "counter story telling" and personal narrative as a tool of inquiry and meaning making (Solórzano and Yosso 2002). She also frequently discussed her own identity as a black woman with incarcerated relatives, focusing on aspects of racial violence and encounters with the police and other systems, but also noting that as a woman her experience with police was different. She spoke about identity as complex also in relation to the clip where gender was foregrounded, although here she kept repeating "I've never been a mother," as the clip concerned care responsibilities interfering with paid labor. She was careful to say how she saw some commonalities without collapsing difference. Most interestingly, she categorized the clip showing a person in a wheelchair as an experience outside her understanding, an interesting side note on the challenges for disability studies. Finally, when I asked her what she might imagine about the writings of the other students, her tone changed markedly, and she slumped a bit in her seat. She gave an account of her time at the university that expressed frustration with her fellow students and the discursive spaces of her classroom, including the way in which minority voices were both silenced and asked to over-represent their communities.

The second student, the liberal feminist, would probably not have been comfortable with that label, as she explicitly disavowed feminism. Liberal feminism considers gender equality as a matter of fairness, arguing against discrimination and that "gender justice ... requires us, first, to make the rules of the game fair and, second, to make certain that none of the runners in the race for society's goods and services is systematically disadvantaged" (Tong 2013, vi). However, I am labeling the student as such because the positions she advanced were those of liberal feminism: everyone should have equal political rights and social respect, and we should combat legal and political discrimination, including in the workplace. For example, she reacted strongly to the precourse clip with the mother struggling at work and suggested that parental leave policies needed to be improved. Unprompted, she then discussed her own goals for a marriage of partnership and friendship, and swung back around to the depiction of working-class masculinity, which involved a man who could barely afford his medical copay for a prescription drug. Her response to him seemed to be one of pity rather than identification or even empathy, but nonetheless she was torn about whether it was his fault or someone else's ("big banks? the financial crisis? I'm not sure how it works") that he was struggling to pay for medical care after a financial hardship. She talked about her own identity as "average" and "normal" and did not mention her gender. Her manner was relaxed throughout.

The last student, who expressed a "post-ism" approach was the most critical of the individuals in the clips and in general blamed them all, although less so the wheelchair-bound person, for their plight. The idea that we are beyond discrimination make up a twenty-first century worldview I am summarizing as "post-ism." It is a view that "[d]espite the racialized and gendered nature of all aspects of American life, including media coverage ... we are beyond, past, or "post-" notions of race-, gender-, and sexuality-based discrimination" (Joseph 2009, 238). My student vacillated between a more libertarian view of the world and a more neo-reactionary rejection of "political correctness [which] is everywhere." He mentioned that "things are moving beyond questions of identity and globalization makes all people blend together," suggesting that race and identity have no meaning under global capitalism. In the clips, there were few details to explain exactly why the characters met difficulty; post-ism supplied his own broader narrative which frequently used the word "choice," followed closely by "opportunity." He wrote, in response to the clip showing a black woman discussing her reincarceration. "Who you are, your group or race ... identity is irrelevant today. I mean, maybe in the Middle East or Africa or something it matters, but not in the United States and not in Wisconsin. I knew all sorts of people in high school and they made their own choices and they ended up where they are now. She could have gotten a job instead."

Although he seemed nervous about discussing race and shied away from the subject, he was less nervous about discussing gender. He claimed that "the feminists I know want special privileges," although he would not give details beyond "laws that benefit them, like in divorce."

After these interviews, I was reflecting on the central question of "for whom" should I teach? These three students, although they all became slightly more thoughtful about the complexity of identity by the second writing, generally stayed in their same positions. Do I want to reach the "post-ism" thinker, whose conceptualization is from my point-of-view the most problematic? Or should I engage with the liberal feminist, who is arguably a more likely target? Or should I be teaching toward the critical race theorist, who expressed with real pain her experience at a majority-white school? Before the interviews, I would have said very directly that it is the color-blind and post-feminist students who most need to understand inequality and intersectionality. However, the affective dimensions of the experience left me most connected to the critical race theorist, and most concerned about how teaching about race can be done in a way that builds joyous communities around learning and engagement with difference. I hope that I can pursue the insights of my students in the spirit of "loving perception" which begins from difference rather than negating or problematizing it.[2]

Is there a pedagogy that helps all three of these students to learn, or is this a choice with trade-offs? When considering "for whom" a pedagogy works, both the power dynamics and hierarchies of the classroom and local area and the broader conversation are in play. And if, as my quantitative research shows, it is very difficult to teach or experience the complexity of students' views on race and gender, what does this mean for learning possibilities in courses where these themes are important?

This problem brings us back to the questions about the gendered subject in political theory; not only do popular methods of SoTL potentially cover over the richness of student subjectivity and experience, but treating the classroom like an idea or public sphere space of liberal neutrality does as well. Faculty are criticized for "political correctness" or shutting down free-speech when they, for example, require students use the pronouns that correspond to other students' gender identities or oppose or even disallow comments that are manifestly racist, sexist, or otherwise dehumanizing to marginalized people. The liberal defense of free-speech in the classroom argues that the best ideas will win, and "the best cure for bad speech is more speech." I can imagine a classroom where all students have the standing and the expertise to present their positions and all can judge based on shared standards of reason, and I can also imagine a classroom where my authority as a professor is whittled down such that I am one voice among many, but it is hard to point to any actually functioning classrooms like this. In my classrooms, I am particularly troubled by my role in relation to the marginalized students either in the classroom, who by definition are potentially isolated, and to perspectives that aren't represented at all. It is my job, as a sort of "democracy enforcing" nondemocratic figure, to protect and extend these voices. But how to choose? If I use the category of advocating for marginalized opinions, does this mean any unpopular opinion, from climate change denial to, in my classrooms, #BlackLivesMatter? One starting place is to develop intentional relationships with colleagues, students, and community members of color to build capacity to "world travel" in our everyday lives (Lugones 2003). These practices reflect the insights of work in WGS, and even political science, which delineates which voices and perspectives are most likely to be excluded from our textbooks, professorate, and politics—as my fellow authors do in this volume. Non-neutral SoTL can inform our non-neutral, gender-forward classrooms, but just as students struggle to learn about intersectional identity from theory, we as instructors need to learn about identity through experience with diverse others, rather than imaginging their views.

So, when the next student comes to my class and cries about the syllabus, I'll show her the new section I have added: "Although these general rules guide the classroom, grading, and assignments, they are open for revision through collaborative work with the professor and the class. We can change the rules together for all students, or with consultation and discussion, assignments can be swapped for alternative assignments to better meet an individual student's needs. Although all students may not do identical work, the goal of a just classroom will guide these negotiations and our classroom." I hope this can be an invitation to, in a small way, coalition-build.

Appendix Acita

Each video clip was chosen because it both showed *primarily* one identity, either as a speaker self-identified or showed several traits associated with a group (such as skin color and race), but also implied or included the other aspects of identity that might cause someone to think intersectionally.

Video Clip Set 1 (prior to class)

1A Class: From the 2012 film *Take Shelter*, a scene where a man needs to pay a copay for his purchase of a sedative, and is surprised by the price. He can barely find the $47.54 in his wallet.

2A Gender: From the 2011 film *I Don't Know How She Does It*, where a woman and a man discuss an upcoming business opportunity they are competing for which will involve more travel. Although he also has four children, he suggests this will cause problems for her two children.

3A Race: From *The Fresh Prince of Bel Air*, "Mistaken Identity," a clip shows two black men in a fancy car who are pulled over for going too slowly; the cop assumes they have stolen the car.

4A Ability: From *Breaking Bad*, "Down," a scene where a disabled young man (cerebral palsy) is berated by his father, who is teaching him to drive, for driving with both feet instead of just one.

Video Clip Set 2 (after class)

1B Class: From *King of the Hill*, 1993, a teenage boy in a rundown hotel cuts out photos of food and arranges them in place of actual food for a Thanksgiving dinner.

2B: From *Thelma and Louise* (1991), a scene where a trucker makes obscene gestures at the two women as they drive in their car; they force him off the road.

2C Race: From *Orange Is the New Black*, "Fool Me Once," an incarcerated black woman tells her friend how she ended up back in prison after being released.

2D Ability: From *Archer*, "El Contador," a hapless man is given the job of a skilled secret agent because the skilled man has been paralyzed and is in a wheelchair.

ALISON KATHRYN STAUDINGER is Assistant Professor of Democracy and Justice Studies, Political Science, and Women's and Gender Studies at the University of Wisconsin–Green Bay. She teaches courses in American Political Thought, Gender and the Law, and Democratic Theory.

Notes

1. Students of color were just under 15 percent in 2014, according to the UWGB Factbook.
2. Feminist theory and philosophy has continued to expand notions of subjectivity far beyond these initial critiques of liberalism. Following the pioneering works of Gloria Anzaldúa (1987) and other feminists of color (Moraga and Anzaldúa 2015), feminists like Maria Lugones have advanced powerful conceptions of pluralist identity which seek practices of "world-traveling" and multiplicity in their approach to intersectionality (1987, 2003) or, as in the work of Mariana Ortega (2016), through a phenomenology of the self as multiplicity. AnaLouise Keating has extended this challenge in her reading of post-oppositional politics (2012), which also has implications for identity in the classroom. This work deserves full exploration in the space of teaching and learning, but I offer a beginning here in trying to attend to the experiences of my students and the relationships I hope to develop with them.

References

Ambrose, Susan A., Michael W. Bridges, Michele DiPietro, Marsha C. Lovett, and Marie K. Norman. 2010. *How Learning Works: Seven Research-Based Principles for Smart Teaching.* Hoboken, NJ: Wiley.
Anzaldúa, Gloria E. 1987. *Borderlands/La Frontera.* San Franciso, CA: Aunt Lute.
Baines, Beverley, Daphne Barak-Erez, and Tsvi Kahana. 2012. *Feminist Constitutionalism: Global Perspectives.* Cambridge: Cambridge University Press.

Beard, Charles A. [1913] 2012. *An Economic Interpretation of the Constitution of the United States.* New York: Simon and Schuster.

Benhabib, Seyla. 2013. *Situating the Self: Gender, Community and Postmodernism in Contemporary Ethics.* Hoboken, NJ: Wiley.

Biesta, Gert. 2007. "Why 'What Works' Won't Work: Evidence-Based Practice and the Democratic Deficit in Educational Research." *Educational Theory* 57 (1): 11–22.

Bloch-Schulman, Stephen. 2016. "A Critique of Methods in the Scholarship of Teaching and Learning in Philosophy." *Teaching & Learning Inquiry* 4 (1): 1–15.

Bloch-Schulman, Stephen, Susan Wharton Conkling, Sherry Lee Linkon, Karen Manarin, and Kathleen Perkins. 2016. "Asking Bigger Questions: An Invitation to Further Conversation." *Teaching & Learning Inquiry* 4 (1): 1–7.

Bowleg, Lisa. 2008. "When Black + Lesbian + Woman ≠Black Lesbian Woman: The Methodological Challenges of Qualitative and Quantitative Intersectionality Research." *Sex Roles* 59 (5/6): 312–25.

Chick, Nancy. 2014. "'Methodologically Sound' under the 'Big Tent': An Ongoing Conversation." *International Journal for the Scholarship of Teaching and Learning* 8 (2): Article 1.

Cole, Elizabeth R. 2009. "Intersectionality and Research in Psychology." *American Psychologist* 64 (3): 170.

Cook-Sather, Alison, Catherine Bovill, and Peter Felten. 2014. *Engaging Students as Partners in Learning and Teaching: A Guide for Faculty.* Hoboken, NJ: Wiley.

Cowan, Brian. 2001. "What Was Masculine about the Public Sphere? Gender and the Coffeehouse Milieu in Post-Restoration England." *History Workshop Journal* 51: 127–57.

Delgado, Richard, and Jean Stefancic. 2012. *Critical Race Theory.* New York: New York University Press.

Dahl, John, dir. March 29, 2009. "Down." *Breaking Bad*, season 2, episode 4.

Easton, Lee, and Kelly Hewson. 2012. "Have You, My Little Serpents, a New Skin? Transforming English Studies and the Scholarship of Teaching and Learning." *Collected Essays on Learning and Teaching* 5: 75–79.

Fraser, Nancy. 1990. "Rethinking the Public Sphere: A Contribution to the Critique of Actually Existing Democracy." *Social Text* 25/26: 56–80.

Frazer, Elizabeth. 2008. "Political Theory and the Boundaries of Politics." In *Political Theory: Methods and Approaches*, edited by David Leopold and Marc Stears, 171–95. New York: Oxford University Press.

McCarthy, Andrew, dir. July 11, 2013. "Fool Me Once." *Orange is the New Black*, season 1, episode 12.

Gilpin, Lorraine S., and Delores Liston. 2009. "Transformative Education in the Scholarship of Teaching and Learning: An Analysis of SoTL Literature." *International Journal for the Scholarship of Teaching and Learning* 3 (2): 11.

Giroux, Henry A. 2003. "Spectacles of Race and Pedagogies of Denial: Anti-Black Racist Pedagogy under the Reign of Neoliberalism." *Communication Education* 52 (3/4): 191–211.

Grauerholz, Liz, and Eric Main. 2013. "Fallacies of SoTL: Rethinking How We Conduct Our Research." In *The Scholarship of Teaching and Learning in and across the Disciplines*, edited by Kathleen McKinney, 152–68. Bloomington: Indiana University Press.

Habermas, Jürgen. 1991. *The Structural Transformation of the Public Sphere: An Inquiry into a Category of Bourgeois Society*. Cambridge, MA: The MIT Press.
Hancock, Ange Marie. 2011. *Solidarity Politics for Millennials: A Guide to Ending the Oppression Olympics*. New York: Palgrave Macmillan.
Hubball, Harry, and Anthony Clarke. 2010. "Diverse Methodological Approaches and Considerations for SoTL in Higher Education." *Canadian Journal for the Scholarship of Teaching and Learning* 1 (1): 2.
Huber, Mary Taylor, and Sherwyn P. Morreale. 2002. *Disciplinary Styles in the Scholarship of Teaching and Learning: Exploring Common Ground*. Sterling, VA: Stylus Publishing.
Joseph, Ralina Landwehr. 2009. "Tyra Banks Is Fat": Reading (Post-) Racism and (Post-) Feminism in the New Millennium. *Critical Studies in Media Communication* 26 (3): 237–54.
Keating, AnaLouise. 2012. *Transformation Now: Toward a Post-Oppositional Politics of Change*. Urbana: University of Illinois Press.
Landes, Joan B. 1988. *Women and the Public Sphere in the Age of the French Revolution*. Ithaca, NY: Cornell University Press.
Levinson, Sanford. 2006. *Our Undemocratic Constitution: Where the Constitution Goes Wrong (and How We the People Can Correct It)*. New York: Oxford University Press.
List, Christian, and Laura Valentini. 2016. "The Methodology of Political Theory." In *The Oxford Handbook of Philosophical Methodology*, edited by Herman Cappelen, Tamar Szabo Gendler, and John Hawthorne, 525–53. New York: Oxford University Press.
Lugones, Maria. 1987. "Playfulness, 'World'-Traveling, and Loving Perception." *Hypatia* 2 (2): 3–19.
———. 2003. *Pilgrimages/peregrinajes: Theorizing Coalition Against Multiple Oppressions*. Lanham, MD: Rowman & Littlefield Publishers.
Moraga, Cherríe, and Gloria Anzaldúa, eds. 2015. *This Bridge Called My Back: Writings by Radical Women of Color*. New York: Suny Press.
McGrath, Douglas, dir. 2011. *I Don't Know How She Does It*. The Weinstein Company. DVD (2012), Anchor Bay Entertainment.
Melman, Jeff, dir. 1990. "Mistaken Identity." *The Fresh Prince of Bel Air*, season 1, episode 6.
Miller-Young, Janice, and Michelle Yeo. 2015. "Conceptualizing and Communicating SoTL: A Framework for the Field." *Teaching and Learning Inquiry* 3 (2): 37–53.
Mills, David, and Mary Taylor Huber. 2005. "Anthropology and the Educational 'Trading Zone' Disciplinarity, Pedagogy, and Professionalism." *Arts and Humanities in Higher Education* 4 (1): 9–32.
Nichols, Jeff, dir. 2011. *Take Shelter*. Sony Pictures Classics. DVD (2012), Sony Pictures Classics.
Okin, Susan Moller. 1991. *Justice, Gender, and the Family*. New York: Basic Books.
———. 1994. "Political Liberalism, Justice, and Gender." *Ethics* 105 (1): 23.
Ortega, Mariana. 2016. *In-Between: Latina feminist phenomenology, multiplicity, and the self*. New York, NY: SUNY Press.
Pateman, Carole. [1988] 2014. *The Sexual Contract*. Hoboken, NJ: Wiley.
Rawls, John. [1971] 1999. *A Theory of Justice*. Rev. ed. Cambridge, MA: Harvard University Press.
———. 2001. *Justice as Fairness: A Restatement*. Cambridge, MA: Harvard University Press.
———. 2005. *Political Liberalism*. New York: Columbia University Press.
Reed, Adam, dir. January 26, 2012. "El Contador." *Archer*, season 3, episode 5.

Ritter, Gretchen. 2006. *The Constitution as Social Design: Gender and Civic Membership in the American Constitutional Order*. Redwood City Stanford, CA: Stanford University Press.

Rodabaugh, Rita Cobb. 1996. "Institutional Commitment to Fairness in College Teaching." *New Directions for Teaching and Learning* 66: 37–45.

Schwarzenbach, Sibyl A., and Patricia Smith. 2012. *Women and the US Constitution: History, Interpretation, and Practice*. New York: Columbia University Press.

Solórzano, Daniel G., and Tara J. Yosso. 2002. "Critical Race Methodology: Counter-Storytelling as an Analytical Framework for Education Research." *Qualitative Inquiry* 8 (1): 23–44.

Tong, Rosemarie. 2013. *Feminist Thought: A Comprehensive Introduction*. Boca Raton, LA: Routledge.

Waldstreicher, David. 2010. *Slavery's Constitution: From Revolution to Ratification*. New York: Macmillan.

Weber, Brenda R. 2010. "Teaching Popular Culture through Gender Studies: Feminist Pedagogy in a Postfeminist and Neoliberal Academy?." *Feminist Teacher* 20 (2): 124–38.

Wilson-Doenges, Georjeanna, and Regan A. R. Gurung. 2013. "Benchmarks for Scholarly Investigations of Teaching and Learning." *Australian Journal of Psychology* 65 (1): 63–70.

Wilson-Doenges, Georjeanna, Jordan D. Troisi, and Robert A. Bartsch. 2016. "Exemplars of the Gold Standard in SoTL for Psychology." *Scholarship of Teaching and Learning in Psychology* 2 (1): 1–12.

Young, Iris Marion. 1990. *Justice and the Politics of Difference*. Princeton, NJ: Princeton University Press.

———. 1994. "Gender as Seriality: Thinking about Women as a Social Collective." *Signs* 19 (3): 713–38.

———. 2001. "Activist Challenges to Deliberative Democracy." *Political Theory* 29 (5): 670–90.

9 Thinking through Movement: Embodied Learning as Feminist Pedagogy for the Social Sciences

Valerie Barske

Thinking through Embodied Learning

Despite significant strides in the scholarship of teaching and learning (Evans, Davies, and Rich 2009; Freiler 2008; Horn and Wilburn 2005), the concept of embodied learning remains undertheorized, particularly as a meaningful, feminist pedagogical approach for the social sciences. Practitioners in leadership training and management workshops have come to define "embodied learning" most simply as "the ability to take new actions" (Strozzi Institute 2013). Sociologist Hui Niu Wilcox employs the terms "embodied learning," "embodied knowledge," or "embodied pedagogy" interchangeably "to signal an epistemological and pedagogical shift that draws attention to bodies as agents of knowledge production" (2009, 104). In this chapter, I extend this theoretical move one step further to fill a gap in Scholarship of Teaching and Learning (SoTL) literature thus far by linking strategies for teaching in the social sciences to the scholarly notion of "dynamic embodiment" (Farnell and Varela 2008). I then trace the process of designing, executing, and assessing results of a SoTL research case study focused on how embodied learning proved central for students to grapple with competing historical narratives and gendered memories of the past. In the end, I argue that teaching and learning to "think with and through movement" (Farnell 2012) may be utilized as a gender-forward strategy based on high-impact practices that create spaces for multimodal learning as feminist activism in the social sciences.

My research on embodied learning seeks to participate in historical discussions of embodiment in social theory. Challenging Eurocentric ideas of what constitutes knowledge and humanity, socio-cultural anthropologist Brenda Farnell subtitled her most recent work on embodied social theory "I Move Therefore I Am" (2012). This transformative statement represents an ontological shift that locates agency in human movement. Farnell disrupts the legacy of the Enlightenment through a meta-theoretical move away from René Descartes' philosophy of *"cogito ergo sum"* (I think therefore I am; *Je pense, donc je suis*, 1637), which infamously promoted a dualistic split and fostered the binary of "mind versus body." The very history of social scientific notions of personhood has remained haunted by the disembodied *spectre* of this Cartesian bifurcation. As feminist activist and human sexuality scholar Tamsin Wilton explains, "Cartesian dualism is, famously, premised on the irreconcilable differentness of the material body from that which inhabits and motivates it" (Wilton 2000, 239). She adds that Descartes' notion of a mind/body split underpins some of the greatest "anomalies of modern science," which "bequeathed feminists and queers a difficult legacy" (Wilton 2000, 239). Similarly, in her work on embodied ways of knowing, Wilcox draws from feminist theorist Elizabeth Grosz (1994) to explain that "the Eurocentric, patriarchal power in Western knowledge production is maintained via the willful disembodiment of white male scientists (known for their brilliant, objective minds), and via the equation of women and those in other marginalized groups to bodies (deemed as passive objects incapable of knowing or reason)" (Wilcox 2009, 106). In this way, Cartesian dualism grounds scientific knowledge in inherently gendered and racialized assumptions, historically located in European Enlightenment ideals. Descartes' legacy fosters social theory that privileges "the mind," as associated with the male, masculine rational thought, and "Western" imperial knowledge, over "the body," as equated with the female, feminine irrational emotion, and "non-Western," colonized, primitive, traditional, natural, or pre-linguistic practices (Barske 2009; Butler 1993; Grosz 1994; Farnell 2001).

Rather than privileging mind over body, or body over mind, as in phenomenological approaches, the concept of dynamic embodiment as a social theory is a "theory of *Moving Being*—a principle of which is that the *somatic is necessarily semiotic*" (Farnell and Varela 2008, 221). The semiotic significance of the moving body serves as the foundation of the "second somatic revolution," articulated by Drid Williams, a professional dancer trained as a social anthropologist under E. E. Evans-Pritchard at Oxford University. Williams (1979) developed "semasiology," the anthropological study of human movements as "action signs," by drawing from renowned social theorist Rom Harré (1970), especially his theory of causal powers. Williams argues that the moving body functions as a signifier of meaning and movements are laden with various cultural and semantic values, which represent both a reflection of and an active engagement with producing the beliefs, values, and histories of a given people at a given time (Williams 1995, 52). In this sense, human beings may be best defined as "dynamically embodied meaning-making agents" (Farnell 1999, 341).

My theorization of embodied learning relies directly on Farnell's conclusion that "dynamically embodied acts thus belong at the heart of social theory" (Farnell 2012, 7). Following Williams and Farnell, I seek to expand standard assumptions of discourse and knowledge by arguing that the impact of embodied learning lies in an epistemological shift of "thinking with and through movement" in which "human movement is *in itself* imaginative, conceptual and metaphorical, and thinking with movement is fundamental to dynamically embodied personhood" (Farnell 2012, 3–5). Discourse and knowledge are inherently multimodal and encompassing various modes of meaning-making, such as visual, aural, spatial, embodied, and so forth. Embodied learning, in a sense, offers a chance to erode the seemingly impenetrable wall between gendered categories of knowledge creation and dissemination (mind versus body) by combining various modes of learning as simultaneously cognitive and somatic. This approach provides an integrated view of learning and the learner with great possibilities for all scholarly teachers. The idea of embodied learning as thinking with and through movement opens new avenues for any discipline to train students in performing disciplinary actions, as well as challenging the gendered assumptions within the discipline, including political science.

Viewing students as "dynamically embodied meaning-making agents" who "think with and through movement" highlights the importance of challenging how "knowledge" has been defined and conveyed in academia. Especially in traditionally male-dominated fields of political science and history, embodied learning helps to revolutionize the ways in which we approach both the content and format of our classrooms as inherently gendered and politicized. As Wilcox notes, "most feminist educators have yet to see what they do in the classroom through the lens of embodiment," and therefore "consider somatically engaging our students outside of our responsibility" (2009, 107). She argues that by failing to recognize "multiple intelligences," feminist pedagogues may even "reproduce the very system of power that we claim to critique" (Wilcox 2009, 107). In this sense, actively embracing multimodal teaching strategies as central to learning serves as an example of feminist praxis, reflection plus action, in the classroom. Following a similar line of argument, Diana Gustafson defines embodied learning as a form of feminist pedagogy, linking embodiment to "politics, power, and transformation" (2009, 250). She highlights how embodied learning not only challenges "*what* is learned" but also "*how* it is learned" (Gustafson 2009, 251). Especially relevant for social scientists working in cross-cultural contexts, Gustafson emphasizes that embodied learning "contests the primacy of androcentric, Eurocentric institutionalized knowledges as a way of knowing our bodies, ourselves, and our world" (Gustafson 2009, 251).

For my SoTL case study, Gustafson's work on challenging Western biomedical assumptions about the body-as-object also proves particularly useful in terms of emphasizing how embodied learning helps students to experience the constructed nature of knowledge as producers rather than simply consumers. When embodiment serves as both the content and pedagogy, Gustafson demonstrates that students are able to challenge normalized ways of seeing the world.

This approach dovetails directly with discussions on how to define a "signature pedagogy" for the interdisciplinary field of Women's and Gender Studies (WGS) and extends the value of the former to improve teaching and learning in many traditional social science disciplines, especially political science and history. The embodied and experiential nature of learning proves necessary for conceptualizing gender-forward teaching and essential to feminist pedagogies as outlined by Holly Hassel and Nerissa Nelson. Hassel and Nelson highlight the key components of feminist pedagogies as focusing on "participatory learning, validation of personal experience, development of political/social understanding and activism, critical thinking/open mindedness, reflexivity (consciousness-raising), action orientation (social change), social construction of knowledge, attention to affect (refusal to separate the rational from the emotional), use of situation at hand (local and global connections), empowerment, inclusion, collaboration, community and leadership" (2012, 145–146). Beyond simply a list of feminist tools in the classroom, I argue that the mechanism by which these high-impact practices achieve both learning outcomes and feminist activist goals is the engagement of embodiment as central to accessing multiple knowledges. These practices also echo broader calls to social scientists by anthropologist Michael Wesch (2009) who promotes teaching students how to be knowledge-able by moving beyond simply subjects to teaching subjectivities or ways of being in the world. This educational approach helps feminist social scientists to create a greater link between what they achieve in their disciplinary research, namely challenging standard assumptions about power and knowing, and what they accomplish in the classroom as a space to do more than simply reproduce oppressive structures. Learning to think through and with movement, recognizing humans as dynamically embodied agents, also changes how we move in the world.

Feminist Research for Teaching, Learning, and Moving in the World

Reflecting my personal anthropology as a scholarly teacher nestled between the fields of feminist history, sociocultural anthropology, Asian studies, and global studies, I contend that what, how, even why we teach in the classroom reflects what, how, why we act in our disciplinary research. Before explaining my SoTL case study on embodied learning, I briefly situate my work in a specific "personal is political" context. In writing this chapter, in teaching my classes, I bring with me the gendered ways of acting and moving gained from my participant observational experiences. Since 1998, through several extended research stays including as a Fulbright IIE Fellow (1998–1999) and a Fulbright-Hays Fellow (2005–2006), I have been conducting ethnographic research with female peace activists in Okinawa, Japan. My scholarship examines gender in Okinawa, formerly the Ryukyu Kingdom (ca., 1429–1879) transformed into a colonial governorship under imperial Japan (1879–1945), at the crossroads of competing empires. The site of one of the bloodiest ground battles in World War II (April 1 to June 23, 1945), Okinawa suffered further atrocities under the US military occupation, which continued officially until 1972. Situated in a complex geopolitical position between China and Japan, contemporary Okinawa maintains an estimated 50,000 US troops, despite returning to Japanese sovereignty under a peace constitution that prohibits a standing military. In terms of conceptualizing gender and politics, I study the politicization of dancing and other cultural performances, especially the targeting of women's bodily practices, as central to understanding the ongoing struggles with decolonization in post-World War II Okinawa. The women utilize dancing as a means of both grappling with the past, but also constructing meaningful identities to address current political struggles (Barske 2003).

Together with feminist leaders Ginoza Eiko, a thirty-five-year veteran of teaching in Japan's compulsory education system, and Takazato Suzuyo, former Naha City assemblywoman, I participated in fieldwork training at local sites of historical trauma. For example, the most impactful experiences often involved visiting abandoned caves where civilians lived and died during World War II, some through the complex practice of "compulsory group suicide" (shudan jikestu). The Chibichiri Gama in Yomitan has become a site for memorializing loss as well as trans-generational trauma. On April 2, 1945, the day after US forces stormed the Okinawan shores, a group of 140 residents living in the cave refused to surrender. An estimated eighty-three people, mainly women and children under age fifteen, lost their lives at the hands of fellow family members or various forms of suicide, including detonating hand grenades distributed by the Japanese military. Japanese imperial education, made compulsory in colonial Okinawa in the late 1800s, instructed Okinawans to die for the divine emperor, to avoid the shame of surrender, and to sacrifice their families rather than allowing them to be tortured or raped by the enemy (McCormack and Norimatsu 2012). Educators and activists, such as Ginoza and Takazato, struggle with how to convey these kinds of stories to current generations, particularly as cautionary tales for the realities of supporting militarism and allowing the ongoing presence of US military bases in their backyards (Takazato 1994). Their activism recognizes the inherent intersectionality of identities, in particular by highlighting how historical oppressions as well as current political inequities in Okinawa directly link to the intersections of gender, race, and empire.

When I walk into the classroom, I bring these inherently personalized, subjective, and embodied experiences of another time and place with me. As I try to describe the legacies of war to my students, I recall the smell of death inside the caves, the viscerally disturbing sight of broken tea cups symbolizing the everyday lives of people before the war, and the intense darkness in which some mothers chose to take the lives of their own children (and in some cases vice versa). This detail troubles my students and forces me to develop innovative ways of questioning further gendered binaries of feminine = peaceful and masculine = violent. Often survivor testimonies depict women in wartime and particularly women in Okinawa as victims, peacemakers, or nonviolent mothers. However, the realities of the Battle of Okinawa and many other war zones are such that women actively participated in acts of violence intricately entwined with cultural struggles of colonial oppression (Barske 2015). The very meaning of gendered identities, what it meant to be a woman, a mother, or for that matter a diligent son loyal to the imperial nation was profoundly shaped by war. Several generations later, these historical issues have remained politicized as Okinawa still grapples with enduring processes of decolonization, lodged between the vestiges of Japanese imperialism and neocolonial dynamics as a military client state of the United States.

While these particular experiences are specific to my research site, the ability to bring multimodal insights from feminist research into the classroom is directly relevant to all social scientists concerned with fostering cross-cultural competencies, especially empathetic understanding. The import of sharing our own subjectivities as feminist researchers moving in the world is as powerful in comparative politics as it is in world history, WGS, global studies, or international studies classrooms. Through my research topic and methods of embodied learning, I am intentionally moving the students to think differently about gendered actions in historical and cultural context. I teach them movements from traditional Okinawan "women's" dances, which have been reappropriated as part of a complicated ethno-mythomoteur against Japanese imperialism and US military bases. I share experiences of performing these same movements in Okinawa on ancestral lands reclaimed from US control after decades of court battles. When I danced accompanied by activist Chibana Shōichi at a public celebration of his family's land returned in August 2006, he announced that the act of inviting me to perform signifies that he is "not against Americans, but simply against US bases, especially on my family's land" (Barske 2009, 59). And when I helped him cut a clearing of land with a machete to build a peace monument of a Korean mother clinging to her son conscripted to labor for imperial Japan in World War II, he said "now this is literally making history, can you teach your students this in your history class back in the US?" Here, he is implying not only the physical act of constructing the monument. Chibana is asking how will I teach about the complicated history of Okinawans, as both victims and collaborators under Japanese imperialism, building a monument to atone for abuses they inflicted on colonized Koreans as conscript laborers and sexual "slaves." His question remains an active charge in my classroom and raises a salient point for feminist teachers to reflect on: How might scholarly teaching as a feminist praxis incorporate creative forms of embodied learning to bring the realities of complex intersectional identities to life in our courses?

In this way, I embrace the theoretical framework of dynamic embodiment not as theory for theory's sake, but rather for the usefulness of this approach in the critical analysis of my historical and ethnographical focus. The content defines the form and vice versa. By employing notions of dynamic embodiment, I seek to excavate agentic subjectivities as a means of complicating victimization narratives to recognize the ways in which Okinawans negotiate ongoing colonial violence and lingering processes of decolonization. Ultimately, Okinawan activists utilize embodied engagements that at times reproduce and undo imperial regimes of power that seek to subjugate them. Through this new lens, I help the students to move in ways that not only reproduce a kind of simulacra of the real world, but actually produce new meanings of everyday political activism and socialization in a broader global context.

Teaching beyond "Add Women and Stir," SoTL Case Study Proposal

Given my research background and experiences in Okinawa, I began my teaching career with a clear intentionality to integrate pedagogical strategies that highlighted kinesthetic knowledge and activities for engaging embodied learning. However, for my first SoTL research project, I struggled with deciding exactly what teaching problem would generate meaningful evidence to support my use of embodied learning for teaching gender in the world history classroom. While my scholarship on embodied learning in relation to gender holds great applicability across the social sciences, my original SoTL proposal emphasized the enduring gender bias in history and international studies, especially for the subfield of world history. Despite the work of scholars—such as Merry Wiesner-Hanks (2005, 2007), Ulrike Strasser and Heidi Tinsman (2005), Peter Stearns (2006), and Antoinette Burton (2011)—research and teaching on world history remains rather loosely connected with the study of women and gender history. According to a quantitative study conducted by Sharon Block and David Newman (2011) based on abstracts from 1985 to 2005, journal articles addressing women and gender constituted at most 8 percent of all history articles. Within that 8 percent, less than half of the articles addressed women in the world outside of North America. This scholarly trend directly affects the teaching of world history in terms of available course materials and pedagogical approaches. In this context, my case study proposal began by posing the following questions: (1) What pedagogical strategies and course materials prove most effective for engaging students in the study of world history through the lens of gender? (2) How might student learning be enhanced by courses that emphasize gendered themes including embodied histories, personal narratives, and popular cultures? (3) In what ways might global studies courses be restructured to emphasize embodied learning as a vehicle for recruiting and retaining more students, including more female students?

While my initial research questions were rather broad, they hold great implications not only for feminist historians in world history, but indeed for feminist scholars across disciplines and especially in subfields focused on changing mainstream academic assumptions from within the academy. When I raised the issue of recruiting more female students into history and international studies, traditionally male-dominated fields, my university's funding committee responded with highly gendered and inequitable questions such as "Will this research only benefit female students? Then why should we agree to fund this work if it only benefits a small population of our students?" Leaving aside the statistical reality that 52 percent of our students are female, clearly the committee failed to understand the larger fundamental and systemic issues of how integrating feminist pedagogies into our general education curriculum would benefit all students and the campus as a whole. This example further supports the urgency for publishing this book on gender in teaching and learning not only for the social sciences, but also for all fields connected to liberal education more generally.

Since 2008, I have taught sections of world history each semester, most often with a class size of forty, but at times with double sections as large as ninety. The course fulfills not only general education requirements for historical perspectives and global awareness, but also serves as an option for foundational courses in the international studies major and minor. I selected a textbook, *Worlds Together, World Apart*, which specifically identifies "gender" as a major theme and "one of the most important factors shaping the evolution of societies" (Tignor et al. 2008, xxxii). The textbook includes primary sources for students to examine the writings of great women. In my original proposal, I raised this issue: Am I really accomplishing anything different from so-called traditional courses criticized for emphasizing the "history of dead white men" (Cohen 2009, C1) simply by stirring a few examples of women into the confusing pot of narratives around the globe? This teaching problem (Bass 1999) echoes broader feminist philosophical discussions about the purpose of education: Is it merely enough to talk more about individual women or should the study of gender change how we teach and the very questions we pose in our scholarly learning?

Drawing directly from my experiences with ethnographic research studying the political, cultural, and historical meanings of performance, I hypothesized that in order to reach more students and accomplish gender-forward activism, we must change how we define knowledge and our approach to teaching. I sought to move beyond a format for social science courses that often overemphasizes male-centered narratives of top-down nation-state politics. In contrast, I hoped to embed feminist interventions focused on the body and embodied experiences, social histories of the people, and the everyday realities of empires across the globe (Ballantyne and Burton 2005). Building on these gendered themes, I theorized that students learn more about how the past is gendered and politicized by examining the centrality of subjectivities in history through activities that incorporate experiential learning, cocurricular studies, team-based learning, or other forms of high-impact teaching practices. These activities do not necessarily require explicitly topicalizing women, but rather recognize how a gendered lens helps students experience greater depth, diversity, and difference in multimodal representations and engagements with the past.

Research Methods: Embodied Learning as Gender-Forward Teaching

Through the support of the Wisconsin Teaching Fellows and Scholars program, I participated in group workshops and training sessions for SoTL research in Summer 2012. My project evolved into a more concentrated focus on embodied learning as a feminist pedagogy. I received IRB approval to conduct my study starting in Fall 2012. With the help of a student research assistant, I administered a presurvey and postsurvey questionnaire with both open-ended questions and Likert scale responses to a control group of 200 students enrolled in face-to-face, 100-level, general education, world history courses (See table 9.1).[1] The survey questions intentionally avoided terms such as "gender" or "feminism" to prevent creating an unfair bias of embodied learning before these connections could be contextualized. Rather, the survey included spaces for students to discuss how they understand themselves as learners, how they have experienced learning by doing, and what might constitute learning by doing or embodied learning in a global studies classroom. My class of eighty-four students in Fall 2012 and two classes totaling 116 students in Spring 2013 received both the presurvey and postsurvey and the teaching intervention (See table 9.2). The final project featured small groups conducting original research with a performative component where students synthesized primary and secondary sources to produce their own representations of a cave scene in the World War II Battle of Okinawa situated in world historical context. Along with the open-ended survey questions, I gathered qualitative data from indirect assessment measures, including student self-reflections linked to the final project.

Throughout the semester, students participated in graded, content-embedded, embodied learning activities, along with self-selected, experiential-learning, cocurricular events. The very ways in which I structured the course as a gender-forward, action-driven class served as the teaching intervention for my SoTL case study. I sought to transform intentionally the standard history survey model by weaving embodied learning activities throughout the semester as scaffolding for the final performance-based project. I combined theater techniques adapted from the work of Augusto Boal (1985, 1992, 1998) along with new disciplinary moves in

Table 9.1. Presurvey and Postsurvey Questions.

Please *circle* the Number That Best Reflects How You Personally Respond to Each Statement	Strongly Agree	Agree	Somewhat Agree	Somewhat Disagree	Disagree	Strongly Disagree
Individual experiences and biases affect how we view the past.	6	5	4	3	2	1
Students should be encouraged to recognize how individual experiences and opinions shape history.	6	5	4	3	2	1
Students should be taught to question and to challenge historical accounts of the past.	6	5	4	3	2	1
Only professional historians can produce history.	6	5	4	3	2	1
Students should be encouraged to produce historical knowledge.	6	5	4	3	2	1
History involves a complex process that reaches beyond stating facts.	6	5	4	3	2	1
Historians should acknowledge the personal lens through which they view the past.	6	5	4	3	2	1
Historians analyze a variety of evidence including personalized accounts, oral testimonies, and even embodied experiences.	6	5	4	3	2	1
Students should be encouraged to learn history by doing history.	6	5	4	3	2	1

Table 9.1. (continued).

Please *circle* the Number That Best Reflects How You Personally Respond to Each Statement	Strongly Agree	Agree	Somewhat Agree	Somewhat Disagree	Disagree	Strongly Disagree
Students can only learn history with their minds not with their bodies.	6	5	4	3	2	1

1. Please describe in your own words how you think of yourself as a learner. How do you learn best?
2. Please explain one example of any skill or knowledge in your life that you learned by doing.
3. In a large survey course (80–90 students), how might students learn by doing in World History?
4. Another term for "learn by doing" might be "embodied learning." Embodied learning sees learning as the ability to perform actions previously unavailable to us and results from new practices that we commit our body to, not only in gathering information. Please take a moment to reflect on this idea and then please try to provide an example of how embodied learning might be used in a History course.
5. What does "History" mean for you? Please provide one example of what comes to your mind when you think of learning "History."

teaching history. These activities allowed students active ways to explore gender and history as "threshold concepts" (Meyer and Land 2003). The threshold component of these terms is recognizing that they are both inherently pluralized and products of social construction, a troubling notion that pushes students in the social science classroom to grapple with competing voices on the past and present (Adler-Kassner, Majewski, Koshnick 2012). Along with the social construction of gender, Christie Launius and Holly Hassel (2014) highlight feminist praxis as a threshold concept for teaching gender studies. In my case study, embracing learning as multimodal and embodied actions as knowledge *is* a feminist praxis that allows students to reconceptualize their own roles as dynamically embodied meaning makers capable of enacting social change.

My use of the term "gender-forward" indicates a movement-based, action-driven approach to teaching. This move recognizes the centrality of subjectivities beyond gender-neutral and pushes one step further than merely gender-sensitive to reflect a more integrative curricular strategy, as suggested in the introductory chapter of this book, as well as in Alison Staudinger's chapter on questioning neutrality in the classroom. I also intend the term "gender-forward" as an action sign that indexes an alternative move to the recent faux-feminist image of "lean in" (Sandberg and Scovell 2013). In her book entitled *Lean In: Women, Work, and the Will to Lead*, Chief Operating Officer of Facebook Sheryl Sandberg offers "practical advice for women on how to believe in themselves, pursue any goal and take a seat at any table" (Sandberg 2016). Sandberg characterizes, in her own words "naively," a world that "did not need feminists anymore," where feminism is defined as simply achieving "gender equality" within the existing social system. Feminist scholar and social activist bell hooks contends that we must "dig deep" to unpack the very foundations of the current social system. She critiques Sandberg's "fantasy" in which "the structures of imperialist white supremacist capitalist patriarchy need not be challenged" (hooks 2013, 2).

Clearly Sandberg's call for women to simply lean in with hopes of a trickle-down theory that more women at the top would mean *all* women could reap the benefits of corporate capitalism fails to account for the reality of intersectionality. In fact, hooks argues that Sandberg refuses to pay meaningful attention to "racialized class differences" and even implies that a call to solidarity for women to run the world might be interpreted as "a call to support and perpetuate first world imperialism" (hooks 2013, 2). Rather than uncritically leaning in, hooks' charge for feminists to "dig deep" to truly unpack why Sandberg has been championed as a neoliberal "feminist icon" opens avenues for critique that should be foundational to a global studies or comparative politics course. Inspired by hooks, I therefore propose the idea of digging deep in a gender-forward classroom that embraces embodied learning as a feminist pedagogical strategy where approaching knowledge as multimodal disrupts Cartesian dualism and creates a space for embracing intersectionality.

Content-Embedded Multimodal Activities as a Feminist Teaching Intervention

In Fall 2012, my gender-forward, world history class was backward designed to focus on gender, history, and feminist praxis as threshold concepts, where learning to embrace knowledge as pluralized, socially constructed, and multimodal served as a feminist activist intervention. Our course began with establishing ground rules for interaction, to help build a sense of community and create a safe learning space. The students co-generated guidelines that included showing "mutual respect for different perspectives" and a "right to egress" clause for when someone feels unable to participate. On the first day, we performed movement activities that emphasized kinesthesia as an overlooked but crucial human sense, historically celebrated in various cultures across the globe. For example, working in pairs, students took turns closing their eyes and allowing their partner to spin them around in place.[2] We then discussed the experience focusing on how, even without our eyesight, even without being fully in charge of our own movements, we still have a clear way of knowing which way is up and a sense of where our bodies are in space.

The next activity served as a jumping-off point for developing a meaningful working definition of embodied knowledge. The students stood up in class and practiced first drawing a plus sign (+) in the air with their right hand. Then they tried to draw an "x" in the air simultaneously with the left hand. We then topicalized why this task is not so easy and what it might take to perfect these skills. The students concluded that it would simply require regular practice to learn to move in new ways. Linking directly to our movement activities, I primed students to understand that their conclusion is the very basic foundation for embodied learning in this class. The course would require students to practice moving in new ways, to learn to take new actions such as developing disciplinary-specific moves, and to embrace kinesthetic experiences as knowledge worthy of being taught and learned in a social science classroom.

Building on a workshop that I attended by theater scholar Suzanne Burgoyne entitled "Engaging the Whole Student: Interactive Theatre in the Classroom" (Burgoyne 2003), our content-embedded, embodied activities utilized movement to help students access and analyze complex historical issues. I introduced the students to the historical foundation of these theater techniques, namely the work of Brazilian dramatist Augusto Boal, especially his *Theatre of the Oppressed* (1985). Boal's title recalls the work of his mentor, pedagogue Paulo Freire who published *Pedagogy of the Oppressed* in Portuguese in 1968. Freire popularized the now famous pedagogical critique that students do not come to the classroom with blank heads into which teachers simply pour or "bank" knowledge in an empty space. Freire also emphasized "conscientization" as learning to perceive social, political, and economic contradictions to take action against the oppressive elements of reality (Freire 2000). Drawing from Freire, Boal focuses on breaking standard hierarchies of power and authority between the actor and spectator, teacher and student, oppressor and oppressed, and so forth. His strategies rely on games with clear rules of interaction that may be readily applied to nontheater courses.

Although some feminists have critiqued the limitations of Boal's work, others such as Ann Elizabeth Armstrong (2006) and Berenice Fischer (1994) contend that the theater of the oppressed techniques offer feminists meaningful pedagogical tools. For example, to help make real for students the unequal power dynamics that have defined the politicized social construction of history, I adapted Boal's strategy called "Columbian Hypnosis" (1985). Early in the semester, we embraced the name of the exercise literally to dislodge the personage of Christopher Columbus, and by extension Euro-American male-dominated imperialism, as the point of origin for modern global history. Working in pairs, one student leads as the imperial "hypnotizer" by placing their hand five to ten inches away from their partner's face. The hypnotized then follows the leader's movements striving to maintain the same distance between their face and the leader's hand. The students take turns being the imperial leader and complicating the relationship by adding subcolonial powers, other students who follow one leader while that leader follows another.

Our initial debriefing focused on the students' own subjective experiences, how they felt being in control, relinquishing power, following or being followed, and so forth. Then we broadened our reach with discussions about agency, the ability to act, or, as some students showed, the choice not to act, as central to understanding complex political and historical power dynamics. The activity provides a new angle for addressing intended learning outcomes in our general education program, namely that the students will be able to "identify the role of human agency in shaping historical change." In this example, embodied learning "works" because the students could more readily access and imagine palpably these power dynamics once they reproduced them on a microlevel with their own bodily actions. This activity also served as a meaningful launching point for discussing history and gender as threshold concepts as we considered the intersection of multiple unequal power relationships such as colonizer and colonized, male and female, civilized and barbaric, which came to define the Columbian Exchange in a global context.

In addition to theater techniques, I employed a learning strategy popularized by historian Lendol Calder (2006). Calder promotes "think alouds" for uncovering historical ways of thinking, rather than simply covering chronological details as facts. Calder utilizes this strategy as a means of transforming the standard history survey model by allowing students to grapple more with primary source content. However, Calder does not challenge disciplinary assumptions, including those based on Cartesian dualism, quite enough. He concludes that think alouds allow students to expose the "inner workings of a mind trying to make sense of the past" (2006, 1368). Rather than reifying the gendered notion that thinking in history happens in some mental space of the inner mind, I argue that the think aloud approach proves useful because it requires students to focus on the processes of analysis by embodying, performing what scholars do often tacitly or without concrete verbalization. Students learn to take new actions, to think with and through performing disciplinary moves, which is how and why embodied learning works as a pedagogical device for any and every discipline.

Our first in-class think aloud featured the students working in pairs to practice decoding sources such as a Chinese wheel map from the eighteenth century (Tignor et al. 2008, 613). The map appears sideways with north facing the cardinal direction of West in our textbook, so part of the activity was for students to articulate aloud questions about how to approach an image they cannot read. In this case, the inability to decipher Chinese proved metaphorically useful for helping students to problematize assumptions about all images. The exercise resulted in students rotating the map, literally changing their vantage point physically, and then posing new questions about what they could perceive. At the most basic level, how we look at a source, physically wondering which way is up, serves as a crucial skill for challenging standard narratives of the past, particularly those grounded in Eurocentric notions of gender, race, or other historically specific categories of civilized versus barbaric. The exercise also allowed us to topicalize the embodied nature of critical thinking and analysis by engaging multiple modes of discourse and knowledge. The visual map with written textual ideographs along with images of landscapes inscribed on paper as an artifact required tactile manipulation in order to allow for a new way of seeing to generate verbal articulations of meaningful historical questions.

We returned to think alouds throughout the semester when students encountered gendered and politicized representations. And each time the complexity of the students' questions and their ability to include comments that demonstrated a developing understanding of the intersections between gender, race, and empire markedly increased. For example, the students co-generated in their think aloud pairs questions to problematize portrayals of alternative masculinities in depictions of the Mughal leader Akbar (1604) and to unpack eroticized images of women in Japanese woodblock prints about 1700 (Tignor et al. 2008, 606, 614). In this sense, the embodied and coconstructed components of learning to take new disciplinary actions through think alouds served as a feminist pedagogical intervention that helped students engage with gendering global historical awareness as producers rather than simply consumers of knowledge.

Finally, the last content-embedded embodied learning activity that I will present here functioned as more of a direct confrontation of the gendered nature of Eurocentric Enlightenment thought in the late eighteenth century. The students analyzed primary sources on the gendered roles of women by Enlightenment thinker Jean-Jacques Rousseau (1712–78) read through and against the works of Mary Wollstonecraft (1759–97).[3] Before selecting roles, we discussed historically based definitions of gender and contemporary theories on the constructed nature of gender in historical and cultural context. Encouraged to reflect on how they position and perform their own gendered identities, students self-identifying as women embodied the role of Rousseau in historical context, those self-identifying as men, Wollstonecraft, and students preferring to self-identify in additional gendered categories (gender nonconforming, nonbinary, etc.) were allowed to choose either side. The students prepared notecards with three main points from relevant primary sources authored by their character on the front and three rebuttals or counter points from the opposite character on the back side (Rousseau 1979; Wollstonecraft 1999). Then we mixed up the classroom, moving students around in space to create even pairings or groups of three combining students embodying Wollstonecraft and those performing the role of Rousseau.

Drawing from their prepared cards and the primary sources, students debated in historical context gendered perspectives promoted by their characters on the role of women in Enlightenment thought and how women and girls should be educated in the 1700s. The students then posted on the white board summaries of their main points for each character and the best rebuttals. Next, we debriefed with Clicker questions and a written worksheet that posed issues about how gender was socially and historically constructed in the context of Enlightenment Europe. Students also reflected on their own experiences portraying a different gendered perspective in historical context. Based on the shared learning outcomes for the Gender Debate activity, my Fall 2012 class responded with the following poll statistics:

This embodied learning activity on gender in World History improved my ability to

Challenge my own gender-based assumptions about women's roles in history	16 percent
Deepen my understanding of the gendered nature of Enlightenment thought by analyzing primary sources in an innovative way	45 percent
Broaden my perspective on how competing ideas shape global issues	39 percent

The students also responded to the relative difficulty they faced in portraying a different gendered perspective in historical and cultural context. Roughly 44 percent of the students found the activity challenging, 44 percent relatively easy, and the remaining 12 percent "the same as expressing my own gender-based perspective." We had a lively discussion about how some students struggled to embody arguments that challenged their own beliefs about gender roles. On the other hand, other students argued that it was easier to play the opposite-gendered perspective because they already knew all too well the mainstream social assumptions about women, which sadly the students stated have not changed radically enough from the context of 1700s Europe. Overall, this activity situated in historical and cultural context offers an important scaffolding step toward the students formulating their own depictions of gendered subjectivities in the final project. The content of the activity also allowed students to come full circle in the class, critiquing the meaning of Enlightenment thought, which included primary sources documenting how women were not considered capable of "rational" thought. The student self-assessments supported the success of the activity as providing a chance to deepen an understanding of the gendered nature of political discourses. In addition, the multimodal focus of the activity created a space for the students to engage as dynamically embodied meaning-making agents who help to produce their own readings of the past and present.

Final Project: SoTL Research, Survey Results, and Student Self-Assessments

The final project involved two weeks of in-class group preparations where students conducted original primary source research on media representations of the Pacific War using the *New York Times* newspaper database. Students were also assigned specific secondary and primary sources that represented various historical, political, and cultural views on how to depict the World War II Battle of Okinawa in global context. The students read secondary sources that explained the ways in which depicting the past invokes specific contemporary political positions. The perspectives reflected various gendered and national vantage points, including the male soldiers from the US and Japan, Okinawan female survivors, Japanese male politicians, contemporary US historians (gender not specified), female Okinawan peace activists, and museum curators (gender not specified). For example, for examining masculinity and male soldiers in the US, students engaged with the primary source "Ordeal at Okinawa" from *Yank: The Army Weekly* June 29, 1945. The source features details about how individual soldiers showed "a lot of guts" to endure one night of fighting on the island by hiding in caves and tombs (Wylie 1945, 3). Another source features an image of a child's shirt with blood stains and an explanation for how the child suffered fatal wounds at the hands of a Japanese soldier hiding in a cave with civilians.

The project was presented as an authentic assignment to create a museum diorama for the Pacific War Memorial Association in Hawaii. Drawing from my own adaptation of Boal's (1985) *tableau* images to approach sensitive political topics, students workshopped how to utilize their own bodies not only to commemorate past events, but also to recognize the historical complexities of current political struggles. In particular, students analyzed testimonies in translation by female Okinawan survivors, including young nurses such as Miyagi Kikuko who witnessed incredible atrocities on the battlefield (Cook and Cook 1992, 354–62). On our final performance day, we started with movement exercises, including a few Okinawan dance movements and other actions that recalled the embedded, embodied learning activities throughout the semester. For example, we resurrected the Columbian Hypnosis activity to recall the issues of power and agency we topicalized at the very beginning of the course. A professional photographer captured the student groups performing the completed dioramas with props, costumes, and creative use of their bodies. At the end of the workshop, we formed a circle and cleansed ourselves of any residual trauma, ensuring that we did not re-inscribe violence. The students were encouraged to recognize that we had walked in the footsteps of real people and their real-life experiences. To cleanse the space and to physically "dance through" trauma (Barske 2010; LaCapra 2004), we learned to perform *suriashi* sliding steps enacted by biologically male dancers in embodying the ideals of femininity on the court stage in the former Ryukyu Kingdom (Okinawa before 1879). The slow intentional movements created time and space for us to think about what we accomplished in this activity. Students then reflected further on their experiences in their small groups, created a caption for their diorama, and completed a final analysis of the scene in a written reflection format.

The combination of the small group assignments and primary source research with images embodied activity with movement exercises. Then, the written reflection created a multimodal context for enacting critical thinking and specifically for understanding multiple perspectives, while recognizing the importance of gendered subjectivities and feminist praxis. At the end of the semester, the postsurvey revealed some notable dynamics for understanding the impact of this teaching intervention (See table 9.2). For example, compared to 13 percent in the presurvey, 31 percent of the students "strongly agreed" that "students should be encouraged to produce historical knowledge." Similarly, 45 percent of the students in the postsurvey, in comparison to 11 percent in the presurvey, "strongly disagreed" that "students can only learn history with their minds not with their bodies." Approximately 45 percent of the students in the postsurvey, in contrast to 33 percent in the presurvey, selected "strongly disagree" for the statement "only professional historians can produce history." However, for the open-ended postsurvey questions, one self-identified female student highlighted ongoing struggles for instructors working for gender-forward teaching in the social sciences. In Fall 2012, she noted in the section under "describe how you learn best" that "I learn well when we are able to have group debates or educational games." And yet, in the section on "what does 'History' mean for you," she admitted that still history means mainly memorizing "wars, names, and dates." Here the student still could not articulate a connection between "thinking with and through movement" in our classroom with the larger mainstream and disciplinary meanings of knowledge in history at large. This response also suggests that she has not yet grasped fully the threshold concept of "history" as multiplicity, as a process of social construction that involves competing narratives and unpacking gendered assumptions about knowledge.

Overall, student self-assessments and responses demonstrate that they were personally engaged, even to the point of expressing a sense of responsibility and commitment to the project. This component speaks to the threshold concept of feminist praxis and recognizing political socialization as part of the learning process. In addition, many students commented on how their final *tableau* performance was most greatly influenced by the narratives of female survivors who described their lives in the Okinawan caves. This approach seemed to aid students

Table 9.2. Presurvey and Postsurvey Result Comparisons by Question.

	Presurvey Results						Postsurvey Results				
	Strongly Disagree	Disagree	Somewhat Disagree	Somewhat Agree	Agree	Strongly Agree	Strongly Disagree	Disagree	Somewhat Disagree	Somewhat Agree	Agree	Strongly Agree
Students should be encouraged to produce historical knowledge	37.500%	45.31%	2.63%	43.42%	40.79%	13.16%			1.56%	15.63%	51.60%	31.25%
Only professional historians can produce history		32.47%	9.38%	4.69%	3.13%		44.87%	41.03%	11.54%	1.28%	1.28%	
Students can only learn history with their minds, not with their bodies	11.69%	32.47%	15.58%	5.19%		2.60%	45.31%	25.00%	9.38%	10.94%	1.56%	8.81%

in moving beyond US-centered depictions. For example, one self-identified female student from the Spring 2013 class wrote a particularly detailed summary of the sources that resonated most and influenced how her group chose to perform:

> I think the most persuasive sources for me were the people who were actually in the war and suffered through it. My source was from an interview of a woman who was a girl at the time and she described her and her family's experience. Other sources talked about nurses that were in the war. I think they were the most convincing because they actually saw what was happening. They weren't observing from afar or hearing it from other people; they were in the middle of the war. The imagery they laid out was incredibly detailed and hard not to believe, so for me these accounts were the most persuasive. The aspects that resonated most with me would probably be the cave scenes and the horror some of the Okinawans suffered from. The way they were described really stood out to me and it was even hard to read at some points. In my source the woman talked about walking around only at night and not being able to see then suddenly realizing she was surrounded by bloody body parts. The way she described how much she hated living in the caves was incredibly horrific. The caves smelled terrible, there was little food, it was crowded, there were dead bodies around them, and they were in constant fear. These aspects resonated the most with me mostly because of how graphic they were described and how terrible the conditions were around them.

This description made clear to me as the instructor that the specific kinds of sources also greatly affected what students selected to embody. By featuring oral history narratives that included first-hand depictions of detailed embodied experiences, students tended to seek meaningful ways of representing these components in their final embodied projects.

Similarly, a self-identified male student in the same class reacted to the primary source by a young girl nurse. He articulated the importance of recognizing and yet not dismissing the biased nature of historical narratives. He wrote:

> I found the personal account of the young Okinawan girl acting as a nurse to affect me the most as I can scarcely imagine what it would have been like to go through all of that. Individual perspective strongly influences the act of producing history… Different people are attracted to different subjects and the one we choose was one we were drawn to. Personal bias also comes in when we recount that history and condemn or praise certain actions.

He also added a meaningful assessment of the embodied activity, for him not as revealing new knowledge, but rather reconfirming conclusions he had already reached. He explained:

> Personally, I didn't learn from the embodied experience as much as it reconfirmed ideas that I had about the nature of war from independent study and analysis. War is a complicated and nasty thing. Usually fought by opposing

governments but it is the civilians and those not directly involved who bear much of the burden. In this case, the worst of fighting on land in the Pacific Theater did not even take place on the soil of Japan, but rather on its colonies and territories. It is especially ironic to think about how two groups of people (in this case American soldiers and Okinawan civilians) feared each other because both have been told that the other hates them and is willing to do anything to kill. This leads to desperation and evil acts committed by all involved.

His comments highlight how even in a 100-level general education course, the students begin to recognize complexities of studying human actions including how political conflicts often involve colonial populations whose interests are not always central to the major national powers.

The theme of recognizing personal bias and the subjective aspects of studying social sciences was in general well-articulated by students in their self-assessments. For example, a self-identified male student wrote:

> Well we each had sources from different perspectives so that helped to paint a picture for us. We had accounts of citizens getting grenades and chocolate so we wanted to combine those two in our final work. We could see the importance of accurate portrayal of events and how the argument over what is accurate is still going on today. We realized that we must try to show different angles in our embodied performance since we have no way of knowing the complete story. It is like painting a picture with only half the puzzle pieces ... The personal accounts weighed a lot with me as I felt for those involved, whatever way they were involved. Then I also came to realize that the personal lens is a very slim lens and can be greatly skewed due to bias. That's when I saw the importance of the puzzle and each source as a piece to try and add it together and construct history. I can see how there is controversy because there is no right or wrong way to produce history and so many perspectives to draw from that it is virtually impossible to create an objective point of view. We are always going to lean more one way than another or favor one group over another. So essentially, there will always be debate over history.

This statement demonstrates that some students, through the process of grappling with what perspectives to embody and how, actively engaged with the threshold concept of accepting multiple, subjective, and biased views that require ongoing and often controversial or politicized negotiations in the construction of historical narratives of the past. Another student further emphasized the significance of the active component of constructing the final project. She noted:

> Personally, I really enjoyed our embodied learning experience. It was beneficial to actually plan out and organize a scene during [class] time. I learned more from actually "doing history" than just having dates and a lot of information thrown at me during lecture. It was a different perspective and it really helped me better understand this moment in history. By doing embodied research on World War II in Okinawa we were able to discover many different

perspectives, including different views based on nationality and gender. I came to understand those perspectives by talking about them with my group and by planning out the scene we wanted to do. When planning the scene, we had to account for all the perspectives and pick the most convincing one.

This response summarizes the direct connection between the embodied, active "doing" as central to the process of learning, meaning-making, and understanding. The group project here serves as a clear example of how students assessed their own experiences of learning to "think with and through movement." The student also highlights how embodied research links specifically to discovering competing gendered perspectives. In this way, student self-assessments show that for some students the multimodal and embodied learning activities functioned as a vehicle for bringing feminist teaching and research goals alive in the classroom.

Concluding Remarks: Moving Gender-Forward Teaching Forward

In the end, my case study highlights some important dynamics for theorizing and implementing embodied learning as a feminist pedagogical for gender-forward teaching in the social sciences. First, although the specific SoTL research assessment was primarily focused on the final project as the measured teaching intervention, the scaffolding of other activities seems crucial to the overall impact of the intervention. The use of smaller activities, such as think alouds and the Columbian Hypnosis, coupled with the Enlightenment debate activity specifically on gender prove critical in combination as a broader critique of Euro-American–centered approaches to defining knowledge and knowledge production. This perspective would be central not only for a world history class to move beyond a Western civilization model, but also for any course in the social sciences that grapples with cross-cultural, transnational, or global issues.

Additionally, if one of the key feminist moves is to employ embodied learning to teach students how to challenge the unequal gender dynamics perpetuated by the Cartesian binary of mind versus body, then it is insufficient to isolate only kinetic or kinesthetic components in a single activity. It becomes necessary to layer various multimodal engagements where students grapple with personalized narratives, learn to value subjective perspectives, as well as experience politically provocative images and textual descriptions. Echoing Hassel and Nelson (2012), these strategies constitute the signature pedagogies of WGS, but also speak to the foundation of social science education as linked to feminist praxis and activism.

Moving forward, there remains much work to be done in terms of gaining headway for integrating more seamlessly the use of embodied learning as gender-forward teaching across the social sciences. One component that continues to be underdeveloped is how to connect these teaching concerns with a more concentrated treatment of masculinity and embodiment. For my own research on scholarly teaching, I noticed that a majority of students did not articulate enough the ways in which gender functioned in their primary sources authored by men or in their embodied choices for representing male perspectives in the final project. While they could discuss gendered expectations and memorializing techniques of women, the lens of gender appeared irrelevant to their discussion of male politicians, historians, or military men. I suspect that in the future a more focused discussion of masculinity, potentially embedded in the content presentation related to Rousseau and Wollstonecraft, might help shed a greater light on this issue. Then, in the context of the final project, questioning various meanings of masculinity in World War II propaganda and in the actions of individual military personnel in different nationalistic contexts could be a useful starting point. In particular, I would also emphasize a complication of the feminine versus masculine binary in relationship to the intersections of gender and militarism (Fruhstuck 2014).

Beyond my case study, the issue of linking masculinity and embodiment for teaching in the social sciences has a broader reach. For example, in the field of history, scholars such as Lendol Calder (2006), David Voelker (2008), and Joel Sipress (Sipress and Voelker 2009, 2011) have made great strides in moving toward an active uncoverage model that involves creating a Socratic influenced history lab approach. However, integrating a gendered critique would require analyzing specifically how even this innovative approach might re-inscribe the privileging of historically masculine actions as central to scholarly knowledge production. Similarly, in the field of political science, embodied learning in the form of simulations has proven successful for encouraging students to "think like political actors" (Bernstein 2012, 91). The pedagogical possibilities for simulations thus far fail to tease out the mechanism of how embodiment functions and also fail to problematize sufficiently the male-gendered disciplinary actions students learn to embody. In the end, I would maintain that what should be explored further are specific cases of how gender-forward teaching, including analyzing masculine actions, benefits from encouraging students to actively think with and through movement as central to undoing Euro-American assumptions about knowledge and personhood. As students engage their own subjective experiences with multimodal activities, they begin to understand themselves as dynamically embodied meaning-making agents who possess the power for social change, a perspective that directly supports feminist praxis in action.

VALERIE H. BARSKE is Associate Professor of History and International Studies at the University of Wisconsin–Stevens Point. Her research and scholarly teaching on women activists in Okinawa Japan has received funding from two Fulbright grants, a Blakemore Foundation award, and a fellowship with the Institute for Research in the Humanities.

Notes

1. A special thank you to my student research assistant Bobbie Walker.
2. This activity has been adapted from my experiences training under Brenda Farnell as a graduate student at the University of Illinois, Urbana-Champaign. She uses this activity is courses such as "Body, Personhood, and Culture."
3. I have adapted this activity and added even more interactive components from the *Women in World History Curriculum* website. Lyn Reese, "Mary Wollstonecraft Debates Jean-Jacques Rousseau 1791," *Women in World History Curriculum*, July 10, 2016. www.womeninworldhistory.com/lesson16.html.

References

Adler-Kassner, Linda, John Majewski, and Damian Koshnick. 2012. "The Value of Troublesome Knowledge: Transfer and Threshold Concepts in Writing and History." *Composition Forum* 26: 1–17.
Armstrong, Ann Elizabeth. 2006. "Negotiating Feminist Identities in Theatre of the Oppressed." In *A Boal Companion: Dialogues on Theatre and Cultural Politics*, edited by Mady Schutzman and Jan Cohen-Cruz, 173–83. New York: Routledge.
Ballantyne, Tony, and Antoinette Burton, eds. 2005. *Bodies in Contact: Rethinking Colonial Encounters in World History*. Durham, NC: Duke University Press.
Barske, Valerie. 2003. "Nuchibana: Okinawans Dancing for Peace." *Journal for the Anthropological Study of Human Movement* 12:4 (Autumn): 145–65.
———. 2009. "Performing Embodied Histories: Colonialism, Gender, and Okinawa in Modern Japan." PhD diss. University of Illinois at Urbana-Champaign.
———. 2010. "'Dancing 'through' Historical Trauma: Okinawan Performance in Post-Imperial Japan." *Intersections: Gender and Sexuality in Asia and the Pacific* 24. http://intersections.anu.edu.au/issue24/barske.htm.
———. 2015. "Dancing Postcolonial Trauma and Rupturing Gendered Binaries in Okinawa, Japan." *Journal for the Anthropological Study of Human Movement* 22 (2): 15–34.
Bass, Randy. 1999. "The Scholarship of Teaching: What's the Problem?" *Inventio* 1:1 (February). www.doiiit.gmu.edu/Archives/feb98/randybass.htm.
Bernstein, Jeffrey. 2012. "Signature Pedagogies in Political Science." In *Exploring More Signature Pedagogies: Approaches to Teaching Disciplinary Habits of Mind*, edited by Nancy Chick, Aeron Haynie, and Regan Gurung, 85–96. New York: Stylus Publishing.
Block, Sharon, and David Newman. 2011. "What, Where, When, and Sometimes Why: Data Mining Two Decades of Women's History Abstracts." *Journal of Women's History* 23 (1): 81–109.
Boal, Augusto. 1985. *Theatre of the Oppressed*. New York: Theatre Communications Group.
———. 1992. *Games for Actors and Non-actors*. London: Routledge.
———. 1998. *Legislative Theatre: Using Performance to Make Politics*. London: Routledge.
Burgoyne, Suzanne. 2003. "Engaging the Whole Student: Interactive Theatre in the Classroom." *Toward the Best in the Academy* 15 (5): 1–5.

Burton, Antoinette. 2011. *Empire in Question: Reading, Writing, and Teaching British Imperialism*. Durham, NC: Duke University Press.
Butler, Judith. 1993. *Bodies that Matter: On the Discursive Limits of "Sex."* New York: Routledge.
Calder, Lendol. 2006. "Uncoverage: Toward a Signature Pedagogy for the History Survey." *The Journal of American History* 92 (4): 1358–70.
Cohen, Patricia. 2009. "Great Caesar's Ghost! Are Traditional History Courses Vanishing?" *The New York Times* June 11.
Cook, Haruko, and Theodore Cook. 1992. *Japan at War: An Oral History*. New York: New Press.
Evans, John, Brian Davies, and Emma Rich. 2009. "The Body Made Flesh: Embodied Learning and the Corporeal Device." *British Journal of Sociology of Education* 30 (4): 391–406.
Farnell, Brenda. 1999. "Moving Bodies, Acting Selves." *Annual Review of Anthropology* 28: 341–73.
———. 2001. *Human Action Signs in Cultural Context: The Visible and the Invisible in Movement and Dance*. Metuchen, NJ: Scarecrow Press.
———. 2012. *Dynamic Embodiment for Social Theory: "I Move Therefore I Am."* London: Routledge.
Farnell, Brenda, and Charles Varela. 2008. "The Second Somatic Revolution." *Journal for the Theory of Social Behaviour* 38 (3): 215–40.
Fischer, Berenice. 1994. "Feminist Acts: Women, Pedagogy, and the Theatre of the Oppressed." In *Playing Boal: Theatre, Therapy, Activism*, edited by Mady Schutzman and Jan Cohen-Cruz, 185–227. London: Routledge.
Freiler, Tammy. 2008. "Learning through the Body." *New Directions for Adult and Continuing Education* 119 (Fall): 37–47.
Freire, Paulo. 2000. *Pedagogy of the Oppressed*. New York: Continuum.
Fruhstuck, Sabine. 2014. "The Modern Girl as Militarist: Female Soldiers in and beyond Japan's Self-Defense Forces." *The Asia-Pacific Journal* 12 (November 10).
Grosz, Elizabeth. 1994. *Volatile Bodies: Toward a Corporeal Feminism*. Bloomington: Indiana University Press.
Gustafson, Diane. 1999. "Embodied Learning: The Body as an Epistemological Site." In *Meeting the Challenge: Innovative Feminist Pedagogies in Action*, edited by Maralee Mayberry and Ellen Cronan Rose, 249–74. New York: Routledge.
Harré, Rom. 1970. *The Principles of Scientific Thinking*. Chicago: University of Chicago Press.
Hassel, Holly, and Nerissa Nelson. 2012. "A Signature Feminist Pedagogy: Connection and Transformation in Women's Studies." In *Exploring More Signature Pedagogies: Approaches to Teaching Disciplinary Habits of Mind*, edited by Nancy Chick, Aeron Haynie and Regan Gurung, 143–55. New York: Stylus Publishing.
hooks, Bell. 2013. "Dig Deep: Beyond Lean In." *Feminist Wire*, October 28. www.thefeministwire.com/2013/10/17973/.
Horn, Jim, and Denise Wilburn. 2005. "The Embodiment of Learning." *Educational Philosophy and Theory* 37 (5): 745–60.
LaCapra, Dominick. 2004. *History in Transit: Experience, Identity, Critical Theory*. Ithaca, NY: Cornell University Press.
Launius, Christie, and Holly Hassel. 2014. *Threshold Concepts in Women's and Gender Studies: Ways of Seeing, Thinking, and Knowing*. New York: Routledge.
McCormack, Gavan, and Satoko Oka Norimatsu. 2012. *Resistant Islands: Okinawa Confronts Japan and the United States*. Lanham, MD: Rowman & Littlefield.

Meyer, Jan, and Ray Land. 2003. *Threshold Concepts and Troublesome Knowledge: Linkages to Ways of Thinking and Practicing within the Disciplines.* Edinburgh: University of Edinburgh.

Reese, Lyn. 2016. "Mary Wollstonecraft Debates Jean-Jacques Rousseau 1791," *Women in World History Curriculum*, July 10. www.womeninworldhistory.com/lesson16.html.

Rousseau, Jean-Jacques. 1979. *Emile: Or, on Education.* New York: Basic Books.

Sandberg, Sheryl. 2016. "About Us." Lean In. Org. http://leanin.org/about/.

Sandberg, Sheryl, and Nell Scovell. 2013. *Lean In: Women, Work, and the Will to Lead.* New York: Alfred A. Knopf.

Sipress, Joel, and David Voelker. 2009. "From Learning History to Doing History: Beyond the Coverage Model." In *Exploring Signature Pedagogies: Approaches to Teaching Disciplinary Habits of Mind*, edited by Regan Gurung, Nancy Chick, and Aeron Haynie, 19–35. Sterling, VA: Stylus.

———. 2011. "The End of the History Survey Course: The Rise and Fall of the Coverage Model." *Journal of American History* 97 (4): 1050–66.

Stearns, Peter. 2006. *Gender in World History.* London: Routledge.

Strasser, Ulrike, and Heidi Tinsman. 2005. "Engendering World History." *Radical Historical Review* 91 (Winter): 151–64.

Strozzi Institute. 2013. "Why Embodied Learning?" *Strozzi Institute.* www.strozziinstitute.com.

Takazato, Suzuyo. 1994. "Trials of Okinawa: A Feminist Perspective." *Race, Poverty & the Environment* 4/5 (4/1): 10.

Tignor, Robert, Jeremy Adelman, Stephen Aron, Stephen Kotkin, Suzanne Marchand, Gyan Prakash, and Michael Tsin. 2008. *Worlds Together, Worlds Apart: A History of the Modern World from the Mongol Empire to the Present.* 2nd ed. Volume 2. New York: Norton.

Voelker, David. 2008. "Assessing Student Understanding in Introductory Courses: A Sample Strategy." *History Teacher* 41 (August): 505–18.

Wesch, Michael. 2009. "From Knowledgeable to Knowledge-able: Learning in New Media Environments." *Academic Commons*, January 7.

Wiesner-Hanks, Merry. 2005. "Women's History and World History Courses." *Radical Historical Review* 91 (Winter): 133–50.

———. 2007. "World History and the History of Women, Gender, and Sexuality." *Journal of World History* 18 (1): 53–67.

Wilcox, Hui Niu. 2009. "Embodied Ways of Knowing, Pedagogies, and Social Justice: Inclusive Science and Beyond." *National Women's Studies Association* 21 (2): 104–20.

Williams, Drid. 1979. "The Human Action Sign and Semasiology." *Dance Research Collage* (CORD Dance Research Annual, X): 39–64.

———. 1995. "Space, Intersubjectivity, and the Conceptual imperative: Three Ethnographic cases." In *Human Action Signs in Cultural Context*, edited by Brenda Farnell, 44–81. Metuchen: Scarecrow Press.

Wilton, Tamsin. 2000. "Out/Performing Our Selves: Sex, Gender and Cartesian." *Sexualities* 3 (2): 237–54.

Wollstonecraft, Mary. (1792) 1999. *A Vindication of the Rights of Woman.* New York: Bartleby.

Wylie, Evan. 1945. "Ordeal at Okinawa." *Yank: The Army Weekly* 4 (2): 1–4.

Gender Forward: Momentum for the Future

Ekaterina M. Levintova and
Alison Kathryn Staudinger

IF, AS THIS book suggests, political science as a professional and educational field is both deeply troubled and full of opportunities to change how we teach gender, the question of how to respond remains. Several authors have offered their pedagogical and theoretical prescriptions. In our last chapter, we wish to highlight and extend those prescriptions that will help us more fully embrace gender mainstreaming and gender forwardness, instead of the current practice of gender neutrality that might mask and actually reinforce gender inequities. We also point to some of the remaining challenges that require additional scholarly work and activism, both within and beyond the discipline of political science. Because this book is less about the status of gender in political science and more about the issues of gender as they affect teaching and learning and the scholarship about them, we focus our prescriptions on these areas of our profession. Coincidently, these are the areas where change is both likely and promises to yield the biggest payoffs.

Because the Scholarship of Teaching and Learning (SoTL) and political science are both methodologically and substantively heterogeneous fields, this book reflects the tension between traditional political science (and social science, broadly defined) methodology and feminist methodology, inspired by our focus on gender as it manifests itself in teaching and learning in political science and cognate disciplines. This tension extends to the various research problems (national-level teaching and learning issues that serve as an institutional context for more micro-level classroom SoTL puzzles) and types of theories and methodologies that our authors adopt (content analysis, statistical analysis, interpretative methods, embodied knowledge, etc.), as well as the very decision to use anonymous data (a standard in social sciences and SoTL) versus the engendered and non-anonymous data that feminist methodologies and epistemologies might require. Likewise, our prescriptions reflect a similar tension and highlight the challenges that we, as a discipline that is still failing to achieve gender mainstreaming, might face when we introduce gender forwardness. Using SoTL to uncover persistent and often unexpectedly gendered aspects of our discipline invites not only dialog about the desirability of gendering our curriculum, but also discussions about the next steps that we need to contemplate if we are to change the status quo.

The SoTL recommendations that we propose in this chapter are not necessarily disruptive; rather they are reflective, collaborative, and collegial. Rather than seeing the inclusion of gender mainstreaming and gender forwardness in teaching and learning as a zero-sum gambit that might result in the dropped coverage of other, equally important topics, we envision a collaborative discourse resulting from a sincere discussion of our disciplinary insensitivity to gender and the woeful omission of gender from our curriculum. Rather than seeing a drawback, we see such a discourse as a logical denouement that stays true to the dual purposes of this book and eschews traditional dichotomies, zero-sum solutions, and frustrated defeatism. Even if the change that this volume advances is incremental and largely discursive, it will be a welcome improvement and a transformative development in its own right. We see graduate schools (not limited to political science); interdisciplinary centers for teaching excellence; inclusivity and diversity centers; and various SoTL workshops, conferences, and programs as natural allies and catalysts of change.

It did not take long for the authors of this book to establish the pervasive nature of gender inequity in teaching and learning in political science and its cognate disciplines. Gender bias extends to the classroom and reinforces traditional societal gender roles and other axes of inequality. In fact, unwittingly, we all might be modeling the very social, political, and economic problems we teach about in a quite direct and powerful way, perpetuating existing gender fault lines for future participants in a democratic process. Do we want to continue to enable historic disadvantages or should we, men and women alike, do something about it? Is not teaching the best way to effect change, if, as we anticipate, few would argue we need to do better for the sake of our discipline, and, more importantly, for the sake of democracy and its principle of equality? Gender awareness in the classroom will have an effect not only on the students we teach, but also on us, as teachers and humans, ensuring that change can come sooner rather than later.

What are the best ways to consider how what and why we teach may help close the gender gap in politics, economics, and the social norms of our discipline and then society? Does it require only the inclusion of female voices, perspectives, and topics, like poverty or war, that disproportionally affect women? It is the first step, for sure, but is it the end of our efforts? Should we also think about our textbooks, student expectations, evaluative criteria for faculty performance, high impact practices, and the very structure of the discipline as often unacknowledged and informal barriers that are nonetheless real and need to be dismantled for the true equity to take root in our discipline? Do we (students, professors, and administrators) often expect women to perform in particular ways in the classroom, both as students and instructors? Do we have preconceived notions about female political positions, roles in politics, and political attitudes? We believe our book gives affirmative answers to all these questions.

But this volume is not just about documenting gender biases in our field of study and related disciplines. It is more about seeing gender in often unexpected ways, overhauling existing gender-neutral cultures, and finding new solutions to teaching and learning that are both truly gender equitable and conform to the best pedagogical practices. In other words, gender mainstreaming calls on us to reconsider the entire curriculum and discipline in a holistic way, rather than just touch up particular courses. As a discipline concerned with power and powerlessness, it is incumbent on us to emphasize gender throughout our curriculum, including extracurricular and high-impact practices (e.g., service-learning), not just individual courses. As Ingrid Bego writes in chapter 1, we need to consider our discipline in an institutionalist sense to truly uncover the often informal social and cultural norms that loom over our efforts to be more inclusive.

New Ways to Think and Talk about Gender in Our Professional Conversations

How can our disciplinary social, cultural, and professional norms and practices be changed? First, our book suggests that we need to be aware of the current bottlenecks preventing us from attaining gender equality: depictions of gender in textbooks that mirror reality but perhaps should present more diverse role models; unequal division of academic labor; student biases in evaluating instructors; and prohibitive norms defining certain research topics as exclusively male or female. Second, we should depart from our current emphasis on gender neutrality, as attractive as it might have once been, in favor of more gender forwardness and gender sensitivity. This means more interaction with the work of Women's and Gender Studies (WGS) scholars, including moving toward (and maybe beyond) their dominant paradigms such as intersectionality. In this book, Rooks, Barske, and Staudinger have done some of that work, but more is needed. We need to be proactive and incorporate feminist pedagogies, classroom management techniques, assignments, and topics of discussion that will not only expose gendered assumptions and role expectations, but will correct them. To this end, each chapter offers not only a description of gender biases, but specific, if at times modest, solutions.

The idea of gender across the curriculum has been more popular in the rest of the world than in the United States and this should change.[1] It can be modeled after similar efforts in writing across the curriculum (Bazerman and Russell 1994; Bazerman 2005) and citizenship across the curriculum (Smith, Nowacek, and Bernstein 2010). Yet, we are also deeply concerned that, as critics of these curricular reform movements have claimed, writing, citizenship, or gender analysis could become thin or even nonexistent when spread widely. We are likewise wary that students could expect only gender-tagged classes to include considerations of gender, whereas we are arguing that there is *no* political science course that could not benefit from considering gender. We should continue to support requirements that students take specific courses, as part of general education programs but also within our disciplines, that are primarily devoted to gender and to the politics and theories of women and sexual minorities. Indeed, gender mainstreaming may be *too* easily depoliticized and accepted; we may need to advocate for mainstreaming feminism or other ways of conceptualizing gender justice and equality. In short, gender across the curriculum would need to be supported by explicit training in feminist pedagogy, with substantive attention to the content of courses and their consideration of the intersections of gender and other factors. It would also, given the complex interplay between gender, identity, and sexuality, require that faculty reeducate themselves on the justice issues that matter to today's gender pioneers. Training in feminist pedagogy, epistemology, and methodology should first start in our graduate schools, as it is currently inadequate and it is unrealistic to expect that current faculty will have adequate means and incentives to educate themselves.

What is it about the reconceptualization of how we collectively teach (and learn about) important concepts like gender or citizenship that makes it compelling? Does it require a new lens or a new way to teach it? Our book strongly suggests that we have informal and often unexamined gender barriers that call for a new and different focus and, more important, pedagogy. As shown by the interrelationship of the two sections—national and classroom via institutional and departmental transition—this change cannot be the work of individual teachers, but must instead comprise a more activist and collective refashioning of higher education, as Curtin has argued from the perspective of New Zealand. Indeed, as higher education comes under threat, just as women and minorities gain access, we must respond to outside "disruptions" with gender-forward thinking and intersectional coalition-building. To do this, we also need to change how graduate education constructs and reflects gendered mentoring and subfield choice, as Williams and Jenkins argue.

We cannot simply teach more or more consistently about gender in each individual class in political science and related disciplines; we need a real transformation. This transformation needs to not be carried out by political science alone. At the heart of both earlier "across curriculum" movements is the idea that teaching and learning are not about simply a transfer of disciplinary content or even habits of mind, as suggested in the previous paragraph. "Across curriculum" approaches call for dialogue about particularly thorny issues that resonate with a wide variety of educators. Thinking about gender-forward curricula in a variety of disciplines makes clear the uneasy relationship between identity and academic bodies of knowledge and their embedded understandings of what counts as good work in a particular field. As WGS and other identity-focused programs that are increasingly deemed ideologically suspect or unnecessary in our supposedly "post" world have discovered, the question of how other disciplines will incorporate and advance work that has been marginalized is a core one. Political science might initially seem like an odd place to do this incorporation, because from the behaviorist revolution to the recent dominance of rational choice and other economic methods, it has often strived to appear ideologically neutral and emulate the harder sciences. It has also, however, been a place where scholars have questioned the possibility of scientific neutrality in dialogue with feminist critiques of science. One example of this is the Caucus for a New Political Science, most active in the late 1960s and early 1970s, and dedicated to a more engaged and politically relevant discipline. In the 1990s the Perestroika Movement, which began as an email accusing powerful institutions such as the *American Political Science Review* (*APSR*) of methodological suppression, spawned a great deal of debate about pluralism and engagement (Monroe 2005). Although the Perestroika Movement, which engendered criticism as well as praise, failed to fundamentally shift the discipline, participants did gain access to powerful positions within the discipline, create a new journal, *Perspectives on Politics*, and change expectations at the *APSR* (Dryzek in Monroe 2005).

Similarly, many political scientists do work that is informed by political questions and normative values, including gender debates. One relevant approach is "phronesis," a value-oriented research practice that Bent Flyvbjerg (2001) adapted from Aristotelian roots to fit the problem-focused needs of democratic communities. Phronesis can be powerfully linked with critical pedagogy to both inform and shape education that addresses real problems, including those identified in this book. Similarly, a newly emerged approach called "civic studies" is committed to the interlocking importance of facts, values, and strategies for research. This new subfield assists and clarifies people-led democratic change and nourishes a commitment to a political science (or an academy) that is multidisciplinary, normatively engaged, and of practical use to actual citizens. We can continue to support institutional structures that allow graduate students and scholars to carry out this work.

Another way to start thinking about gender in a new light is to treat it as a threshold concept that has yet to be incorporated into mainstream political science. The term threshold concept, pioneered in the works of Meyer and Land (2003) and further developed by Wimshurst (2011), Morgan (2012), and Fouberg (2013), among others, refers to a concept without which one cannot truly master a discipline or way of thinking. Gender is not one of these concepts for political science as it stands: one could and can get a PhD in political science without thinking seriously about any of the issues raised in this book or taking any classes with gender as a primary focus of analysis and discussion. In fact, few contributors to this volume were trained to competently apply feminist methodologies or pedagogies, despite being sensitive to gender in the political science classroom; instead they used the traditional methods in which they were trained. This is not an accidental deficiency; rather it is a reflection of the systemic omission of gendered ways of knowing and transferring knowledge. In a sense, there is an entire world of political science that faculty miss out on because they haven't crossed this threshold. This glaring omission leads to the perpetuation of gender inequality on both professional and normative levels, as generations of political scientists, the very experts on the world of politics, themselves operate in a discipline in which gender neutrality masks persistent exclusion and subtle discrimination. It is little wonder that we, as instructors, tend to marginalize gender—an intellectually uncomfortable threshold concept few of us understand and feel comfortable with—in our classes, entire curricula, criteria for tenure and promotion, and political socialization of college-educated voters.

We propose a shift in our professional training and expectations that centralizes gender as a threshold concept similar to other pivotal, if often invisible, categories of analysis such as justice or power. In fact, since gender is related to both of these concepts, it stands to reason that we start introducing gender in our professional conversations as an important construct on all levels of the educational ladder, from undergraduate classrooms to doctoral programs. The current volume is a first step to crossing this invisible barrier and our own call to recognize that, as instructors, we also face threshold concepts that we then tend to pass on to our students.

As a result, our book has implications well beyond our own disciplinary boundaries and well beyond those of the social sciences in general. We would welcome bringing our insights to a broad and animated debate about gender in the academy, which already includes heated discussions of gender discrimination in the sciences, technology, engineering, and mathematics (STEM); the feminization of the arts, social work, and humanities disciplines; and the economic inequalities associated with these gender divisions on campuses. Our hope is that this book will rekindle broader conversations about gender in higher education as it brings our own discipline to the table.

Making Implicit and Unexamined Gender Barriers Visible to Students, Ourselves, and Our Administrators

The findings reviewed here suggest that we first need to start mainstreaming gender in our curriculum, increasing the number of Gender and Politics classes and infusing gender in all of our classes well beyond occasional and isolated lectures on the topic. Surely, we can do better than the current 12 percent of our curriculum that is devoted to gender and politics. But mainstreaming goes further, as any "across curriculum" reconceptualization would imply. It also means insuring that "gender" doesn't just mean "women" conceived of as a preexisting group with definite characteristics. A more inclusive political science studies LGBTQ+ politics and integrates queer perspectives; it allows in considerations of how class and race interact with gender that we sometimes leave to sociology. We also need to bring scholarship on intersectionality into the political science mainstream, as scholars like Hancock (2016) have done. Indeed, partnership with cognate disciplines is a great way to advance this work.

Starting with textbooks, students need to see a more gender sensitive approach to women in politics. Granted, textbooks and pictorial representations reflect existing political reality, but this state of affairs provides powerful teaching opportunities to examine and discuss the gender inequality in and outside our political science classrooms. Also, what we see as political colors what gets pictured and who. As instructors and students we should engage in these dialogues so students know that not only are we aware of gender inequalities, but that we welcome discussions of what the reasons are behind them and what should be done to address them. This intellectual honesty with students will have an effect on political gender expectations.

Making students more aware of their own gender biases vis-à-vis teaching, mentoring, and advising (reported in chapter 5) is more challenging, since few people want to acknowledge their own biases, and asking students pointed personal questions is adversarial and counterproductive in our profession. The use of hypothetical situations, characteristic scenarios, and case studies illustrating similar bias might inspire some students to examine their own beliefs, but these techniques are unlikely to be universally effective. It is also challenging to ask faculty to behave contrary to their teaching, mentoring, and advising styles if these conform to and reinforce gender biases. We must make a concerted effort in student orientation sessions and our own departmental culture to stress that the same expectations and level of professional respect be afforded to both men and women. Students should be aware that the honorific titles of professor or doctor apply to both genders, understand that the female instructors are not providers of additional nurturing, and recognize that equal work deserves equal respect. Administrators and faculty colleagues should be aware of student gender biases and weigh them when analyzing student course evaluations, a type of data that has a crucial impact on retention and promotion.

As instructors and peers, we need to understand unequal patterns of participation in the classroom, which may reinforce existing political gender roles and spill into political participation patterns outside the classroom. Existing research, including new data reported in Rinfret and Pautz's chapter in this volume, demonstrates that male students not only start their political science education with greater willingness to discuss politics in class and participate politically, but also benefit the most from the participatory learning objectives we incorporate on our syllabi and in our classroom. In other words, our classrooms, regardless of the format of delivery, might not be as successful in closing the gender participation gap as we think. The problem is even more pressing in online instruction, a direction where higher education is currently moving, and should therefore be a topic of conversation as we consider converting traditional classes into online offerings.

Closely related is the persistent gendering that occurs outside the classroom, even in the rightfully touted high-impact practices, like service-learning and study abroad. These high-impact educational experiences appear to perpetuate gender biases that exist in the world outside the college campuses. As instructors, we should be aware of some unexpected and counterintuitive learning outcomes that occur even when our intentions are to develop valuable skills such as civic engagement, empathy, independence, cross-cultural communication, and efficacy. As Daisy Rooks discovered in her service-learning courses, the female students not only are confronted with traditional (and often unwanted) gender expectations, but also struggle to negotiate and deal with unwelcome and unprofessional interactions. One might very well extend these findings to other types of experiential extramural learning, including internships and study abroad. Orientation and debriefing sessions that often book-end these experiences must therefore include discussions of gender inequalities and strategies for dealing with inappropriate expectations. We need to warn and prepare students rather than hope that the proven benefits of these learning opportunities will outweigh the potential harm of experiencing gender discrimination. To assume that experiential learning is always empowering and transformative might be a dangerous illusion, especially when it comes to gender equity.

Finally, gender sensitivity also applies to how we see women in professional settings beyond a particular classroom and it too needs reconsideration. Do we, as students and faculty, recognize the implicit division of teaching and research labor that essentializes gender by assigning women to particular "gender-friendly" subfields, courses, and research topics within our discipline? Acknowledging this fact, documented in chapters 2 and 4, is a starting point, but we need more mentoring and advising to reverse these patterns, starting with undergraduate education. We need to be more intentional. These changes, however, also require substantive institutional and departmental commitment to gender equity in job searches, course assignments, and research funding decisions.

Changing Existing Classroom, Institutional, and Disciplinary Cultures

The task of changing culture is a difficult one, especially when the status quo benefits particular ways of approaching research problems and classrooms. However, the plurality of political science opens up space for this work to be done even by relatively less powerful graduate students and assistant professors when they are armed with rigorous research methods and self-reflexive awareness of the pitfalls. Some of these pitfalls come from the lack of attention to gender as a complex phenomenon in graduate training and scholarly publishing in political science; if graduate programs do not have the faculty who can teach such concepts confidently, they should send students to disciplines like sociology, women's and gender studies, psychology, human biology, and even English and comparative literature to learn more.

Several chapters in this book (Rooks, Staudinger, and Barske) urge the adoption of gender-conscious or even gender-forward pedagogies, not only as correctives to the gender inequality identified in this book, but as a new and long-overdue approach to teaching and learning. We argue for these new pedagogical solutions not only because they level the playing field for both male and female students, change the extant patterns of classroom socialization and participation, and create a more inclusive classroom, but also because these pedagogies are based on best practices, take into account new educational research, and result in effective content acquisition. Gender-conscious pedagogies are not only about teaching valuable skills and working toward equity; they are about good teaching. They also take us outside the classroom and into the community.

Specifically, our contributors suggest readings, assignments, and conversations that explicitly address gender in our subject area and as part of our identity. These readings and conversations will not occur without careful planning, given what our chapters have shown about how gender is portrayed in textbooks and how it matters for research design. In areas that are associated with masculinity, such as foreign and defense policies or game theory, the instructors will need to seek out coverage by or about women, or that uses alternate methodologies. Or, in courses on topics such as ancient political theory, it will require instructors to ask questions about what gender does (or doesn't do) in the foundational texts, which are mostly written by cis-gendered Western men. To overturn false impressions of gender neutrality, instructors can adopt approaches like that used by Carole Pateman (1989), who expands feminist theory by engaging with texts that ignore or subsume women.

Beyond the individual classroom, clearly a focus of this book, there are other advantages of mainstreaming and promoting gender in our discipline and its cognates. The benefits of gender-forward political science also lie in increasing the explanatory power and relevance of our research and the political socialization of our students. These instrumental benefits are perhaps not as important as the goal of producing a democracy where more have voice, access, and representation, but are still imperative. Political science cannot advance the study of politics, whether conceived as a scientific process or humanist inquiry, without prioritizing the intersectional relationships of gender and other inequalities. As teachers, this means not only making clear how assumptions about gender work and what they do in our teaching materials, but also offering students tools and habits of mind that help them, as future citizens and future political scientists, challenge these assumptions in their own professional lives. For example, showing how divisions of labor in the political world and in the profession tend to rest on unquestioned gender norms, or how polling is oriented around heteronormative assumptions, helps the students concretely understand how bodies are disciplined in our world. It is not shifts to more advanced statistical methods, or emulation of economics, that can give political science deep relevance for students and policy-makers, but rather attentive and grounded research that addresses concerns of actual citizens.

Central to our case is that political science is often a source of political socialization, perhaps particularly for nonmajors who encounter politics only peripherally until they take a general education political science course. These courses are commonly introductions to American government, international politics, or even political science more generally; they rarely, if ever, focus on questions of gender and politics. When we make gender more visible in these entry-level courses, we frame how college graduates conceptualize politics and what matters.

There are of course challenges to be overcome. As noted above, diffusion of gender questions into the curriculum cannot work without institutional support and faculty leadership that creates a space to reflect and, yes, even assess whether this approach is working. It also cannot substitute for the in-depth explorations of gender and sexuality that emerge from scholars in WGS or political scientists who specialize in women's politics or feminist political theory. Without more graduate training on gender, it will be hard for political science departments to be truly gender-forward in every class. There is also at least a perceived danger of blurring the boundaries of political science such that it ceases to have a focus distinct from cognate disciplines like sociology or even WGS, which are also highly focused on questions of politics and power. How alarming this is depends on one's orientation to the disciplines themselves. It certainly may mean that it is difficult for junior scholars to do the gender-critical work they want to do in departments with tenure and promotion standards that are wary of work that is too interdisciplinary, or with informal departmental norms that frown on politically engaged or social-justice oriented teaching and scholarship. This also means there is a danger that those who do the most work to advance gender-forward curricular changes will be the same workhorses (workmares) who already bear more of the burden of service obligations or the SoTL work.

Far from suggesting that gendering our discipline can only occur in partnership with our colleagues from WGS, we also argue for broad collaborations across social science disciplines. In other words, we need to branch out to both WGS and traditional fields. The former is an established ally, whose insights we urgently need to truly mainstream gender in both political science and cognate disciplines. On the other hand, even though social science fields need to be "enlightened" to cross the gender threshold (as we argued earlier), they too offer important intellectual contributions to the gender-forward momentum. In fact, each social science domain has vital insights to share to create a full and realistic picture of gender in the classroom. We need more gender lessons from history, anthropology, economics, psychology, sociology, and communication. For instance, history tells us about the evolution of gender norms and expectations; economics highlights existing and persistent gender inequities in social and economic status, sociology reveals social construction of gender, anthropology illuminates cultural components of gender treatment, communication documents differences in discourses when discussing gender, and so forth. Since gender is a central concept in so many social science disciplines, we need more collaboration across curricula and more interdisciplinary conversations about gender in our teaching and learning. This book already includes enlightening discussions from historians and sociologists who speak to the very problems that plague our discipline and offer practical and long-overdue solutions that are widely applicable beyond the political science classroom. This book demonstrates that mainstreaming gender in our fields means making it central, not relegating it to ghettoized corners of the traditional disciplines. This can only be achieved if we get buy-ins from all allies, both traditional and already gender-centered.

Agenda for the Future

There is much work to be done on gender in the evolving field of SoTL, in political science, and beyond. At the 2014 ISSOTL meeting in Quebec City, Canada, there were only thirteen presentations out of approximately two hundred and sixty that dealt with gender—often tangentially. Political scientists were also underrepresented, suggesting an opportunity. Sociologists already have their own SoTL professional group, so our field can learn from its sister disciplines. Research on the learning of the working class and first generation students is still lacking, despite the fantastic work of Sherry Linkon (1999). SoTL projects considering sexuality or queer theory are also rare. These omissions reflect similar lacunae in political science, where, as Smith and Lee (2015) argue in "What's Queer about Political Science?," sexuality and gender are still treated as marginal concerns. Political scientists who work on gender and teaching have the opportunity to advance not only their own discipline, but to improve and shape the future of gender-forward SoTL as well.

What to do now? Why not try one of the specific exercises, assignments, or approaches outlined in this book in your own classroom, whatever you teach? Consider starting a campus or discipline-wide group that tackles how gender could be more "forward" on your campus or in your curriculum. Think about how gender neutrality or the assumption that individual choice, rather than institutional structures, explains inequality might creep into your worldview or teaching. And consider what SoTL work you could do to advance how we teach, learn, and produce gender in political science.

Our proposals in this chapter, including efforts to address gender through SoTL, gender across the curriculum initiatives, unmasking gender barriers, on-campus discussions, changes in curriculum and faculty performance evaluation criteria, and identifying gender as a disciplinary threshold concept can only bear fruit if we acknowledge the biggest political issue. So, we would like to close this volume with an argument for what meaningful gendering of our curriculum might mean in the broadest sense of privilege and disadvantage, existing hierarchies and exclusion, in terms of efficacy and equity as big ideals, not limited to political science or even social science broadly defined. This argument goes beyond the benign neglect inherent in threshold concepts discussions, for example. As epistemology of ignorance theorists convincingly argue (Tuana and Sullivan 2007), the willful, intentional, and strategic lack of knowledge or negative knowledge (stereotyping, lack of terms, different expectations, etc.) about certain groups leads to the exploitation and marginalization of these groups and the silencing of their intellectual contributions. As a result, we deprive entire disciplines or areas of human activity (in our case, political science and politics) from true advancement. Marginalization stifles the dissemination of diverse and stimulating ideas as well as the intellectual challenges that might come from excluded groups. Likewise, due to historical and contemporary discrimination against women, failure to recognize their work, ideas, and value to society, and (as amply demonstrated in our book) persistent construction and perpetuation of inequitable gender treatment in our own teaching and learning, the gender-forward change is long overdue. Women are still stereotyped as teachers, mentors, and advisors; implicitly discouraged from certain subfields and associated methodologies; overlooked in classroom participation; expected to bear the brunt of formal and informal service obligations; and inadequately represented in textbooks. Women's specific ways of knowing and analyzing are marginalized. The epistemology of ignorance has much to say about gender.

The political history of our discipline and the history of what counts as disciplinary knowledge have resulted in gender being a persistent setback to achieving true equity and social justice. The chapters of this book clearly detail the gendered nature of privilege and disadvantage in our discipline. Arguing for greater inclusion and promotion in political science, as we do in this volume, might imply that privileged others may need to cede their exalted positions. Would people on the top of the disciplinary pyramid risk re-evaluating the system that has granted them this status? What might compel them? After all, our graduate training and professional norms are still gender insensitive and ostensible gender neutrality masks inequality. In other words, while the call for change is powerful, the forces of resistance are also entrenched and might not be ready to give up their benefits. Perhaps most promising for the authors of this book, the lack of transformation appears to be primarily the consequence of inertia and the absence of meaningful discussion. This can definitely be changed and this volume is an important step in this direction. Appeals to moral responsibility and arguments for justice are often effective. This volume, along with the intersectionality scholarship and epistemology of ignorance literature, should go a long way toward shedding light on the normative problems of inequity, at least in our teaching and learning, that for too long have been implicitly silenced and overlooked. Understanding why and how change has not happened, well established by the epistemology of ignorance theorists, including Tuana and Sullivan (2007), is not enough. We hope that we have made a compelling case that the moral imperatives of both efficacy or empowerment and equity or social justice are important enough (normatively, socially, and professionally) to warrant changes in our discipline and beyond.

EKATERINA M. LEVINTOVA is Associate Professor of Political Science, University of Wisconsin–Green Bay, where she teaches comparative politics, political behavior, and international relations courses. Her research on political sociology of post-Communist transitions has been published in *Party Politics*, *Europe-Asia Studies*, *Slavonic and East European Review*, *Journal of Communist and Post Communist Studies*, and in two edited volumes. Her SoTL-related work has appeared in *The Journal of Political Science Education* and *Canadian Journal for the Scholarship of Teaching and Learning*. She also coedited *From Peasant to Patriarch: An Account of the Birth, Upbringing, and Life of Nikon, Patriarch of Moscow and All Russia*.

ALISON KATHRYN STAUDINGER is Assistant Professor of Democracy and Justice Studies, University of Wisconsin–Green Bay, where she studies democratic theory and practice generally and in the classroom. She regularly teaches courses on gender and the law, American political thought, and social justice. Her SoTL research has appeared in *Teaching and Learning Inquiry*, and her teaching has been recognized by an NEH Enduring Questions Grant. She is a speaker for the Wisconsin Humanities "Shoptalk" series, where she has presented her research on constitutional change in the early twentieth century among other topics.

Notes

1. Commonwealth Countries in particular have used this language. See Morley (2007).

References

Bazerman, Charles. 2005. *Reference Guide to Writing across the Curriculum*. West Lafayette, IN: Parlor Press.
Bazerman, Charles, and David R. Russell, eds. 1994. *Landmark Essays on Writing across the Curriculum*. Davis, CA: Hermagoras Press.
Flyvbjerg, Bent. 2001. *Making Social Science Matter: Why Social Inquiry Fails and How It Can Succeed Again*. Cambridge: Cambridge University Press.
Fouberg, Erin H. 2013. "'The World Is No Longer Flat to Me': Student Perceptions of Threshold Concepts in World Regional Geography." *Journal of Geography in Higher Education* 37 (1): 65–75.
Hancock, Ange-Marie. 2016. *Intersectionality: An Intellectual History*. New York: Oxford University.
Linkon, Sherry Lee, ed.1999. *Teaching Working Class*. Amherst: University of Massachusetts Press.
Meyer, Jay, and Ray Land. 2003. "Threshold Concepts and Troublesome Knowledge: Linkages to Ways of Thinking and Practicing Within the Disciplines." *ETL Project*. https://commons.georgetown.edu/m/media/resources/ETL-Report4-Meyer-andLand2.pdf.
Monroe, Kristin Renwick. 2005. *Perestroika!: The Raucous Rebellion in Political Science*. New Haven, CT: Yale University Press.
Morgan, Hannah. 2012. "The Social Model of Disability as a Threshold Concept: Troublesome Knowledge and Liminal Spaces in Social Work Education." *Social Work Education* 31 (2): 215–26.
Morley, Louise. 2007. "Sister-matic: Gender Mainstreaming in Higher Education." *Teaching in Higher Education* 12 (5–6): 607–20.
Pateman, Carole. 1989. *The Disorder of Women: Democracy, Feminism, and Political Theory*. Stanford, CA: Stanford University Press.
Smith, Michael B., Rebecca S. Nowacek, and Jeffrey L. Bernstein, eds. 2010. *Citizenship across the Curriculum*. Bloomington: Indiana University Press.
Smith, Nicola J., and Donna Lee. 2015. "What's Queer about Political Science?" *The British Journal of Politics and International Relations* 17 (1): 49–63.
Tuana, Nancy, and Shannon Sullivan, eds. 2007. *Race and Epistemologies of Ignorance*. Albany: SUNY Press.
Wimshurst, Kerry. 2011. "Applying Threshold Concepts Theory to an Unsettled Field: An Exploratory Study in Criminal Justice Education." *Studies in Higher Education* 36 (3): 301–14.

Index

Page numbers with an f refer to a figure; t refers to a table, and n refers to an endnote.

active learning, 168–169
"active postures," 171
Adams, Maurianne, 50
Adler, Patricia A., 171
Adler, Peter, 171
advising, 149
Alexander-Floyd, Nikol G., 46
American Economic Association (AEA), gender mainstreaming as model, 41, 50
American Political Science Association (APSA): best practices of, 42; changes in, 18; Committee on the Status of Women, 41; on diversity/inclusivity, 1; gender mainstreaming models for, 41; president's statement, 60; Teaching and Learning Conference, 10; Women and Politics Research section, 34; women as conference participants, 67–68; women as officers in, 13
American Political Science Association (APSA), publications by: *Perspectives on Politics*, 63; *Politics & Gender*, 34; *PS: Political Science and Politics*, 2, 63; report on state of political science, 40–41; shortcomings of, 63; Task Force Report (2011), 33
American Political Science Review, 62–63, 68, 138, 267
American Political Thought, freewriting in, 218
American politics: analysis of textbooks in, 93, 94–95t, 95–96, 102f; definition of, 84n1; gender identity limitations in, 5–6; job listings in, 22n2; methodologies in, 74f, 75–77, 75t, 81t; New Zealand politics as alternative to, 118; PhD degrees in, 72, 72f; as specialty, 5

American Psychological Association, gender definition, 140
American University, Nigeria, 142
Andersen, Kristi, 68
Anderson, Kristin J., 141–142
androcentrism, in political science, 66
anonymity, shortcomings of, 221, 263
anti-rationalist approach, 67
Anzaldúa, Gloria, 233n2
APSA (American Political Science Association). *See* American Political Science Association (APSA)
Armstrong, Ann Elizabeth, 249
Astell, Mary, 122
Atchison, Amy, 44, 49
auditing. *See* gender auditing
Australia: gender mainstreaming in, 116, 119; women faculty in, 127
Australian Political Science Association, Women's Caucus, 119
authorship by gender: in New Zealand, 121–122, 133n10; US, 68, 69, 90, 101–102f

bachelor's degrees: data for, 64; in New Zealand, 128t; in political science, 42, 43f, 64
Barrett, E., 200
barriers, exposing, 268–270
Barske, Valerie, 6, 20, 265
bathroom bills, 3–4
Beard, Charles A., 218
Beckwith, Karen, 44–45, 76, 130
Bego, Ingrid, 8, 19
Beijing, UN Conference on Women, 32, 44, 116
Bell, Lee Anne, 50
Benhabib, Seyla, 225

Bernstein, Jeffrey L., 7; *Citizenship across the Curriculum*, 138
best practices: APSA, 42; gender-forward pedagogy in, 271; methodology transparency as, 78
bias: of faculty, 91; pervasiveness of, 263–264; in student course evaluations, 11, 14; toward faculty, 4, 140–144, 150, 265
Biesta, Gert, 218
blended learning. *See* hybrid class format
Bloch-Schulman, Stephen, 221, 222
Block, Sharon, 243
Boal, Augusto: *Theatre of the Oppressed*, 249
book reviews, 123
Bos, Angela L., 2, 49
bottlenecks, as barriers, 7
Breuning, Marijke, 68, 90
Brintnall, Michael, 22n2
Bucy, Erik P., 69
Burgoyne, Suzanne, 249
Burrell, Barbara, 13
Burton, Antoinette, 243
business settings, gender in images of, 106
Butler, Judith, 8

Cabinet ministers, feminist, 130–131
Calder, Lendol, 250–251, 259
Canada, women faculty in, 127
Carroll, Susan J., 36, 91
Cartesian dualism, 238
Caspi, Avner, 200
Cassese, Erin C., 2, 49
Caucus for a New Political Science, 267
caves, in Okinawa, 241, 253
Chajut, Eran, 200
change resistance, 31–32
Chatelain, Marcia, 53
Chibana Shoichi, 242
Chibichiri Gama, Yomitan, suicide at, 241–242
"chilly classroom climate," 48, 50, 200
Chrisler, Joan C., 142
Chronicle of Higher Education, 138
citations, unequal rates of: in New Zealand, 118; in US, 14, 61, 75–76, 90, 125
citizen engagement, classroom as model for, 196–197. *See also* political participation

Citizenship across the Curriculum (Smith, Nowacek, and Bernstein), 138
civic studies, as field, 267
class: as factor for analysis, 218; socioeconomic, 15, 38; as unprotected in US jurisprudence, 228
classroom participation: as civic engagement driver, 198–199; gender differences in, 138, 170, 199, 205–208, 205–208t, 269–270; reconfiguration for, 198
classrooms, gender in all classes, 265–266
class structuring: around economic/social inequality, 38; around gender or sexual orientation, 37, 38t; around race/ethnicity/nationality, 38
client interactions: scenarios (in-service), 192nn9-16; student comfort levels with, 170, 175–182, 184, 188–191
coding protocol, 71f
Colby, Anne: *Educating for Democracy*, 197
Cole, Elizabeth R., 219
Collings, Lynn H., 142
Collins, Patricia, 9
colonial oppression, violence entwined with, 242, 243
"Columbian Hypnosis" (Boal), 249, 258
Columbus, Christopher, dislodging, 249–250
comfort levels: with ambiguity/complexity, 210; in political discussions, 204–205, 209; in service-learning courses, 170, 175–182, 184, 188–191
communities of practice, 18
community partners, service-learning impact on, 169
community service. *See* service-learning courses
comparative politics: analysis of textbooks in, 93, 94–95t, 95–96, 102f; gender identity limitations in, 5–6; job listings in, 22n2; methodologies in, 74f, 75–76, 75t, 82–83t; in New Zealand, 122; PhD degrees in, 72, 72f; as specialty, 5
compulsory group suicide, 241–242
conflict, in healthy political system, 7
Connell, R.W., 191n4
constitutionalism, intersectionality and, 219

contingent faculty, gender imbalance in, 4, 13
course format, 199–200, 202, 203t, 204–205, 211
course logistics, 198
Cousins, Margaret, 127
Cowell-Myers, Kimberley, 130
Crenshaw, Kimberlé, 9
"critical junctures," 31
critical race theory, 229, 231
Crocco, Margaret S., 17
cross-cultural awareness, 41–42, 91–92
cultural interpretation, male/female as, 8
curriculum: in Australia, 119; content in, 49, 97–102, 111–112, 265, 271–274; data on. *See* data; gender mainstreaming in, 44, 47; hidden, 32–33, 50; indigenous views in, 133n2; LGBTQ+ perspectives in, 268–269; in New Zealand, 117–119, 120, 128–129, 130, 133n4; omission of gender in, 268; women's role in, 126–127
Curtin, Jennifer, 17, 20, 33, 52

daily life, gender in images of, 107–108
Dancer, Diane, 198
dancing, for grappling with past/present, 241–242, 253–254
data: anonymous/non-anonymous, 221, 263; for degrees, 64; on faculty, 52; on gender and politics courses, 47; for graduate education gender disparities, 69–76, 80–83; national, 37–40, 38–40t; pluralistic, 217; for self-evaluation, 52
date invitations, 176–177
deflecting gendered interactions, 179–180
degendering, 32
degrees. *See* bachelor's degrees; honors qualification; master's degrees; PhD degrees/programs
Democracy in New Zealand (Miller), 122
demographics: of class format study, 203, 203t; by gender, 80t; impending changes, 40–41; by methodologies, 80t; of service-learning students, 186t, 193n17; in student perceptions study, 144t, 145; by subfield, 80t
demonstrations, gender in images of, 105

Descartes, René, 237–238
Deutsch, Francine M., 171
Dewey, John, 197
discomfort, from service-learning, 170, 188
dissertation methodologies. *See* methodologies
Dittmar, Kelly, 130–131
Doherty, Leanne, 44, 51
downplaying gendered interactions, 178–179
Driscoll, Adam, 141
Dudley, Janice, 121
Duncan, Lauren E., 2, 49
dynamic embodiment, 237, 238, 243

Easton, Lee, 222
economics: AEA gender mainstreaming as model, 41, 50; gender studies in, 141
economic status, as unprotected in US jurisprudence, 228
Educating for Democracy (Colby), 197
education, value/expense of, 10
educational settings, gender in images of, 108
education journals, gender in, 10
elected officials, 95, 119
electoral politics, 3, 35
embodied learning, 237–240; content-embedded multimodal activities, 248–253; feminist research for, 240–243; research methods in, 245–248; SoTL in, 243–245, 253–258; summary, 258–259
emergency personnel, gender in images of, 104
emotional experiences, in fieldnotes, 173
employability as graduate attribute, in New Zealand, 120
engineering, barriers in, 12
Enlightenment, gendered roles in, 251, 258
essentialism, 6, 8
ethics, gender in, 77
ethnicity/nationality discussions, 38–40
ethnographic fieldnotes. *See* fieldnotes
Euro-American male-dominated imperialism, dislodging, 249–250
Eurocentric Enlightenment, gendered roles in, 251, 258

Evans, Heather K., 69
Evans, Peter, 5
Evans-Pritchard, E. E., 238
expectations: career path from, 171–172, 188, 191n3; faculty gender in, 14, 142; graduate student gender in, 12; neutrality and, 223
experiential learning: embodied learning in, 245; gender bias in, 270; in service-learning courses, 168, 169

faculty: in Canada, 127; communication styles, 199; contingent/tenure-track gender imbalance, 4, 13; critiques of, 62–63; diversity in, 132n1; expectations for, 269; by gender, 143–144; gender as student choice factor, 147; gender bias of, 91; gender imbalance in, 13, 63; impact on female students, 147–148, 148t; in New Zealand, 123, 126–129, 130; political correctness of, 231; at Rutgers University, 138; student bias toward, 4, 140–144, 150; student evaluations of, 11, 14; teaching style differences, 149; at University of Wisconsin–Green Bay, 139; women as, 13, 41, 52
faculty of color, 41
faculty scenarios: female, 144t, 153–154, 156–160t; male, 144t, 153, 156–160t
Faculty Survey of Student Engagement, 37
faculty traits: expectations of, 151–152; gender differences in, 149–150; student perceptions of, 145–147, 146t
fairness, neutrality and, 214–215, 222
family: socialization by, 171, 224; Young on, 36
Farnell, Brenda, 237–238
female peace activists (Okinawa, Japan), 240–241
feminist epistemology, 64, 66–67
feminist international relations, 122
feminist movement: APSA evolution contemporaneously with, 33; exclusion questions raised by, 34; impact on APSA, 33
feminist pedagogy, 50–51, 266
feminist political theory, 122–123

feminist politics/theory/international relations, 124
feminist praxis, 8
feminist research methods, 19
feminist study, SoTL in, 10
"femocrats" (feminist bureaucrats), 116
Ferguson, Ann Arnett, 171
Ferguson racial tensions, classroom exercise on, 53
fieldnotes, 173–180, 174t
Fischer, Berenice, 249
Flyvbjerg, Bent, 267
Fouberg, Erin H., 267
Foucault, Michel, 8, 22n3
Fourteenth Amendment jurisprudence, 222
Fox, Richard L., 15
Fraser, Nancy, 225
Freire, Paulo: *Pedagogy of the Oppressed*, 249
Fritschner, Linda Marie, 198

game theory, 62
García Bedolla, Lisa, 45–46
"gay" topics/activism, risks in, 12
gender: across curricula, 265; APA definition of, 140; in disciplinary socialization, 12–15; implications of, 15–18; increased scholarship in, 14; in political science, 4; sex vs., 8; as social structure attribute, 35–37; as swampy lowland, 217. *See also* textbooks; threshold concepts
gender and politics, as subfield, 125
gender auditing: course websites, 133n7; journals, 123, 124; public policy, 121; textbooks, 119
gender-conscious/gender-neutral pedagogy, 188–189
gendered expectations. *See* expectations
gendered interactions, in service-learning courses, 174–175; responses to, 177–180, 184–186; types of, 174t, 175–177
gender equality messages, for adolescents, 170–171
gender forward momentum, 263–265; changing the culture, 270–273; dynamic embodiment in, 237; future of, 273–275; making barriers visible, 268–270;

professional conversations, changes in, 265–268
"gender-friendly" subfields/research, 270
gender impact assessment, 44
gendering, 32, 44–45; of classrooms, 52; New Zealand lag in, 117
gender justice, SoTL in, 11
gender mainstreaming, 43–44, 265; in Australia, 116; as budget cuts/austerity justification, 1–2; in New Zealand, 116–117, 129–132; at systemic level, 52; as a tool, 48–49; UN definition of, 32
gender-matching theory, 141, 142, 149–150
gender-neutral pedagogy: as counterproductive, 172; gender-conscious pedagogy vs., 188–189; gender forward momentum vs., 263, 265
gender norm acquiescence, 184
gender role training, 171
gender/sexual orientation discussions: in class, 37, 38t, 39; outside class, 38, 39, 39t, 40t
gender socialization: as counterproductive, 188; education and, 170–172; undoing, 182–183, 185–186
Gilpin, Lorraine S., 222
Ginoza Eiko, 241
globalization: opportunities for, 42, 49; of US political science, 62
Good, Jessica J., 92
Goodin, Robert, 124–125
Gould, Thomas, 200
graduate education, gender disparities, 60–64; data for, 69–76, 80–83; leaky pipeline from, 12; reasons for, 64–69; summary, 76–79. *See also* data; degrees; methodologies; PhD degrees/programs
Gramsci, Antonio, 7, 22n3
Griffin, Pat, 50
Grosz, Elizabeth, 238
Gruberg, Martin, 67–68
Gunnell, John G., 71
Gurung, Regan A. R., 216
Gustafson, Diana, 239–240
Gutiérrez y Muhs, Gabriella, 9

Habermas, Jürgen, 223, 224–225
Hall, Roberta, 48
Hancock, Ange-Marie, 6, 46, 269
Harding, Sandra, 66
hard sciences, barriers in, 12
Harman, Elizabeth, 121
Harré, Rom, 238
Hartwick College, 211n2
Hassel, Holly, 8, 61, 240, 247, 258
Hawkesworth, Mary, 66–67, 79
Helms, Marilyn, 200
Hero, Rodney, 60, 63, 64
Hesli, Vicki L., 13, 64
Hewson, Kelly, 222
hidden curriculum, 32–33, 50
higher education: gender imbalance/discrimination in, 137–138; status quo perpetuated by, 31–32, 191n3
Hill, Shirley A., 170–171
Hoffman, Florian, 141
homelessness, sexual assault risk and, 173
honors qualification, 128t
hooks, bell, 248
Htun, Mala, 45
humanities: cross-pollination with, 5; gender concepts in, 2–3; political science as link for, 5, 18
human movement, in embodied learning, 239
hunger and homelessness. *See* service-learning courses
Hunt, Andrea, 141
hybrid class format, 199–200, 202, 203t, 205–206, 206t, 211n1

identities: among multiple axes, 217; intersectional, 45–47; overlapping/multiple, 9, 48; pluralist, 233n2; relevance of, 37; as swampy lowland, 217
ignoring gendered interactions, 178
inappropriate physical contact, 177
inclusivity, 46
incumbency, impact on electoral success, 35
inequality, intersectionality and, 229–232
influence, male dominance of, 103–104
innate talent, as requirement, 77
in-person class format, 199–200, 202, 203t, 206, 207t
institutional culture, barriers in, 13–14

282 | Index

institutional inertia: missed opportunities from, 42; in New Zealand, 130; power asymmetries in, 36; status quo perpetuated by, 31–32
Institutional Review Boards (IRB), expectations of, 221
intercoder reliability, 96
International Political Science Association, 119
international relations: analysis of textbooks in, 93, 94–95t, 95–96; gender identity limitations in, 5–6; job listings in, 22n2; methodologies in, 74f, 75–76, 75t, 83t; in New Zealand, 122; PhD degrees in, 72, 72f; as specialty, 5
International Women's Year, 44, 123
internships, in New Zealand, 120–121
interpretive methods, 65–66, 66t, 74t, 77, 78, 80t
interruptions, by male faculty/male students, 199, 206
intersectionality, 45–47; and constitutionalism, 219; as difficult to represent, 217; inequality and, 229–232; in political science classrooms, 45–48; relevant measures of, 220t; in SoTL research, 9; teaching of, 218; as threshold concept, 8, 61, 217
IRB (Institutional Review Boards), expectations of, 221

Jackson, Mary Jo, 200
Jackson, Philip W., 200
Jenkins, Laura Dudley, 13, 17, 19, 217
Jennings, Carolyn Dicey, 77
job market, marginalization of women in, 90–91
journal article authorship by gender: in New Zealand, 118, 123, 133n10; US, 68, 69, 77, 90
journal articles, methodology homogeneity in, 62–63
The Journal of Political Science Education, 10
Journal of Women, Politics and Policy, 34, 52

Kamvounias, Patty, 198
Kane, Catherine C., 199

Kantola, Johanna, 91
Keating, AnaLouise, 233n2
Keller, Jean, 191n3
Kettler, David, 70–71
Kikuko, Miyagi, 253
Kless, Steven J., 171
Koenig, Rebecca, 200
Krause, Sharon, 5
Krupnick, Catherine G., 200

labor, gender in images of, 106
Lally, V., 200
Land, Ray, 90, 267; *Threshold Concepts within the Disciplines*, 7
Landes, Joan, 225
Lasswell, Harold, 31
Launius, Christie, 8, 61, 247
Lawless, Jennifer L., 15
leadership, career path from, 171–172
leaky pipeline: in graduate programs, 12; impact of, 89; women/marginalized groups thinning with, 4
Lean In: Women, Work, and the Will to Lead (Sandberg), 248
Lee, Donna, 273
legal profession, political science and, 48
Leslie, Sara-Jane, 77
Levintova, Ekaterina, 11, 20, 61, 167, 168, 201
LGBTQ+ community: discrimination against, 12, 13; perspectives of, 268–269
LGBTQ+ studies, 2
liberalism, 214, 222–226
"Liberal Learning and the Political Science Major" (Wahlke), 1, 18, 47
Libresco, Andrea S., 17
Linkon, Sherry, 273
Liston, Delores, 222
Locke, John, 223
Lodge, Juliet, 127
Lugones, Maria, 233n2
Lyle-Gonga, Marsha, 44

MacNell, Lillian, 141
mainstreaming gender. *See* gender mainstreaming

Index | 283

males: gender expectations impact on, 191n4; prevalence in supervisory roles, 12–13; standards set by, 66
Maliniak, Daniel, 90, 128
Maori women, 122
master's degrees: data for, 64; by gender, 61; in New Zealand, 128t, 133nn3–4
matching-gender theory, 141, 142, 149–150
Mathews, A. Lanethea, 68
McGlen, Nancy E., 13
mentoring: faculty gender differences in, 149; improving, 49–50; lack of, 14
Merkel, Angela, 95
Mershon, Carol, 52
methodologies: by demographics, 80t; dissertation explanations of, 78; feminist critiques of, 216; and feminist epistemology, 66–67; feminist interventions in, 244–245; gender as focus of, 142–143; graduate education training in, 79; mixed, 74t, 80t; prior to 1998, 68–69; by subfield, 74f, 75, 76–77, 81–83t; types of, 73f; women's choices in, 61–63, 65–66, 73–74, 74f, 76
Meyer, Jan, 90, 267
Meyer, J. H. F.: *Threshold Concepts within the Disciplines*, 7
military, gender in images of, 104
Miller, Raymond: *Democracy in New Zealand*, 122; *New Zealand Government and Politics*, 121
Minority Fellows Program, 41
mismatching gender in the classroom, 150
Moloney, Pat, 124
The Monkey Cage, 138
Monroe, Kristen R., 63
Morgan, Hannah, 267
Moulder, A., 69
"Mr. Perestroika," 62
Mueller, Daniel, 10, 17, 20
Mulgan, Richard: *Politics in New Zealand*, 121
museum diorama, as class project, 253

National Service-Learning Clearinghouse, 168
National Survey of Student Engagement, 37
Nelson, Nerissa, 240, 258

Nelson, Sheila, 191n3
neutrality: fairness and, 214–215, 222; liberalism and, 222–226; structural inequalities and, 223
neutral policies, harm caused by, 215
Newman, David, 243
New Political Science, 18
New Right, 3
New Zealand: evolution in, 52; gender mainstreaming in, 116–117, 129–132; political science in, 117–121; textbooks/source materials in, 121–126; universities in, 132n2; US system in, 17; women faculty in, 126–129, 128t; women's suffrage in, 119
New Zealand Government and Politics (Miller), 121
New Zealand Political Studies Association, 118, 129, 130
Nicholl, Rae, 127
Nowacek, Rebecca S.: *Citizenship across the Curriculum*, 138

occupational settings, gender in images of, 106
Okin, Susan Moller, 223–224
Okinawa, Japan: discussions of, 254, 256–258; student role playing, 253–254; studies in, 240–241
online education: class format, 199–200, 202, 203t, 206–207, 208t, 209; conversion to, 270; gender bias testing with, 141
Ontai, Lenna L., 171
oppression: intersectionality in, 46; in political science teaching, 9
Oreopoulos, Philip, 141
Ortega, Mariana, 233n2
Oxford Handbook of Gender and Politics, 125
Oxford Handbook of Political Science, 124–125

Pacific War Memorial Association (Hawaii), museum diorama for, 253
"passive postures," 171, 185
Pateman, Carole, 223, 271
Pautz, Michelle, 16, 20, 167, 269

Pedagogy of the Oppressed (Freire), 249
Perestroika Movement, 18, 62, 267
Perspectives on Politics, 10, 63, 267
PhD degrees/programs: in American politics, 72, 72f; in comparative politics, 72, 72f; critiques of, 62–63; data for, 64; by gender, 61, 71–72, 72f; in international relations, 72, 72f; in New Zealand, 128t, 133nn3–4; in political science, 43f; in political theory, 72, 72f
Phillips, Anne, 126
philosophy, gender disparities in, 77–78
phronesis, 267
police, gender in images of, 104
policy formulation, gender in, 116
political correctness, in student responses, 227, 230, 231
Political Engagement Project, 197
Political Liberalism (Rawls), 224
political participation: by economic class/gender, 15–16; by fostering citizen/female engagement, 196–197; literature review, 197–200; research, 201–208; summary, 208–211
political parties, women/men in, 35
political rallies/events, gender in images of, 106
political science: boundary blurring, 272; change forces in, 51–52; deep gender differences in, 138; diversity/shortcomings in, 42, 47; female percentages of, 42; feminist methodology vs., 263; gender as setback in, 274; goal setting for, 50; implications of, 15–18; in New Zealand, 117–121; transformation within, 266–267; US global impact in, 125–126; WGS/LGBTQ+ studies integration into, 2. *See also* curriculum; faculty; political participation; scholarship of teaching and learning
Political Science, 123, 130
political science books, chapters by gender, 68, 90
political science classroom, 1–5; gender as threshold concept, 5–9; gender socialization in, 12–15; implications of, 15–18; SoTL in, 9–12; summary, 18–21

political science classrooms, 31–33; APSA reports, 40–42; data for, 37–40; future of, 48–51; gender and, 33–37; gendering/gender mainstreaming, 43–45; intersectionality, 45–48; summary, 51–53
political science departments, marginalization of women in, 91
Political Science in the Twenty-First Century (APSA), 63, 129
The Political Science Teacher, 10
political socialization: classroom role in, 210; by gender participation, 16; implications of, 15–18; in textbooks, 17
political space, inequalities masked in, 224
political theory: absence of textbooks in, 93; feminist theory in, 5; by gender, 77; job listings in, 22n2; methodologies in, 74f, 75–76, 75t, 77, 81–82t; in New Zealand, 122; PhD degrees in, 72, 72f; as specialty, 5
politics: barriers in, 3; division of labor in, 16; gender in, 34–35
Politics & Gender (APSA), 34, 66, 124
Politics in New Zealand (Mulgan), 121
positive discrimination, 32
positivist (rationalist) methods, 65, 66, 67, 76–77
post-graduate career, 64
post-rationalist (interpretive) methods, 67
Poverello Center. *See* service-learning courses
power: asymmetries in, 36; male dominance of, 103–104; as threshold concept, 7
Powers, Ryan, 90
preconceived notions, 264–265
private sphere, 36
privilege: ceding, 274–275; as demonstrated in classrooms, 51; masculine understandings as, 125; oppression and, 8
professionalization practices, 17
professional norms, graduate student gender in, 12–13
promotions, unequal rates of: in New Zealand, 130, 131, 133n8; US, 14–15, 61, 268
proportional representation, impact on women's electoral success, 35

PS: Political Science and Politics (APSA), 2, 52–53, 63
psychology, research methods of, 216
publication venues, gender disparities in, 14
public policy: analysis of textbooks in, 93, 102f; for hunger and homelessness, 172
public/private spheres, 36, 224–225
publishing, by gender, 14, 68, 69, 91

quantitative methods, 76
questionnaires: presurvey/postsurvey, 245, 246–247t, 255t; of student gender bias, 154–155
Quina, Kathryn, 142
quotas, in European political parties, 35

race: critical race theory, 229, 231; discipline differences for, 171; discussions of, 38–40
racialized class differences, 248
Raffaelli, Marcela, 171
Ralph Bunch Summer Institute, 41
Randall, Vicki, 67
rationalist (positivist) methods, 65, 66, 67, 76–77
Rawls, John: *Political Liberalism*, 224; *A Theory of Justice*, 223
rebranding, of gender and politics, 49
redistricting, 3
reflection, 169, 173, 187
refugees, gender in images of, 108–109
relationship status queries, 176
religious settings, gender in images of, 107
research: methods of, 19; privilege reinforced by, 125; topics by gender, 265, 270. *See also* methodologies
research-based teaching, in New Zealand, 123
resisting gender role training, 172
reticence, at Poverello Center, 180–181
Rey-Cao, Ana, 93
Rinfret, Sara, 16, 20, 167, 269
Rocca, Kelly A., 198, 199, 200
role playing, 251–252
Rooks, Daisy, 11, 20, 265, 270
Rousseau, Jean-Jacques, 251
Rudolph, Susanne Hoeber, 65, 66t

rules, at Poverello Center, 181–182
Rutgers University, faculty/student grievances at, 138
Ryukyu Kingdom. *See* Okinawa, Japan

Sadker, David, 17
Sandberg, Sheryl: *Lean In: Women, Work, and the Will to Lead*, 248
Sanders, Kathryn, 68, 90
Sandler, Bernice, 48
Saporta, Kelly, 200
Sarkees, Meredith Reid, 13
Saunders, Kent T., 141
Saunders, Phillip, 141
Saxon, Susan E., 171
scholarship of teaching and learning (SoTL): current strength of, 138; in embodied learning, 243–245, 253–258; equitable/just classrooms of, 50; political science and, 9–12; research by gender, 9–10; in STEM fields, 21n1; student perceptions in, 139–144; as trading zone, 2–3
scholarship of teaching and learning (SoTL), beyond gender neutrality, 214–215; of intersectionality/inequality, 229–232; liberalism and, 222–226; methods in, 215–222, 226–228
scholars of color, 64
Schuck, Victoria, 67–68
Schumpeter, Joseph, 7, 22n3
Schwartz-Shea, Peregrine, 68–69
Schwitzhebel, Eric, 77
scientific mode of inquiry, 65–66, 66t
Scott, Joan, 66
"second somatic revolution," 238
Sedowski, Leanne, 22n2
self-reported gender differences, 149
service-learning courses, 51, 167–168; benefits of, 191n2; bias in, 270; discussion, 184–186; experiences shaped by gender, 175–180; gender-conscious, 180–183; literature review, 168–172; methods and data, 172–175; summary, 187–189
sex, as biological state, 8, 35
sexuality: increased scholarship in, 14; marginalization of, 273

sexual orientation, 3
Shapiro, Ian, 71
Simien, Evelyn M., 46
single-sex high schools/colleges, 172
Sipress, Joel, 259
Sjoberg, Laura, 75–76
Smith, Gabriel, 141–142
Smith, Jan: *Threshold Concepts within the Disciplines*, 7
Smith, Michael B.: *Citizenship across the Curriculum*, 138
Smith, Nicola J., 273
social construction of gender, 8
socialization, gender in, 137, 152
social sciences: cross-pollination with, 5; diverse perspectives in, 38, 39t; gender concepts in, 2–3; gendering collaboration among, 272–273; methodologies of, 143; political science as link for, 5, 18; undergraduate diversity in, 42t. *See also* methodologies
socioeconomic class: political participation and, 15; as unprotected in US jurisprudence, 228
sociology, barriers in, 12
SoTL (scholarship of teaching and learning). *See* scholarship of teaching and learning
spectrums, gender and sex as, 8
sporting events, gender in images of, 107
Status of Women in the Profession, Committee on, 14
status quo: eliminating, 270–273; and institutional inertia, 31–32, 191n3
Staudinger, Alison, 9, 20, 61, 168, 247–248, 265
Stearns, Peter, 243
STEM fields, SoTL in, 21n1
stereotypes: classroom reinforcement of, 16; faculty challenges of, 90; in hidden curriculum, 33; impact on student performance, 92; in textbooks, 89–90, 109–110; of women, 274. *See also* expectations
Strasser, Ulrike, 243
structural inequality, 46, 215, 223
structured reflection, 169, 185

student course evaluations, gender bias in, 11, 14
student perceptions, 137–139; by class format/gender, 197; course format impact on, 211; of intersectionality/inequality, 219–220, 229–232; of mismatching gender in the classroom, 150–151; quotes from, 156–160t; research in, 139–144; results, 145–150; summary, 150–152
student performance, stereotypes impact on, 92
students: comments on appearance, 175; confidence levels of, 198; diverse perspectives of, 38, 39t; as dynamically embodied agents, 239; out-of-state, 186t, 193n17, 193n18; primary/secondary sources for, 253; self-examination by, 269. *See also* comfort levels
students of color, 186t, 193n18
study abroad, bias in, 270
suicide, 241–242
Sullivan, Shannon, 275
suriashi sliding steps, 254
surveys: pretest/posttest, 202, 203–208t, 208–209, 210–211; of student gender bias, 154–155, 156–160t
"suspect classes," 222

Táboas-Pais, Maria, 93
Takazato Suzuyo, 241
Tannen, Deborah, 199
Teaching, Research, and International Policy (TRIP) project, 127–128
teaching awards, 14–15
teaching style expectations, by gender, 141–142
tension, between majority/minority, 7
tenure-track faculty, gender imbalance in, 4, 13
textbook research, 89–92; content analysis, 97–102; interpretation, 103–109; methods, 93–97; summary, 109–112
textbooks: in Australia, 119; challenging stereotypes in, 89–90, 109–110; content choices, 111–112, 265; gender in, 49, 93, 95–102, 98t, 269; in New Zealand, 121–126, 133n6; revamping of, 52; shortcomings in, 120–122

Theatre of the Oppressed (Boal), 249
A Theory of Justice (Rawls), 223–224
"The Teacher Symposium" (APSA), 2
"think alouds" (Calder), 250–251
Thinking and Learning Inquiry (symposium), 221
threshold concepts, 6–8; feminist praxis as, 248; gender as, 5–9, 15, 117, 140, 247–248, 267–268; in graduate education disparities, 61; history as, 247, 248; intersectionality as, 217–218; linking disciplines with, 18; patriarchy as, 11; in subfields, 119; transformation from, 90
Threshold Concepts within the Disciplines (Land et al.), 7
Tinsman, Heidi, 243
Tolleson-Rinehart, Sue, 91
trading zone: political science as, 2–3; SoTL as, 215–216
traditional service-learning courses, 169. *See also* service-learning courses
trauma cleansing, 253–254
Treaty of Waitangi, 122, 133n2
TRIP (Teaching, Research, and International Policy) project, 127–128
Tuana, Nancy, 275
2016 election, 3

undergraduate education: diversity in, 42t; gender bias in, 91; impact from faculty methodologies experience, 78; in New Zealand, 128t, 133n4; women in, 42t
United Kingdom, women faculty in, 127
United Nations (UN): Conference on Women, 32, 44, 116; gender mainstreaming as outgrowth from, 43
United States: Constitutional law, 222; impending demographic changes, 40–41; military occupation of Okinawa, 241, 253
University of Dayton, 211n2
University of Wisconsin–Green Bay, gender imbalance/male dominance at, 139

verbal reflection, 169
violence, gender in images of, 104–105
"virtuous feedback loop," 49

Voelker, David, 259
volunteerism. *See* service-learning courses
voting: gender in images of, 105; women's record of, 137

Wade, Rahima C, 199
Wahlke, John: dra, 1; "Liberal Learning and the Political Science Major," 18, 47
Walsh, Denise, 52
Walter, Barbara F., 90
Washington Post, gender disparities described by, 138
Weldon, S. Laurel, 6, 46, 47
welfare/social services, in New Zealand, 119
Wesch, Michael, 240
WGS (women's and gender studies). *See* women's and gender studies
Wick, Rachel, 191n3
Wiesner-Hanks, Merry, 243
Wilcox, Hui Niu, 237, 239
Williams, Drid, 238
Williams, Paul, 7
Williams, Rina Verma, 13, 17, 19, 217
Wilson, Angelia R., 9
Wilson-Doenges, Georjeanna, 216
Wilton, Tamsin, 238
Wimshurst, Kerry, 267
Wingfield, Lylan C., 92
Wollstonecraft, Mary, 122, 251
women: hunger and homelessness impact on, 185; as lead authors, 69; stereotypes of, 274; teaching awards and, 14–15; voting participation by, 137; writings of, 244. *See also* journal article authorship by gender
Women and Politics. See Journal of Women, Politics and Policy
women in politics: exclusion of, 34; global studies of, 33; Merkel, 95; in New Zealand, 119
women of color, as 'space invaders,' 46
Women's Advancement in Political Science (APSA), 63
women's and gender studies (WGS): budget cuts/austerity and, 1–2; in New Zealand, 116; role of, 215, 265; signature pedagogy for, 240; threshold concepts in, 8

Women's Caucus for Political Science, 33
women's experiences, male vs., 126, 127, 170
women's methodologies, mixed use of, 62
Women's Policy Agencies (WPAs), 44
women's suffrage, in New Zealand, 119
Women Talking Politics, 120
Woodzicka, Julie A., 92
Worlds Together, World Apart, 244
World War II, in Okinawa, 241, 253

WPAs (Women's Policy Agencies), 44
Wright, Richard A., 199
written reflection, 169, 187

Yanow, Dvora, 63, 65, 68–69
Young, Iris Marion, 36, 225–226

Zittleman, Karen, 172
Zivkovic, Jelena, 142

Lightning Source UK Ltd.
Milton Keynes UK
UKHW02n0631220718
326082UK00010B/402/P